The Hieroglyphics of Space

'Spatial images', wrote the German cultural theorist Siegfried Kracauer, 'are the dreams of society. Wherever the hieroglyphics of any spatial image are deciphered, there the basis of social reality presents itself.' But how exactly are these spatial images to be deciphered?

This volume addresses this question with a series of insightful essays on some of the great metropolitan centres of the world. From political interpretations to gendered analyses, from methods of mapping to filmic representations, and from studies in consumption to economic surveys, the volume offers a range of strategies for reading and experiencing the modern metropolis.

Neil Leach teaches at the Architectural Association, London, and the University of Bath, where he is Professor of Architectural Theory. He is the author of *The Anaesthetics of Architecture* and *Millennium Culture* and editor of *Rethinking Architecture, E-Futures* and *Architecture and Revolution*.

The Hieroglyphics of Space

Reading and experiencing the
modern metropolis

Edited by Neil Leach

London and New York

First published 2002
by Routledge
11 New Fetter Lane, London EC4P 4EE

Simultaneously published in the USA and Canada
by Routledge
29 West 35th Street, New York, NY 10001

Reprinted 2002

Routledge is an imprint of the Taylor & Francis Group

Typeset in Galliard by Taylor and Francis Books Ltd
Printed and bound in Great Britain by Biddles Ltd, Guildford and
King's Lynn

British Library Cataloguing in Publication Data
A catalogue record for this book is available from the British Library

Library of Congress Cataloguing in Publication Data
Library of Congress Data for this book has been applied for

ISBN 0–415–19891–7 (hbk)
ISBN 0–415–19892–5 (pbk)

This volume is dedicated to the memory of the victims of the attacks on the World Trade Center and the Pentagon on 11 September 2001. These attacks demonstrated – with tragic consequences – the potential of architecture to convey a level of symbolic meaning beyond the materiality of its fabric.

Contents

List of illustrations

Every effort has been made to obtain permission to reproduce copyright material. If any proper acknowledgement has not been made, or permission not received, we invite copyright holders to inform us of the oversight.

Contributors

Iain Borden is Director of the Bartlett School of Architecture, UCL, where he is Reader in Architecture and Urban Culture. He is co-editor of *Architecture and the Sites of History* (1995), *Strangely Familiar* (1996), *Gender Space Architecture* (2000), *The City Cultures Reader* (2000), *InterSections* (2000), *The Unknown City* (2001) and *New Babylonians* (2001). He is the author of *Skateboarding, Space and the City: Architecture and the Body* (2001), and co-author of *The Dissertation: an Architecture Student's Handbook* (2000).

Sarah Chaplin is a qualified architect and has a Masters in Architecture and Critical Theory. She is Senior Lecturer in Visual Culture and Media at Middlesex University where she set up the MA Digital Architecture in 1998. She is also a Director of the design consultancy *evolver*. Her publications include: chapters in I*ntersections, Feminist Visual Culture, Images of the Modern Woman in Asia*, articles in *The Journal of Architecture, Leonardo, Space and Culture, Urban Design International, Architecture*, and *Architectural Design* and she is the author of two books: *Visual Culture, an Introduction*, co-authored with John A. Walker, and *Consuming Architecture*, which she co-edited with Eric Holding.

Natasha Chibireva is currently working as an architect in private practice. She was trained in architecture at the Moscow Institute, Russia, and won a President Yeltsin scholarship to undertake postgraduate research at the University of Nottingham, England, leading to doctoral research on 1930s' classical architecture and its connection to extremist political regimes. She has published articles and design work, and has collaborated in art installations with the Russian avant garde group, Art Blaye.

Barry Curtis is Professor of Visual Culture and Director of Research and Postgraduate Studies in the School of Art, Design and the Performing Arts at Middlesex University. He is researching the relationship between architecture and film, and his most recent publications are: 'That Place Where' in *The Unknown City* (MIT 2001), a contribution to a book on 'Location Envy' and an essay, 'Out of Babylon' in *New Babylonians*, eds. Borden and McCreery (Wiley/Academy 2001).

Lieven de Cauter studied Philosophy and History of Art, and was awarded a PhD for a study of Walter Benjamin. He teaches part-time at the department of Architecture and Urban Design (ASRO) of the Catholic University of Leuven, as a member of OSA, and teaches philosophy of culture in several art schools and universities. He is the author of *Het hiernamaals van de kunst (The Hereafter of Art)* (1991), *Archeologie van de kick: verhalen over moderniteit en ervaring (An Archaeology of Kicks: Tales on Modernity and experience)* (1995), *De Dwerg in de schaakuatomaat Benjamin's verborgen leer (The Dwarf in the Chess Machine. Benjamin's Hidden Doctrine)* (SUN 1999) and *De Capsulaire beschaving: Over de stad in het tijdperk van het transcendentaal kapitalisme (The Capsular Civilization: On the City in the Era of Transcendental Capitalism)* (forthcoming). He is also the co-editor of an anthology of twentieth–century key texts on architecture *Dat is architectuur!* 010, Rotterdam (forthcoming). He collaborated on the controversial television talkshow *Container* (BRT 1989). He has also published a collection of poems *De Dageraadsmens (Man of Dawn)* (2000), and is now working on a science fiction story.

David Frisby is Professor of Sociology at Glasgow University. His publications include *Fragments of Modernity* (Cambridge: Polity Press, 1985), *Simmel and Since* (London: Routledge, 1992) and *Cityscapes of Modernity* (Cambridge: Polity Press, 2001), and he is the editor of Georg Simmel's *The Philosophy of Money* (London: Routledge, 1991) and co-editor (with Mike Featherstone) of *Simmel on Culture* (London: Sage, 1997). Forthcoming publications include (with Iain Boyd Whyte) *The Metropolis: Form and Culture 1880–1940: A German Sourcebook* (Berkeley: University of California Press) and *Metropolitan Architecture and Modernity: Otto Wagner's Vienna* (Minneapolis: University of Minnesota Press).

Graeme Gilloch is Senior Lecturer in Sociology at the University of Salford. He is author of *Myth and Metropolis: Walter Benjamin and the City* (Cambridge: Polity Press, 1996) and *Walter Benjamin: Critical Constellations* (Cambridge: Polity Press, 2002). With the support of a Leverhulme Trust Study Abroad Fellowship he is presently undertaking research at the Deutsche Literaturarchiv Marbach am Neckar and is writing an intellectual biography of Siegfried Kracauer.

Jonathan Hale is an architect and Lecturer in Architecture at the University of Nottingham. A former Fulbright and Thouron Scholar at the University of Pennsylvania (1994–6) and recipient of the RIBA Silver Medal (1989), he is the author of *Building Ideas: An Introduction to Architectural Theory* (Wiley/Academic, 2000). Currently he is conducting research on the relationship between philosophy and technology in architecture.

Eric Holding is a freelance architect, a Research Associate in Architectural Studies at Middlesex University and a director of *evolver*, a multidisciplinary design consultancy based in London. His recent publications include *Consuming Architecture* which was co-edited with Sarah Chaplin and *Staged*

Architecture, a monograph on the architect Mark Fisher. He has published numerous articles in the architectural press and been an invited speaker at conferences and schools of architecture in the UK, USA, Australia and Japan.

Neil Leach teaches at the Architectural Association and the University of Bath, where he is Professor of Architectural Theory. He has also been Reader at the University of Nottingham and Visiting Professor at Columbia University, New York. He is author of *The Anaesthetics of Architecture* (MIT, 1999) and *Millennium Culture* (Ellipsis, 1999); editor of *Rethinking Architecture: A Reader in Cultural Theory* (Routledge, 1997), *Architecture and Revolution: Contemporary Perspectives in Central and Eastern Europe* (Routledge, 1999) and *E-Futures: Designing for a Digital World* (Wiley, 2002); and co-translator of L.B. Alberti, *On the Art of Building in Ten Books* (MIT, 1988).

Anna Notaro was from 1995 to 1997 Leverhulme Research Fellow at Royal Holloway, University of London, working on the project: 'Imperial Cities: Landscape, Space and Performance in Rome and London, 1850–1950'. She is currently a Research Fellow in Visual Culture working on the 'Three American Cities' Project (http://www.3cities.org.uk) in the School of American and Canadian Studies at the University of Nottingham. Areas of current research include: American and European Visual Culture, Art History (American and European avant-garde movements, 1915–35, American painting, especially New York), Film Studies (Cinema and the City, Cinema and Architecture) and Theories of Representation and Architectural History.

Claire Pajaczkowska is a Senior Lecturer in Visual Culture at Middlesex University. Her most recent books are *Perversion* and *Feminist Visual Culture*. Her current research is on the mundane sublime in popular culture.

Doina Petrescu is a Lecturer at the University of Sheffield and a research fellow at the Centre of Women's Studies, University of Paris 8. She studied architecture in Bucharest, and went on to study philosophy with Jacques Derrida and women studies with Hélène Cixous in Paris. She is an architect, curator and writer. She is co-founder of ReDesign studio in Paris, co-author of *l'Association (des pas)* (Syndicat mixte du Familistre Godin, 2001) and editor of *Alterities: Feminine Practices, Technology and Poetical Politics of Space* (forthcoming).

Constantin Petcou trained as an architecture in Bucharest, before going on to take an MA in Semiotics at the University of Paris 8. He is an architect and media theorist, and currently teaches at Ecole d'Architecture Paris Malaquais and in the Media Department of the University of Paris 8. He has published several articles and lectured in various countries. He is co-founder of ReDesign studio and a member of Atelier d'Architecture Autogere in Paris.

Steve Pile is Lecturer in the Faculty of Social Sciences at the Open University. His recent books include *The Body and the City* (1996) and *City Worlds*

(1999, co-edited with Doreen Massey and John Allen), and *Unruly Cities?* (1999, co-edited with Chris Brook and Gerry Mooney). Now, he is looking forward to getting down to some serious dreaming.

Jane Rendell is Lecturer in Architecture at the Bartlett School of Architecture, University College London. An architectural designer, historian and theorist, she is author of *The Pursuit of Pleasure*, (Athlone Press, 2001). She is also editor of 'A Place Between', *Public Art Journal*, issue 2 (October 1999) and co-editor of *Strangely Familiar: Narratives of Architecture and the City* (Routledge, 1995), *Gender Space Architecture: An Interdisciplinary Introduction* (Routledge, 1999), *Intersections: Architectural Histories and Critical Theories* (Routledge, 2000) and *The Unknown City: Contesting Architecture and Social Space* (MIT Press, 2000). She is currently researching two new books, *A Place Between: Art, Architecture and the Urban* for Reaktion Press, and another collection of essays on art, space and gender.

Adrian Rifkin is Professor of Visual Culture and Media at Middlesex University, and is author of *Street Noises - Parisian Pleasure 1900-1940* (1993) and *Ingres Then, and Now* (2000).

Mireille Rosello works on French and Francophone cultures, gender studies and post-colonial theories. Her recent books are *Littérature et identité créole* (1993), *Infiltrating Culture: Power and Identity in Contemporary Women's Writing* (1996) and *Declining the Stereotype: Representation and Ethnicity in French Cultures* (1997). She is currently studying the political and philosophical connections between immigration, hospitality and generosity.

Douglas Tallack is Professor of American Studies and Pro-Vice-Chancellor at the University of Nottingham, UK. His publications are *City Sites: Multi-Media Essays on New York and Chicago* (co-ed.) (2000), *Critical Theory: A Reader* (ed.) (1995), *The Nineteenth-Century American Short Story* (1993), *Twentieth-Century America* (1991), *Literary Theory at Work* (ed.) (1987), and articles and chapters on Intellectual History, Visual Culture, Critical Theory, and American Literature. He has twice won the Arthur Miller Prize for the best article in American Studies. His current research is a monograph on Visual Culture in New York City. He is Director of the AHRB 3Cities project based at the Universities of Nottingham and Birmingham.

Peter Wollen is a film-maker, film scholar and Professor at the Department of Film and Television, UCLA. He has curated several international exhibitions (Kahlo and Modotti; The Situationist International; 100 Years of Art and Fashion; Global Conceptualism). He co-wrote Antonini's *The Passenger* and has co-directed many other films. His most recent feature was *Friendship's Death*, a science fiction movie. His books include *Signs and Meaning in the Cinema*, *Singin' In the Rain* and *Raiding the Icebox*.

Introduction

This volume contains a collection of essays which attempt to analyse the modern metropolis. The metropolis is understood here as a '*mater polis*', a 'mother city', a substantial conurbation, which exceeds the scale of the traditional city. As such it attracts its own problems. The metropolis constitutes a complex web of social interaction. It is difficult to navigate and difficult to understand. But so too the metropolis plays an important role in contemporary society. It features prominently in the public imagination as the very site of modernity. And within an age of global tourism, advertising and marketing, the great examples of the metropolis – London, New York, Paris, Berlin and so on – take on an international significance beyond their regional status. They have become world cities on a world stage, emblems of their nations, symbols of civilisation. To understand the metropolis is – to some extent – to understand our present age. In looking at a number of examples of the metropolis from a range of different perspectives, the essays in this volume therefore attempt to shed some light on our contemporary condition.

'Spatial images', writes the German cultural theorist Siegfried Kracauer (1889–1966), 'are the dreams of society. Wherever the hieroglyphics of any spatial image are deciphered, there the basis of social reality presents itself.'[1] This is the premise on which this volume is based. It is also the premise that lies behind much research in cultural theory as a whole. What we see on the surface, so any marxist-inspired cultural theorist would argue, is the product of deeper underlying forces, and in order to understand these forces we need to interpret the surface level. This applies to all aspects of cultural production. Kracauer goes on to articulate this general principle: 'The surface-level expressions ... by virtue of their unconscious nature, provide unmediated access to the fundamental substance of the state of things. Conversely, knowledge of this state of things depends on the interpretation of these surface-level expressions.'[2]

This statement carries with it an obvious Freudian allusion. The 'unconscious nature' of surface-level expressions reveals the hidden logic behind these phenomena like a slip of the tongue. Indeed it is precisely because Kracauer focuses his attention on the more marginal and seemingly mundane phenomena of everyday life, such as hotel lobbies, shopping arcades, cinemas, dance halls and so on, that these 'unconscious' visual clues are likely to reveal themselves.

Like the notion of the 'optical unconscious' explored by Walter Benjamin whereby the marginal details in a photograph can often be seen to expose provocative secrets, so the unconscious nature of surface-level expressions would more readily give up their most revealing insights into the 'fundamental substance of the state of things'.

The metropolis, then, can be understood as an amalgam of objects of cultural production, and as such presents itself beyond the limitations of any strictly positivistic outlook as a repository of meaning. For the metropolis is more than a collection of transportational networks, buildings, parks, rivers and so on. It is a patchwork quilt of traces of human existence. The task of any theorist intent on analysing the metropolis thus is to act like a detective, interrogating these traces and divining their secrets – 'botanising on the asphalt', as Walter Benjamin describes the role of the *flâneur*. For to analyse the traces is to analyse the lives of those who left those traces. The metropolis therefore lends itself to serve in textual terms as an object of research. It constitutes a series of spatial images – hieroglyphics – which may be deciphered in order to provide access to deeper underlying questions about society.

Knowing the metropolis

How, then, might we go about this process of 'deciphering' these 'hieroglyphics' of space? This volume does not attempt to prescribe any particular approach to this question. But as the subtitle suggests, it posits in general terms two alternative models of knowing the metropolis – those of 'reading' and 'experiencing'. The first is a broadly semiological model, which would also include psychoanalytic readings. We might define a semiological approach in terms of the structuralist paradigm which sought to understand the world in terms of 'signs', composed of 'signifiers' and 'signifieds'. Here 'signifiers' refer to the forms – in the case of the metropolis, the architectural elements – and 'signifieds' refer to their content or meaning. The metropolis, then, might be 'read' – its forms deciphered and its meanings understood. Poststructuralist theorists have sought to revise this model by problematising the simple one-to-one relationship of signified to signifier, and highlighting the provisionality and multiplicity of readings that might be made. Meaning, for them, is never fixed, but always in a state of deferral.[3]

The second model is a broadly phenomenological one. Theorists adopting a phenomenological approach seek to highlight the 'experience' of our engagement with the world. The problem with 'reading' the environment as a codified system of meaning is that this approach effectively privileges the visual, and makes little allowance for the full ontological potential for human experience. This leads, so critics such as Henri Lefebvre argue, to a shallow, superficial level of perception. But it is not simply a question of opening up to the other senses – smell, taste, touch and sound – but rather being open to the possibility of some revelatory moment in which some deeper underlying truth might be revealed. In the context of this volume, it is through a more holistic way of engaging with the metropolis, by the ontological experiences of spatial practices, in particular, that another way of understanding the city might be opened up and revealed.[4]

This volume, then, explores such ways of 'reading' or 'experiencing' the metropolis. All the while it is acknowledged, however, that this may be a some-what fragile distinction. Too often the two models collapse into one another. How, for example, does any discourse of phenomenology fully escape the problem of 'reading'? While thinkers such as Henri Lefebvre criticise the tendency in Western cultural discourse, since the invention of perspective, to privilege the eye, one wonders how any phenomenological discourse might exist which does not rely primarily on optical reception. Equally, one is left wondering how the phenomenological might impact upon a semiological 'reading' of an architectural space. Can there be any 'pure' semantic analysis devoid of any ontological concerns, and if so, is this not a highly impoverished way of engaging with the world to the point where, perhaps, it fails to provide a true engagement? The distinction, then, between the semiological and the phenomenological – between 'reading' and 'experiencing' the metropolis – remains a tentative and somewhat compromised one. Rather than reinforcing this distinction, we should recognise the links between the two. 'Reading' and 'experiencing' should not be seen as mutually exclusive, but as interdependent models of understanding the metropolis. It is a question, then, not of 'reading' *or* 'experiencing', so much as 'reading' *and* 'experiencing' the metropolis.

What this suggests is that there is no single way of understanding the metropolis. It is not just a question of *how* we view the metropolis. We must also take into account *who* is viewing it. How, then, might we 'know' the metropolis? The answer lies, perhaps, in the multi-layered sedimentation of meaning that Italo Calvino conveys so persuasively in *Invisible Cities*;[5] here one city – Venice – is read and re-read by different people from a series of perspec-tives, such that it no longer appears to be the same city. It is both one city and a plurality of different cities. In reading cities or indeed any cultural artifice, meaning is never univocal. A city – any city – is always open to a variety of inter-pretations. Meaning must always remain plural and contested.

Cixous captures this with her evocative description of Prague, 'Attacks of the Castle'. For Cixous such cities exist first as a form of dream, imagistic, 'phantom cities' envisaged well before the actual cities have been visited, to the point where it is almost impossible to match up the actual city with one's projected mental image of it. So it is when Cixous actually visits Prague – Prague, the city of her dreams, the literary world of Kafka and others – that she senses that she has not really been there. Prague itself, and so too the 'spirit of the city', has evaded her: 'I was in Prague for the first time and Prague was not there…. We dream of going to Prague. We do not know how to go. We fear. We go. Once inside we do not find it.'[6]

For Cixous, a Prague is a city of traces, memories and meanings erased by repetition. It is a city that can never be fully captured by the onto-hermeneutical process. It is not Prague, but Pragues, promised Pragues to which the author might never gain entry. 'Promised Pragues. You dream of going. You cannot go.

What would happen if you went?' The theme of Prague as a city of multiple interpretations echoes Cixous' earlier observations on Monet's twenty-six paintings, each an attempt to 'capture' Rouen Cathedral. The 'truth' of Rouen Cathedral is in fact twenty-six cathedrals, the 'truth' of Prague a series of varying and overlapping impressions that can never be resolved to provide any totalising description of Prague. But so too, we might add, the truth of Prague can never be contained by a purely semiological approach, no matter how many 'readings' are offered. It must always be open to a more overtly phenomenological approach. To 'know' Prague is to 'experience' it as much as to 'read' it.

This, too, is a question addressed by Roland Barthes. For Barthes the city can be analysed in semiological terms like a language, and yet it is a language that must be 'lived' rather than 'decoded' in any literal way. To 'live' the city is to engage in some symbiotic relationship with it, to listen to it and speak to it, but above all to wander through it and experience its spaces. To this extent, although primarily a semiological thinker, Barthes would appear to be open to a more phenomenologically oriented approach: 'The city is a discourse and this discourse is truly a language: the city speaks to its inhabitants, we speak our city, the city where we are, simply by living in it, by wandering through it, by looking at it.'[7] And in reading the city one must be alert to the provisionality of any such reading, and to the dangers of attempting to present any totalising and over-determined account of the meanings of a city. 'Historically', Barthes notes, 'these signifieds are always extremely vague, dubious, and unmanageable ... In this attempt at a semantic approach to the city we should try to understand the play of signs, to understand that any city is a structure, but that we must never try and we must never want to fill in this structure.'[8]

To Barthes the answer to these problems lies in the multiplicity of 'readings' of the city:

> if we want to undertake a semiology of the city, the best approach, in my opinion, as indeed for every semantic venture, will be a certain ingenuity on the part of the reader. Many of us should try to decipher the city we are in, starting if necessary with a personal rapport. Dominating all these readings by different categories of readers (for we have a complete scale of readers, from the native to the stranger) we would thus work out the language of the city. This is why I would say that it is not so important to multiply the surveys or the functional studies of the city, but to multiply the readings of the city, of which unfortunately only the writers have so far given us some examples.[9]

The reader, the 'lover' of cities, must therefore be open to a range of 'readings' which go well beyond straightforward, rational analyses to open up the 'poetry' of the city: 'For the city is a poem, as has often been said and as Hugo said better than anyone else, but it is not a classical poem, a poem tidily centred on a subject. It is a poem which unfolds the signifier and it is this unfolding that ultimately the semiology of the city should try to grasp and make sing.'[10]

To this it could be added, perhaps, that we should multiply not only the ways in which we 'read' the metropolis, but so too the ways in which we 'experience' it. This, at any rate, is the premise behind this volume. Just as 'the metropolis' itself does not exist, and can only be understood through its various manifestations, so too there can never be any exhaustive method of 'knowing' any metropolis. All there can be are a series of strategies or tactics, engaging with different examples of the metropolis at different levels, pursuing a range of theoretical models. The various sections into which this volume has been divided offer a number of such models. They consider in turn how the metropolis might be perceived as 'legible', and how one might trace one's way through it; how the metropolis might be read as 'political', and how its spaces might be seen to be gendered; how the image of the metropolis might be 'represented' and 'promoted' in marketing terms; how the metropolis might be perceived through films, and finally how the various spaces of the metropolis might be read in economic terms. But these sections do not offer an exhaustive range of possible ways of 'knowing' the metropolis. They merely offer a few suggestions, examples of how specific moments in each individual metropolis can be put together to form a 'constellation' of readings and experiences that will form the basis for a more generalised theory for how any metropolis might be perceived as a series of spatial hieroglyphics.

The legible metropolis

In his piece, 'The metropolis as text: Otto Wagner and Vienna's "Second Renaissance"', David Frisby outlines how Walter Benjamin and Siegfried Kracauer perceive the metropolis as a form of hieroglyphic text to be decoded. This, of course, is not an unproblematic position, in that not only does the text presuppose a reader, but so too it presupposes legibility. It is precisely this question of legibility that Frisby addresses in turning his attention to the specific question of turn-of-the-century Vienna. Otto Wagner's comment that the metropolis was 'unintelligible' to the reader opens up the question of how modernist architects sought to transcend the stylistic cacophony of nineteenth-century Vienna with the clear and 'intelligible' language of modernism. Frisby describes how the cool, modernist outlines of Wagner's architecture were intended to be 'read' by the swiftly moving inhabitant of the modernist metropolis with its new transportational systems. And yet Wagner's vision was perhaps somewhat optimistic. Not everyone shared his faith in 'modern life', and turn-of-the-century Vienna remained a complex mix of old world values and new world aspirations. It is hardly surprising, then, that Wagner's new 'legible' architecture would not have found favour with everyone.

In 'Cognitive mapping: New York vs Philadelphia', Jonathan Hale looks at the question of spatial orientation. He explores how the grid of the metropolis might be read, in Fredric Jameson's terms, as a form of 'cognitive map', considering how the clear, symmetrical layout of Philadelphia would appear to offer a clearer framework for orientation than the homogeneous grid of New York, but in fact proves somewhat disorientating and less easy to navigate. But the importance of 'cognitive mapping' for Jameson is not simply that the metropolis should be legible – in the manner explored, say, by Kevin Lynch – but that this legibility might form part of a broader project in which the individual might be able to resist the homogenising force of late capitalism, and find his or her place in the world. Paradoxically, then, it is New York – the archetypal space of monopoly capitalism – which, according to Hale, ends up giving us a more legible model in terms of 'cognitive mapping'.

In 'Benjamin's London, Baudrillard's Venice', Graeme Gilloch makes a comparison between two stories of a pursuit through a metropolis: the story of Edgar Allen Poe's 'Man of the Crowd' set in London and related by Walter Benjamin, and the project in Venice, *Suite vénitienne*, by the French artist, Sophie Calle, on which Jean Baudrillard has commented extensively. Gilloch compares and contrasts the two episodes, drawing a distinction between the concept of 'mimesis' that underpins Benjamin's account and the concept of 'seduction' which underpins that of Baudrillard. Mimesis, the attempt to seek meaning in the chaotic world of nature, offers a model of how to interpret and make sense of the 'puzzling hieroglyphics, strange inscriptions [and] obscure traces' of the enchanted modern metropolis, the 'city of signs'. But seduction, Gilloch notes, constitutes a less critical mode of engagement. To be seduced by the metropolis is not to discern its meaning, but to give way to fascination. Both modes of engagement, however, illustrate ways of navigating and tracing one's way through the metropolis.

The political metropolis

In 'Resurrecting an imperial past: strategies of self-representation and "masquerade" in fascist Rome (1934–1938)', Anna Notaro looks at attempts in fascist Italy to refashion and re-present Rome. She considers the attempts of Mussolini to create an architecture of classical monumentality that evokes the memory of Rome's imperial past, and contrasts it to the Futurist/Modernist vision of the Liberal government. Architecture here is seen as the embodiment of political ideals, as a form of 'word in stone', as Adolf Hitler has described it. The self-conscious re-evocation of classical architecture serves as a form of 'masquerade', a strategy of self-representation which has much in common with other fascist regimes in the twentieth century.

The notion of architecture as the embodiment of political ideals is further explored by Natasha Chibireva in 'Airbrushed Moscow'. Here she considers the site of the cathedral of Christ the Saviour in Moscow, which became a battlefield for political ideals. The original cathedral was demolished to make way for the ill-fated Palace of the Soviets, whose abandoned foundations were subsequently converted into a giant open-air swimming pool. Eventually, the swimming pool was itself demolished, and the cathedral reconstructed hastily in what might be read as an act of repentance. This process of demolition and reconstruction, Chibireva argues, can be understood within the broader context of writing and rewriting the past within Russian history.

Continuing the focus on Central and Eastern Europe I look at the dilemma of how to deal with buildings which bear the stigma of associations with previous, now-discredited regimes in 'Erasing the traces: the "denazification" of post-revolutionary Berlin and Bucharest'. The ways in which the cities of Berlin and Bucharest have dealt with the architectural monuments to their communist pasts are compared, the physical erasure of the wall being contrasted with the symbolic reappropriation of Ceauşescu's palace. Drawing upon Freud's concept of the 'screen memory' I attempt to account for the way in which the palace has been recoded from monument to a repressive dictator to emblem for a new Romania. It is not necessary, I conclude, to actually demolish structures in order to erase the traces of evil. Indeed in our present 'culture of amnesia' it is all too easy to forget the past. Perhaps, then, the problem is not how to forget the past, but how to remember it, and learn from its lessons.

These questions are reconsidered in my further piece, 'Erasing the traces: the "denazification" of post-apartheid Johannesburg and Pretoria', where I compare two structures, the Johannesburg Central Police Station, the notorious site of numerous breaches of human rights under apartheid, and the Voortrekker Monument just outside Pretoria, the foremost emblem of Afrikaanerdom. What makes the case of South Africa so interesting is the singular figure of Nelson Mandela, who – as a universally recognised force for good – is able to reappropriate emblems of the apartheid regime for the new democratic South Africa, highlighting the strategic potential of these acts. What is required, I argue, is not demolition or architectural alterations, but the reappropriation of these buildings. Indeed many would argue that these buildings must not be destroyed. They act as necessary reminders of an important – if regrettable – moment in South Africa's history.

The gendered metropolis

In 'The pursuit of pleasure: London rambling', Jane Rendell considers how particular sites within the metropolis might be read from a feminist perspective. Through the figure of the rambler she attempts to analyse spatial practices within the Burlington Arcade and other spaces in nineteenth-century London which were the sites of often highly charged gendered encounters. Her analyses of these spaces – bazaars, arcades and other sites of exchange – and the activities that take place there remind one of Walter Benjamin's work on nineteenth-century Paris. These are spaces in which women are seen as objects of exchange, and it is precisely through the activities and spatial practices that prevail there that these spaces can be read as gendered.

In 'Gay Paris: trace and ruin' Adrian Rifkin looks at Paris as the site of gendered encounters. The metropolis must be understood not in terms of often superficial 'reading' of facades, but in terms of the spatial practices that take place there. In the context of Paris, the privatisation of previously contested spaces – doorways, courtyards and gardens – through the medium of the digi-code and other tactics of exclusion have eroded the potential sites of gay exchange. Instead we find a tidied-up, post-AIDS scare, clinical world of blandness and conformity, in which former heterotopias have become sanitised spaces of consumption that have something in common with EuroDisney.

The representational metropolis

In ' "Waiting, waiting": the hotel lobby, in the modern city', Douglas Tallack makes a comparison between two works, both titled 'The Hotel Lobby', an article from the 1920s by German cultural theorist, Siegfried Kracauer, and a painting from the 1940s by American artist, Edward Hopper. Although Kracauer and Hopper adopt differing theoretical outlooks, they share similar interests. The hotel lobby represents for them the quintessential space of modernity, which is characterised, for Kracauer, by a form of transcendental homelessness, captured with such accuracy in Hopper's painting. The hotel lobby is the space where silence reigns, and where guests bury themselves in their newspapers to avoid exchanging glances. It is by deciphering the hotel lobby as a social space, that we might grasp the essence of modernity.

Barry Curtis and Claire Pajaczkowska explore the theme of the mask in the representation of Venice in 'Venice: masking the real'. Through its literary associations Venice has often been associated with the figure of death. And so too, in terms of its perilous physical condition, Venice has been read as a doomed city. But Venice remains inscrutable, a place of concealed mystery. In fact it has survived and prospered, exploiting a new industry – that of tourism. The mask can be taken as the emblem for Venice. Through the mask the city has been read in gendered terms as the site of seduction and intrigue, but so too through the mask the city can be read as a city of self-representation. The real secret of Venice is the way in which it has re-invented and re-presented itself from decaying monument to the past to archetypal tourist city of the present.

In 'Benjamin's Moscow, Baudrillard's America', Graeme Gilloch makes a telling comparison between Walter Benjamin's essay on Moscow, and Jean Baudrillard's travelogue *America*. Both share common features, and both are written purportedly from an 'untheorised' perspective, although this would seem to amount to little more than a sublimation of theory, which may be detected too easily beneath the surface. Benjamin reads Moscow as a series of fragments – *Denkbilder* – which give clues to the whole, while Baudrillard views America as though through the lens of a camcorder as a 'real-time' road movie. These are fleeting, imagistic impressions of these cultures, perceptive enough, but ultimately somewhat constrained by their own limited framework.

Sarah Chaplin and Eric Holding explore the notion of the post-urban, in their piece, 'Addressing the post-urban: Los Angeles, Las Vegas, New York'. The post-urban city is one which 'has entered a critical self-aware stage with regard to the marketable status and image of the city'. The shift is from a naturalistic way of understanding the city to a promotional one: 'The post-urban city is not what it is, but what it is made out to be.' Highlighting how a city

might be promoted as a space of consumption through its own cinematographic representation, they contrast the tactics behind various commercial
developments in Los Angeles, Las Vegas and New York. In a culture where
advertising has come to suffuse our entire symbolic horizon, the importance of
'promoting' a city becomes paramount. The success of various enterprises
promoting the city as theme park forces us, they conclude, to reconsider some
of the more pejorative approaches to the representation of cities.

The filmic metropolis

In 'The "Problem of London", or, how to explore the moods of the city',
Steve Pile examines the potential of reading the hieroglyphic space of the city
through the documentary film by Patrick Keiller, *London* (1993), which is
composed of a series of Benjaminian 'postcards' – still shots accompanied by a
social commentary. These 'fragments' are stitched together by Keiller to
provide a provocative reading of London. Yet, according to Pile, the film
remains a collection of abstract musings about the city. There are, Pile
suggests, other more fertile ways of 'experiencing' London, and psychogeography might be used as a means of accessing the spirit of the city, and of
divining the ghosts and dreams that pervade it: 'It is not by seeing the city as a
fixed space', Pile concludes, 'or as a space of perpetual (speeding up) motion
that we will catch sight of these ghosts and dreams. It is only through spatial
practices which trace out the city, which map-make it, that the experiences of
haunting and of desire can be discerned.'

In '*Playtime*: "Tativille" and Paris', Iain Borden reconsiders the implications
of Tati's *Playtime*, which some have read as a critique of the modernist
metropolis in the manner of *Alphaville*. According to Borden, however, not
only does Tati make efforts to give a positive gloss to modern architecture, but
his films are 'overtly positive attempts to reassert the poetic aspects of modern
lives latent within modernist urbanism'. Far from denigrating modernism, these
films 'help unlock the experiential and comic potential of modern architecture'.
As Borden argues, to understand the filmic metropolis we must go beyond a
simplistic 'reading' of it. We must be open to reading its ironies and revelries,
but so too we must be open to its spatial experiences, its 'reflections, visions,
utterances, noises, rhythms, journeys [and] exchanges'.

In '*Blade Runner* : "Ridleyville" and Los Angeles', Peter Wollen examines
the re-presentation of Los Angeles as the fictional setting for the cult film *Blade
Runner*. The film presents a form of generic metropolis, composed of elements
of both New York and Los Angeles, although modelled more closely on the
latter. It is a form of hybrid world city, incorporating features common to other
'command-and-control centres for global capitalism', whose composite
languages reflect its status as a magnet for immigrants and ethnic minorities.
The dystopian image of the city in *Blade Runner* served to update the noir
image of Los Angeles, but the city is not quite Los Angeles. 'In a way', Wollen
comments, 'it is both the city which Los Angeles wishes to be, perceived in

boosterish, optimistic terms from the vantage-point of an elite, and yet fears it will become, looked at in noir, pessimistic terms from the point of view of its critics and its immigrant and underclass population'. 'It reflects', Wollen concludes, 'both the vision of Los Angeles as a future world city and the unsustainable dystopia which that would involve.'

The economic metropolis

Mirielle Rosello focuses on the failure of a dream for the inner-city in post-war Paris in 'French *bidonvilles* around 1960's Paris: urbanism and individual initiatives'. She questions the whole politics of representation, and the drive to rid the city of its shantytowns – *bidonvilles* – championing instead the strategies of resistance of those who inhabit these spaces. These *bidonvilles*, seemingly chaotic clusters of buildings, dismissed as unhealthy slums and objects of embarrassment by the state, and not even recorded on official maps, nonetheless followed their own logic, and managed to survive until eventually bulldozed, reflecting the resourcefulness of their inhabitants. Moreover, the erasure of the *bidonvilles* to make way for prestigious state buildings did not solve the problem. The inhabitants of the *bidonvilles* were displaced to high-rise estates where they found themselves in new ghettos which lacked the *bidonvilles'* sense of community. The question which should therefore be asked is whether a better strategy might have been to support the upgrading of the *bidonvilles*, rather than pursue a utopian vision for the high-rise estate, a vision which, as we know in hindsight, clearly failed.

In 'Pl(a)ys of marginality: transmigrants in Paris', Doina Petrescu addresses the spatial tactics of a new breed of temporary migrants colonising the space of Paris. Romanians peasants – neither political exiles, nor economic refugees – are engaging in short-term strategies for exploiting social security systems in the West. But this should be understood not as some cynical contemporary economic strategy, but as part of a cultural tradition of migrant working that stretches back through history. As Petrescu puts it: 'For these Romanian peasants, the transmigrational practice functions within an ancient vocabulary of mobility'. But so too these tricks and ruses have been honed by years of attempting to resist and subvert a totalitarian regime.

In 'The Capsular city', Lieven de Cauter develops the notion of 'capsular architecture', the architecture of the generic city. With transcendental capitalism our cities are held in a tension between 'Disneyfication' of the centre and 'Bronxification' of the periphery. The Disneyfied centre is obsessed with zoning, with safety and control. The 'cellular city' emerges, composed of capsular architecture which aims to exclude all that is undesirable, and to create its own artificial ambience. The postmodern atrium is but one example of this social 'cocooning'. And these exclusionary 'cellular cities' bear witness to the great social inequality that still exists today.

In 'Media-polis/media-city', Constantin Petcou explores the concept of 'extra-territoriality' in the media city of today. Neither territorialised nor deterritorialised in Deleuzian terms, 'extra-territoriality' refers to an ever-emerging condition, 'an extra-contextual anonymity' that is beginning to engulf our metropolitan centres. Architecture is ensnared within this condition, no less than transnational corporations and marketing outlets. Buildings are no longer place-dependent, but rather they exist within a nebulous extra-territorial realm of which Peter Eisenman's buildings offer a perfect example. The consequence of this is that extra-territoriality is becoming the new rule of social, economic, cultural and political contextualism, such that referentiality itself has lost its hegemony.

Notes

1 Siegfried Kracauer, 'On Employment Agencies', in *Rethinking Architecture*, ed. Neil Leach, London: Routledge, 1997, p. 60.
2 Kracauer, 'The Mass Ornament', in *The Mass Ornament: Weimar Essays*, trans. and ed. Thomas Y. Levin, Cambridge, MA: Harvard University Press, 1995, p. 75.
3 For a more complete description of structuralism and post-structuralism, see *Rethinking Architecture*, ed. Leach, pp. 163–4, 283–4.
4 For a more complete description of phenomenology, see *Rethinking Architecture*, ed. Leach, pp. 83–4.
5 Italo Calvino, *Invisible Cities*, trans. William Weaver, London: Vintage, 1997.
6 Hélène Cixous, 'Attacks of the Castle', in *Rethinking Architecture*, ed. Leach, pp. 306–7.
7 Roland Barthes, 'Semiology and the Urban', in *Rethinking Architecture*, ed. Leach, p. 168.
8 Barthes, 'Semiology and the Urban', pp. 171–2.
9 Barthes, 'Semiology and the Urban', p. 171.
10 Barthes, 'Semiology and the Urban', p. 172.

Part I
The legible metropolis

1 The metropolis as text

Otto Wagner and Vienna's 'Second Renaissance'

David Frisby

The metropolis as text

The notion of the city, its streets, its architecture, its populace, as a text is to be found in various forms in the work of many writers since at least the nineteenth century.[1] In particular, the conception of the city as text rests upon a number of presuppositions. Amongst these is that the city possesses features of textuality – at the basic level, a potentially decipherable constellation of signs and symbols. In its most basic form, a language is presupposed, a system of hieroglyphics. The city as text presupposes a reader or readers. Although since Baudelaire the reader has often been identified with the figure of the *flâneur*[2] (and much more rarely the *flâneuse*), it should be recognised that readership is stratified, partly on the basis of access to the text (mediated by power relations in the city), but certainly according to gender, social class, ethnicity, generation, etc. In turn, the city as text presupposes legibility in principle. This may not necessarily be at the present time but in the future (Walter Benjamin speaks of 'the coming to legibility' of the nineteenth century in our own century, for example).[3] Again to follow Benjamin, legibility in principle does not exclude erroneous readings (where the object – in this case, the city as text – is 'riddled with error').[4]

In order to identify some of the problems and themes that emerge from the conception of the city as text, it may be fruitful to review a number of the ways in which the city as text has been discussed. The examples chosen are all associated with writers who are also concerned with the delineation of features of modernity. This is not a fortuitous connection. Rather, a case can be made for assuming that the activity of reading the city as text itself emerges out of a desire to know and to analyse that which is new in the modern metropolis. The metropolis since the mid-nineteenth century at least has been one of the crucial sites of modernity – to be explored as a result of its quantitative and qualitative transformation. The interest in reading the metropolis may be documentary, poetic, political, social, etc.

For Baudelaire, for example, the modern metropolis was the site of modernity, and associated with the transitory, fleeting and fortuitous elements of existence within it. The features of modernity within the modern metropolis require interpretation and representation – by 'the painter of modern life' – insofar as they are represented symbolically. When Baudelaire declares that 'Man traverses a forest of symbols that look back at him with a familiar regard', then this implies that although human beings have created this forest of symbols, they are not thereby necessarily immediately intelligible.[5] Indeed, Baudelaire's conception of modernity as the transitory, the fleeting and the fortuitous also implies the discontinuous or disintegrating experience of time as transitory, space as fleeting, and causality as replaced by the fortuitous and the arbitrary. It is the task of the painter of modern life to capture the fleeting beauty of these dimensions of metropolitan modernity that nonetheless contain elements of 'the eternal and the immutable'.[6]

This transitory dimension of modern metropolitan experience is more broadly accentuated in Marx's analysis of modernity, with its focus upon the revolutionary new destruction of the past, the ever new destruction of the present, and the ever same reproduction of the 'socially necessary illusion' of the commodity form as the barrier to a qualitatively new future.[7] Although Marx spends too little time analysing the modern metropolis, the features of modernity that he outlines do nonetheless have relevance for reading the city as text. The destruction of the past in the metropolis is one of the central themes in the dispute surrounding the emergence of a new discipline of *Städtebau* in the late nineteenth century. In particular, the volumes by Camillo Sitte and Joseph Stübben published in 1889[8] and 1890[9] respectively are both responding – negatively in the case of Sitte – to Baron Haussmann's earlier transformation of Paris and its 'creative destruction'.[10] The destruction of the present takes the form of the accumulation of urban capital and the necessary increasing circulation of capital and commodities in the metropolis. The destruction and reconfiguration of the built environment that is implied in these processes have important implications for the constraints imposed upon metropolitan architecture, to maximise output of units and, where appropriate, to cheapen such units (as in the rental barracks [*Mietskaserne*]). In turn, the commodified (and the non-commodified) built forms are also given a representative, symbolic value in material and social hieroglyphics. As Marx remarks in the context of the commodity form – but also applicable to the non-commodified built form that owes its existence to the political production and reproduction of the built form – 'Value does not have its description branded on its forehead. Rather, it transforms every product of labour into a social hieroglyphic.'[11] In terms of the discussion here, the implication is that metropolitan architecture reveals constellations of hieroglyphics that require to be read.

If Marx did not spend sufficient time on the analysis of metropolitan modernity, the same cannot be said of the early Futurists, for whom the modern city was not merely the epitome of modernity but also one of the crucial showcases of modern technology. For Marinetti, the new configuration of everyday technologies both transforms the modes in which we experience the modern metropolis and creates new sets of entities in the urban landscape that require to be read. Writing in 1913, Marinetti notes that:

Whoever today makes use of the telegraph, the telephone, the gramo-phone, the train, the bicycle, the motorbike, the ocean liner, the airship, the airplane, the cinema, the major daily newspaper (synthesis of a day in the world) does not think of the fact that these diverse types of communi-cation, transport and information exercise a decisive influence upon a person's mind.[12]

What Marinetti does not mention here in this context is the dramatic increase in the street furniture and the plethora of things, signs and other entities that are produced for the modern metropolis and the increased circu-lation of its traffic and its individuals. One of the tasks of the new discipline of *Städtebau* (city planning) was not merely to facilitate the creation of this new system of objects but also to read its significance. In a quite fundamental manner, the alignment of streets, the provisions for categories of traffic, the furniture of this street *exterieur* all serve to condition not merely how we perceive the city and its streets but also our bodily movement and deport-ment within them.[13]

It remained for others to raise some of the issues involved in reading this increasingly complex text of the modern metropolis. In his volume *Spazieren in Berlin*,[14] Franz Hessel – with whom Benjamin had originally embarked upon writing a couple of short articles on the Parisian arcades – quite explicitly oper-ates with a notion of the city as text to be read by the *flâneur*. Hessel views the activity of the *flâneur* as follows:

> *Flânerie* is a kind of reading of the street, in which human faces, shop windows, cafe terraces, street cars, automobiles and trees become a wealth of equally valid letters of the alphabet that together result in words, sentences and pages of an ever-new book. Hessel, however is less interested in the syntax and semantics of the city's signifiers than in the images them-selves. Despite the dangers of *flânerie*, he assumes that the city as text can be read immediately by the *flâneur*.[15]

This assumption is not made by Hessel's contemporary, Siegfried Kracauer. Trained as an architect himself, Kracauer does not merely relate to the city as text, as a labyrinth of often fragmentary signs, but also raises the problem of deciphering the metropolitan text as a constellation of images. The city as text must be read in such a way as to uncover or reveal what is hidden. For Kracauer, 'spatial images are the dreams of society. Wherever the hiero-glyphics of any spatial image is deciphered, there the basis of social reality presents itself.'[16] Elsewhere, Kracauer distinguishes two types of spatial images that are to be deciphered. The fact is 'consciously formed' and to be found in plans and guidebooks. The second are 'fortuitous creations' – configurations of buildings, streets and figures which the individual confronts.[17] Both contribute in different ways to our knowledge of the city, although it is the second type that is merely likely to reveal 'the basis of social reality'. This knowledge is not directly available but mediated through the images themselves: 'Knowledge of cities is bound up with the deciphering of their dream-like expressive images.'[18] In a more positivistic reading of the city, Wagner's critique of historicist façades led him to denounce their 'dream' as 'a lie'.

The city as dream 'text' was already developed by Louis Aragon in his *Paris Peasant*, exploring the decaying world of the Parisian arcade in the 1920s.[19] There Aragon declares that 'our cities are peopled with unrecognized sphynxes'[20] whose significance remains to be read. Although drawing initially upon Aragon, it was in fact Walter Benjamin who most fully explored the possibility of reading the city as text, as well as drawing attention to intertextuality in this context. If the city is a text, then the reflexive possibility can be posited of the text possessing affinities with the city: 'that which is written is like a city, to which the words are a thousand gateways'.[21] Although there are many instances of Benjamin reading the contemporary city in *One Way Street*,[22] *Moscow Diaries*[23] and elsewhere, it was his unorthodox historical projects reconstituting his childhood – in *Berlin Childhood Around 1900*[24] and *Berlin Chronicle*,[25] and above all his textual reconstruction of 'Paris: Capital of the Nineteenth Century'[26] that are testimony to his detailed analysis of the city – its architecture, streets, population, traffic, street furniture, interiors, etc. As Graeme Gilloch has demonstrated,[27] Benjamin's reading of the metropolis is a multi-faceted one in which the city is explored as physiognomy ('a space to be read'), phenomenologically ('the city is a monad, a fragment within which the totality of modern life may be discerned'), as mythology, as history, as politics and as text. The city as text, as 'a linguistic cosmos' (Benjamin),[28] as 'a secret text to be read' (Gilloch) requires a special kind of reader of modern metropolitan life. Benjamin states his task as that of Hugo von Hofmannsthal: '"Read what was never written". The reader called to mind here is the true historian.'[29] For Benjamin's project to be successful, he would have to train *readers of his texts* to read the labyrinth of the phenomenal world of the metropolis.

This brief intimation of some of the issues – which could be extended – arising out of the concept of reading modern metropolitan existence is intended to indicate that 'reading' modern life cannot be viewed unproblematically. As Peter Fritzsche suggests in his reconstruction of a reading of Berlin around the turn of the century based upon newspaper texts, 'texts do not speak for themselves in one voice, and they are not understood in the same way by all readers'.[30]

In the present context, that draws in part on Otto Wagner's readings of modernity in Vienna in the late nineteenth century, it may be necessary to distinguish between the professional and the lay person's reading of modern life and the modern metropolis. Here we might draw upon a distinction which Michel de Certeau, in 'Walking the City',[31] made between reading the city as a 'geometrical' or 'geographical' space of visual, panoptic or theoretical constructions – which might be associated with architects' or city planners' readings – and reading 'an opaque and blind mobility characteristic of the bustling city – in which a migrational or metaphorical city thus, slips into the clear text of the planned and read-able city' – which might be associated with a lay person's everyday reading.

However, there are two relevant problems with this distinction. The first, which draws upon phenomenological and ethno-methodological insights, is that the first reading rests ultimately upon the second, or at least that the grounds for privileging the first reading must be demonstrated and not taken for granted. The second problem arises from the notion of 'the clear text of the planned and readable city' which already concedes the 'clarity' of geometrical or geographical space. The first problem should lead us to inquire further into the location or siting of the professional's reading of the city or modern life (is it really a reading from above, for instance?). The second should lead us to ques-tion whether the building of cities (*Städtebau*) ever commenced from or created the clarity which de Certeau ascribes to it.

If de Certeau's distinction is transposed to the reading of 'modern life', then it has affinities not merely with a distinction between a conscious and a fortuitous reading (and therefore possessing similarity with Kracauer's distinction indicated above), but also with a distinction between two different readings of modernity. Modernity as a process of rationalisation (and progressive abstraction) and modernity as disintegration of basic categories of time, space and causality, and experience as 'transitory, fleeting and fortuitous' (Baudelaire) are ostensibly two distinct conceptions of modernity. But the first might well emanate from a desire to regulate the second, to control the implications of its dynamic and disinte-grating movement. For the architect of modern life – and this is how Otto Wagner viewed the role of the modern architect, and was certainly his own aim – the task of giving expression to modern metropolitan life itself contained tensions that remained to be resolved. This task for the architect of modern life may well be construed as different from that of Baudelaire's 'painter of modern life'.

If the city is a text, then it should be read – amongst others – by those who seek to create, shape, and transform it. Their *reading* of the city crucially condi-tions their *writing* of the city text, its buildings, its streets, its street furniture, etc. Texts and cities can be read from a distance in which only their general contours are visible and which, therefore, might only appear abstract. They can also be read closely bringing out precise details. Both readings generate meaning out of a plethora of signifiers. As Franz Löwitsch argued for the Berlin street network in 1931, it is 'not a chaos of meaningless lines but rather a script that is to be deciphered'.[32]

Readings of the city confront one another in space and time. There can be different temporal readings of the spatial configurations and physiognomy of the city as old (to be preserved) and as new or modern (involving the destruc-tion of the old). The mode in which the juxtaposition and the confrontation of old and new take place conditions the manner in which modernity is expressed in the metropolis. This is significant for, amongst others, those who wish to create a modern architecture for the modern metropolis that is appropriate to, and even mirrors, modern life. A striking early exemplar is Otto Wagner in Vienna in the 1890s (see Figure 1.1).

Figure 1.1   Wagner's bird's-eye view of projected development of Danube canal quay
and projected Wagner Avenue from southern end of the Ringstrasse towards
the Stephansdom: reading from the city above.

Reproduced by kind permission of the Historisches Museum der Stadt Wien and the Direktion der Museen
der Stadt Wien.

Wagner and Vienna's 'Second Renaissance'

In the mid-1890s Wagner produced a critique of the Viennese architecture of
recent decades in which he maintained that much recent and current architecture was responsible for the low esteem accorded to architects in Vienna. In
particular, Wagner argued that

> The main cause of the lack of full appreciation of the significance of the
> architect lies in *the world of forms* employed by him up to now, in his
> *language directed to the mass of the people* which in most instances *remains
> completely unintelligible* to them.[33]

There are a number of sources of this unintelligibility that render much of
recent architecture unreadable, but Wagner is at pains to suggest that the indif-
ference of the masses is not responsible for this state of affairs. Where
construction has been increasingly given over to engineers rather than architects
there has been a tendency to produce structures lacking in aesthetic form.
However, the principal reason for unintelligibility lies in the absence of architectural forms that are appropriate to modern needs and representations of
modern life.

Indeed, instead of an architecture appropriate to modern life, recent decades have witnessed a 'rush through all stylistic tendencies', 'a jumble of styles',[34] a morbid recall of past, dead styles, and an appropriation of specific historicist styles for particular buildings (churches should be Gothic, for example). Historicist facades are often the expression of 'artistic lies', creating the impression in rented apartment blocks that everyone lives in a palace. The 'stuck on facade' of many a historicist apartment block produces 'the swindle-like dimensions abounding in lies reminiscent of Potemkin villages'[35] – a reference taken up in 1898 by Adolf Loos in his 'Potemkin City'.[36]

Such a critique of historicist architecture leads to the conclusion that recent architectural practice has created the basis for erroneous readings of the city, the construction of a 'false' text. Its Viennese context is summed up in Hermann Bahr's statement that 'Otto Wagner is the opposite of the Ringstrasse. There everything starts out from effect, in Wagner from expression. There arbitrariness, here necessity. There swindle, kitsch, theatre, here always merely what the object will be.'[37] The historicist search for effect in earlier forms contrasts with Wagner's claim that new, practical and modern needs cannot be accommodated in old forms – the latter are no longer appropriate and new forms must be created. Such a view contrasts with the notion still to be found throughout the 1890s that it is possible, for instance, to have new buildings fulfilling new tasks but totally in Renaissance form.[38] For Wagner, the search for new forms must be undertaken on the premiss that 'the sole departure point for our artistic work can only be modern life.'[39] And what is true for individual structures must also be true for the metropolis as a whole since 'a great modern city cannot and should not have the appearance of Ancient Rome or of old Nuremburg'.[40] Indeed, for Wagner, the opposite premise is his starting point: 'The most modern of that which is modern in architecture are indeed our present day metropolitan cities.'[41] Modernity in modern architecture means addressing modern needs, applying modern building materials, creating structures appropriate to modern life, with an accord between interior and exterior (and not the false motifs of apartment block 'palaces'), and interiors that are appropriate to modern human beings (and not historicist, illusory backdrops to modern life).

At no point in his critique of Viennese architecture of recent decades does Wagner reveal his own earlier contribution to this architecture, its interiors or his collaboration with, for example, Hans Mackart.[42] Rather, Wagner appears to argue for a complete break with the past, including his own previous 'somewhat free Renaissance style'.[43] In keeping with this break with the past, Wagner sees the present period of the mid-1890s not as a 'Renaissance of the Renaissance' but as a 'Naissance'.[44] However, contemporaries such as Feldegg, the founder and editor of the avant-garde Viennese architecture journal *Der Architekt* since 1895, probably expressed contemporary views more accurately with his notion of 'Vienna's Second Renaissance'[45] in the 1890s. What was the significance of the contrast between the 'first' and 'second' Renaissance in Vienna? As Hermann Bahr's judgement on Wagner intimated, a distinction was being drawn between the first enlargement of the city of Vienna after 1857 and the construction of the Ringstrasse and the zone surrounding it, and the second extension of the city in 1890 and the consequent expansion of building programmes in the ensuing decades. Feldegg drew a distinction between Vienna's first Renaissance associated with the building of the Ringstrasse as aristocratic in tone with individual monumental works as a primary feature, on the one hand, and, on the other, the second Renaissance in the 1890s as democratic in impulse with whole building complexes as monumental. The assemblage of public monuments often in open spaces on the Ringstrasse is contrasted with whole street perspectives of rented apartment blocks, for example, as manifestation of a democratic impulse. What is noteworthy is that the Ringstrasse monuments – with the possible exception of the stock exchange – are all public and state-dependent monuments.[46] In terms of building types, those which contemporaries viewed as manifestations of modernity, such as department stores and railway stations, are absent from the Ringstrasse. And whereas the historicist variations in building styles along the Ringstrasse were not conducive to creating the effect, at least, of a *Gesamtkunstwerk*, one of the most prominent of the structures erected between 1894 and 1898 and designed by Wagner and his students – the *Stadtbahn*, the city railway – as a symbol of circulation in the modern metropolis (and for reasons of military security, the railway ran *around* the centre of the city), could lay claim to being a *Gesamtkunstwerk*, a total work of art on a monumental scale.[47]

The fact that the modern city railway runs around the old city centre has more than military significance. The second extension of the city boundaries after 1890 opened up renewed debate on the nature and boundaries of 'Old' and 'New' Vienna, on the challenge of modern architecture and the possibility of Vienna as a modern metropolis. This debate coincided with a related but ostensibly more theoretical confrontations on the nature and purposes of city planning, literally city building (*Städtebau*), especially after the publication of Camillo Sitte's volume on city planning in 1889. The preservation of the inner city's Renaissance and Baroque structures and the layout of its streets and squares was simultaneously a confrontation with the modern, taking on increasingly hostile tones after Wagner's students at the Academy of Fine Arts from 1894 onwards achieved some successes, and especially after the establishment of the Vienna Secession in 1897 and its heavily contested exhibition building designed and erected by Olbrich – a Wagner student – in 1898.[48] There were no major avenues constructed through the centre of the city (such as the projected Riehl avenue from the Stephansdom to the Prater), no underground railway (under discussion in the decade prior to the First World War) and not one of Wagner's projects completed (several Museum designs, hotel complex or department store) in the most disputed area around the Karlsplatz with the exception of his city rail station. The Ringstrasse, itself largely completed by 1890 with the exception of the Stuben area, remained the most monumental street complex and contained no 'modern' structures with the exception of Wagner's Post Office Savings

Bank (which was itself set back from the main thoroughfare), yet which faced the Ministry of War designed by the conservative Ludwig Baumann (designs by Wagner, Adolf Loos and others were rejected).

Despite Wagner's search for support from the Christian Social Party Mayor, Karl Lueger (whose populist programme combined strong currents of anti-Semitic ideology with local public sector projects),[49] increasing opposition in Vienna resulted in none of his major public projects being realised (even the Kirche am Steinhof was approved by the Lower Austrian parliament and not the Viennese authorities).

Yet amongst his contemporaries, it was Wagner who published the first modernist manifesto on architecture (his *Modern Architecture* of 1896) and who, in effect, produced a reading of modern, metropolitan life that was to have been the foundation for a modern architecture responsive to modern needs. What were the salient features of Wagner's reading of modern life and how did he propose to render architecture intelligible?

Transcending the 'unintelligible'?

In order for modern architecture to be intelligible once more it must be a reflection of its times. As Wagner declared in his 1894 Inaugural Lecture, 'the starting point of every artistic creation must be the need, ability, means and achievements of our time'.[50] In a somewhat naive manner, Wagner assumes that the creation of a structural homology between modern life and modern architecture will render the latter intelligible. In turn, modern architecture's success in this respect depends upon an 'accurate' (and there are strong positivist strands in Wagner's reflections) reading of modern life. What were its features as recognised by Wagner?

Although there is no systematic and ordered presentation of the features of modern life in Wagner's writings, it is possible to draw them out from various sources. It will then be possible to inquire as to their common features and the problems which their realisation in modern metropolitan architecture might raise. Wagner's reading of modern life is a general one, comprising the following features: an unbounded expansion of the metropolis, permanent progress, technological advance, democratisation, levelling (of life styles, for example), purposive orientation to time and money, increasing mobility and movement in transport systems (and the transformation of time–space relations), monumentalism (including the street as monument), increasing significance of fashion and the domination of the rented apartment block (in its variants that include the dwelling and commercial block and its abstract form the 'conglomerate of cells') (see Figure 1.2). Of perhaps greater interest are some of the implications contained within these somewhat abstract tendencies in modern life and their consequences for the transformation of modern experience.

Since his submission for the general plan of Vienna competition in 1894,[51] Wagner had conceived of the modern metropolis as a constantly expanding network; a radial city with distribution centres (reminiscent of Gottfried Semper's *Stellen*) at appropriate points, expanding commensurate with population increases and accompanied by corresponding increases in troops stationed in the city (the military and modernity in this context appear contradictory until the fear of revolution and insurrection is taken into account). The modern metropolis of straight-lined avenues and plain surfaces, the continuous rows of (economically viable) apartment blocks, creates the modern street as itself monumental (and this aside from Wagner's permanent call for more public monuments, themselves contingent upon *political* support for their construction). Modern metropolitan constructions should avail themselves of new technological developments both in the use of new materials (steel, aluminium) and new modes of construction. In this context, Wagner calls for a greater co-operation between architect and engineer (as is apparent in his own contributions to the city railway and the Nussdorf

Figure 1.2 Completion of Wagner's 'Majolika' apartment block, 1899: similar but not identical lifestyles.

Reproduced by kind permission of the Historisches Museum der Stadt Wien and the Direktion der Museen der Stadt Wien.

sluice on the Danube canal), thereby alleviating one of the grounds for the 'unintelligibility' of contemporary architecture (by giving engineering structures a modern architectural form).

In terms of reading modern life, Wagner places emphasis upon its *tempo* and its distinctive *goal orientations*, epitomised in the slogan 'time is money'. The acceleration of interactions and transactions requires a new orientation to metropolitan life. First, architects must concern themselves precisely with the economic needs of the building process (accurate and detailed costings), with the speed of construction and with the whole problematic of building investment (the rented apartment block's purpose, as Wagner recognises, is to function as an interest-bearing investment – not merely a rented block [*Miethaus*] but also an interest-generating block [*Zinshaus*]). Second, a general acceleration in economic and other transactions *(Verkehr)* is also implicit in this slogan, and above all in the sphere of circulation, exchange and consumption. The metropolis is not merely the site of accelerating circulation of commodities but also human beings (even Sitte saw the Ringstrasse as 'a traffic highway of human beings in motion'). Therefore, the infrastructure for safe, mass circulation in all its forms must be a priority. Third, our actions are conditioned by our orientation to ends in many spheres of life. What Max Weber later saw as purposive rational action requires, for Wagner, a new orientation in architecture: the development of a utility style *(Nutzstil)* and an art directed to needs and ends *(Zweckkunst)*. Such orientations were vehemently contested by those who maintained that the artistic sphere should remain an autonomous sphere.

The identification of such general features of modern life with common orientations to action are associated, for Wagner, with a process of *levelling* in our conditions of life – a questionable general thesis in the context of a society increasingly differentiated by social class. The assumption of the increasingly similar mode of living will lead to the increasing *uniformity* of the rented apartment block and the destruction of the external differentiation of the palace-like facades of the historicist blocks (by size and degree of ornamentation). Similarly, the development of the electric lift leads to a potential equalisation of floors in the rented apartment block. This is perhaps the context within which we may understand Wagner's assertion of the *democratisation* (probably in a formal sense) of modern life. A mode of equalisation at least is presupposed by the emergence of a mass private housing market – with the apartment block as a 'conglomerate of cells' – and the only differentiating feature of this and other building types (including the city railway) being a standard, uniform price to pay for entry.

In many respects most disturbing for his contemporaries is Wagner's positive association of modern architecture with *fashion*. Arguing against the disharmony between historicist styles and modern life, Wagner asserts that this is manifested in a disharmony between fashion (which always responds to new tendencies) and style (which becomes rigidified and more difficult to influence). Modern human beings are extremely sensitive to fashion changes and the built environment should be appropriate to this sensibility (rather than placing modern clothed individuals in imitation Louis XV or other settings). And although Wagner's examples of fashion are male, this argument is with reference to modern human beings in general. The archaeology of styles favoured by historicism ensures that the language of art remains unintelligible. The clear implication of Wagner's argument is that modern architecture should heed *the language of fashion* if it wishes to create works for *our* times.

What are the implications of Wagner's unsystematic explorations of modern life for the transformation of modern experience? The levelling and democratisation thesis implies the exchangeability and replicability of individuals and a tendency towards the creation of a mass society. At the same time, this replicability of individuals and life styles is accompanied by increasing *abstraction of signifiers* – a feature which is expressed architecturally in the predominance of the straight line and the simple surface or abstract ornamentation (whose monumental effect is produced by viewing the whole avenue of built structures). In this context, the modern metropolitan dweller in the apartment block is more prepared 'to disappear in the crowd as a "number"'[52] – as a means of securing individual freedom – than to long for the individual family house (and unwelcome contact with neighbours). Anonymity secures individual freedom.

This putative levelling and uniformity in life style and, above all, in street profiles and major open squares could have other consequences, some of which are hardly addressed by Wagner. It is Sitte who sees a correlation between broad empty streets and huge open squares and agoraphobia, whereas the small, old enclosed squares create a feeling of cosiness[53] (which Wagner would view as claustrophobia). In any event, the pathologies of space (and Freud was shortly to investigate the uncanny[54]) as part of a wider pathology of modern life were entering contemporary discourse, to be joined by a pathology of loss in relation to the past (amnesia),[55] in relation to things (Simmel's association of hyperaesthesia with the money economy), and monomania in relation to the self (which Sitte ascribes to Wagner's obsession with straight streets).

All too briefly, Wagner touches upon the optical and perspectival transformation of our metropolitan experience arising, in part, from the fact that we are ourselves in motion in new ways. Beatriz Colomina has suggested that 'the mode of perception is what becomes fleeting. Now the observer (the *flâneur*, the train traveller, the department store shopper) is what is transient. This transience, and the new space of the city in which it is experienced cannot be separated from the new forms of representation.'[56] Wagner had already reflected upon the modern eye's loss of the small intimate scale, its becoming accustomed to changeable images, to longer straight lines, broader surfaces and larger volumes. Yet Wagner did not examine here these optical, perspectival and panoramic changes in relation to transport systems such as his own city railway, even though later in his essay on the metropolis he was to emphasise the fact that 'the "city's physiognomy" has the greatest influence upon the image of the city'.[57] There he is emphatic too that the city itself, and its streets, should be works of art, and not be confined to the 'art storage spaces' of metropolitan museums.

Contradictory texts

If it is the case that Wagner's general delineation of metropolitan modernity, of modern life can be characterised as emphasising abstraction, circulation and movement, and monumentality – however contradictory these features might be when set alongside one another – then they do possess a further common feature insofar as none of them are specific to Vienna. The modern metropolis is cosmopolitan, not rooted inexorably in the past. Wagner's reading of modern life as a foundation for a modern architecture had to confront an alternative reading of Vienna's 'Second Renaissance', sometimes based on a closed, anti-modern high culture, afraid of an unlimited metropolis (such as Berlin). The 'second' architectural renaissance heralded by Wagner, his students and others and epitomised by the Secession movement could be read by conservatives as 'arbitrariness', 'complete anarchy', the absence of 'a kind of logical grammar of forms', social levelling without 'reverence',[58] and so on. Others might reflect that the modern movement should confine its attention to building private villas in the suburbs since 'outside, one does not need to seek out its buildings'. In the heart of the city – and especially in the Karlsplatz area – this 'sudden, powerful tearing away from all tradition' must be resisted.[59] Yet others might lament Wagner's one-sided emphasis upon the *modern* that ignores the need for the development of a mature *national* art, a regard for national consciousness and, with the decline in the influence of religion, the need for a new ideal – love of fatherland.[60] Such opposition to modernity reveals that the desire to create a 'New Vienna' confronted an 'Old Vienna', a confrontation heightened by tensions between capitalist and quasi-feudal social formations, vertical and horizontal stratification of social classes and ethnic groups and an emergent labour movement.

At the same time, Wagner's own reading of metropolitan modernity contains contradictions and problems that he failed to address. The positivistic tendency to maintain that modern architecture should 'mirror' modern life entails that this mirror does indeed reflect everything in modern life including its contradictions. Contemporary life in Vienna in the 1890s contains both modernising and anti-modern dimensions. In this sense, 'modern' life is not yet established in Vienna whilst, at the same time, a delineation of modern life that did address its historical specificity would have to confront deep contradictions in its social, economic, political and cultural configurations.

Wagner's optimistic assumption that we are all 'modern' human beings is contradicted by his own assertions that large sections of the public – including much of the 'educated' public – are not yet capable of recognising architecture's language of forms. His assumption is more seriously qualified by Adolf Loos' reflections on the non-contemporaneity of the contemporaneous in Vienna. Loos maintained that:

> The rate of cultural development is held back by those that cannot cope with the present. I live in the year 1908, but my neighbour lives approximately in the year 1900, and one over there lives in the year 1880.[61]

Figure 1.3 Construction of section of Wagner's city railway and regulation of the River
Wien, and Olbrich's Secession building, 1898: 'Vienna is now being
demolished into a metropolis' (Kraus).

Reproduced by kind permission of the Historisches Museum der Stadt Wien and the Direktion der Museen
der Stadt Wien.

The temporal differentiation of readings of the contemporary metropolis
must be taken into account. So too must the prior knowledge or 'stock of
knowledge at hand' (Alfred Schutz) in recognising a modern language of
forms. Similarly, the loss or threatened loss of orientation by the destruction
of the past requires new facilitators for the acquisition of a new language.
Although writing in 1897 with a different aim, Karl Kraus comments that
'Vienna is now being demolished into a metropolis (see Figure 1.3).
Together with the old houses *the last pillars of our memories* are falling, and
soon an irreverent spade will have also leveled the venerable Cafe Griensteidl
to the ground.'[62] The new Vienna emerging alongside old Vienna gave a
stimulus to nostalgia. Not merely was a 'new' Vienna in the process of being
developed but also the ideology of 'old Vienna' was being renewed.

Thus, beneath Wagner's confident and often very general reading of
modern life as precondition for a modern metropolitan architecture that
would be appropriate to it, the issues associated with rendering a reading
possible and intelligible were clearly more complex than he appeared to indicate. However, without reducing the significance of his writings, it is
Wagner's modern architecture itself which displays a very close reading of the
immediate space within which it is located.

Notes

1 See James Donald, 'Metropolis: The City As Text', in *Social and Cultural Forms of Modernity*, ed. Robert Bocock and Kenneth Thompson, Cambridge, 1992, pp. 418–61.

2 See Charles Baudelaire, *The Flâneur*, ed. Keith Tester, London, 1994.

3 See Susan Buck-Morss, *The Dialectics of Seeing*, Cambridge, MA, 1989.

4 See Walter Benjamin, *Charles Baudelaire: A Lyric Poet in the Era of High Capitalism*, London, 1973, p. 103.

5 See Charles Baudelaire, *The Painter of Modern Life and Other Essays*, London, 1964.

6 For a brief discussion of this task in the context of exploring modernity, see David Frisby, *Fragments of Modernity: Theories of Modernity in the Work of Simmel, Kracauer and Benjamin*, London and Cambridge, MA: Polity Press, 1985, chap. 1.

7 Marx's analysis of modernity is also examined in Frisby, *Fragments of Modernity*, Cambridge, 1985, chap. 1.

8 Camillo Sitte, *City Planning According to Artistic Principles*, trans. George and Christine Collins, New York, 1985.

9 Joseph Stübben, *Der Städtebau*, Braunschweig and Wiesbaden, 1990.

10 On Haussmann see most recently David P. Jordan, *Transforming Paris. The Life and Labors of Baron Haussmann*, New York, 1993.

11 Cited in Frisby, *Fragments of Modernity*, p. 21.

12 Cited in Manfred Smuda, 'Die Wahrnehmung der Grossstadt als ästhetisches Problem des Erzählens', in *Die Grossstadt als Text*, ed. Manfred Smuda, Munich, 1992, p. 131.

13 As an instance of the significance of street furniture in the nineteenth century see Stübben, *Der Städtebau*.

14 Now re-titled and available as Franz Hessel, *Ein Flâneur in Berlin*, Berlin, 1984.

15 Hessel, *Ein Flâneur in Berlin*, p. 145.

16 Cited in Frisby, *Fragments of Modernity*, p. 109.

17 See Frisby, *Fragments of Modernity*, pp. 135–6.

18 Cited in Frisby, *Fragments of Modernity*, p. 136.

19 Louis Aragon, *Paris Peasant*, London, 1980.

20 Aragon, *Paris Peasant*, pp. 28–9.

21 Cited in Baudelaire, *The Flâneur*, p. 106.

22 Walter Benjamin, *One Way Street*, London, 1979.

23 Walter Benjamin, *Moscow Diaries*, Cambridge, MA, 1983.

24 Walter Benjamin, *Berliner Kindheit um Neunzehnhundert*, Frankfurt, 1950.

25 In Benjamin, *One Way Street*, pp. 293–346.

26 The incomplete project was assembled, Walter Benjamin, *Das Passagenwerk*, Frankfurt, 1982.

27 Graeme Gilloch, *Myth and Metropolis. Walter Benjamin and the City*, Oxford, 1996.

28 Cited in Gilloch, *Myth and Metropolis*, p. 181.

29 Gilloch, *Myth and Metropolis*, p. 181.

30 Peter Fritzsche, *Reading Berlin 1900*, Cambridge, MA, 1996, p. 47.

31 Michel de Certeau, *The Practice of Everyday Life*, Berkeley, CA: University of California Press, 1984, pp. 91–110.

32 Franz Löwitsch, 'Die Idee Berlin', *Wasmuth's Monatsheft*, XV (1931): 424.

33 Otto Wagner, *Modern Architecture*, trans. (and amend.) Harry Mallgrave, Santa Monica, 1985, p. 65.

34 Otto Wagner, 'Moderne Architektur', in *Otto Wagner. Das Werk des Architekten*, I, ed. Otto A. Graf, Vienna, 1985, pp. 172 and 173.

35 Otto Wagner, 'Moderne Architektur', p. 281.

36 Adolf Loos, 'Potemkin City', in *Spoken Into the Void*, Cambridge, MA, 1982, pp. 95–6.

37 Hermann Bahr, 'Otto Wagner', *Essays von Hermann Bahr*, ed. Heinz Kindermann, Vienna, 1960, pp. 283–4.

38 See, for example, Fritz Schumacher, 'Die Sehnsucht nach dem "Nenen"', *Deutsche Bauzeitung*, 31 (1897): 629–32.

39 Otto Wagner, 'Moderne Architektur', p. 263.

40 Otto Wagner, *Modern Architecture*, p. 109.

41 Otto Wagner, *Modern Architecture*, p. 103

42 See Otto A. Graf, *Der Baukunst der Eros*, Vienna, 1996, for details of Wagner's early work and the personal context.

43 Otto Wagner, *Einige Skizzen, Projekten und ausgeführte Bauwerke*, Tübingen, 1987, p. 17.

44 Otto Wagner, *Modern Architecture*, p. 79.

45 Freiherr von Feldegg, 'Wiens zweite Renaissance', *Der Architekt*, I, (1895): 1–2.

46 For a discussion of the symbolic significance of the Ringstrasse, see Carl E. Schorske, *Fin-de-Siècle Vienna*, London, 1980.

47 On the city railway in detail see Günter Kolb, *Otto Wagner und die Wiener Stadtbahn*, Munich, 1989.

48 On the increasing opposition to Wagner see Peter Haiko, *Otto Wagner und das Kaiser Franz Josef-Stadtmuseum*, Vienna, 1988.

49 On Lueger's policy see John W. Boyer, *Culture and Political Crisis in Vienna*, Chicago, IL, 1996.

50 Otto Wagner, 'Anttritsrede Otto Wagners, 1894', in Marco Pozzetto, *Die Schule, Otto Wagners. 1894–1912*, Vienna, 1980, pp. 144–6.

51 See Graf (ed.), *Otto Wagner*, I, pp. 88–122.

52 Otto Wagner, *Die Grossstadt*, Vienna, 1911, p. 21.

53 See Sitte, *City Planning*.

54 On Freud, see Anthony Vidler, *The Architectural Uncanny: Essays in the Modern Unhomely*, Cambridge, MA, 1992.

55 See Christine M. Boyer, *The City of Collective Memory*, Cambridge, MA, 1996.

56 Beatriz Colomina, *Privacy and Publicity*, Cambridge, MA, 1994.

57 Wagner, 'Die Grossstadt', in Graf (ed.), *Otto Wagner. Das Werk*, II, p. 641.

58 See the articles on architecture in A.F. Seligman, *Kunst und Künstler von gestern und heute*, Vienna, 1910.

59 See Joseph Bayer, 'Die Moderne und die historische Baustyle', *Neue Freie Presse*, 3 April 1902.

60 See Karl Henrici, 'Moderne Architektur', *Deutsche Bauzeitung*, XXXl, (1897): 14–20.

61 Adolf Loos, 'Ornament and Crime', in *The Architecture of Adolf Loos*, London, 1897, p. 101.

62 Karl Kraus, 'The Demolished Literature', in *The Vienna Coffee House Wits 1890–1938*, ed. Harold B. Segel, West Lafayette, 1993, p. 65.

2 Cognitive mapping
New York vs Philadelphia

Jonathan Hale

Introduction

In the essay 'Cognitive Mapping', published in 1988, cultural theorist Fredric Jameson sets out the possibilities for a new kind of Marxist aesthetic. By considering the pedagogical function of the work of art as providing a sense of orientation towards the larger and in itself unrepresentable social totality, Jameson attempts to rehabilitate the project of political change through the media of visual and spatial form. The inspiration for this view of the work of art as a 'mental map' for the process of political action springs from two very different sources: one directly political and the other urbanistic and architectural. The first is the statement from Louis Althusser that defines ideology as 'the Imaginary representation of the subject's relationship to his or her Real conditions of existence'.[1] The second source is presented as an analogue to the first and comes from the work of architect and urban theorist Kevin Lynch on the process of spatial orientation in city centres.[2] Jameson highlights the parallel between the two ideas in the opening chapter of his book *Postmodernism, or, The Cultural Logic of Late Capitalism*:

> There is, for one thing, a most interesting convergence between the empirical problems studied by Lynch in terms of city space and the great Althusserian (and Lacanian) redefinition of ideology ... Surely this is exactly what the cognitive map is called upon to do in the narrower framework of daily life in the physical city: to enable a situational representation on the part of the individual subject to that vaster and properly unrepresentable totality which is the ensemble of society's structures as a whole.[3]

By taking the notion of the cognitive spatial map into the realm of political activity – 'projected outward onto some of the larger national and global spaces' that he is concerned with in his work[4] – Jameson is aiming, ultimately, at a means to realise a coherent socialist political project. As against what he sees as the forces of fragmentation at work in society due to the dominant, 'late capitalist', ideology of the present, he claims that an orientation towards the social whole is the key to the organization of effective political action.[5] As he makes

more explicit in the earlier essay on 'Cognitive Mapping' already referred to, the necessary function of ideology as a means of orientation in the social realm might be understood more clearly through a comparison with Lynch's empirical research:

> The conception of cognitive mapping proposed here therefore involves an extrapolation of Lynch's spatial analysis to the realm of social structure, that is to say, in our historical moment, to the totality of class relations on a global (or should I say multinational) scale. The secondary premise is also maintained, namely, that the incapacity to map socially is as crippling to political experience as the analogous incapacity to map spatially is for urban experience. It follows that an aesthetic of cognitive mapping in this sense is an integral part of any socialist political project.[6]

Having said this, quite how an aesthetic of cognitive mapping is meant to be realised as part of this larger objective remains unclear in Jameson's writing. As Colin MacCabe has written in the preface to Jameson's more recent book on *The Geopolitical Aesthetic*: 'cognitive mapping is the least articulated but also the most crucial of the Jamesonian categories. Crucial because it is the missing psychology of the political unconscious, the political edge of the historical analysis of post-modernism and the methodological justification of the Jamesonian undertaking.'[7] In an attempt to develop some of the possibilities for the aesthetic of cognitive mapping that Jameson is suggesting in his writing, I will return to one of the sources of his thinking in order to examine more closely the contribution that spatial form might offer to the debate concerning the analogy with political orientation.

Images of the city

In his book entitled *The Image of the City*, Lynch developed the notion that orientation in the urban environment is dependent on the construction of a mental or 'cognitive' map. Every inhabitant of the city develops their own version of the map, dependent on their individual activities, but most people rely on common physical characteristics as reference points for their particular acts of imaginary representation. From a series of questionnaires and interviews conducted with the residents of three American cities, Lynch identified five categories of significant components or 'building-blocks' that contributed to the formation of a navigational or cognitive urban map. These were: Paths, Edges, Nodes, Districts and Landmarks. Those features that people most often referred to when describing or drawing their city centre from memory tended to fall into one of the above categories. Some of these categories overlapped, as when major paths also formed distinctive edges to districts, or when the districts themselves were centred on a memorable landmark, as well as possessing a dominant building type or functional distinction such as industrial, retailing or residential uses. While other categories of spatial form could perhaps be added to the list above and the characteristics might vary between different cultures, the theoretical claim would remain substantially the same: orientation in a complex environment is fundamentally dependent on a sense of the larger, yet 'invisible', whole. For Lynch this sense of orientation springs from the *image-ability* of the urban scene – the perceptual clarity and vividness of the characteristic spatial elements that allow their use by the inhabitant's imagination. Once an overall framework has been constructed out of a series of distinctive and 'legible' components, any journey across the city can be measured according to its relationship to a relatively stable and complete 'environmental image' of the whole.[8] While Lynch's work remains constrained, as Jameson suggests, due to its being 'locked within the limits of phenomenology',[9] it might be possible to draw out the significance of his basic insights by considering their historical antecedents. Jameson himself suggests the importance of the temporal dimension in his outline of what he calls a 'spatial analysis of culture', set out at the beginning of the essay on 'Cognitive Mapping'. Jameson identifies three phases in the historical development of capitalism – 'classical' or market capitalism, 'monopoly' or imperialist capitalism, and the current phase of global or 'late-capitalism', described in somewhat apocalyptic terms as: 'a moment in which not merely the older city but even the nation-state itself has ceased to play a central functional and formal role in a process that has, in a new quantum leap of capital, prodigiously expanded beyond them, leaving them behind as ruined and archaic remains of earlier stages in the development of this mode of production'.[10] Jameson's further claim is that each of the previous stages of capitalist development had found expression in – and even been partly constituted by – a corresponding spatial form. However, under present conditions we have lost this correlation, leaving us without a means to navigate in the wider 'geopolitical' realm. Rather than dismissing these earlier forms as 'ruins' or 'archaic remains' a closer examination of the characteristics of these residual forms might yield further possibilities for their meaningful survival in the present situation. As Lynch's studies also suggest, the process of cognitive mapping is reinforced by this kind of correlation between the patterns of use and movement in a city and its patterns of visual and spatial order. By considering the historical development of this relationship I will attempt to open up a further possibility, that of the *operable* as opposed to the *imageable* city, to go some way towards answering Jameson's call for an aesthetic of orientation that would allow effective operation within an otherwise unrepresentable totality.

Patterns of thought/patterns of order

The first phase of market capitalism in Jameson's three-part schema found its spatial counterpart in what he calls 'the logic of the grid, a reorganisation of some older, sacred and heterogeneous space into geometrical and Cartesian homogeneity, a space of infinite equivalence and extension ...'.[11] This understanding of the history of the grid in city planning overlooks the important distinction between two alternative traditions in Greek and Roman practice that have influenced the way the grid has been perceived down to the present day. The two ideas which I would like to draw out from these traditions arise from the ambiguous dialectical relationship between spatial form and political structure that was characteristic of the city grid even prior to its large-scale exploitation by the colonising Romans. The initial spread of the grid layout is generally attributed to the most famous of the Greek town-planners, Hippodamus of Miletus, who laid out the sea-port of Piraeus near Athens in the fifth century BC. But while the original authorship of the grid diagram is by no means historically certain – as the architectural historian Joseph Rykwert has taken care to point out[12] – what is clear from the Greeks' deployment of the grid system is the importance of the spatial and social correlation referred to above. As the urban historian Spiro Kostof has stated, using the words of Aristotle:

> Aristotle writes that Hippodamus discovered 'the divisioning of cities,' …
> and that 'he was the first man of those not actually involved in politics to
> make proposals about the best form of constitution.' Now, since
> Hippodamus could not have *invented* the grid, one possible interpretation
> of Aristotle's words is that he advocated a special instance of it and
> combined it with a social theory of urbanism. Indeed, Hippodamus, it
> would seem, proposed a political system 'whereby the population of the
> town was divided into three classes – craftsmen, farmers and soldiers – and
> the land divided into three portions, the first sacred, the second public (to
> support the soldiers) and the third private (to be owned by the farmers)'.[13]

Extending the significance of the ordering power of the grid beyond the pragmatic concerns of everyday spatial organization, Hippodamus' work also provides the first clues to the cosmological capacity of the form of the city to provide an orientation to just the kind of 'unrepresentable totality' that Fredric Jameson was attempting to come to terms with. It is this neglected cosmological dimension of Greek city planning that Joseph Rykwert draws close attention to, citing the French scholar Jean-Pierre Vernant's comparison of Hippodamus with another noteworthy Milesian, Anaximander, the reputed 'father' of Greek philosophy. The tiny fragment of Anaximander's sixth-century BC treatise which provides the first recorded words of Western philosophy betrays a clear preoccupation with the principle of flux and the ordinance or 'arrangement' of time[14] that was also to prove highly influential for subsequent Greek philosophers. In addition to his cosmological writings he is reputed to have been something of a scientist – devising the gnomon for telling the time by the shadow of the sun, constructing the first map of the world drawn out on the upper surface of a solid cylinder and also producing a celestial globe, though the last is more difficult to substantiate. The preoccupation with movement and change in Anaximander's thinking appears in another guise in the open-ended grids of those cities like Miletus and Priene where the layout of the streets is randomly cut back to suit the ragged outlines of the local topography. A flexibility of growth is built into the Greek system, restricted only by the need for military fortifications and the limits of the natural geography. This flexibility seems to be generated by a sensibility towards the principles of growth and change at the core of the Greeks' understanding of the cosmos – bearing in mind in particular the origin of the term *cosmos* in the processes of ordering, arranging and adorning.[15]

In contrast to the principles of Greek cosmology – as partly constituted through the form of the gridded city plan – a second idea emerges from the Roman use of the grid layout, showing an altogether different interpretation of the notion of the city as a 'microcosm'. The Romans deployed the grid plan in their colonial expansion emblematically, as a fixed and finite form, as a reminder of their spiritual origins as much as an efficient organisation of land use. As a tool of political domination as well as psychological orientation, the image of the city of Rome – from which all roads inevitably led – could be seen drawn out across the landscape of Europe in the shape of even the most temporary of colonising settlements. The military camp ground or *castrum*, with its two principal routes crossing at right-angles at the centre, formed an emblem of the structure of the Romans' conceptual world. Each new town became itself a new 'centre' by reiterating the structure of the absent 'mother city' through a diagrammatic idealisation rather than a literal representation of Rome as it actually appeared – more a reminder of the perception of the original metropolis in its role as the 'centre of the world'. In the hierarchical Roman grid layout the central north–south street or *cardo* ('hinge') represented the axis of the earth's rotation. The main east–west route across the city also marked out the path of the sun across the sky.[16] The resulting pure geometry embodied in the Roman grid – complete and finite as a form, in the image of a finite cosmos – shows little of the Greeks' sensibility towards principles of flexibility and flux. The status of the boundaries of the Roman city also betrays this urge towards fixity and completeness of form due to its emphasis on the marking of the earth. As a means of making visible what for the Romans was the fundamental underlying order behind the chaos of immediate appearances, this marking out of an emblematic pattern on the ground had a particular, persistent significance. The rituals of city foundation and the setting out of religious enclosures both involved cutting into the surface of the ground, most notably the marking of the boundary of the city with a ploughed rectangular furrow defining the lines of the four city walls. At the crossing of the four main routes into the city the plough would be ceremonially lifted above the ground and carried to the other side, thereby preserving the sanctity of the boundary while allowing the inhabitants to pass in and out. Here the city gates would be erected, addressing the cardinal points of the compass, with each of the breaches in the wall protected by the image of a deity. As the sequence of choosing the site and the rituals of town foundation were also seen as a re-enactment of the founding of Rome itself, the colonial outpost would have taken on something of the status of a temple – a sacred, protected realm allowing communication with the spiritual legacy of Roman history. In addition to reiterating a cosmological model and providing a conceptual diagram of the larger spatial whole, the sense of familiarity provided by the standardization of the layout also allows an instant grasp of geographical orientation, as well as a sense of security, in an otherwise unfamiliar environment. As suggested by the legend of the shipwrecked philosopher Aristippus, washed up on the shore of Rhodes, finding a geometric pattern marked out in the sand was cause for rejoicing – signifying not just another life, but the reassuring presence of a civilised human intellect.[17]

Rules and models

It should be clear from this account of the Roman appropriation of the Greek city grid that the process described by Fredric Jameson of a linear transition from a sacred to a secular geometry in city planning is more complex than he seems to suggest. Elements of both sacred and secular sources for the gridded city plan survive into the present as clues towards the kind of aesthetic of orientation that Jameson is suggesting, and to understand their possibilities we must consider the dialectical relationship between thought patterns and spatial forms that was already hinted at in the work of Hippodamus. The distinctions between flux and fixity in the two examples of grid planning discussed so far might also be considered under a different rubric, such as that suggested by the historian Françoise Choay in her writing on the theory of architecture and urbanism entitled *The Rule and the Model*, published in French in 1980 and only recently translated into English.[18] Choay's basic thesis concerns the Renaissance reinterpretation of the classical traditions of both architecture and city-building, seen in terms of the inheritance of two distinct methodologies. One involves the application of principles and rules and is best represented by the tradition of the architectural treatise inaugurated by L.B. Alberti in the fifteenth century. The other is concerned with the reproduction of complete spatial models and is part of an alternative strategy for the generation of built space inspired by Thomas More's *Utopia* published in 1516. As Choay says in comparing the two approaches:

> As a quantified topographical schema, the device of the utopian spatial model allows everyone to be assigned to, and identified with, a particular place, and thus it can be applied freely to the entire domain of human activity. In this sense it is as universal in scope as Alberti's rules, even if its function is to control specific kinds of practice and not to accommodate new projects ... However, this in turn constitutes a fundamental limitation. Whereas the Albertian rule is an operator which ... engenders infinitely variable spaces according to circumstances and desires, the Morean model, a model space and a model of space, is condemned to be replicated in perpetuity.[19]

The central thesis of Choay's work appears to support the earlier criticism of the limitations of the Roman hierarchical city – along with the fact that few of the cities laid out as 'perfect' geometric forms have survived the ravages of subsequent development – and she also points out the inherent flexibility of a design method based on the application of rules and principles, continually adaptable to different spatial and temporal situations, as in the Greeks' use of the open-ended grid. Having said this, the persistence of the literary and artistic tradition of representing ideal political communities embodied in pure and finite geometric structures provides a telling illustration of the power of this idea, hence perhaps Jameson's attraction to the idea of Lynch's *imageable* city. From Plato's 'lost city' of Atlantis, described in the dialogue *Critias* as a series of concentrically arranged islands encircled with canals,[20] through to Tommaso Campanella's seventeenth-century vision of a *Città del Sole*, centred on a circular temple, the connection between pure form and political ideology has been a close one. One of the reasons for the strength of this relationship is the 'imageability' of physical form that started off this whole discussion, but the actual medium of these descriptions must also be taken into account. As a manifesto for political change through the act of city building the traditional utopian text is an almost literal example of the sort of cognitive mapping that Fredric Jameson was alluding to. However, rather than studying the fixed form of the city as described by Françoise Choay, perhaps there is another lesson hidden in the operation of the texts themselves as a stimulus to the workings of the imagination and the exercise of the processes of memory. As Frances Yates has attempted to demonstrate, in describing Campanella's creation in her history of mnemonic techniques entitled *The Art of Memory*, the relationship between ideas and forms that surfaced earlier in this discussion deserves a further, more deliberate, definition:

> This is the kind of encyclopedic lay-out of a universal memory system, with a 'celestial' organising basis, with which [Giordano] Bruno has made us very familiar. And Campanella repeatedly stated that his City of the Sun, or perhaps some model of it, could be used for 'local memory', as a very quick way of knowing everything, 'using the world as a book'.[21]

This tradition of 'reading' buildings provides a useful clue to the survival of the classical 'arts of memory' as described by Frances Yates, in the similar operation of images in association with a sequence of architectural spaces. The technique involved the memorising of spoken passages such as long Homeric storylines or great political orations, by the matching of images from the speech concerned with a series of places in a building or a city. Whether real or merely imagined, the setting would be traversed in the mind of the orator during the recounting of the literary work and as each place in turn was visited, the image discovered there was meant to inspire recollection. The method effectively functions like a 'cinematic' record, in its relating of visual images to the content of spoken dialogue, but the use of a spatial armature for the structuring of the sequential memory provides another parallel to the cognitive map as Jameson initially described it. The Roman rhetoricians who set out this methodology were careful to describe the ideal environments for the technique to be most effective, with qualities like distinctiveness and vividness of place, and particularities of lighting and ornamental effects. Each of the characteristics that reinforce memorability sound remarkably similar to those that Kevin Lynch was concerned with – albeit in his system of navigation the place is recognised through the image, rather than the image through the place.[22] The key point to draw out of Yates' observations on the traditional techniques of memory involves a further distinction between static form and dynamic action in the consideration of urban space. The use of a time-structured 'sequential' model for the mapping of city form highlights again the importance of the open-ended, rule-based, principles that Françoise Choay was describing. Likewise, Campanella's use of the analogy of the 'world as a book' also brings to light a parallel tradition in the realm of both sacred and civic architecture that reached a peak with the medieval tradition of iconographical and allegorical interpretation of church buildings. Prior to the advent of the printed Bible, the texts of the scriptures would be known by most of the church worshippers only through the 'reading' of the form and ornamentation of the structure of the building itself. As Victor Hugo most memorably declared, seeing the downfall of a meaningful architecture in the face of the mass availability of books:

> It was a presentiment that human thought, in changing its form, would also change its method of expression, that the leading idea of each succeeding generation would no longer be inscribed with the same tools and in the same manner, that the book of stone, so solid and lasting, would give place to the book of paper, more solid and more lasting still. Looked at in this connection, the vague formula of the archdeacon had a further meaning; it signified that one art was on the eve of dethroning another. What it wished to say was, 'printing will kill architecture!'[23]

American excursus

Notwithstanding Hugo's pessimistic prognosis it should have become clear from the preceding observations that the two realms are in some sense continually obliged to refer to one another. The kind of cognitive mapping proposed by both Jameson and Kevin Lynch is dependent on the dialectical interplay between a level of conceptual structure and a level of spatial structure that both constitute and are constituted by the experience of the other.

In concluding this discussion, I want to return to the question of the 'rule' versus the 'model' in city planning in the hope of illustrating the kind of cognitive mapping that I believe goes some way towards meeting Jameson's tentative definition. Considering the transition between the

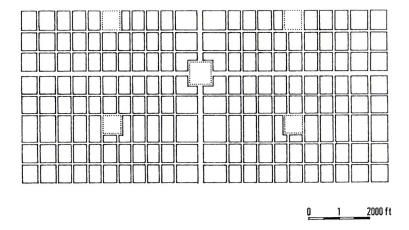

0   1   2000 ft

Figure 2.1 Plan of Philadelphia (re-drawn by the author after William Penn's Plan for
        Philadelphia, Pennsylvania, 1682)

gridded street layout of Philadelphia, established in 1682 (see Fig. 2.1), and
the later New York Commissioners' grid plan for Manhattan of 1811 (Fig.
2.2), it is clear that a shift has taken place in both intention and resulting
effect. The original inspiration for the city of Philadelphia, like many colonial
settlements, was the desire to found an 'ideal' religious community, though
in William Penn's case the founding of a free society of fellow Quakers also
allowed the exercise of his architectural imagination.[24] Having experienced
the crowding and disorder of Restoration London, as well as the great
disaster of the fire of 1666, Penn was inspired by the visions of a re-planned
city being proposed by Sir Christopher Wren among several others. Along
with most of the schemes for the City of London Penn began with a grid of
streets for his new colonial city, and like the plans of Richard Newcourt he
included five substantial public open spaces. His experience of London's few,
pre-Georgian, open squares like Covent Garden and Lincoln's Inn Fields also
gave his conception a more 'suburban' quality, though he set it out on a
grand metropolitan scale. Like an archetypal Roman cosmological diagram
Penn's two major streets meet at right-angles at the central 'city hall', sub-
dividing the two-mile wide layout into four equal sections, with a large
public space towards the centre of each quarter. This structure creates a
'perfect' formal hierarchy in the original grid layout which was soon lost in
its rapid and undisciplined extension. Penn's 'green country town', as he
began by describing it, soon became a sprawling port city, as the strip of
dense development along the harbour front broke out beyond the original
north and south boundaries of the plan during the second phase of construction in the eighteenth century.

Seen in comparison with the early American settlements like Philadelphia,
the nineteenth-century gridding of Manhattan seems to have sprung from the
opposite intention. The commissioners' grand proposals in the plan of 1811

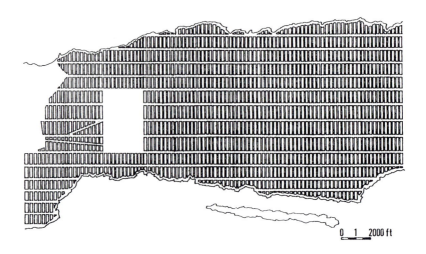

0   1   2000 ft

Figure 2.2 Plan of Manhattan (re-drawn by the author after the Commissioners' Plan of
New York City, 1811)

seem bewildering at first sight and superficially contain nothing of William
Penn's sense of overall hierarchy and structure. A vast chequered blanket has
been thrown over the Indians' 'Island of Many Hills' with the effect of hiding
any underlying natural features.[25] Where Penn was happy to shift his main
north–south street to sit along the high ground off-centre of the original plan,
the New York city planners ignored even the established routes around the
island, which, apart from Broadway, were never again to reappear. At first
glance the grid seems relentless and intimidating and it wasn't until much later
in the nineteenth century that Central Park appeared on the plan providing a
hint of a larger-scale order. What is not so clear from the two-dimensional
drawing, but which has a major effect on the experience 'on the ground', is the
shift in the orientation of the grid. Instead of Penn's square city blocks and
identical width streets, the New York plan uses an asymmetrical system, with the
wider 'avenues' running north–south and the more closely spaced streets going
east–west, providing a critical distinction between routes at each corner which,
except at the centre, the Philadelphia plan never allows. Apart from the two
principal streets at 100 feet wide, all the others in Penn's scheme were meant to
be exactly half that size, with the effect of making orientation very difficult
while moving through the grid – unless one can follow the street signs. Even
with the image in mind of Penn's distinctive *Roma quadrata* layout there are
few clues to direction available at street level. With the pure 'fixed' form of the
original being extended without structure, this problem is made worse as one
moves away from the centre – losing contact with the main axes and any visual
connection with the four open squares, one soon suffers a disquieting loss of
direction.

Conclusion

The 'inflected network' of the New York grid layout poses an interesting possibility for the notion of cognitive mapping, like the comparison between the rule and the model, concerning the relationship between fixity and flux. Compared with the 'quartered cosmos' of the Philadelphia four-square plan, the openness and extendibility of the Manhattan grid system, cut to suit the limits of its natural topography, might provide a clue to a new kind of cognitive map – the *operable* as opposed to the *imageable* city of Kevin Lynch's work. As a way of navigating through a complex and 'unrepresentable' environment an operational understanding of the structure of the system should be more useful than an all-encompassing image. One great lesson from the teachings of the Classical rhetoricians is the use of the journey as the basis of their method. Based on the unfolding of a rhizome-like series of spaces and events, each memory yields the clue to the next – instead of fixing the limits of the form, new components can be added and assimilated through the sequence of their encounter. For Jameson's concept of cognitive mapping to prove useful for its purpose, it might develop along the lines of the 'inflected network' suggested by the Manhattan grid. As the distinction that Michel de Certeau makes clear, between small-scale tactics as opposed to large-scale strategies, the spatial and social practices of navigation are best understood at the most local level – in the unfolding relationships between image and place. As he writes in the introduction to the book *The Practice of Everyday Life*:

> Many everyday practices (talking, reading, moving about, shopping, cooking, etc.) are tactical in character. And so are, more generally, many 'ways of operating': victories of the 'weak' over the 'strong' (whether the strength be that of powerful people or the violence of things or of an imposed order, etc.), clever tricks, knowing how to get away with things, 'hunter's cunning,' maneuvers, polymorphic simulations, joyful discoveries, poetic as well as warlike. The Greeks called these 'ways of operating' *metis*. But they go much further back to the immemorial intelligence displayed in the tricks and imitations of plants and fishes. From the depths of the ocean to the streets of modern megalopolises, there is a continuity and permanence in these tactics.[26]

What I have attempted to demonstrate in the above discussion is that a rule-based rather than a model-based approach to cognitive mapping – as suggested by the Greek as opposed to the Roman tradition of city-planning – yields a powerful yet paradoxical possibility. Instead of the fixed form of the 'Roman' Philadelphia's ideal religious community, now lost amidst subsequent expansion, the more Greek-inspired Manhattan grid – the archetypal space of monopoly capitalism in Jameson's argument – can also be seen as giving rise to its opposite: an operative or tactical, rather than strategic, urban map, born out of a subtly inflected network of differences that allows any individual to navigate within it according to its rules. The clarity and flexibility of the open-ended

New York grid goes a long way to demonstrate how an understanding of the rules by which a system has developed provides a much more useful means of understanding the rules by which to subvert it.

Notes

1 Quoted in Fredric Jameson, 'Cognitive Mapping', in *Marxism and the Interpretation of Culture*, ed. C. Nelson and L. Grossberg, Chicago: University of Illinois Press, 1988, pp. 347–57 (p. 353).
2 Kevin Lynch, *The Image of the City*, Cambridge, MA: MIT Press, 1960.
3 Fredric Jameson, *Postmodernism, or The Cultural Logic of Late Capitalism*, London: Verso, 1991, p. 51.
4 Jameson, *Postmodernism*, p. 51.
5 Jameson, 'Cognitive Mapping', p. 353.
6 Jameson, 'Cognitive Mapping', p. 353.
7 Frederic Jameson, *The Geopolitical Aesthetic: Cinema and Space in the World System*, London: British Film Institute, 1992, xiv.
8 Lynch, *The Image of the City*, pp. 6–13.
9 Jameson, 'Cognitive Mapping', p. 353.
10 Jameson, 'Cognitive Mapping', p. 350.
11 Jameson, 'Cognitive Mapping', p. 349.
12 Joseph Rykwert, *The Idea of a Town*, Cambridge, MA: MIT Press, 1988, pp. 86–7.
13 Spiro Kostof, *The City Shaped: Urban Patterns and Meanings Through History*, London: Bulfinch, 1991, p. 105.
14 Jonathan Barnes, *Early Greek Philosophy*, London: Penguin, 1987, p. 75.
15 Indra Kagis McEwan, *Socrates' Ancestor: An Essay on Architectural Beginnings*, Cambridge, MA: MIT Press, 1993, p. 43.
16 Rykwert, *Idea of a Town*, pp. 41–71.
17 Retold by Vitruvius in the preface to Book VI of *De Architectura*, trans. Frank Granger, 2 vols, Cambridge, MA: Harvard University Press, 1985, II, 3.
18 Françoise Choay, *The Rule and the Model: On the Theory of Architecture and Urbanism*, ed. Denise Bratton, Cambridge, MA: MIT Press, 1997.
19 Choay, *The Rule and the Model*, p. 145.
20 See Plato, *Timaeus and Critias*, trans. Desmond Lee, London: Penguin, 1977, pp. 154–5. Plato suggests the combination of the functional and symbolic qualities of geometry – describing the circular capital city accompanied by a hinterland of gridded irrigation canals.
21 Frances Yates, *The Art of Memory*, London: Pimlico, 1966, p. 289.
22 Yates, *The Art of Memory* , pp. 22–28.
23 Victor Hugo, *Notre Dame de Paris*, London: J.M. Dent and Sons, 1910, p. 165.
24 John W. Reps, *The Making of Urban America*, Princeton, NJ: Princeton University, 1965, pp. 160–5.
25 Reps, *The Making of Urban America*, p. 298.
26 Michel de Certeau, *The Practice of Everyday Life*, trans. Steven Rendall, Berkeley, CA: University of California Press, 1984, pp. xix–xx.

3   Benjamin's London, Baudrillard's Venice[1]

Graeme Gilloch

Introduction

The writings of Walter Benjamin and Jean Baudrillard suggest a number of fruitful points of comparison which have yet to be fully explored by contemporary critics. Drawing upon Benjamin's interpretation of Edgar Allan Poe's 'The Man of the Crowd' and Baudrillard's reading of Sophie Calle's *Suite vénitienne*, this chapter takes as its point of departure one particular shared motif – the pursuit of a stranger through the labyrinthine urban environment. The complex interplay of pursuer and pursued is explored with respect to Benjamin's understanding of the mimetic faculty and Baudrillard's concept of seduction. It is argued that antithetical moments of mimesis are at play in these writings, namely, interpretation and imitation. The elusive and confounded hope of mimetic reading in Benjamin, to 'read what was never written', is counterposed to the mimetic compulsion of seduction in Baudrillard, the enticing invitation to 'please follow me'.

Mimesis and *flânerie*

> *Was nie geschrieben wurde, lesen* – 'To read what was never written'.
>
> (Hofmannsthal)

This enigmatic statement appears in at least three places in Walter Benjamin's writings: in his 1933 fragment on the origin of language, 'On the Mimetic Faculty';[2] as one of the epigrams to 'Konvolut M The *Flâneur*' of his now renowned yet unfinished and fragmentary study of nineteenth-century Paris, the *Passagenarbeit*;[3] and in the initial notes for his 1940 'Theses on the Concept of History'.[4] These locations point to a fundamental set of connections between these texts; namely, that elements of the so-called mimetic faculty described by Benjamin are somehow reconfigured in the activities of the flâneur, the perambulating pedestrian of the modern metropolis, and that they thus come to form a model of critical practice for the social theorist and historian. The mimetic faculty is a constitutive element of the phantasmagoria of modernity, which paradoxically points to a method for disenchanting the mythic.

For Benjamin, mimesis is concerned with the primordial human capacity to discern and create resemblances, similarities, correspondences within and between elements of the natural and cultural domains. One may distinguish two moments of the mimetic faculty: interpretation and imitation.

First, mimesis refers to particular forms of perception and recognition, 'the gift of seeing resemblances'.[5] The mimetic faculty is the human ability to identify correspondences between diverse phenomena and, moreover, to interpret these connections as signs, omens and portents. Mimesis involves our capacity for the perception of patterns, figures or configurations in nature which can be deciphered and read. Benjamin regards the identification of such magical signs, such non-sensuous correspondences, as the very origin of script and thus of reading itself:

> 'To read what was never written.' Such reading is the most ancient; reading before all language from the entrails, the stars or dances. Later the mediating link of a new kind of reading, of runes and hieroglyphs, came into use. It seems fair to suppose that these were the stages by which the mimetic gift, which was the foundation of occult practices, gained admittance to writing and language.[6]

The mimetic faculty involves the translation of superficial elements of the natural world, the realm of appearances, into manifestations and intimations of a hidden text, the 'book of nature'. Mimesis is bound up with discovering and unfolding meaning lodged within the seemingly chaotic, disparate, daemonic world of nature. Mimetic reading is the divination of the secret from the surface.

The second moment of the mimetic faculty refers to the capacity for imitation. Human beings do not simply 'read' natural phenomena, but also copy and mimic them. Humankind was subject to 'the powerful compulsion in former times to become and behave like something else',[7] to actively engage in the creation of similarities. Humankind did not merely register resemblances, but also reproduced them. Benjamin notes that this notion of imitation is most apparent in those ancient rituals, dances and rites in which participants performed like, or gave representational form to, animals and natural phenomena in order to worship or gain magical power over them. He detects vestiges of this corporeal, sensuous, mimetic activity even today in children's play, which is 'everywhere permeated by mimetic modes of behaviour'.[8] In play children pretend to be other people, natural objects or elements of the built environment. Benjamin observes that 'the child plays at being not only a shopkeeper or teacher but also a windmill and a train'.[9]

Benjamin points out that the mimetic faculty can be seen to have both an ontogenetic and a phylogenetic history: it is manifest in the childhood stage of the human individual and in the early phases of human history. He is at pains to point out, however, that although 'the observable world of modern human beings contains only the minimal residues of the magical correspondences and analogies that were familiar to ancient peoples',[10] the mimetic faculty has not vanished as such, but rather has been subject to transformation and reconfiguration. Just as modernity itself for Benjamin involves nothing less than a re-articulation and reactivation of mythic powers, so too, as Michael Taussig points out,[11] does magical reading, the deciphering of myth, adopt new forms and modes. Benjamin writes in 'Konvolut M' of the *Passagenarbeit*:

> 'primal history of the nineteenth century' – this would be of no interest, if it were understood to mean that forms of primal history are to be recovered among the history of the nineteenth century. Only where the nineteenth century would be presented as the originary form of primal history – in a form, that is to say, in which the whole of primal history groups itself anew images appropriate to that century – only there does the concept of a primal history of the nineteenth century have meaning.[12]

Indeed, the notion of mimetic reading becomes an essential model for Benjamin's own deciphering of the recent past, his prehistory of modernity. In his historiographical reflections Benjamin notes: 'The historical method is a philological one based on the Book of Life. Hofmannsthal states: "To read what was never written." The reader called to mind here is the true historian.'[13] For Benjamin, the enchanted modern metropolis, where the most modern and most ancient interpenetrate, is to be understood as an unwritten text, a 'linguistic cosmos'[14] of puzzling hieroglyphs, strange inscriptions, obscure traces, magical names to be identified, read and interpreted. In 'Konvolut N' of the *Passagenarbeit*, Benjamin notes: 'The expression "the book of nature" indicates that we can read the real like a text. And that is how the reality of the nineteenth century will be treated here. We open the book of what happened'.[15] Baudelaire's primeval and mystical 'forest of symbols' finds its corollary in Benjamin's modern, but equally mythical 'city of signs'.

The epigram 'To read what was never written' clearly identifies the key figure who claims to decipher the elusive and enigmatic clues to the modern metropolitan environment and population: the *flâneur*. The *flâneur* combines the pleasures and distractions of solitary walking in the metropolis with the intriguing possibilities of deciphering this environment. It is the *flâneur* who turns the urban setting into a landscape which is to be negotiated and navigated through the attentive reading of its inconspicuous features. Benjamin opens his 1932 essay 'A Berlin Childhood Around 1900'[16] with a reflection on *flânerie*:

> Not to find one's way in a city means little. But to lose oneself in a city as one loses oneself in a forest requires practice. Then the street names must call out to the lost wanderer like the snapping of dry twigs, and the small streets of the city-centre must reflect the time of day as clearly as a mountain hollow. I have learned this art of straying only recently.[17]

The heroic *flâneur* possesses the sharp eye and keen senses of the hunter, the detective, pursuing the traces and clues left by others.[18]

Moreover, the *flâneur* reads 'what was never written' in his self-appointed role as the great urban physiognomist, the supposedly shrewd reader of character from the faces of passers-by, and, above all, the expert interpreter of the multiple, ever-changing and bewitching countenances of the city itself.[19] Benjamin notes: 'The phantasmagoria of the *flâneur*: to read from faces the profession, the ancestry, the character, of passers-by',[20] and points out that the *flâneur* 'made his study from the physiognomical appearance of people'.[21] '"Botanising" on the asphalt',[22] the *flâneur* was the author of 'physiologies', inane journalistic pen-portraits which appeared in the *feuilleton* section of newspapers.[23]

The *flâneur* as hunter, as physiognomist, transforms the modern metropolis into a landscape, a countenance, a text. In so doing this figure takes on the alluring role of the detective.[24] Benjamin observes: 'The detective is prefigured in the *flâneur* ... Preformed in the figure of the *flâneur* is that of the detective. ... It suited him very well to see his indolence presented as a plausible front, behind which, in reality hides the riveted attention of an observer, who will not let the unsuspecting malefactor out of hi sight.'[25] This notion of the *flâneur* as a phantasmagorical hunter/physiognomist/detective finds its fullest articulation in Benjamin's discussion of Edgar Allan Poe's 1840 tale 'The Man of the Crowd'.[26]

Seductive strangers

The narrator of Poe's story sits in the window of a London coffee-house studying, with the eager eyes of the physiognomist, the spectacle of the urban crowd thronging the city's streets. Suddenly:

> there came into view a countenance (that of a decrepit old man, some 65 or 70 years of age) – a countenance which at once arrested and absorbed my whole attention, on account of the absolute idiosyncracy of its expression. Anything even remotely resembling that expression I had never seen before.[27]

The narrator, 'aroused, startled, fascinated',[28] is overcome by a 'craving desire to keep the man in view – to know more of him',[29] to learn the secret of this ominous apparition, and he decides in an instant 'to follow the stranger whithersoever he should go'.[30] Maintaining a discreet distance so as to remain undetected himself, the narrator pursues the stranger through the murky nocturnal streets of the capital, noticing how he always keeps to its most populated spaces, whether the bustling squares or, later, the teeming back-streets of its most ruinous and villainous quarters. 'Resolute not to abandon a scrutiny in which I now felt an interest all-absorbing',[31] the narrator remains 'at a loss to comprehend the waywardness of his actions'.[32] The hours pass, night gives way to day and 'as the shades of the second evening came on I grew wearied unto death, and stopping fully in front of the wanderer, gazed at him steadfastly in the face'.[33] This direct physiognomical scrutiny yields nothing new, however: '"This old man," I said at length, "is the type and genius of deep crime. He refuses to be alone. He is the man of the crowd. It will be in vain to follow; for I shall learn no more of him, nor of his deeds."'[34] The tale ends where it begins, with the observation that this figure, this face 'lässt sich nicht lesen' – does not permit itself to be read. 'There are some secrets which do not permit themselves to be told'.[35]

What is the significance of this peculiar story? Benjamin comments:

> Poe's famous tale 'The Man of the Crowd' is something like the X-ray picture of the detective novel. In it, the drapery represented by the crime has disappeared. The mere armature has remained: the pursuer, the crowd, and an unknown man who arranges his walk through London in such a way that he always remains in the middle of the crowd.[36]

As Benjamin recognises, the 'man of the crowd' himself is no *flâneur*.[37] Rather it is the pursuer as detective who is the *flâneur*, led by curiosity born of a chance encounter to wander the urban labyrinth in the quest to comprehend the sinister stranger, to discover his secret. As such, 'The Man of the Crowd' encapsulates the clearest combination of the two moments of the mimetic faculty in the modern city: interpretation (the fruitless attempt to decipher the face) and imitation (the compulsion to mimic and copy) – for what is this uncanny urge to follow, to shadow the other's movements if not the most precise instance of the imperative to become similar? In the pursuit of the 'figure that fascinates', mimetic reading and mimetic compulsion are not anti-thetical moments but complementary ones promising identification.

Even though the stranger's visage 'does not permit itself to be read', the figure is nonetheless identifiable – he is simply the 'man of the crowd', the 'genius of deep crime'. Poe's tale thus points not to the impossibility of reading as such, the ultimate impenetrability of surfaces, but rather to a recognition of the very limit of reading. The secret is not revealed, stripped bare before us, but rather it is recognised as a secret, as that which simply does not permit itself to be known. Or perhaps the secret here is that there is no secret, nothing to fathom. This constitutes the clearest limit of mimetic reading, for such reading fails where there is no secret beneath the surface to be divined. Perhaps this is why it would be in vain to pursue the stranger further – his meaning is exhausted in the apprehension of his surface, there is simply nothing more to be known. Ironically, the 'figure that fascinates' is one who reveals simply that he will reveal nothing or has nothing to reveal.

The stranger gives no clue, leaves no trace behind for the detective. The countenance, singular and inscrutable, of the 'figure that fascinates' is an exemplary instance of the 'auratic', that 'strange weave of space and time: the unique appearance or semblance of distance no matter how close the object may be'.[38] Benjamin notes this opposition between trace, the legible, and aura, that which eludes or defies reading: 'Trace and aura. The trace is the appearance of a nearness, however far removed the thing that left it behind may be. Aura is the appearance of a distance, however close the thing that calls it forth. In the trace, we gain possession of the thing; in the aura it takes possession of us.'[39] Indeed, it is not the stranger who leaves a trail (he has no desire to be followed), but the narrator. After all, what is reading if not the act of deciphering those textual traces, the non-sensuous correspondences of script, left by the narrator, which lead and lure us towards an unsuspected destination? The narrator is not the only one to pursue the stranger's secret. The hapless reader of the tale too is most assuredly compelled to follow, as a witness, the textual twists and turns of this singular narrative in the hope of illumination.

If 'The Man of the Crowd' is an 'X-ray' of the detective story, then Sophie Calle's *Suite vénitienne* (1983),[40] with its painstaking chronology of events and movements interspersed with sequences of secretly taken photographs, appears to be a simulation of the surveillance report.

Calle's story begins in Paris, where, as a photographer, she is undertaking a rather peculiar enterprise. She writes:

> For months I followed strangers on the street. For the pleasure of following them, not because they interested me. I photographed them without their knowledge,[41] took note of their movements, then finally lost sight of them and forgot them. At the end of January 1980, on the streets of Paris, I followed a man whom I lost sight of a few minutes later in the crowd.[42]

Coincidentally encountering this man (Henri B.) again the same evening and discovering that he is about to visit Venice for a few days, Calle travels there herself to follow and photograph him secretly. Disguising herself, trying various ruses and enlisting the help of various acquaintances there, Calle spends three days attempting to establish Henri B.'s whereabouts, roaming the streets, squares and alleyways of the sinking city, enquiring casually in its hotels and bars. Her approach becomes more systematic: she phones the city's hotels one by one and, discovering where Henri B. is staying, hesitates: '*My investigation was proceeding without him. Finding him may throw everything into confusion, precipitate the end. I'm afraid.*'[43] Nevertheless, the following two mornings find her waiting for him outside his hotel (the Casa de Stefani) on the Calle del Traghetto,[44] but to no avail. Finally, at 10.05 am on Monday 18 February 1980, she notices him emerging from the hotel and the pursuit begins.

Calle follows Henri B. at a distance, exhaustively listing his itinerary, carefully mapping his route, sometimes photographing him, sometimes the people he encounters, sometimes what he photographs: 'he crouches to snap a shot of the canal, or perhaps of that passing boat? After several seconds, I imitate him, trying my best to take the same picture.'[45] She becomes his shadow for an hour before losing sight of him once more. This playful intermittent pursuit, this game of urban hide-and-seek continues into the evening and the next day until Calle senses that she is 'perhaps ... weary of playing this out alone'.[46] No longer maintaining her distance, he suddenly recognises her beneath the disguise and speaks to her: "'Your eyes, I recognise your eyes; that's what you should have hidden.'"[47] As they walk together briefly, his attempts to lure her into conversation elicit no response. Calle notes: 'I like the awkward way he's hiding his surprise, his desire to be master of the situation. As if, in fact, I had been the unconscious victim of his game, his itineraries, his schedules.'[48] They fall silent, they part. Calle writes:

> We simply say good-bye. I believe he smiles ever so slightly. He walks away under the arcades. I photograph his back and let him go. What did I imagine? That he was going to take me with him, to challenge me, to use me? Henri B. did nothing, I discovered nothing. A banal ending to this banal story.[49]

She can follow him no longer, but this is not quite the end. She retraces her steps: 'Alone, I wander back over the routes we took together these last two days, Henri B. and I',[50] and then discovers that he is about to return to Paris. She decides to leave Venice, arranging her journey back so as to arrive at the Gare de Lyon a few minutes before him. She hurries to the platform to await the arrival of the Venice train:

> 10.08 am ... I photograph him one last time as he passes through the station gate, I will go no farther. He moves away, I lose sight of him. After these last thirteen days with him, our story comes to a close.

10.10 am: I stop following Henri B.[51]

Suite vénitienne is explored by Jean Baudrillard in his accompanying essay 'Please Follow Me'.[52] Baudrillard treats Calle's tale as an exemplary instance, a model of seduction. *Se-ducere*: to lead astray, 'to take aside, to divert from one's path'[53] – to seduce is to lure, to entice, to intrigue, to lead the other astray through fascination, the deployment of a special charm, the manipulation of signs. For Baudrillard, there is no depth to seduction; seduction is the superficial and delight in the superficial. Seduction is a 'strategy of appearances',[54] a grand game of surfaces,[55] 'a conspiracy of signs'.[56] As a form of diversion, seduction is playful: it is nothing more nor less than an 'arbitrary and absurd game',[57] a series of stratagems, ruses and reversals, deceptions and duplications.[58]

Venice, home of the carnival, last haunt of *flânerie*, provides the perfect setting for such ludic pursuits. Baudrillard writes:

> The city is built like a trap, a maze, a labyrinth that inevitably, however fortuitously, brings people back to the same points, over the same bridges, onto the same plazas, along the same quays. By the nature of things, everyone is followed in Venice; everyone runs into each other, everyone

recognizes each other (hence the quite reasonable hope of finding someone there without any directions) ... Better yet, the only way not to meet someone in Venice is to follow him from a distance and not lose sight of him.[59]

In Venice, pursuit of the other is a method for preventing any encounter. For this to succeed, Calle must disguise and hide herself. The pursuer must not be recognised by the pursued, she must not permit herself to be read by him. Baudrillard notes: 'This is why the violent moments of the narrative, the dramatic moments, are those where the followed person, seized by a sudden inspiration, as they say, turns around, making an about face like a cornered beast. The system reverses itself immediately, and the follower becomes the followed.'[60] When Henri B. turns, she must avert her eyes to avoid recognition: 'Don't look now!'. When she knowingly returns his gaze, she is finally unmasked by the object of her pursuit. Baudrillard compares this moment to that in a game of hide-and-seek, when the child suddenly jumps out from his/her place of concealment for fear, not of being found, but of never being found.[61] In the play of seduction, all roles, 'all appearances are reversible'.[62]

For Baudrillard, seduction involves the 'invisible dance'[63] of signs and appearances unburdened by meaning. Unlike Poe's tale, we are no longer particularly concerned with understanding the man pursued. The stranger and his reasons for being in Venice are of little interest to the reader, in part because they appear to be of no interest to the narrator. Calle insists that she finds Henri B. neither particularly intriguing nor especially desirable.[64] Her surveillance is not to discover any secret double life that he might be leading; indeed for Baudrillard, it is precisely Calle's pursuit, her mirroring, that doubles his life. He writes:

> It does no good to discover, while shadowing someone, that he has, for instance, a double life, save to heighten curiosity – what's important is that it is the shadowing itself that is the other's double life. To shadow another is to give him, in fact, a double life, a parallel existence. Any commonplace existence can be transfigured (without one's knowledge), any exceptional existence can be made commonplace. It is this effect of doubling that makes the object surreal in its banality and weaves around it the strange ... web of seduction.[65]

Our attention is drawn not to Henri B. but to Calle. It is *she* who perplexes and perturbs us. What are *her* motives and intentions? In this game of seduction, the pursuer becomes the 'figure that fascinates'. We scrutinise *her* words and images, images which are often nothing but imitations of his images. We follow *her* mysterious movements and meanderings in the hope of discovering *her* secret. This is in vain, of course, for Calle's motives are not hidden in *Suite véni-tienne*. Rather it is the very absence of hidden motives which is puzzling.[66] She confesses everything and nothing, namely, that she has nothing to confess.

There is no secret, only the furtive strategies of secrecy: 'seduction lies in the aura of secrecy produced by weightless, artificial signs and not in some natural economy of meaning, beauty or desire'.[67] Mimetic reading does not so much fail here, as fall into the depthlessness of appearance, 'the superficial abyss'.[68] In this sense, Calle and her story, like the stranger's inscrutable visage, do not permit themselves to be read.

In seduction 'every discourse is threatened with this sudden reversibility, absorbed into its own signs without a trace of meaning'.[69] As a form of absorption or implosion, seduction is the enemy of both the production and interpretation of meaning. Baudrillard writes of production thus:

> Its original meaning, in fact, was not to fabricate, but to render visible or make appear ... To produce is to materialize by force what belongs to another order, that of the secret and seduction. Seduction is, at all times and in all places, opposed to production. Seduction removes something from the order of the visible, while production constructs everything in full view, be it an object, a number, or concept. Everything is to be produced, everything is to be legible, everything is to become real, visible, account-able.[70]

Interpretation, the search for hidden meanings, 'neglects and destroys' the 'charm and illusion of appearances'.[71] Baudrillard writes: 'This is why interpretation is what, par excellence, is opposed to seduction, and why it is the least seductive of discourses. Not only does it subject the domain of appearances to incalculable damage, but this privileged search for hidden meanings may be profoundly in error.'[72] Interpretation pretends to discover or generate sense where there is only 'non-sense', the ludic. Interpretation is an imposter which falls prey to dissimulation, the deception of depth rather than the seduction of surface. The pursuit of meaning is led astray, paradoxically, by its denial of seduction. This is its banality, the very banality which Calle's story eludes so long as it does not permit itself to be interpreted.

If Calle has no interest in Henri B., if this figure fails to fascinate, why follow him? One might be tempted to answer that Calle is a photographer, that she is accumulating photographs for an exhibition,[73] for a publication like *Suite véni-tienne*. Her motives are instrumental – this is her job. But this is prosaic, unseductive. For Baudrillard, Calle's puzzling pursuit is for the pure playfulness of following itself, the 'aesthetic intensity of seduction'.[74] She is seduced, not by Henri B., but by seduction itself. Seduction seduces and it does so through the challenge it presents. This challenge of seduction seduces others too. Baudrillard notes how the fleeting acquaintances she makes in Venice fall under the spell of seduction and become her willing accomplices.[75] Baudrillard writes:

> it is necessary that Sophie, herself, have no reason; that her overture make no sense, in order to have a chance of success in this sphere of strangeness, absurd complicity, fatal consent. We are tired of solidarity, contracts, and

exchange. We are very willing to consent to anything, provided it be absurd – we are very willing to submit ourselves to anything, as long as the request is irrational. It is because Sophie, herself, submits to an absurd task, because she prostitutes herself, as it were, to a senseless enterprise that requires more patience, servitude, boredom, and energy than any amorous passion, that she effortlessly obtains from others this irrational complicity that no consideration for her well-being could ever have inspired. It is to the challenge that people respond; it is the absurd they obey.[76]

We are helpless not to help when confronted by the challenge of seduction. In the final instance, the reader, too, becomes an accomplice, or perhaps a victim, the only victim of this cunning, tantalising text. No longer a mere witness to seduction, an innocent bystander, the reader is seduced: the reader is intrigued and lured by Sophie Calle in her pursuit of Henri B., the reader unerringly follows her deceitful trail, duped by the traces left behind. It is the reader who unwarily falls into the 'abyss of the surface' and is fatally caught in the 'web of appearances'.[77] The reader, too, is seduced by seduction.

Mimesis and seduction

If Poe's tale and Calle's narrative appear to have certain correspondences, then so too do the mimetic faculty and seduction: fascination, the compulsion to follow, shadowing, mirroring. But, if in Poe's tale we see the two moments of the mimetic faculty, interpretation and imitation combining in the unfulfilled promise of identification, the notion of seduction exemplified by Calle's story polarises these moments. Indeed, perhaps the mimetic faculty is torn asunder by seduction. Seduction involves the infinite postponement and deferral of meaning. Interpretation is, for Baudrillard, nothing other than the spurious attempt 'to read what was never written', to discover a meaning beneath the surface which is not there, to bring a premature close to the endless game of appearances. Seduction aestheticises the mundane. The fatal theorist sacrifices interpretation and privileges the seductive allure, the singular joys, the enchanting aura of the game itself. The seductive does not permit itself to be read – and this is what makes it seductive. Seduction is delight in the futility of reading. There is no invitation to interpretation, only to further seduction: 'Please follow me'.[78]

Benjamin recognises but warily resists the spell of seduction. Whatever the fleeting pleasures of pursuit, its purpose must not implode in intoxication. That reading fails is not a reason to abandon it. The critical theorist is not so fickle. The sober imperative of interpretation remains: we must decipher the trace, not succumb to aura. Benjamin retains and redeems the elusive promise of interpretation, the hope 'to read what was never written' even when 'it does not permit itself to be read'. The futility of reading is not a source of indulgent delight, but a melancholy reminder of enduring hope, for, as Benjamin observes, 'only for the sake of the hopeless ones have we been given hope'.[79] Please read me.

Notes

1 This paper was originally presented at the International Walter Benjamin Association Congress, 24–26 July 1997, Amsterdam. I am very grateful to Tim Dant and Bernadette Boyle for their comments, suggestions and help during its writing.

2 Walter Benjamin, *One-Way Street and Other Writings*, London, 1985, p. 162.

3 Walter Benjamin, *The Arades Project*, trans. Howard Eiland and Kevin McLanghlin, Cambridge, MA, 1999, p. 416, Schweppenhäuser, 7 vols, Frankfurt, 1991, ed. Rolf Tiedemann and Hermann.

4 Walter Benjamin, *Gesammelte Schriften*, I, 1238.

5 Benjamin, *One-Way Street*, p. 160.

6 Benjamin, *One-Way Street*, p. 162.

7 Benjamin, *One-Way Street*, p. 160.

8 Benjamin, *One-Way Street*, p. 160.

9 Benjamin, *One-Way Street*, p. 160.

10 Benjamin, *One-Way Street*, p. 161.

11 He writes: 'modernity provides the cause, context, means and needs, for the resurgence – not the continuity – of the mimetic faculty' (Michael Taussig, *Mimesis and Alterity: A Particular History of the Senses*, London: Routledge, 1993, p. 20).

12 Benjamin, *The Arcades Project*, p. 463.

13 Benjamin, *Gesammelte Schriften*, I, 1238.

14 Benjamin, *The Arcades Project*, p. 522.

15 Benjamin, *The Arcades Project*, p. 464.

16 In a letter to Gershom Scholem of 28 February 1933 Benjamin notes that 'On the Mimetic Faculty' was 'formulated while I was doing research for the first piece of the Berliner Kindheit' (*The Correspondence of Walter Benjamin*, ed. Gershom Scholem and Theodor W. Adorno, trans. Manfred Jacobson and Evelyn Jacobson, Chicago, IL, 1994, p. 403).

17 Benjamin, *Gesammelte Schriften*, IV, 237.

18 Benjamin writes: 'Whoever follows traces must not only pay attention; above all he must have given head already to great many things. (The hunter must know the hoof of the animal whose trail he is on; he must know the hour when that animal goes to drink; he must know the course of the river to which it turns and the location of the ford by which he himself can get accross)' (*The Arcades Project*, p. 801).

19 Benjamin notes: 'no face is surrealistic in the same degree as the true face of the city' (*One-Way Street*, p. 230).

20 Benjamin, *The Arcades Project*, p. 429.

21 Benjamin, *The Arcades Project*, p. 430.

22 Walter Benjamin, *Charles Baudelaire: A Lyric Poet in the Era of High Capitalism*, trans. Harry Zohn, London, 1983, p. 36.

23 See Benjamin, *The Arcades Project*, p. 372 and 447, and *Charles Baudelaire*, pp. 38–9.

24 Owing to the influence of Cooper, it becomes possible for the novelist in an urban setting to give scope to the experiences of the hunter. This has a bearing on the rise of the detective novel' (*The Arcades Project*, p. 439).

25 Benjamin, *Gesammelte Schriften*, V, 554.

26 See Benjamin, *Charles Baudelaire*, pp. 126–8.

27 Edgar Allan Poe, 'The Man of the Crowd', in *The Fall of the House of Usher and Other Writings*, ed. David Galloway, London, 1986, pp. 179–88 (p. 183).

28 Poe, 'The Man of the Crowd', p. 184.

29 Poe, 'The Man of the Crowd', p. 184.

30 Poe, 'The Man of the Crowd', p. 184.

31 Poe, 'The Man of the Crowd', p. 187.

32 Poe, 'The Man of the Crowd', p. 186.

33 Poe, 'The Man of the Crowd', p. 187.

34 Poe, 'The Man of the Crowd', p. 188.
35 Poe, 'The Man of the Crowd', p. 179.
36 Benjamin, *Charles Baudelaire*, p. 48.
37 Benjamin notes: 'Baudelaire saw fit to equate the man of the crowd, whom Poe's narrator follows throughout the length and breadth of nocturnal London, with the *flâneur*. It is hard to accept this view' (*Charles Baudelaire*, p. 128).
38 Benjamin, *One-Way Street*, p. 250.
39 Benjamin, *The Arcades Project*, p. 447.
40 Sophie Calle/Jean Baudrillard, *Suite vénitienne/Please Follow Me*, trans. Dany Barash and Danny Hatfield, Seattle, WA, 1988.
41 To do this Calle uses 'a Squintar, a lens attachment equipped with a set of mirrors so I can take photos without aiming at the subject' (Calle/Baudrillard, *Suite vénitienne*, p. 4).
42 Calle/Baudrillard, *Suite vénitienne*, p. 2.
43 Calle/Baudrillard, *Suite vénitienne*, p. 16.
44 *Calle* is Italian for alleyway.
45 Calle/Baudrillard, *Suite vénitienne*, p. 30.
46 Calle/Baudrillard, *Suite vénitienne*, p. 50.
47 Calle/Baudrillard, *Suite vénitienne*, p. 50.
48 Calle/Baudrillard, *Suite vénitienne*, p. 50.
49 Calle/Baudrillard, *Suite vénitienne*, p. 51.
50 Calle/Baudrillard, *Suite vénitienne*, p. 51.
51 Calle/Baudrillard, *Suite vénitienne*, p. 72.
52 This appears in two shorter versions with minor differences: in *Fatal Strategies*, ed. Jim Fleming and trans. Philip Beitchman and W.G.J. Niesluchowski, London and New York, 1990, pp. 128–31, under the title 'The Gray Imminence'; and, as 'Pursuit in Venice', in *The Transparency of Evil: Essays on Extreme Phenomena*, trans. James Benedict, London, 1993, pp. 156–60. The key difference in 'The Gray Imminence' is that Calle continues her pursuit of Henri B. after the return to Paris: 'She doesn't abandon the trail, and contacts the people who work with him, a writer with whom he's going to collaborate as a photographer. But things turn out badly. Two or three times he has noticed her following him; there was an incident in Venice. In Paris it's even more serious; he becomes violent. The charm is lost and she gives up' (Baudrillard, *Fatal Strategies*, p. 130).
53 Jean Baudrillard, *Seduction*, trans. Brian Singer, London, 1990, p. 22.
54 Baudrillard, *Seduction*, p. 8.
55 Baudrillard, *Seduction*, p. 111.
56 Baudrillard, *Seduction*, p. 2.
57 Calle/Baudrillard, *Suite vénitienne*, p. 79.
58 Thus 'seduction … is not of the order of the real' (Baudrillard, *Seduction*, p. 46).
59 Calle/Baudrillard, *Suite vénitienne*, p. 83.
60 Calle/Baudrillard, *Suite vénitienne*, p. 83.
61 Baudrillard writes: 'What a thrill to be hidden while someone is looking for you, what a delightful fright to be found, but what a panic when, because you are too well hidden, the others give up looking for you after a while and leave. You are forced to come out on your own when they don't want you any more. … Therefore it is better not to know how to play too well' (Calle/Baudrillard, *Suite vénitienne*, p. 84). Benjamin makes a similar point in his 'One-Way Street' collection and later in 'A Berlin Childhood Around 1900'. Interestingly, he links this with the child's capacity for imitation: 'Standing behind the doorway curtain, the child becomes himself something floating and white, a ghost. The dining table under which he is crouching turns him into the wooden idol in a temple whose four pillars are the carved legs. And behind a door he is himself a door, wears it as his heavy mask and as a shaman will bewitch all those who unsuspectingly enter.

At no cost must he be found ... indeed, without waiting for the moment of discovery, he grabs the hunter with a shout of self-deliverance' (Benjamin, *One-Way Street*, p. 74).

62 Baudrillard, *Seduction*, p. 8. Baudrillard later writes: 'Every structure can adapt to its subversion or inversion, but not to the reversion of its terms. Seduction is this reversible form' (*Seduction*, p. 21).

63 Baudrillard, *Seduction*, p. 111.

64 Baudrillard writes: 'She wants nothing. No mystery story, no love story' (*Transparency of Evil*, p. 159).

65 Calle/Baudrillard, *Suite vénitienne*, pp. 78–9.

66 In this sense, the story moves beyond both simulation and dissimulation to a higher order of the image: the final stage in which the image neither stands for, nor hides the absence of, the real, but rather has nothing to do with the real at all: the hyper-real, 'the pure simulacrum' (Jean Baudrillard, *Selected Writings*, ed. Mark Poster, Cambridge, 1988, p. 170).

67 Baudrillard, *Seduction*, p. 90.

68 Baudrillard, *Seduction*, p. 54.

69 Baudrillard, *Seduction*, p. 2.

70 Baudrillard, *Seduction*, p. 34.

71 Baudrillard, *Seduction*, p. 53.

72 Baudrillard, *Seduction*, pp. 53–4.

73 *Suite vénitienne* was originally published in book form in 1983. It was subsequently been staged as an exhibition consisting of 81 photographs with accompanying texts, 12 September–18 October 1997 at White Cube, London.

74 Calle/Baudrillard, *Suite vénitienne*, p. 78.

75 One of these acquaintances asks Calle to follow them: '"Follow me, then," she was told, "I am more interesting to follow than the housewife on the corner"' (Calle/Baudrillard, *Suite vénitienne*, p. 78).

76 Calle/Baudrillard, *Suite vénitienne*, pp. 80–1.

77 Baudrillard, *Seduction*, p. 87. Baudrillard writes: 'What destroys people, wears them down, is the meaning they give their acts. But the seductress does not attach any meaning to what she does nor suffer the weight of any desire. Even if she speaks of reason or motives, be they guilty or cynical, it is a trap' (*Seduction*, p. 82).

78 Calle/Baudrillard, *Suite vénitienne*, p. 86.

79 Walter Benjamin, *Selected Writings*, vol. 1, eds. Marcus Bullock, Michael Jennings *et al.*, Cambridge, MA, 1996, p. 356.

Bibliography

Baudrillard, Jean, 1988, *Selected Writings*, ed. Mark Poster. Cambridge: Polity Press.

Baudrillard, Jean, 1990a, *Fatal Strategies*, ed. Jim Flemming, trans. Philip Beitchman and W.G.J. Niesluchowski, London and New York: Semiotext(e).

Baudrillard, Jean, 1990b, *Seduction*, trans. Brian Singer, London: Macmillan.

Baudrillard, Jean, 1993, *The Transparency of Evil: Essays on Extreme Phenomena*, trans. James Benedict, London: Verso.

Benjamin, Walter, 1983, *Charles Baudelaire: A Lyric Poet in the Era of High Capitalism*, trans. Harry Zohn, London: Verso.

Benjamin, Walter, 1985, *One-Way Street and Other Writings*, trans. Edmund Jephcott and Kingsley Shorter, with an introduction by Susan Sontag, London: Verso.

Benjamin, Walter, 1991, *Gesammelte Schriften Vols I–VII*, ed. Rolf Tiedemann and Hermann Schweppenhäuser, Frankfurt: Suhrkamp Verlag.

Benjamin, Walter, 1994, *The Correspondence of Walter Benjamin*, ed. Gershom Scholem and Theodor W. Adorno, trans. Manfred Jacobson and Evelyn Jacobson, Chicago, IL: University of Chicago Press.

—— 1996, *Selected Writings*, vol. 1, eds. Marcus Bullock, Michael Jennings *et al.*, Cambridge, MA, Harvard University Press.

—— 1999, *The Arcades Project*, trans. Howard Eiland and Kevin McLaughlin, Cambridge, MA: Belknap Press of Harvard University Press.

Calle, Sophie/Baudrillard, Jean, 1988, *Suite vénitienne/Please Follow Me*, trans. Dany Barash and Danny Hatfield, Seattle, WA: Bay Press.

Poe, Edgar Allan, 1986, *The Fall of the House of Usher and Other Writings*, London: Penguin.

Smith, Gary, ed., 1989, *Benjamin: Philosophy, Aesthetics, History*, Chicago, IL: University of Chicago Press.

Taussig, Michael, 1993, *Mimesis and Alterity: A Particular History of the Senses*, London: Routledge.

Part II
The political metropolis

4 Resurrecting an imperial past

Strategies of self-representation and 'masquerade' in fascist Rome (1934–1938)

Anna Notaro

tanta vis admonitionis est in locis

(Cicero)

Figure 4.1 Mussolini starts demolition work on the Via dell'Impero (credit: Farabolato).

Introduction

This chapter will focus on the reconstruction of the Piazzale Augusto Imperatore zone next to the Tiber, linking this development to the *Mostra Augustea della Romanitá* (1937) and the visit of Hitler (1938). My concern will be to compare the ways that these fascist developments negotiate existing imperial meanings (Classical and Papal) in Rome to the ways in which the previous Liberal government had negotiated the same imperial heritage. I think that the negotiation between existing imperialist/urbanistic discourses on the one hand, and changing contemporary cultural discourses (Beaux Arts in the case of Liberal Italy, Futurism/Modernism in the case of the Fascists) on the other – all in the nationalism/imperialism context – might represent a useful perspective in order to look behind the familiar iconography of fascist architecture. My argument is that by choosing in the end the rhetoric of classical monumentality over futurist radicalism in pursuit of what should have been a truly 'fascist style' (or *stile littorio*), Fascism resorted to a strategy of self-representation which, to borrow literary terminology, I will call 'masquerade', this in order to cover up its always shifting and oxymoronic ideological core.[1] As we shall see, Rome was the victim but, paradoxically, also the accomplice in such a strategy, which would indelibly alter not only her urban landscape but also her symbolic perception in the nation's collective imagery.

Mussolini, the new Augustus

As I have pointed out elsewhere,[2] after its annexation Rome became a space of contestation in which the contrasting discourses of the Classical Roman empire, the Papacy of a universal Church and the secular Savoyard monarchy of the tiny Kingdom of Italy were articulated. It is thanks to Mussolini's shrewd policy that what might have become a continuous source of problems (that is, the relation between the Italian state and the Catholic Church) found a provisional solution with the Lateran Accords of 1929. Such accords worked smoothly not only on the political level but also on the ideological one, and in particular, as I shall argue further on, with the Church's active role in resurrecting the Augustan myth.

As Giorgio Ciucci has observed, the key issues of planning in the 1930s had been well established before the fascist era.[3] Already in Liberal Rome it appeared to be very difficult to find a feasible compromise between conservation and demolition; one needs only to remember the clearances and road-widening associated with the Victor Emanuel monument. Not surprisingly, in some of his speeches Mussolini himself oscillates between a double logic of conservation and demolition. On one occasion he maintains that his age 'must respect to the highest degree that which represents the living testimony of the glory of old Rome' (speech of 18 March 1932); on another that 'The millennial monuments of our history must loom gigantic in their necessary solitude' (speech of 31 December 1925). The master plan of 1931 aimed at reaching a settlement of the many divergent views on the matter, a sort of 'conservation through isolation', but, as Kostof points out, it was viewed only as a conceptual frame; in fact some interventions were carried out according to an individual action plan, and often differed from the layout of the master plan itself.[4] However, some general lines were drawn on which everyone agreed. Among the most important was the view that archaeological sites (especially those of the Augustan era) were of the utmost importance in the self-representation of Fascism. The call for a revival of the classical spirit was nothing new of course in the country's (and the city's) history; what was new was the scale of realisation and the forms in which it expressed itself (be it in the concrete monumentality of the marble or on a cinematographic screen).

The idea of freeing the Mausoleo di Augusto was again first advanced in Liberal Italy, in the plan of 1909. In 1925–6 the original plan was revised and it was proposed that the three churches around it, SS. Ambrogio e Carlo al Corso, San Girolamo degli Schiavoni and San Rocco were also to be freed from the surrounding constructions; moreover, a zone of silence had to be created by burying the existing tramlines. Unfortunately the idea of Enrico del Debbio to create picturesque vistas through old buildings and not to build 'pompous and inexpressive new palaces' was swept away by the 1931 plan and the Augusteo was left as we see it today, a huge rectangular piazza lined precisely with those pompous and inexpressive palaces del Debbio so strongly despised. According to the project devised by the architect in charge, Vittorio Morpurgo, new porticoed buildings of the National Fascist Institute of Social Insurance were to define the piazza on the north and east sides. A wide street piazza was created between the churches of San Girolamo and San Rocco. Moreover a Latin inscription recording part of the testament of Augustus (the *Res gestae*), copied from the Temple of Augustus in Ankara, was added, together with the reconstruction of the *Ara Pacis* in a site between the Augusteo and the Tiber.[5] In 1938 it was located in a glazed protective building (an example of rationalist architecture in sharp contrast with its classical content) between via Ripetta and il Lungotevere.[6] The works were finished in three months and ten days, just in time for the inauguration on 23 September, the last day of the Augusto Bimillennial and right at the opening of the Augustan Congress which would last for four days.

One of the first reflections one could make on the freeing of the Augusteo concerns the contamination of two disciplines, archaeology and urban planning, where the latter always has the upper hand. Since fascist urban planning had to fulfil the goals of the regime, the consequence is that archaeology too had to comply with the same principles.[7] As well as this, the new Piazzale Augusto Imperatore which emerged after the work was completed is interesting for the purpose of this chapter because it is one of those places in Rome where the intersection of different cultural and ideological discourses has deeply altered the urban landscape.

It all started on 22 October 1934 (the twelfth anniversary of the March on Rome), when *Il Duce* climbed on the roof of a building, seized a pick and gave the official start to the demolition that would bring the great mausoleum to light again. Undoubtedly, the iconography of the pick, reproduced in photograph, painting and the newsreels of the Istituto Luce, became as powerful as that of the dagger and machine gun in the monumental art of the period (see Fig. 4.1). In fact, one could say that a frenetic 'demolition mania' replaced that wave of 'monumentomania' that had characterised post-Unification Italy. In the years immediately following the First World War until the early 1930s we see a slow decline of the traditional allegorical/realistic monument. One of the last in the series is the statue of the *Bersagliere*, which was located on the commemorative column at Porta Pia in 1932, an obvious link with the values of the Risorgimento viewed by the regime in terms of ideological continuity.

From the early 1930s onwards the celebratory intentions of the regime no longer concentrated on the single monument, since the shift, as I have already pointed out, was towards a concerted intervention in the whole city. The kind of 'political pedagogy' which had brought together in a perfect syncretism aesthetic and ideological discourses serving the Liberal establishment so well had to find new means to speak to the masses, a sort of double voice discourse (to borrow a literary term) that would adopt the language of the avant garde but also that of Classical Roman architecture, often giving rise to striking juxtapositions.

By the time the works at the Augusteo were finished the revival of the *culto della Romanitá* was in full gear, and it was as if time were running out in that very peculiar race in which the city of the present had to match the glory and the beauty of the city of the past. Historic events and mythological recollections often conflated in an overproduction of images, books, slogans etc., and a whole new narrative was created at the core of which was an explicit parallelism between the fascist regime and its Augustan antecedent.[8] Urban planning was of course a way in which such narrative weight was made explicit. If we go back to Piazzale Augusto Imperatore and have a closer look at those buildings which surround it, at their mosaics, sculpture panels, inscriptions, we might start 'reading' it simply like another text, one of the many of the period, which tells us how great the Italian people are. One of the inscriptions actually reads: 'The Italian people are the immortal people who always find a new spring for their hopes, their passion, their greatness'. The very fact that such an inscription is located on a building so close to Augustus' own inscription, the *Res gestae*, establishes a link that is not only physical, but ideal. The Italian people are immortal and we have the archaeological records to prove it – they are there for everyone to see. The reason for this immortality is that such a people, by a strange caprice of nature, seem to be both old and young at the same time; they have survived through the centuries because they have always kept alive the enthusiasm and the passion of youth, but also the wisdom that lies in the memory of the past. Needless to say, the whole place was intended as 'an exercise in memory', and moreover the old/young dichotomy reminds us of the contrasting binarism which is at the base of fascist ideology. Fascism used to propose itself as young, exuberant, revolutionary, but also as conservative, respectful of old customs and traditions. The implicit syllogism here is that the Italian people were fascist even before Fascism, it is just that they did not know it.[9]

Another link with Augustus is constituted, as Kostof has rightly pointed out, by the fact that the Roman Emperor revived the cult of the ancestral gods and respect for them; the parallel with Mussolini's policy of appeasement with the Vatican is clear, even more so if we consider the presence of three churches on the Piazzale.[10] In a way, this presence gave a symbolic blessing to the marriage of Fascism and Classical/Imperial heritage.

Clearly, a common denominator between the Church and the fascist regime was found not only in the field of moral values but also in the imperial ambitions of *Il Duce*. From a Catholic point of view, Italian imperialism was in fact justified on the basis of Aquinas' doctrine of 'the just cause', often used to corroborate Mussolini's aspiration to expand Italy's '*spazio vitale*' and in terms of demographic expansion. The belief that if the population decreased ,no empire was possible and the country was doomed to become a colony was held by many Catholic intellectuals and is strongly related to a moral primacy of the Italian people and of the whole country.[11] An explicit comparison was drawn with an imperial power like Protestant England (nicknamed the 'new Carthage') whose imperialism had a merely utilitarian and mercantile character. In a sense, the same idea of an ethical empire represented the unifying factor of two different traditions, the Classical/Roman on one side and the Catholic on the other, for both aimed at an expansion of their range of influence. So, to go back to the inscription on the Social Insurance building analysed earlier, the reason for the immortality of the Italian people lies not only in keeping up the binarism of youth/old age, but also in the moral and spiritual supremacy innate in these people which justifies the empire of the past as well as the empire of the present.

On a different level, if we look at the place from a vertical as well as from a horizontal perspective, I would argue that the works at and around the Mausoleo aimed at an imperial legitimation of the regime through the stratigraphy of a sacred place – after all, the Mausoleo itself was a burial site not only for Augustus, but for many of his relatives and perhaps also for Claudius and Tiberius. There was a concerted action of archaeology and urban planning, working respectively in what, to simplify, I will call the 'under' and the 'above' dimension of space. The archaeological excavations into the very viscera of the earth stand side by side with the erection of new buildings, as if diving deep into the past was propaedeutic to a projection into the future. For the sake of memory, a whole new landscape is invented, a complex interaction of imaginative and material aspects, something that should make people dream of past glories and hope for future ones. But the empire 'in the mind' is perhaps just as difficult to create as the one outside geographical borders. The artificiality of the whole ideological construction was soon to be exposed since the mask of an empire based purely on morality could not be worn forever.

Undoubtedly, Piazzale Augusto Imperatore, one of the largest squares in Rome, must have had a propaganda impact at the time, although the result was not equal to the expectations from both a scientific and an imaginative point of view. Certainly, there were better ways to fire people's imagination and the *Mostra Augustea della Romanitá* was to be one of them.

Exhibiting the Empire

The Mostra opened on 23 September 1937, in the same Palazzo delle Esposizioni on Via Nazionale where with Modernist enthusiasm the tenth anniversary of the March on Rome had been celebrated in the *Mostra della Rivoluzione Fascista* of 1932. It ran for a year and was a success, being visited by thousands, among them Hitler in May 1938.[12]

The pedagogical aspect of such events is obvious; what is worth examining is the way in which cultural discourses, especially architectural tendencies, of the time were appropriated by the regime in order to create a sort of powerful 'mythopoeic machine', though such a machine cannot mask Fascism's inner-most irreconcilable contradictions. I have already hinted at the dichotomies – tradition/revolution, modernity/antiquity – which characterise the regime's ideological core, a dualism that, according to Asor Rosa, is typical of post-Unification Italy.[13] From this perspective, the exhibitions do nothing but expose such contradictions, for those willing to see them, of course. It is precisely by analysing these exhibitions that Fascism's 'masquerade' strategy of self-representation will become apparent.

I will start by looking at the façades that in 1932 and 1937 covered the front of the Umbertine Palazzo delle Esposizioni, since they are the most impressive visual concretisation of what has been just said. The covering of the front in 1932 had a symbolic meaning: the Risorgimento was definitively over and a new page in the country's history had to be turned. It is not accidental in fact that the *Mostra della Rivoluzione fascista* replaced a major exhibition dedicated to Garibaldi, an exhibition which ran until 5 August 1932. The palace's beaux arts interiors and exterior which still echoed Liberal Italy's past grandeur and failures were disguised by a Modernist black, red and silver façade (a huge mask, if you like) with its four 25-metre tall tin-plate *fasces* and its twin 6-metre X's. As Jeffrey Schnapp has observed, although this Modernist front is far from any building tradition, 'history is permitted to enter … through oblique or indirect allusions … The black *fasces* of the façade, for example, echo the columns of the original Roman colonnade.'[14] I will not dwell here at length on the icono-graphy of the 1932 façade; what I want to do is simply to juxtapose it with the one of 1937. What is immediately apparent is the difference in style. For the 1937 façade, the architect Scalpelli imitated a Roman Triumphal Arch in the monumental style of Novecento architecture; by 1937, in fact, the flirtation with the Futurists was over and Novecento monumentalism had become the official spatial iconography of fascism. History, only obliquely adumbrated in the first façade, now becomes more visible: the four big *fasces* have developed into four pillars which are the replicas of the 'Captive Barbarians', the originals being in the Palazzo dei Conservatori in Campidoglio. On the arch there is the cast of the 'Victory of Metz', whereas on the two sides we have six inscriptions by Classical and Christian scholars (the presence of both traditions is again telling), all exalting the Romans, their *amor patriae* and their civilising mission. Interestingly, in Scalpelli's second project these inscriptions had to be replaced by geographical maps of the empire.

The two façades symbolise two stages in the regime's process of self-representation and masquerade: in the first, Fascism portrays itself as a revolutionary break with any cultural/political traditions of the past; in the second, it seems to find in such a tradition its *raison d'être*. The contradictions were played out more interestingly as far as the idea of Rome was concerned and came to be reflected in the city's landscape. It is worth remembering at this point that, for Marinetti, Rome, like Venice and Florence, was home to *passatismo*, the new futurist city being Milan, a city of velocity where the Kingdom of the Machine could flourish.[15] Mussolini, on the other hand, was obsessed by the idea of Classical Rome even before he came to power.[16] There were, however, a few futuristic elements which survived, although under different guises, in the 1937 exhibition. The most important one is perhaps the futuristic attack on the very institution of the aesthetic, on the museum. Far from being a sort of permanent memorial the museum should have been a provisional rallying point, a 'living monument' capable of being the focus for mass events, happenings, etc. The same masquerade with the Palazzo delle Esposizioni exterior (and interiors) on both occasions is emblematic of such a philosophy, although I would argue that it is reminiscent also of a very old Roman tradition, that of *le macchine pirotecniche* (pyrotechnic machines), beautiful examples, as I have argued elsewhere, of what one might call 'ephemeral architecture', but also a sort of dress rehearsal for future architectural projects.[17] The style of the 1937 façade in fact already envisages a sort of metaphysical, abstract idea of *romanitá* which will characterise the Eur buildings of 1942.[18] The tradition of the *macchine* had flourished again after Unification: Fascism, like the Liberal establishment before, exploited it for its own ends. Again in the cases of the 1932 and 1937 façades we have the impression that we are observing a typical theatrical artefact, that Rome has lent one of her most beautiful palaces to become the stage for an aesthetic/ideological representation in a truly *commedia dell'arte* style. The theme of imperial renewal was expressed by *Il Duce*'s own words on the opening portico: 'Italians let the glories of the past be superseded by the glories of the future'. Such a sentence found an immediate echo in room no. II on the first floor, the Room of the Empire, where another quotation from Mussolini read: 'I don't live in the past, for me the past is only a springboard from which I jump towards a better future.' Undoubtedly, there could not have been a more apt introduction to what was in store inside.

The inside contained about 3000 casts of antique statues, portraits, reliefs and epigraphs made from originals scattered all over the world. The visitors could see models of Roman architecture, engineering and military machines. Large maps of the Roman Empire (which were later affixed to the wall of the Basilica of Maxentius where they can still be seen), didactic panels and quotations by famous authors from Livius to Aurelius Augustinus, from Dante to Mussolini, offered the necessary commentary. An element of novelty stressed by many commentators of the time had to do with the use of modern museodidactic means (drawings, photographic reproductions, a good use of lighting) and the modern adaptations of the Palazzo delle Esposizioni interiors, which made this exhibition different from any other 'where people go just to spend some time and end up learning nothing'. In the end visiting should prove an enjoyable and useful experience both for the archaeologist and the ordinary citizen.[19]

One of the most impressive rooms was no. X dedicated to Augustus.[20] We know that there were several statues of Augustus in this room of about 2 metres in height and located on a pedestal in order to emphasise his *auctoritas* which came from his military victories as well as from his moral strength. Both the illumination, which came directly from the ceiling, and the glass panel to the right add a rationalist touch to a space which seems to be classical and modern at the same time (one of those interferences I mentioned earlier on). Moreover, on the glass panel is written the Christmas story by St Luke who makes an explicit reference to Augustus, the Roman emperor who ordered a census, following which Christ was born in a humble stable of Bethlehem. As one commentator observed, this room was the fulcrum of the exhibition, not only because the Mostra itself was meant to celebrate the bimillenary of the great Emperor, but above all because his age represented a turning-point in the history of humanity, the moment Providence chose for the birth of Christ.[21]

Not surprisingly there was also a Room of Christianity which stressed even more the link between the Classical and the Catholic traditions and the revival of both thanks to Fascism. Such a continuity is symbolised by the lighted cross and testified to by maps, photographic material and several inscriptions which follow the historic development of the Church. Room no. XXVI, aptly entitled 'The Immortality of the Idea of Rome' was also interesting. It contained together with 'The rebirth of Empire in Fascist Italy' the usual inscriptions from Mussolini and several classical scholars, images of recent Fascist rallies and new constructions, like the regime's new towns (Littoria, Sabaudia, etc.) defined as 'truly Roman works of Fascism'.

The *Mostra Augustea della Romanitá* did not close on 23 September, as was first intended, but on 6 November 1938. While it was open it functioned as a 'living monument' and a backdrop for many of the regime's parades and celebrations. This was particularly true in the case of Hitler's visit (3–9 May 1938) when the Palazzo delle Esposizioni became only part of a greater scenographic apparatus that involved the whole city. Besides the use of flags, banners and other traditional decorations on all the public buildings, a whole masquerade made up of 'ephemeral architecture' and ingenious illumination was created along the route that the car with the Führer and Mussolini would follow. One of the major constructions was the provisional pavilion at the Stazione Ostiense where Hitler arrived. Interestingly, this pavilion also reflected that 'double voice' discourse of architecture (monumental and rationalist) which, as we have seen, had already characterised the two exhibitions. One section of the pavilion was in fact porticoed with the classical columns of the *stile littorio*, the other by contrast presented a glass gallery. Again, according to tradition, this example of 'ephemeral architecture' also later found concrete realisation in the works carried out at the Stazione Ostiense and completed in 1940. On the route from the Stazione Ostiense to Termini, where Hitler took the train to Naples, it was an endless sequence of *labari*, Nazi and Italian flags, torches, eagles, a choreography which reached its climax in Via dell'Impero which linked the Colosseum and the Arch of Constantine with Piazza Venezia. With Via dell'Impero the post-Unification project of creating an archaeological landscape was realised, a landscape that on this occasion, more than on any other, had to convey the impression of a powerful fascist Rome. The front of the old Stazione Termini was also covered with a new façade, not just for celebratory reasons but because it was considered obsolete. The works on the new station started soon afterwards. In the days during which he was in Rome Hitler visited both the Mausoleo di Augusto and the *Mostra Augustea della Romanitá*.[22] Special events were also held in Piazza di Siena, a spectacle of ballet and music by Verdi, Bellini and Wagner, and at the Foro Mussolini, where the Führer watched a gymnastic performance, the scenery being that of *Lohengrin* by Wagner. Later there were fireworks in the Piazza del Quirinale. All these events are of course connected to that baroque tradition in which feasts and other popular events used to interact with the urban landscape and the Classical monuments of Rome. The new choreographies adopted this time, some with a typically Nazi character, represent a further step in this longer tradition.

Conclusion

In conclusion, the imperialist perspective is certainly the best starting point to investigate the image that the regime wanted to project both in Italy and abroad and to expose its strategy of self-representation and masquerade. Artists and architects played a key role in the creation of such an image, adopting different cultural discourses to this end: the discourse of the Modernist avant-garde first, and the Classical/Monumental one later. Often the two styles coexisted side by side as we have seen in Piazzale Augusto Imperatore or in the case of the *Mostra Augustea della Romanitá*, where the modernist arrangements of the Palazzo delle Esposizioni interiors contrasted with their content. To make the matter more complicated, sometimes the distinction between the two styles is even difficult to make, at least for somebody who is not familiar with the subtleties of architectural discourses and design. One of the purposes of this chapter, however, was not to draw such distinctions, but rather to expose the modalities of a self-representing process based on an almost inextricable cluster of contradictions. Of course, Fascism 'aestheticized' politics, as Benjamin once put it; however, I tend to agree with Jeffrey Schnapp when he maintains that

> putting forward the first Modern(ist) politics of spectacle, [Fascism] placed the conventional polarities of Marxist and Liberal theory under constant pressure, confusing superstructure with structure, private with public, the State with civil society. Fascism may thus be said to have ushered in a new dispensation in which all oppositions between aesthetics and politics are swept up into a new image politics.[23]

The strategy which best served such image politics – or Fascism's 'politics of spectacle' to quote Schnapp's words – was one of masquerade, which allowed the regime to take up multiple and contradictory positions, performing different roles, while hiding behind an apparently univocal discursive façade. Clearly, there is an element of theatricality, even unintentional carnivalesque comedy, in all this: Rome was transformed by extravagant and over-hasty archaeological campaigns into an antique stage set where every ruin stood as an implicit legitimation of the revived Empire. Archaeology, History, Urban Planning, all such disciplines capitulated to the myth of the new imperial Rome. And the Romans? Some were flattered, some were horrified by what was happening to their city, but then all was done in a climate of nationalistic fervour and with such efficiency, optimism and vigour that it was difficult not to fall into the same delusion. The biggest delusion of Fascism, however, was to believe in its own masquerade and in the constructions of its own mythopoetic machine. It did not understand that, as with any theatrical performance, there is a time when the curtains drop and the lights have to die out. No burst of applause came from the audience.

Notes

1   The concept of masquerade was first theorised in psychoanalysis by Joan Rivière in her essay 'Womanliness as Masquerade', *International Journal of Psychoanalysis* (1929). Such a concept has been at the core of that process of reconceptualisation of gender which emerged from the activism and scholarship of the 1960s and 1970s and whose focus was on the performative aspects of any gender construction. In recent years it has also been extended to the problem of sexual representation in film: see: S. Heath, 'Joan Rivière and the Masquerade', in *Formations of Fantasy*, ed. V. Burgin, J. Donald and C. Kaplan, London: Routledge, 1986, and M.A. Doane, 'Film and the Masquerade: Theorizing the Female Spectator', *Screen* 23 (1982): 3–4.

2   See 'Telling Imperial Histories: Contests of Narrativity and Representation in Post-Unification Rome (1870–1911)', in the electronic journal *Paisano* (University of Texas), June 2000, http://uts.cc.utexas.edu/~phalth/

3   G. Ciucci, *Gli architetti e il fascismo*, Turin: Einaudi, 1989, p. 81.

4   S. Kostof, *The Third Rome, 1870–1950, Traffic and Glory*, Berkeley, CA: University Art Museum, 1973, p. 50.

5   The definitive project is described in detail by Morpurgo himself in his 'La sistemazione augustea', *Capitolium*, 1937; see also E. Ponti, 'Come sorge e come scompare il quartiere attorno al Mausoleo di Augusto', *Capitolium*, 1935 and G. Moretti, 'Lo scavo e la ricostruzione dell'Ara Pacis Augustae', *Capitolium*, 1938.

6   Ugo Ojetti, in the *Corriere della Sera* of 4 October 1938, sharply criticises the glazed building since it lacked a true sense of *romanità*.

7   The goals of the regime and thus of its urban planning policy are listed in F. Ciacci, 'L'urbanistica fascista in Roma mussoliniana ed imperiale', in *Atti v congresso nazionale di Studi romani*, 4 (1937), p. 82. For the effects of fascism's urban planning on the city of Rome, see D. Manacorda and R. Tomassia, *Il piccone del regime*, Rome, 1985.

8   On this point see G. Bottai, 'L'Italia di Augusto e l'Italia d'oggi', *Roma*, 1937 and E. Balbo, 'Protagonisti dell'Impero di Roma, Augusto e Mussolini', *Roma*, 1941 (written 1937).

9   To quote Claudio Fogu's words, this is 'fascism's most truly totalitarian project: the construction of a fascist form of historical consciousness'. See C. Fogu, 'Fascism and

Historic Representation: the 1932 Garibaldian Celebrations', *Journal of Contemporary History* 31, 2 (1996): 335.

10 Kostof, *The Third Rome*, pp. 36–7.

11 On this point see M. Cagnetta, *Antichisti e impero fascista*, Bari: Laterza, 1979, in particular chap. 2, 'Imperialismo demografico'.

12 C. Galassi Paluzzi, 'Perpetuitá di Roma: la mostra augustea della romanitá e la mostra della rivoluzione fascista', *Roma* (1937): 353. For the catalogue of the 1932 exhibition see D. Alfieri and L. Freddi, *Mostra della Rivoluzione Fascista*, Roma, 1933, and for the 1937 exhibition see G.Q. Giglioli, *Mostra Augustea della Romanitá*, Roma, 1938.

13 A. Asor Rosa, *Storia d'Italia*, 4, 'Dall'Unitá a oggi', Turin: Einaudi, 1975, p. 1500.

14 J.T. Schnapp, 'Epic Demonstrations: Fascist Modernity and the 1932 Exhibition of the Fascist Revolution', in *Fascism, Aesthetics and Culture*, ed. R.J. Golsan, Hanover and London: University Press of New England, 1992, p. 26.

15 See F.T. Marinetti, *Futurismo e fascismo*, Foligno, 1924 and *Futurist Manifestos*, ed. Umbro Apollonio, London: Thames and Hudson, 1973.

16 The idea of Rome is recurrent in the Duce's speeches; on this point see *Roma nel pensiero del Duce*, Collezione Capitolini, Governatorato di Roma, *Roma*, 1943.

17 The reference is again to my paper 'Telling Imperial Histories: Contests of Narrativity and Representation in Post-Unification Rome (1870–1911)'. For a history of the Palazzo delle Esposizioni and its exhibitions, see *Il Palazzo delle Esposizioni, Urbanistica e Architettura. L'Esposizione inaugurale del 1883. Le acquisizioni pubbliche. Le attivita' espositive*, Roma, 1991.

18 Already in 1935, at least according to Bottai, the Duce had prophetically anticipated the celebration of the Italian Empire in a world's fair. The fair, known as Eur or E42, was to be held at a huge exhibition site south-west of Rome. Only few buildings were built before work stopped for the war.

19 See M. Pallottino, 'La Mostra Augustea della Romanitá', *Capitolium*, II (1937) and G. Reisoli, 'Ció che si ascolta nella Mostra Augustea della Romanitá', *Roma*, 1938.

20 I am partly indebted for the description of this room to Friedemann Scriba's 'Mussolini's Italy: How to Sacralize the Roman Past', paper given at the conference 'The Sacred Structures of Nationalism and their Transformations in the 18th and 19th centuries', Leipzig, 2–3 July 1993.

21 Pallottino, 'La Mostra Augustea della Romanitá', pp. 522–3.

22 For a detailed description in the press of the complex choreography put up for Hitler's visit see *Il Lavoro Fascista*, IX, 101, 29 April (1938), 104, 3 May (1938), 105, 4 May (1938), 106, 5 May (1938). See also the special illustrated edition of *Il Popolo d'Italia*, 3–9 May (1938) and *L'Illustrazione Italiana*, 19, 8 May (1938).

23 Schnapp, 'Epic Demonstrations: Fascist Modernity and the 1932 Exhibition of the Fascist Revolution', p.3. On the question of Fascism's image strategies see L. Malvano, *Fascismo e politica dell'immagine*, Turin: Einaudi, 1988 and P.V. Cannistraro, *La fabbrica del consenso*, Bari: Laterza, 1975.

5   Airbrushed Moscow

The cathedral of Christ the Saviour

Natasha Chibireva

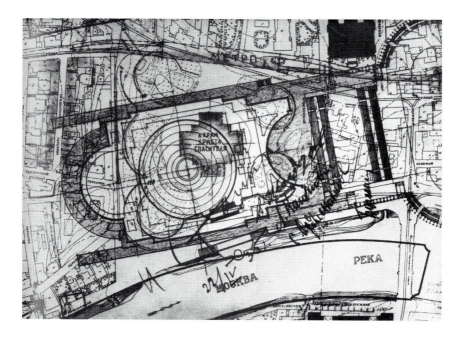

Figure 5.1 Master plan of the Palace of the Soviets, showing a footprint of the Cathedral of Christ the Saviour and signed by Stalin, Molotov, Kaganovich on 22.04.35.

Source: E Kirichenko, 1992, p. 237.

Background

This is the story of a certain site in the city of Moscow, a site which is known to the Western reader, if at all, as that of the abortive Palace of the Soviets. But the story does not begin there. Nor does it end with the abandonment of the project. For up until 1931 the site had been occupied by Russia's largest Orthodox church – the cathedral of Christ the Saviour; this structure was subsequently demolished in order to make way for the proposed Palace of the Soviets, but this project was never completed, and by 1960 the site had been given over to an enormous open-air swimming pool. This in turn was demolished in 1996 in order to make way for the reconstruction of the original cathedral.

As Rem Koolhaas observes in his Bedtime Story about the site: 'No lesson, no allegory, just grasping'.[1]

The site – an afterthought

This site on the river bank a few hundred metres south-west of the Kremlin has proved to be an enduring 'billboard' for the city, constantly being 'repapered' and re-inscribed in a process that embodies the Soviet obsession with writing and rewriting the past. It is perhaps ironic, given its notorious history, that the site itself has only ever been an afterthought. As with all great monuments the idea came first and only then did the energetic search for an appropriate site commence.

Even the cathedral itself had originally been planned for a different site, up on the Vorobievy Hills, and at least four other sites were considered before the final choice was made. The infamous decision to demolish the cathedral in 1931 was taken within a programme of demolitions well before the site was officially approved for the 'monument of all times and all people' and before the preliminary competition had thrown up initial ideas about the architectural character of the Palace.[2] It was as though the idea of the Palace was excuse enough for the inevitable demolition of the cathedral.[3] Significantly, perhaps, the ghost of the proposed Palace of the Soviets tracked the same sites as had been proposed for the cathedral back in the nineteenth century – Red Square, Vorobievy (later Lenin's) Hills,[4] and so on. Finally, the pool which replaced the abandoned Palace of the Soviets was hardly a carefully thought-out project. It was less a question of where to locate the swimming pool than what to do with a particular site.

The cathedral – the national idea

The story of the cathedral – of its competitions, architects and construction – is full of its own tragedies and intrigues. No less dramatic than the later Palace of the Soviets eventually proposed for the site, the cathedral was built to commemorate Russia's deliverance in 1812 from the hands of Napoleon, to mark the end of what was at the time the greatest ever war faced by Russian forces.

The French had occupied the city of Moscow[5] for nearly five weeks, and a great fire had destroyed many of the city's buildings. 'Moscow – it does not exist any more', wrote one of the French troops as he left the city. The subsequent reconstruction of the city proved to be not only a practical necessity, but also a symbol of victory and national revival. The idea of constructing a monument to the 1812 war was hardly controversial. The cathedral of Christ the Saviour served as a form of temple-monument, its function being to serve not only as a church, but also as a national museum and monument.

The imperial decree for its construction was published in December 1812. A competition was held attracting several of the leading Russian architects of

Figure 5.2 The cathedral of Christ the Saviour, Moscow.

Source: E Kirichenko, 1992, p. 87

the time – Voronikhin, Zakharov, Quarengi, Zhilyardi. The winning architect, A.L. Vitberg (1787–1855), who was forced to change faith to the
orthodox religion to meet the stipulations of Alexander *I*, proposed that the
building be sited on the Vorobievy Hills.[6] In 1817 the cornerstone was laid
down, and by 1826 construction had begun. But no sooner had construction
commenced than the new tsar – Nicholas I – called a halt to the works. The
architect was accused of bribery, and in 1835 was exiled to the town of
Vyatka, only to return to St. Petersburg in the 1840s to die in poverty. The
design was abandoned, and the holy 'symbols' were removed from the
Vorobievy Hills and stored temporarily in the main cathedral in the Kremlin.

A second competition was announced. This was won by K.A. Ton
(1794–1881), whose Byzantine design effectively established a new national
architectural style. The site eventually chosen for the second version of the cathedral was one previously occupied by the Alekseevksy Convent order. The
cornerstone was laid down in 1839, and construction continued until 1881. The
new building became a feature in the Moscow cityscape, and its construction

caused no less of a stir than the proposals for the Palace of the Soviets half a century later. But the building was haunted by misfortune. It became something of a tradition in post-revolutionary Russia for art critics to compare the final scheme somewhat unfavourably to the original proposal. Moreover, the consecration of the cathedral, scheduled for 1881, was postponed due to the assassination of Alexander II on the very eve of the day on which Russia was at last to become a constitutional monarchy.[7] When his son, Alexander III, succeeded him, he adopted a very different political stance, convinced as he was that liberal reforms would only encourage opposition to the government. He was, as A.N. Benois once put it, 'a monarch who encouraged the masquerade of nationalism but deeply despised the people'.[8] The official opening of the cathedral was timed to coincide with the coronation of Alexander III in 1883. In 1918 a huge monument to Alexander III on the cathedral square was demolished. The cathedral itself was soon to suffer the same fate.

Soon after the February Revolution of 1917 the Monuments Demolition Committee was founded[9] by the Union of the Art Activists. But the fate of the cathedral of Christ the Saviour was effectively sealed by a split within the Russian Orthodox Church, and by the formation of the rival Vital Church. This led to a haemorrhaging of the clergy of the cathedral of the Christ Saviour to the Vital Church, and even before the persecution of believers had really begun the cathedral had become noticeably empty. Attendance dwindled, and a cathedral originally intended for a congregation of 15,000 disciples now attracted barely a few dozen. Its function came to resemble more and more that of a museum, but even this was to come to an end, as the second stage of this tragedy unfolded: persecution of church activists escalated into the eradication of their buildings.

The agony and death of enormous animals are always disturbing – as in the recent death of the Soviet empire. With the cathedral the latest demolition technique – dynamite – was used. Never mind the fact that building materials were in short supply, and the bricks could have been salvaged for other buildings. When a country is gripped by revolutionary fervour, such concerns are secondary. What was required was demolition – and quickly. Dynamite, when first tested in the Kremlin, had proved very efficient on the most ancient holy places. But with the cathedral the agony was to prove more lasting. The first explosion on 5 December 1931 left the majority of the building still standing. The full moon added to the apocalyptic associations in the terrified minds of the people. The great floundering carcass of the cathedral would not go quietly. Several more charges were needed.[10]

The Palace of the Soviets – a substitution

'Let's build centres of culture instead of centres of mystification' was the popular cry as the sound of demolition charges rang out in religious buildings throughout the land. The very act of replacing these buildings took on a symbolic status. Lenin himself would emphasise the strategic importance of the site where a monument was to be erected. It was this thinking that informed, for example, the decision to site the monument to L. Tolstoy on the precise spot where he had been excommunicated by the Church; or the monument to Radischev, the first to rise up against the monarchy, immediately opposite the Winter Palace in Petersburg; or the monument to Lenin himself at the place where he was assassinated. And it was this thinking that dictated the timing of various events, so that demolition of churches was timed specifically to coincide with key anniversaries of the revolution; the scheduling of the Anti-Christmas at Christmas time, and so on.[11] Thus it came as no surprise that the biggest and most significant cathedral in Russia was to be replaced by a new temple to atheism.

The extraordinary alacrity and impatience with which the authorities approached the project were characteristic of their approach to all forms of commemoration, whether during the revolution itself or during the period of totalitarianism. A replacement had to be found at once, as if by a miracle, to give the impression that it had always been there. To give some examples:

1   From the 1840s onwards, even before they were built, cathedrals would be painted on to views of the city, whether on postcards or in books.[12] And this tactic would later be adopted in the practice of altering paintings, photographs and books under Socialist Realism.

2   In 1928, three years before the cathedral was actually demolished, A. Rodchenko had completed a series of photographs of the cathedral site with the cathedral airbrushed out, and with only the briefest hint of the structure itself, so that for all intents and purposes the cathedral did not exist.

3   In 1935 an underground station was built right by the site using materials from the cathedral, and called the *Palace of the Soviets*, even though the actual palace did not exist. Only when the idea of the palace was eventually abandoned, was the station renamed after one of the streets nearby.

4   In the 1990s the reconstruction of the cathedral proceeded at breakneck speed, which amazed Muscovites and foreigners alike.

5   There was, however, no rush to construct the pool. Nor was there any accompanying governmental propaganda or media hype – a tell-tale sign of the confidence that it would last for some time: the generosity of the victor.

The brief for the design of the Palace was based largely on the 1922 competition for the Palace of Labour – which was also never built. Gigantism and monumentalism were not born in the 1930s. Indeed, the sheer impracticality of the brief for the Palace of Labour was all the more remarkable given the resources available in the country at the time. The story of the Palace of the Soviets is ultimately the story of the four successive rounds of a competition. In early 1931 a preliminary competition was held to clarify the programme. Later that year a second round attracted some 160[13] entries from all over the world. Figures such as Le Corbusier, Gropius, Lubetkin, H. Meyer, Perret, Brasini and Hamilton all entered the competition. Controversially, however, the first prize was awarded jointly to Iofan, Hamilton (USA) and Zholtovsky. By now it was clear that the judges favoured stripped classicism of monumental proportions, and in 1932 Iofan was eventually awarded first prize in the third and final round on the competition.

This was a crucial moment in the development of Soviet architecture. With this competition historicism began to install itself as the official Soviet style, sanctioned in part by the 1932 'historic' Party resolution on the dissolution of all autonomous artistic bodies.[14] But whereas the competition marked the triumphant arrival of Socialist Realism in architecture for the Soviet press, in the eyes of foreign observers it marked a tragic eclipse of Modernism.[15] The results of the competition caused great consternation among Western radicals and their Soviet counterparts alike. As Hans Schmidt, a colleague of Ernst May, wrote: 'the architects of the Soviet Russia will come to their senses eventually'.[16] For Le Corbusier the Soviet decision caused nothing but an 'inexplicable shock, big depression and decline of spirit'.[17] A group of Western architects (Le Corbusier, Gropius, Sert, Gidion, *et al.*) were even so naive as to write a letter to Stalin asking him to intervene so that the design would not be built.[18]

In May 1933 Iofan's design was adopted, and in February 1934, together with Schuko and Gel'freikh, the architect presented the final version – a ziggurat-like creation with a 70-metre tall statue on top of Lenin, taking the overall height to 415 metres, two and half times the height of the cathedral. The master plan was approved in April 1935. Construction began in 1937, and in 1939 the colossal foundations were laid.[19] But the war called a halt to the works. The steel frame was dismantled in 1941–2 to be used in the reconstruction of destroyed bridges and for the construction of anti-tank devices around Moscow.

The pool: functionalism versus symbolism

After the war the riverside site was finally abandoned – 'the thought of resuming work was beyond even the most stalinist of imaginations'.[20] The idea, however, did not die. In 1957–9 a new series of competitions for the Palace of the Soviets was announced for the original site. But nothing was built. Eventually, in 1960, the idea itself was also abandoned. Coincidentally, that same year the site of the former cathedral was turned into a swimming pool.

This was quite unexpected. According to Soviet logic, construction should have continued regardless until the Palace was finally complete. But the original motivation to build had exhausted itself. All that was left was 'an extinguished ideological volcano'.[21] Moreover, as V. Paperny observed,[22] the Palace could – by definition – never be complete; the desire to build an *ideal* building was destined to fail. It could only ever be an endless project, because, were it to be completed, there would be nothing more to do than multiply that ideal model. In fact this process had already started even before the project was abandoned. Despite the extreme conditions of post-war Russia seven skyscrapers were (in)famously built on the radial routes out of Moscow. It was as if the Palace of the Soviets had split into seven smaller palaces. It was as though culture had inverted itself when, instead of the 'highest building in the world', the pool emerged out of a gaping hole.[23]

The Church responded predictably enough. According to Patriarch Aleksii II, the swimming pool was a desecration of a 'holy place', 'a grotesque creation' that represented the 'prominent spiritual void' in society.[24] The ancient Russian expression 'a holy place can never be empty' rang out with a certain irony. When the skeleton of the Palace was eventually dismantled it came to symbolise not only the inadequacies of the communist regime in general, but also the revenge of God. In the eyes of the Church the demolition only confirmed once again the godless nature of the authorities. The pool appeared as a double heresy, and as the eradication of the holy place itself.[25] Yet the infinite void filled with water was perhaps a much stronger image than a huge 'support' for a statue of Lenin disappearing into the clouds.[26] Moreover, the spectacular swirling steam that would hover above the pool in winter was, perhaps, more enigmatic and fascinating than the aggressive, over-decorated, solid monument could ever have been.

Within Soviet dissident circles the pool was seen, if anything, as a rather good thing. It was a form of demonstration against any sort of orthodoxy, be it ecclesiastical or secular. It represented a certain exhaustion of the system. But absence – as in minimalist art – can also represent something. The place was destined to become a symbol to whichever epoch it belonged.

There was a popular joke about the pool:

> During communism, the Soviet intellectuals used to say, 'There used to be a wonderful church here, but now there's a metro and a swimming pool.' And after some time, the intellectuals will say, 'You know, there used to be a wonderful swimming pool here, but now they have gone and built a church.'[27]

The new cathedral – repentance

In the 1990s repentance was in the air, as though there was anything to repent. And the bigger the sin, the bigger the act of repentance. It was the same old story. Just as with the original cathedral and Palace of the Soviets, there was overreaction. The people, after all, were always impressed by anything monumental. And how could they ever repent for the 'crime' that had been committed? Scale seemed the only answer – an enormous building to repent for an enormous crime.

The debate began: what should be done with the bizarre pool? The pool had seen its last days, to be sure. Waterless, monstrous, it lay there, a confused cultural icon, a complete dichotomy, the inside-out concrete manifestation of the absent centre of Russian life. Its days were numbered. In 1989 the idea of redeveloping the site began to circulate in the media, and by 1994 the go-ahead had been given. The pool would be replaced.

Several proposals were made. A steel skeleton of the original cathedral, that somehow echoed the abandoned carcass of the unfinished Palace of the Soviets, which had stood there in its rusting glory, until eventually demolished. A holographic 'virtual' reproduction of the cathedral which echoed the surreal clouds of steam over the site in winter when the pool was open. There was even a proposal to reconstruct the convent that had existed on the site – a fine example of seventeenth-century architecture – before the original cathedral had even been built. But the most popular option was to rebuild the original cathedral, a reinforced concrete 'replica' of Christ the Saviour. Repentance: 'If the temple shines in its former beauty, then truly we are rebuilding what has been taken away from us and destroyed, then Russia is truly being reborn' (Aleksii II).[28] Or so it was thought.

Of course the site could never be quite the same. It no longer enjoyed the same uninterrupted vistas, and the hill on which the cathedral once stood had been levelled to make way for the construction of the Palace of the Soviets. Meanwhile several unseemly Modernist structures had been erected nearby which would ensure that the new-old cathedral would no longer command the surrounding area.

Maybe – if you scratch the surface – you will find that any site will have its own tragic history and be overloaded with symbolism. But what marks out this particular site is that for nearly two centuries it remained a 'battlefield for ideas', a terrain on which the ruling authorities expressed themselves, whether it be the Church, the monarchy, the communist state, or post-communist Russia.

It may be rash to generalise, but the behaviour of all parties, it would seem, was remarkably similar. However contradictory and mutually exclusive the proposals for the site might have been, they all seem to have one thing in common – they were illustrations once more of the inescapable desire to leave one's material mark on the world. They were all guided by the fear of perishing without leaving a trace. Although it hardly makes sense to explore the idea that the site had some mystical properties that attracted the authorities, a certain 'chain reaction' can be observed in the way that substitutions took place: once chosen to demonstrate one ideological position, the site would very likely be chosen to demonstrate another. Architecture – whether one likes it or not – is unique among the arts in playing such a major role in public life, and is the usual vehicle for expressing political power. The site therefore became the victim of successive attempts to 'airbrush' history.

Ghosts and memories of the past remain locked if not into the place itself, then at least into the succeeding structure. The building, then, exceeds what you actually see or experience. It always holds the traces of its tragic history. However, as Nietzsche once observed 'ultimately no one can extract from things, books included, more than he already knows. What one has no access to *through experience* one has no ear for.'[29] But what happens to the object when at some point one finds an 'ear' to listen to its stories?

To make a rather distant comparison, imagine a song in a foreign language which you once grew to like without ever knowing the meaning of its words. In due time you begin to understand the words, and the whole song is suddenly transformed. But the words were always there. Once you recognise the words, you lose your earlier 'disinterest'. The song begins to make sense, and is no longer appreciated for its 'form' alone. The same thing happens with buildings – the 'words', the texts, the stories were always there. It is only the language – or hieroglyphic code – that needs to be deciphered.

Notes

1 Rem Koolhaas, *S, M, L, XL*, London: *Taschen*, 1997, p. 823.
2 The final decision to demolish the structure was taken by the Temporary Technical Advisory Body on 3 June 1931, but the official *Izvestiya* announcement for the competition was not published until 18 July 1931.
3 Interestingly enough it was a group of architects – the ASNOVA group (*Assosiatsia novykh arkhinektorov* (Association of New Architects) founded in 1923) the eventual runners-up in the Palace of the Soviets competition – and not any politician or civic body who in 1924 first proposed this riverside site for a colossus, The Palace of Labour – the workers' parliament. On this see E.I. Kirichenko, *Khram Khrista Spasitelya v Moskve*, Moscow: Planeta, 1992, p. 228.
4 Kirichenko, *Khram Khrista Spasitelya v Moskve*, p. 234.
5 Moscow had ceased to be the capital city from 1703.
6 Kirichenko, *Khram Khrista Spasitelya v Moskve*, p. 31.
7 Kirichenko, *Khram Khrista Spasitelya v Moskve*, p. 142.
8 Benois [1917], quoted by Kirichenko, *Khram Khrista Spasitelya v Moskve*, p. 217.
9 Their primary concern, however, had been for the monuments to the monarchy, rather than church buildings.
10 A documentary of the demolition has survived. For a written account of film director and cameraman, V.V. Mikosha, see Kirichenko, *Khram Khrista Spasitelya v Moskve*, pp. 240–1.
11 For further examples see Kirichenko, *Khram Khrista Spasitelya v Moskve*, p. 219 onwards.
12 Kirichenko, *Khram Khrista Spasitelya v Moskve*, p. 133.
13 There were some 24 entries from foreign architects; on this see S.O. Khan-Magomedov, *Pioneers of Soviet Architecture: The Search for the New Solutions in the 1920s and 1930s*, New York: Rizzolli, 1987; and Paperny, *Culture-2*, [1985], NLO, Moscow, 1996.
14 For a provocative discussion on this, see the account of Russian-born Boris Groys, *The Total Art of Stalinism: Avant-garde, Aesthetic Dictatorship, and Beyond*, [1988], Princeton, NJ, 1992, pp. 34–5: 'It was not Stalin but RAPP and AkhRR, who by the late 1920s and early 1930s had established a virtual monopoly on culture and were responsible for prosecuting all political undesirables' and further: 'Stalin, therefore, really did to some extent justify the hopes of those who thought that direct party control would be more tolerant than the power exercised by individual groups of artists.'
15 This was the last competition covered extensively in foreign publications which has been partly responsible for attracting the participation of world-famous architects.
16 Hans Schmidt, '*Die Neue Stadt*', 1932, no. 6–7; cited in Paperny, *Culture-2*, p. 33.
17 Le Corbusier's letter (1932) to Soviet architects passed via M. Ginsburg; quoted in Paperny, *Culture-2*, pp. 33, 382, quoted from the Russian translation.
18 Paperny, *Culture-2*, p. 33.
19 The marsh-like conditions of the soil on the site had caused the cathedral's builders nearly a century beforehand to make a solid foundation slab of 12m thickness out of

sandstone blocks with lead joints instead of cement (see Kirichenko, *Khram Khrista Spasitelya v Moskve*, pp. 241, 255).

20 Rem Koolhaas, 'Palace of the Soviets. Virtual Architecture. A Bedtime Story', *S, M, L, XL*, pp. 823–4.

21 Koolhaas, p. 824.

22 Paperny, *Culture-2*, p,. 95.

23 The eventual withdrawal of the Palace idea, as Paperny's argument goes, occurred exactly at the time when *Culture-1* was again about to dominate over *Culture-2*. Both – Culture-1 and Culture-2 – are the entirely theoretical, idealised models which he had invented to describe and order some cultural-socio-political events in the Soviet period and were constructed on the material of the 1920s and 1930s–50s respectively. The pool that emerged, according to the model, indicated a shift from Culture-1 to Culture-2, whose attributes were described by the author in a number of binary oppositions including beginning–end, motion–inertia, horizontal–vertical, uniform–hierarchic, etc. In 1995 Paperny interpreted the intended reconstruction as an indication of the Culture-2 return.

24 *http://www.stots.edu/khram.html*, accessed 20/07/99.

25 The idea of the Cathedral of Christ had emerged soon after the devastating fire of 1812. Water, however, seems to have exerted more power than fire during the Soviet regime: stable totalitarianism – the 'hydra' state. Metaphors of water appear throughout. Many churches were submerged by the Volga–Moscow canal, while Khruschev's political reforms of the 1960s were labelled the 'thaw': the system thawed to such a degree that only water was left – the pool. However, the newly constructed temple is in the church's words 'a symbol of the new Russia rising from the Soviet ashes' (but in fact from the Soviet waters).

26 There was a post-war joke about the failure: the country's leaders simply feared that in bad weather Lenin would appear headless. However, the ability to 'influence' the weather was not beyond the wit of the authorities. Clouds could be dispersed with dry ice from aircraft, as it had been for demonstrations and parades during Brezhnev's period.

27 *http://nw3.nai.net/~virtual/sot/church.html* accessed 20/07/99.

28 *http://www.stots.edu/khram.html* accessed 20/07/99.

29 Friedrich Nietzsche, *Ecce Homo: Why I Write Such Excellent Books*, [1878], Penguin Classics, 1992, p. 40.

6 Erasing the traces

The 'denazification' of post-revolutionary Berlin and Bucharest

Neil Leach

Figure 6.1   Checkpoint Charlie, Berlin. (credit: Natasha Chibireva)

If, as Walter Benjamin claimed, to live is to leave traces, what becomes of the traces of lives which were evil? How is one to erase those traces, should one wish to do so? The question is set in perspective by the recent history of 25 Cromwell Road, Gloucester, England, the former home of Fred and Rose West. The house was the site of numerous crimes and murders for which Rose West was convicted, Fred West having committed suicide before he could stand trial. Following the conviction of Rose West, the house was physically eradicated. The building materials were systematically ground down, and a memorial walkway established on the vacant plot.[1]

The eradication of the physical fabric of the building raises a number of questions. If this action was seen somehow to purge the site of the memory of evil, what relationship is there between the physical fabric and the memory associated with it? Furthermore, would there be any alternative method of 'purging' the site? Would it be possible to erase that memory of evil without eradicating the building?

These questions relate on a broader scale to the nation state. How is a nation to deal with the architectural fabric which bears witness to the traumas of a former repressive regime? Some light is thrown upon this complex question by recent developments in Eastern Europe, where two alternative strategies have emerged: the physical eradication of those monuments, on the one hand – in the manner of 25 Cromwell Road – and their symbolic re-appropriation, on the other. These two distinct strategies will be termed here the 'Berlin Wall syndrome' and the 'Bucharest syndrome', respectively.

The 'Berlin Wall syndrome' alludes to the almost complete eradication of the traces of the Iron Curtain around Berlin. Whilst a number of parks have been created on the outskirts of the city to commemorate the Wall, in the centre itself only very limited traces have been left, as once famous Cold War landmarks, such as Checkpoint Charlie and Potsdamer Platz, have been redeveloped for commercial purposes (see Figure 6.1).

The 'Bucharest syndrome' refers here to the re-appropriation and re-use of buildings from a previous regime, of which the most renowned example would perhaps be the palace of the former Romanian dictator, Nicolae Ceauşescu (see Figure 6.2).[2] This building, now known as The People's House, is reputed to be the second largest building in the world behind the Pentagon.[3] It stands at the end of a 4 km long avenue of grand buildings which was driven through the centre of old Bucharest, causing the destruction of much of the historic fabric of the city. Although still unfinished at the time of Ceauşescu's overthrow and execution in 1989, the building has been partially completed, and is now redeployed as the House of the Parliament and as a conference centre. What is remarkable about this building is the way in which a monument so closely associated with an unpopular regime has now been accepted by many as the popular centre of Bucharest.

To borrow a term from Andrew Benjamin, this article will consider the 'denazification' of Central and Eastern Europe following the collapse of communism. This term is used in the very broadest sense to extend beyond the obvious case of National Socialism as such, to include any form of repressive regime. In this context, therefore, 'denazification' means the process of ridding the built environment of associations with a previous unpleasant regime.

The politics of investment

What is supposed by the term 'denazification' is that an object can be 'nazified' in the first place. Yet the precise mechanism by which an object can be invested with political content must be considered, before addressing the question of how it might lose that content.[4] There are, of course, clear instances throughout history, most especially under fascist regimes, when architecture

Figure 6.2   The People's House. (credit: Neil Leach)

does appear to have been used as a political tool. The very physical presence of architecture, it would seem, may serve to reinforce and support a political regime. Yet we must stand back and examine how exactly architecture might perform such a role. Can architectural form *in itself* be political?

One way to address this question is to reflect upon the specific example of Nazi architecture. Here we find a particularly self-conscious use of architecture as a political vehicle. The architecture of the Third Reich took a variety of manifestations. Either it subscribed stylistically to the *völkisch* trend for the vernacular, incorporating local materials and traditional building techniques, so as to invoke a nostalgic sense of a community (*Gemeinschaft*) linked to the soil. Or, in the grandiose, stripped-down classicism of Albert Speer and others, it seemed to allude to a Germany that was seen as the logical inheritor of the Roman imperial tradition. But whatever its particular manifestation, the message was clear enough. The architecture of the Third Reich was a didactic architecture, which played an important role in supporting Nazi ideology. It was, as Adolf Hitler himself proclaimed, a form of 'word in stone'.[5]

Associations have persisted such that the assumption has remained prevalent in post-war Germany that classicism is itself inherently fascistic, an argument that was reputedly used to undermine the competition entry in the 1970s for a museum in Düsseldorf by British architects, Stirling and Wilford, which incorporated the use of columns. But this has not always been the case. Classicism was born in Greece, the very cradle of democracy. How can an architectural style be associated at one moment with democracy, and at another moment with totalitarianism? If, furthermore, we consider the forms of civic architecture popular in other European countries in pre-war Europe – countries, that is, like Britain, in which fascism did not exert a strong influence – we find a certain stylistic affinity with the architecture of Nazi Germany. Two factors begin to emerge which appear to play a crucial role in determining the political content of architectural forms.

First, it is clear that one important factor is that of context – in terms of both time and place. A building with columns which might have served as a temple in ancient Greece, may serve as a Nazi headquarters in 1930s' Germany. Equally, that same building might serve, say, as a civic library or university administration building in 1930s' Britain. To a great extent, then, the 'social ground' of architecture is what lends it meaning. When displaced from the contextual situation that gives it its force, architecture would lose much of its political authority.

Second, it is clear that another important factor is the question of use, since use – the way a building is 'treated' – will determine its associations within a given cultural context. This extends to its political associations. A building assumes a political status through a mechanism of semantic associations, either individually, through its particular politics of use, or collectively, through its stylistic affinities with other buildings associated with a particular politics of use. In other words, a building might be recognised as a Nazi building either because Nazi activities take place there, or because it is stylistically similar to other buildings associated with Nazi activities. By extension, a building once associated with Nazi ideology, such as the 1936 Olympic stadium in Berlin, can be progressively 'rinsed' of those associations, by being used for more mundane activities, such as weekly football matches. Function therefore becomes a crucial factor in determining the 'meaning' of a building. In this sense buildings conform relatively closely to the model of language posited by Wittgenstein, in which meaning is determined by use, to the extent that the way in which buildings are 'viewed' is largely dependent on the way that they are 'used'. We might therefore revise the claim made by Roland Barthes, in the context of the Eiffel Tower, that 'use never does anything but shelter meaning' to read 'use never does anything but *generate* meaning'.[6] Barthes contrasts the *intended* functions of the Eiffel Tower – meteorological station etc. – with the symbolic meaning of the tower as the universal sign of Paris. If, however, we look to the *actual* function of the tower as tourist monument and symbol of Paris, we find that its meaning is precisely defined by its use.

If factors such as use and context are so influential in determining the 'meaning' of a building, we might conclude that architectural form, as Fredric Jameson has observed, is essentially 'inert'.[7] This is not to overlook the relevance of certain physical characteristics, such as size, location and appearance, in influencing the use, and hence meaning of a building – a vast, prominent building, for example, might 'lend' itself to serve as a monument – but rather it is to recognise the underlying neutrality of form against other more significant external factors. Political content is 'projected' on to form. Political content is therefore a question of allegorical content. It is dependent upon a memory of what a particular form is 'supposed' to mean, and as that memory fades, so the meaning is erased.

This does not undermine the fact that at a given time and for a given group of people a building will inevitably be seen as embodying certain political values. This is only to be expected. Indeed, while for Jameson architectural form in itself is 'inert', it must be recognised that architecture is never decontextualised, and is always put to use, even if that 'use' is a non-use. Inevitably, then, a building will be perceived as having a meaning which will be projected on to its form. In the collective imagination, this process of projection on the part of the interpreting agent is somehow overlooked. The very 'ventriloquism' of ascribing a meaning to the building is never fully acknowleged, so that in the hermeneutic moment it seems as though the content is not so much projected on to the building as inherent in the building itself. The building therefore *appears* as the concrete embodiment of certain values.

Erasing the memory

All this would go some way to explaining the rationale behind a policy of physically destroying monuments of a previous repressive regime – what might be termed the 'Berlin Wall syndrome' – as though the evil of that regime were locked into the very bricks and mortar.[8] These monuments are perceived as the embodiment of the values of the previous regime and concrete reminders of its policies, and their destruction would therefore help to erase the memory of that regime. To attack a monument associated with a particular regime is to attack – symbolically – the regime itself. To eradicate the traces of a certain existence somehow helps to erase the memory of that existence. This is what we witness in the almost total destruction of the Berlin Wall and the paraphernalia of the Wall. The physical eradication of the Wall will do much to erase the memory of the Wall.

Contrariwise, monuments have an important potential role in keeping alive the memories – the lessons – of the past. It is against the eradication of monuments to the past, such as the Berlin Wall, that the architect, Daniel Libeskind, has spoken out so vociferously. For Libeskind the Wall is part of the history of Berlin. The removal of the Wall – 'almost overnight' – falls into a pattern of 'erasure of memory' within a country such as Germany which has so often displayed a tendency 'to radically transform society with each political and global change'.[9] Libeskind himself is concerned to resist this tendency, and to preserve a sense of memory. Hence he stresses the need to establish structures which he describes as 'icons' – structures 'which form the texture of living memory'.[10] He emphasises that this memory must remain alive. It must be part of an 'eternal present of transformation and metamorphosis'. But while there is an ethical imperative to retain some sense of memory, the past must not be treated as a 'given' which limits future development. Rather it should be perceived as 'an opportunity pregnant with new relations and urban experiences'.[11] According to Libeskind, then, we should not discard the past, we should not forget its lessons, yet equally we should not be limited by the past, by failing to understand the flexibility with which history has itself unfolded.

Libeskind's own architectural projects have been an articulation of that conviction. One such project, for a competition to design a housing estate on the site of the former Sachsenhausen concentration camp, deliberately ignores the competition brief, and proposes instead a memorial to the victims of that camp. Likewise his Jewish extension to the Berlin Museum attempts to evoke the memory of a culture that has been destroyed. The central void that runs through the zig-zag layout of the museum – a void which visitors are forced to cross and re-cross as they make their way through the museum – is empty of any artifacts. The central exhibit to a culture that has been all but eradicated is an absence of any exhibit. The void becomes a death mask of a culture, the invisible made visible by its conspicuous absence in a physical location that seems to demand its presence.

In some senses, then, the Berlin Wall syndrome – the physical destruction of monuments to a previous regime, and their substitution by monuments to high capitalism – is only too understandable. But what are we to make of the Bucharest syndrome – the retention of a building, and its re-appropriation towards a new political end? What the argument above would seem to support, first and foremost, is that it is quite possible for the political content of a building to shift, since, contrary to appearances, that content is not actually a property of the fabric of the building, but is dictated by external factors such as context and use. As regards context, while a building is clearly unlikely to change its physical location, its temporal context – and with it the cultural values of that context – is constantly shifting. The meaning of a building can never be stable across time. And that meaning is articulated by the way in which the building is perceived in terms of the complex play of its current 'use' and memories of previous 'uses'. In this respect, a change in 'use' and the fading of memories of previous 'uses' will redefine its meaning within the public imagination.

This is precisely what has happened with the case of 'The People's House', and so many other buildings in Central and Eastern Europe that have been re-used. This re-use is quite understandable, and is often dictated by practical concerns. Indeed, it is an economic imperative to put these buildings to new uses in the light of the financial crisis that has hit Eastern Europe. From this point of view the strategic re-use of these buildings will be a significant factor in recoding their 'meaning'.

Turning to the specific example of The People's House in Bucharest, it is clear that with the cultural shift following the collapse of communism, the building will inevitably have changed its meaning. Yet one might have expected that meaning to have changed from 'prospective palace to a current dictator' to 'memorial to a former dictator'. Instead we find the building being re-used as the site of the Romanian parliament, such that the meaning that it derives from its current 'use' comes to overwhelm any previous associations. What is it, then, that allows the building to be re-used so easily in the first place? The crucial factor is surely the question of memory. In the case of the palace at Bucharest, what we have is not a progressive erosion of memory of its previous 'use' over several years – for it is little over twelve years since the removal of Ceauşescu – but a more sudden 'repression' of that memory. It is as though the trauma of the Ceauşescu years, as somehow embodied in that building, has itself been repressed, allowing the building to take on a fresh set of associations.

Screen memories

Some explanation of this process – the repression of one memory and the emergence of another – might be found in Sigmund Freud's notion of the 'screen memory'.[12] The 'screen memory' is a token 'smoke screen' memory which serves as a substitute and a screen for the actual memory which is often too traumatic to endure. This defensive mechanism displaces the actual memory behind a form of decoy. Freud links the 'screen memory' to the 'childhood memory', observing that adult memories often privilege indifferent events over significant ones. This leads Freud to conclude that childhood memories are inherently unreliable. Like 'screen memories' they are 'revisions', whose structure echoes that of a nation's legends and myths:

> One is thus forced by various considerations to suspect that in the so-called earliest childhood memories we possess not the genuine memory-trace but a later revision of it, a revision that may have been subjected to a variety of psychical forces. Thus the 'childhood memories' of individuals come in general to acquire the significance of 'screen memories' and in doing so offer a remarkable analogy with the childhood memories that a nation preserves in its store of legends and myths.[13]

Elsewhere Freud develops this comparison between a nation reconstructing its past through a fantasy collation of myths and legends, and the screen memories that are to be found in the fantasy memories of childhood. Freud makes an explicit comparison between the writing of history and childhood memories. Both are effectively tendentious rewritings of the past, and both amount to a narcissistic reinforcement of 'beliefs and wishes' of the present:

> Historical writing, which had begun to keep a continuous record of the present, now also cast a glance back to the past, gathered traditions and legends, interpreted the traces of antiquity that survived in customs and usages, and in this way created a history of the past. It was inevitable that this early history should have been an expression of present beliefs and wishes, rather than a true picture of the past; for many things had been dropped from the nation's memory, while others were distorted, and some remains of the past were given a wrong interpretation in order to fit in with contemporary ideas. Moreover, the motive of people for writing history was not objective curiosity but a desire to influence their contemporaries, to encourage and inspire them, or to hold a mirror up before them. A man's conscious memory of the events of his maturity is in every way comparable to the first kind of historical writing (which was a chronicle of current events); while the memories that he has of his childhood correspond, as far as their origins and reliability are concerned, to the history of a nation's earliest days, which was compiled later and for tendentious reasons.[14]

In the context of the palace, the actual memory might be understood as the associations with the trauma of totalitarian dictatorship under Ceauşescu, associations, which, as argued above, would have been 'projected' on to the building initially. This 'actual memory' has since been displaced largely by a 'screen memory' which carries with it a new set of associations to mask those original associations. This 'masking', one might suppose, operates within a tension between an unconscious repression of one set of associations and a conscious attempt to 'bury' those associations beneath a new set. The 'screen memory' might therefore be perceived as a gesture which is partly involuntary, and partly deliberate – a defiant act aimed at re-appropriating the building and making it fit the needs of contemporary Romania. In surreptitiously subverting the role of the building, such action helps to veil the quagmire of guilt that surrounds the Ceauşescu years.

The 'screen memory' now projected on to the building would appear to be that of Romanian craftsmanship and materials, which in turn invokes some memory of a greater Romania before the experience of communism. Far from being a painful reminder of the recent past, the building is re-presented as the concrete embodiment of long-standing Romanian qualities. It is recast as a building in which Romanians should take pride. So it is when you visit the palace; the visitor's leaflet stresses the exquisite *Romanian* workmanship and the rich, natural *Romanian* materials.

To quote from the official guidebook to the building:

> The marble of Ruschita sends its reflections from the floors and the columns to the walls and the ceilings. The oak, mahogany and beck wood welcome the visitors with the warmth of their very refined sculptures that may be equalled only by the plaster work or the crystals and the brass of the chandeliers.
>
> Visiting the Palace of Parliament (The People's House), designed and built with great efforts and many sacrifices by Romanian specialists and the whole Romanian industry, anyone may realize that it is not a palace from Aladdin's stories, but a real one, showing the true wealth of Romania: stone, marble and wood from the Romanian mountains and forests.

This return to the supposedly 'authentic', natural order of things evokes the broader restoration of the country to democratic rule after the communist years. It sets up a nostalgic memory which comes to mask the actual memory, and which provides a stable, symbolic order as an escape from the trauma of the genuine memory trace. The building has been recoded not as the decadent legacy of a repressive dictator, but as an articulation of specifically *Romanian* qualities. These become vehicles for a new 'myth of the homeland', a building *of* the people and *for* the people, renamed 'The People's House'.

The People's House therefore comes to stand for a new Romania. It becomes a 'screen' to receive the narcissistic projection aimed at bolstering a new sense of national identity, by evoking a mythic past. Paradoxically this projection achieves its authority by masking the myth that lies behind this claim, the myth, that is, of the Romanian homeland. The very 'myth of the homeland' supposedly embodied in this *Romanian* building, constructed by *Romanian* workmen out of *Romanian* materials, is bolstered up by positing the building as a 'real' building in opposition to the imaginary world of Aladdin. In other words, the building as embodiment of the Romanian homeland gains a certain credibility against the more obviously mythic world of Aladdin. Yet it is precisely in the figure of Aladdin that we might recognise the essentially mythic characteristics of such concepts as the homeland.

Architecture and national identity

What all this reveals is the potential for architecture to play an important role in the formation of national identity, an identity that is itself already mythic. But to understand the relationship between architecture and national identity one has to consider the question of how national identity is itself constituted. This is perhaps a more complex question than might first appear. Let us take the example of contemporary Britain. In the popular imagination, for example, there would appear to be certain objects which are identifiable as symbols of 'Britishness', objects through which British identity is seemingly constituted. Such objects might include the Union Jack, a pint of beer and a pound coin. But what tends to be overlooked in this assumption is that 'Britishness', like any form of national identity – in Lacanian terms – cannot be symbolised. It can only be perceived through the fantasy structure of the homeland. To quote Renata Salecl:

> In the fantasy structure of the homeland, the nation (in the sense of national identification) is the element that cannot be symbolized. The nation is an element within us that is 'more than ourselves,' something that defines us but is at the same time indefinable; we cannot specify what it means, nor can we erase it ... It is precisely the homeland that fills out the empty space of the nation in the symbolic structure of society. The homeland is the fantasy structure, the scenario, through which society perceives itself as a homogeneous entity.[15]

The 'myth of the homeland' therefore becomes a mechanism by which society perceives itself. It becomes the embodiment of that which cannot be symbolised. From this perspective, in order for any national identity to be perceived, it must take some form of material expression. Identity is therefore *cathected* on to an object. It must be embodied. Hence objects such as the pound coin come to embody that identity through a process of symbolic associations. Yet the fact that the pound coin now occupies a role formerly held by the pound note serves merely to illustrate how such symbolic associations are always susceptible to shifts and erasures.

Buildings would fall into precisely this category. They potentially become the visible embodiment of the invisible, the vehicle through which the fantasy structure of the homeland is represented. There are obvious examples of this when we consider the way in which buildings – the Eiffel Tower, Sydney Opera House, the White House, etc. – come to symbolise a city, and even a country. But in terms of national identity it is perhaps more likely that the common, everyday buildings, the familiar streetscapes of our cities and villages, and the landscape of our countryside, will become the embodiment of what we know as 'homeland'.

It is here, then, that we can understand national identity as an identity which is forged around certain objects. This highlights and exposes the necessary role of the aesthetic in the formation of national identity. The nation, in effect, needs to read itself into objects in the environment in order to articulate that identity. What we have here, then, is a two-way process whereby a nation projects on to the environment certain values as though on to some blank screen, and then reads itself back into that environment, and sees itself symbolically *reflected* in that environment, invested as it now is with certain values. This reveals how, in a narcissistic fashion, national identity comes to be grounded in a reflection of the values assigned to aesthetic objects around us.

This process, it would seem, is beginning to take place for many people in Bucharest. The People's House, through a process of 'screen memory' which represses the former traumatic associations with Ceauşescu behind the more palatable recoding of the building as celebration of specifically *Romanian* qualities, of *Romanian* achievement, of *Romanian* workmanship and *Romanian* materials, becomes invested with a new semantic meaning. It becomes a 'screen' on to which this new 'meaning' – of The People's House as the embodiment of a new, nostalgic 'myth of the homeland' – is projected. And it is as such that it plays an important political role in fostering a new sense of Romanian national identity. For it is against the backdrop of The People's House as the seat of government – of The People's House as emblem of a new, democratic Romania – that a new sense of national identity might be forged.

While the physical building of Ceauşescu's palace has not been erased, it should not be forgotten that this palace is itself part of a programme of erasure and rebuilding, a programme, that is, which also embodies the 'Berlin syndrome'. The palace is the final part of that process, following the initial destruction of a substantial part of old Bucharest to clear a site for construction. Renata Salecl has argued that what Ceauşescu sought to do, by razing part of old Bucharest and creating a new architectural form, was to install a new Romanian identity:

> Ceauşescu's creationism tried to undo the old signifying chain in order to establish a totally new symbolic organization. By razing the historical monuments, Ceauşescu aimed to wipe out Romanian national identity, the fantasy structure of the nation that is forged around the historical old buildings, churches, and then to establish his own version of this identity.[16]

What happened with the adoption of this building for the Romanian parliament is that the people have fulfilled Ceaușescu's plan, although not perhaps in the way that he intended. By re-using this building with its novel architectural language as an integral part of the new Romania, the people have forged a new sense of identity, and have managed to 'establish a totally new symbolic organization'.

Conclusion

What, then, is the consequence of all this? The experience of Bucharest would seem to indicate that, while physical demolition is the most effective means of 'denazifying' the built environment, it may not be necessary actually to demolish buildings in order to achieve that end. All that is required is a symbolic re-appropriation of them, which is itself facilitated by the constructive re-use of those buildings.

But the Bucharest syndrome equally points towards a consideration which must be taken into account even by those who seek to retain the monuments of the past as a conscious strategy for keeping memories alive. For there is nothing to guarantee that the true memories and associations will be retained. Indeed the very shift from one temporal context to another necessarily involves a change in meaning. Remains of the Berlin Wall as monument to the Berlin Wall will therefore have a different meaning to the Berlin Wall as Berlin Wall.

But a more far-reaching question arises when we consider the waning of historical sensibility that is often associated with the 'postmodern condition'. For the saturation of information within the 'ecstasy of communication' of our present media society will undermine our potential to absorb individual items of information, such that the way in which we absorb that information is liable to become increasingly superficial. Once perceptions of history have been reduced to a collection of shallow, depthless images, we must question whether we can ever retain any authentic purchase on the past. In a culture of simulation – a hyperreal world of images detached from their original cultural referents – we progressively lose the potential to grasp the ontological reality of the past. In such a context, the authentic is always prone to fold into the inauthentic, and the Berlin Wall is likely to be perceived as the 'Berlin Wall Experience'. Indeed, it is in the tourist souvenir shops which will inevitably spring up to mark the Wall, or rather the absence of the Wall, that we will find the inescapable consequences of this condition. Inauthentic as they may seem, they reveal with a certain authenticity the dominant way in which many people engage with the world today.

The consequence of all this, we might suppose, is that the retention of monuments to evil will not guarantee in themselves that memories of their associations will be kept alive. Underscoring the question of whether or not to retain the physical traces of evil is therefore the more fundamental problem of how to maintain an ability to grasp their significance. If the monuments to evil cannot deliver their message, their lessons will never be learnt. Within a culture of simulation dominated by a form of historical amnesia, evil will always threaten to reappear.

Notes

1   On this see *The Guardian*, 15 July 1997, p. 4.
2   The 'Bucharest syndrome' is, of course, not limited to Bucharest. It applies equally to many monuments in Berlin, just as the 'Berlin Wall syndrome' also applies to other cities.
3   This statistic is based on its gross floor area. In terms of interior volume, 'The People's House' is in fact the third largest building in the world behind the Pentagon and the NASA assembly building in Florida.
4   'Content' should be understood here as content within the public perception. Whilst in practice it will always be subject to deferral and play at the level of the individual, within the context of this discussion, 'content' will be treated in a generalised fashion for the sake of simplicity.
5   Adolf Hitler, quoted in Robert Taylor, *The Word in Stone*, Berkeley, CA: University of California Press, 1974, p. 14.
6   Roland Barthes, 'The Eiffel Tower', in *Rethinking Architecture*, ed. Neil Leach, London: Routledge, 1997, p. 174.
7   'I have come to think that no work of art or culture can set out to be political once and for all, no matter how ostentatiously it labels itself as such, for there can never be any guarantee that it will be used the way it demands. A great political art (Brecht) can be taken as a pure and apolitical art; art that seems to want to be merely aesthetic and decorative can be rewritten as political with energetic interpretation. The political rewriting or appropriation, then, the political use, must be allegorical; you have to know that this is what it is supposed to be or mean – in itself it is inert' (Fredric Jameson, 'Is Space Political?', in *Rethinking Architecture*, ed. Leach, pp. 258–9).
8   The term 'monument' is used here in the extended sense to refer to all physical remnants from a previous regime.
9   Daniel Libeskind, 'Resisting the Erasure of History', interview conducted by Anne Wagner, in *Architecture and Revolution*, ed. Neil Leach, London: Routledge, 1999, p. 131.
10 Libeskind, 'Traces of the Unborn', in *Architecture and Revolution*, ed. Leach, p. 127.
11 Libeskind, 'Traces of the Unborn', p. 127.
12 On this see Sigmund Freud, *The Psychopathology of Everyday Life*, trans. Alan Tyson, London, Penguin, 1991, pp. 83–93.
13 Freud, *The Psychopathology of Everyday Life*, p. 88.
14 Freud, *Art and Literature*, trans. James Strachey, London, Penguin, 1990, pp. 173–4.
15 Renata Salecl, 'The State as Work of Art: The Trauma of Ceasescu's Disneyland', in *Architecture and Revolution*, ed. Leach, p. 102.
16 Renate Salecl, 'The State as a Work of Art', in *Architecture and Revolution*, ed. Leach pp. 102.

7 Erasing the traces

The 'denazification' of post-apartheid Johannesburg and Pretoria

Neil Leach

Figure 7.1 The South African Embassy Projection, Trafalgar Square, London, 1985 (credit: Krzysztof Wodiczko)

If we are to look for a model of the way in which political content in a building might be understood as a form of 'projection' we might consider the work of the Polish-Canadian public artist, Krzysztof Wodiczko, who literally projects politically loaded images on to buildings as a commentary on the politics of use of that building. In 1985 Wodiczko projected the image of a swastika onto the pediment of South Africa House in Trafalgar Square, London (see Fig. 7.1).[1] It is an image which has a particular significance in South Africa, where supporters of apartheid, such as the AWB, would consciously evoke the swastika and other emblems of Nazi Germany, and where critics of the regime would likewise use the emblem in graffiti and other forms of political commentary. This act was intended as a political protest against the trade negotiations then underway between the apartheid government of South Africa and the British government under Prime Minister Margaret Thatcher. The projection of the swastika onto the building raises some interesting questions about the relationship between buildings and politics. In particular it highlights the condition of buildings which have been blemished with the stain of evil. His projection of 'content-laden' images on to monuments and buildings echoes the process by which human beings 'project' their own readings onto them, as though on to some blank cinematographic screen. And it is precisely this image of South Africa House with a swastika projected on to it which provides us with the clue as to how buildings in South Africa can and have been appropriated. The issue becomes the problem of how to make that projected image fade, or how to supplant it with another image which effectively cancels it out. And it is the question of use and associations with use – as outlined earlier – which may dictate these issues.

In the context of South Africa the 'fading', as it were, of the projected image – the associations that have been grafted on to an object – has been effected on occasions by the singular figure of Nelson Mandela. This is what makes the case of South Africa so interesting. It was, for example, through the very action of donning a South African rugby jersey at the finals of the 1995 Rugby World Cup in which the South African national team were taking part, that Nelson Mandela effectively recuperated and re-appropriated – at least temporarily – an organisation such as the South African Rugby Union, which had been seen by some to have been associated too closely with apartheid. As a result black South Africans could identify with their national team, despite the fact that it was composed almost entirely of white players. Likewise, from an architectural perspective, it was the act of Nelson Mandela stepping across the threshold of the Union Buildings in Pretoria as the new president of the Republic of South Africa which effectively rinsed those buildings of their tarnished associations with a government of apartheid, and re-appropriated them for the new South Africa. In so doing Mandela effectively 'recoded' these buildings. It was in these acts that the 'swastika' was removed from these key emblems of South Africa.

Moreover, these acts can be charged with a highly symbolic role. This re-use, this re-appropriation can be an act of defiance. Like the storming and eventual occupation of an enemy stronghold, like the raising of the Russian flag in 1945 above the Reichstag, such gestures extend beyond themselves to become iconic moments that mark the formation of a new South Africa. And yet, to Mandela's credit, these acts are not treated with a degree of triumphalism that might only incite rancour in the vanquished. Instead they are treated with a disarming humility. They become actions intended to embrace all South Africans, actions that are in keeping with the 'softly softly' approach to reform in South Africa.

This extends to the whole politics of place names, and the renaming of sensitively named spaces, to which I shall refer below. By not renaming places with potentially provocative ANC names, but by renaming them with essentially neutral names – Johannesburg International Airport, and so on – the government has avoided much of the potential antagonism that can accompany such gestures. Sensitive, communal re-appropriation can therefore be seen to be a more effective strategy than triumphalist destruction and renewal.

Examples of shifts in semantic associations may be found throughout South Africa. One might point towards the new sites of national pilgrimage, such as Robben Island, which – for much of the white population at any rate – long served as a form of Lazarus for political prisoners, as though it had been tarnished by the stigma of its early days as a leper colony, to perceive how spaces can shift their semantic associations. Likewise one might point towards the now largely discredited political monuments to Afrikaanerdom, such as the Voortrekker Monument, to see this mechanism operating in reverse. What had once been the site of national embarrassment has become the site of pilgrimage, while what had once been the site of national pilgrimage has now become for many – if not all – an object of embarrassment, if not outright contempt.

Figure 7.2 Nelson Mandela's prison cell, Robben Island, Cape Town, South Africa.
(credit: Neil Leach)

What we find in South Africa is similar to what we find in Eastern Europe. The experience of both Bucharest and South Africa would seem to indicate that, while physical demolition is the most effective means of 'denazifying' the built environment, it may not be necessary actually to demolish buildings – in the manner of the 'Berlin Wall syndrome' – in order to achieve that end. All that is required is a symbolic re-appropriation of them – in the manner of the 'Bucharest syndrome' – which is itself facilitated by the constructive re-use of those buildings. The lesson for South Africa would seem to be this. Within the existing constraints buildings must be re-appropriated and not demolished. It is through the re-use and the perceptions of their re-use that buildings may be purged of their traces of evil.

Case Study 1: Johannesburg Central Police Station

A number of strategies have emerged which serve to assist the re-appropriation of discredited buildings. These strategies include renaming, re-cladding and other symbolic gestures aimed at recoding a building. An obvious example of a building where such gestures have been deployed is the Johannesburg Central Police Station, formerly known as 'John Vorster Square'. This building has been the subject of attempts to recode it both before and after the collapse of apartheid. In the mid-1980s the building was given a facelift by the architectural firm GAPP, through the addition, in particular, of 'sun louvres' which were used to clad the building even on the south side. Primarily, of course, this was a defensive measure; the louvres were intended to protect the building from any attack from the adjacent elevated highway. However, they also had a secondary role of improving the appearance of the building. More recently there have been two ceremonies as part of a programme of reform. On Monday 22 September 1997 a bust of John Vorster was removed from the station and taken to Pretoria to be kept in a police museum. The following Wednesday in a ceremony led by the then Gauteng safety and security MEC Jessie Duarte, herself a former detainee at the station, and attended by other former detainees of the infamous 11th floor, the building was renamed Johannesburg Central Police Station.

If the facelift of John Vorster Square had indeed been intended as a public relations exercise, a form of architectural repackaging, an attempt to semantically recode the building, this gesture would raise some interesting questions. Who, for example, would have been fooled by such a superficial gesture? The strategy comes across as particularly naive in the light of our earlier discussion of embodied meaning. If meaning is so dependent on the activities associated with a particular building, what use would be a facelift?[2] The logic of what we have outlined above dictates that unless the facelift were to be backed by a genuine change in policing activities, a shift that had been perceived and accepted by the people, such gestures could be read as cynical attempts to dress up still repressive policing strategies. As such, these gestures threaten only to 'backfire', and to provoke contempt, as their emptiness is exposed. If there are to be any physical works to the building, ideally they should be works which facilitate the new spatial practices within that building. For example, plate glass windows could be installed and physical access improved, so as to offer greater transparency to policing activities and greater accessibility for the public. But even these will prove empty gestures if police activities are not reformed.

In the light of all this a genuine shift in policing activities would be a far more effective means of recoding the building. There is, of course, a whole area of research which has addressed the question as to how the South African Police might be overhauled, but which cannot be broached here.[3] Let us merely suppose that the police force should be pursuing an effective strategy of reforming its activities. Just as the sight of the benign figure of Nelson Mandela emerging from the Union Buildings, as the new president of South Africa, effectively 'denazifies' the fabric of those buildings, so the sight of a police force with genuine community concerns would recode Johannesburg Central Police Station from site of oppression to site of public service.

Nonetheless the representation of police reforms remains as important as the reforms themselves. To this end one can understand the logic of the ceremonial acts of renaming the building and removing the bust of John Vorster. These are two acts that traditionally accompany political shifts.

Renaming acts as a strategic gesture which marks and signals the reappropriation of a space. Renaming, we should not forget, is a strategy that accompanies all revolutions. And here one might cite not only the renaming of certain buildings, but also streets, squares, towns and cities, and even entire countries. Thus, to take an example from Eastern Europe, St Petersburg after the Russian Revolution becomes Leningrad, which in turn reverts to St Petersburg following the collapse of communism.

The renaming of John Vorster Square falls within this logic and relates to the renaming of the police themselves, from South African Police Force to South African Police Service. The police must be seen to 'serve' the public interest if they are to be accepted by that public. The police must be seen to be *of* and *for* the people, if they are to be trusted and taken into the public confidence. Furthermore, by erasing the name of John Vorster and substituting the anonymous name 'Johannesburg Central Police Station', the renaming of the building avoids the risk of triumphalism referred to earlier. The Headquarters for a cosmopolitan police service for a cosmopolitan society must be inclusivist in its self-representation.

The removal of the bust also has parallels in Eastern Europe, with the demise of various statues following the collapse of communism. Here we might make an important distinction between the way in which buildings, as opposed to statues, are treated in moments of transition.[4] For what distinguishes buildings from statuary is not only the fact that buildings do not serve as fixed indexical markers in the same way as statuary, as Laura Mulvey has observed in her documentary film, *Disgraced Monuments* – a statue of Stalin can only represent Stalin – but also the fact that buildings, unlike most statues, may be re-used. It is therefore not surprising that while almost all statues of Stalin have been either destroyed or removed, all Stalinist buildings have remained intact and have been put to new uses.

Case study 2: The Voortrekker Monument, Pretoria

Here we might return to the case of the Voortrekker Monument (Fig. 7.3), as an example of a building which warrants special consideration. The problems of this building are self-evident. The monument, which has long served as a key cultural emblem of Afrikaanerdom, sits prominently on a hill outside Pretoria, quite visible from the offices of the president of the Republic of South Africa. What makes the Voortrekker Monument an interesting case is that it is part building, and part sculpture. It contains sufficient features to ensure that it cannot be easily recoded. A frieze running around the interior tells the tale of the Voortrekkers from when they left the Cape in 1835 to the signing of the Sand River Convention in 1852 when the independence of the Transvaal was recognised formally by the British. It illustrates several key moments in the history of the Afrikaaner nation – the murder of Piet Retief, the Making of the Vow, the Battle of Blood River, and so on. The problem lies, however, in the way that the story is told. Aside from showing in graphic detail the killing of many black South Africans, the frieze offers a highly moralising account of the 'treachery' of the Zulus and the fortitude of the Voortrekkers.

This is reinforced by the actual form of the building, which is designed to allow a ray of sunlight to pierce a hole in the roof at midday on 16 December, the anniversary of the Battle of Blood River, so as to shine in a precise circle on

Figure 7.3 Voortrekker Monument, Pretoria, South Africa.
(credit: Neil Leach)

the centre of the cenotaph which symbolises the last resting place of Piet Retief and all the Voortrekkers who perished during the Great Trek, and to illuminate the words '*Ons vir jou Suid-Afrika*' (We for thee, South Africa). As Riana Heymans remarks in the official guidebook to the monument: 'The ray of sunlight symbolises God's blessing on the work and aspirations of the Voortrekkers.'[5] The monument can therefore be seen to be locked into the cosmological order of the universe, as though the Afrikaner nation had been sanctioned by divine right.

What, then, is to be done with this monument? Several options could be suggested. The most radical would be to demolish the structure and to remove the friezes and other works of art to some remote museum, as was done with the bust from John Vorster Square. Equally the monument could be defiantly re-appropriated as a monument to the new South Africa, and might be converted, for example, into a centre for human rights. But the problem here is that the building constitutes an important shrine for the Afrikaners, a significant section of the South African population. To destroy such a structure, or to re-appropriate it in too controversial a manner would amount to a highly provocative act.

A less radical gesture would be to re-appropriate the structure in a more inclusivist fashion. This could be achieved either by removing the objects which act as fixed indexical markers and re-using the building for less antagonistic and more universal purposes, such as a place of prayer. Alternatively, it could form part of a series of other monuments celebrating the fruits of the pioneering spirit. Were the feats of the Voortrekkers to be celebrated alongside other cultural and scientific feats within the history of the nation – such as the world's first ever heart transplant operation, which was performed by a South African doctor – the structure could be redefined not as a political shrine to a specific political agenda, but as a monument to the pioneering spirit of all South Africans.

However, it may be that the simplest solution is also the most expedient, and that the structure is best left as it is. Here we return to the question of whether indeed it is always appropriate to erase traces of evil. From this perspective it could be argued that South Africa's past should not be hidden or repressed. The monument remains an important legacy in the history of South Africa. To forget the mistakes of the past is to invite their return. Moreover, it should be asked whether indeed the monument is so offensive as it stands. The logic of familiarisation dictates that with time even statues sink into our background horizon of consciousness, such that we hardly notice them. As Fredric Jameson has remarked: 'The statue often seems to stigmatize its moment of the past with a greened and bespattered boredom and stifling dustiness that unmarked glories do not have to contend with.' Moreover we tend to judge such items according to their appearance rather than their political associations. In this sense monuments act like statues. As Jameson adds: 'The commemorative statue, in representational or allegorical form, is so foreign to the contemporary aesthetic that it may well be the style of the art rather than the content of the memorial that drives this dreariness and death of the past so strongly home.'[6] Instead of asking 'Who is offended by the Afrikaner Monument?', we should perhaps ask, 'Who really notices it?'

Moreover, once the flag of the new South Africa has been raised outside the monument, all that the structure once stood for will have been effectively defused. Just as the jingoistic rhetoric of the AWB rings somewhat hollow once a black South African president has been elected democratically, so too the Voortrekker Monument, once the virile emblem of Afrikaanerdom, comes to be read as an impotent stump within the culture of the new South Africa. And once the monument has been inscribed within a revised history of South Africa, and forms part of a different allegorical tale, the monument will serve as an important reminder, not of a glorious past, but of a past which once existed, but which should never return. In this instance, perhaps, the traces of evil should not be erased.

Notes

1   On the work of Krzysztof Wodiczko, see 'Public Projections' and 'A Conversation with Krzysztof Wodiczko', *October*, 38: 3–52.

2   The project can be read, of course, as part of an overall 'Hearts and Minds' campaign to improve the image of the police, a campaign which sought to ingratiate the police to the black community and to give the police an acceptable face – a campaign for which the CIA reputedly acted as image consultants to the SAP, but one might ask of the whole campaign whether anyone was taken in by it.

3   On this see, for example, Gavin Cawthra, *Policing South Africa: The South African Police and the Transition from Apartheid*, London: Zed Books, 1993; Michael Brogden and Clifford Shearing, *Policing for a New South Africa*, London: Routledge, 1993; John Brewer, *Black and Blue: Policing in South Africa*, Oxford: Clarendon Press, 1994.

4   For a discussion of the plight of statues in post-communist Eastern Europe, see Mark Lewis, 'What is to be Done?', in *Ideology and Power in the Age of Lenin in Ruins*, ed. Arthur and Marilouise Kroker, New York, St. Martin's Press, 1991, pp. 1–18.

5   Riana Heymans, *The Voortrekker Monument Pretoria*, Pretoria, 1986, p. 6.

6   Fredric Jameson, 'History Lessons', in *Architecture and Revolution*, ed. Neil Leach, London: Routledge, 1999, p. 72.

Part III
The gendered metropolis

8 The pursuit of pleasure

London rambling

Jane Rendell

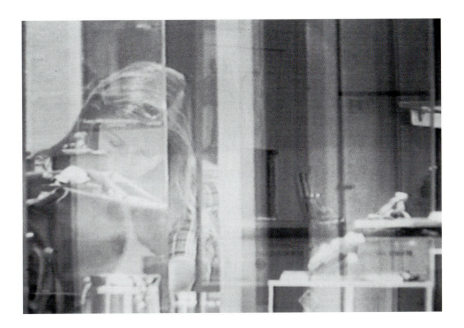

Figure 8.1 Women on display. (credit: Jane Rendell)

Prologue: spatial stories

> In wide arcs of wandering through the city
> I saw to either side of what is seen,
> and noticed treasures where it was thought there were none.
> I passed through a more fluid city.
> I broke up the imprint of all familiar places,
> shutting my eyes to the boredom of modern contours.[1]

In contemporary urban and architectural discourse, we are increasingly obsessed by figures which traverse space: the *flâneur*, the spy, the detective, the prostitute, the rambler, the cyprian. These are all spatial metaphors, representing urban explorations, passages of revelation, journeys of discovery – 'spatial stories'.[2] Through the personal and the political, the theoretical and the historical, we all tell spatial stories, we exchange narratives of architecture in, and of, the city.[3] Inspired by a desire to 'know' the past as a woman, to understand the gendering of architectural space in nineteenth-century London, this chapter tells one such story, a spatial story of the ramble.

Historical epistemology is a complex area; being female complicates it further. Historical knowledge may be characterised as a masculinist pursuit, where the act of knowing does not call the self into question, indeed to know already assumes one knows one's own mind. But for this female subject, historical knowledge is founded in subjectivity; knowing the past involves knowing the self; the two are in dialectic relation. (Who I am makes a difference to what I know; conversely, what I know makes a difference to who I am). For feminists, the personal is an important epistemological site; as a feminist historian it forms a threshold between past and present.

Exchange: ramblers and the pursuit of pleasure

Pleasure and novelty were his constant pursuits by day or by night.[4]

The verb 'to ramble' describes incoherent movement, 'to wander in discourse (spoken or written), to write or talk incoherently or without natural sequence of ideas'. As a mode of movement, rambling is unrestrained, random and distracted: 'a walk (formerly any excursion or journey) without any definite route or pleasure'.[5] In the early nineteenth century, the verb specifically described the exploration of urban space: 'This day has been wholly devoted to a ramble about London, to look at curiosities'.[6] Rambling was concerned with the physical and conceptual pursuit of pleasure, specifically sexual pleasure – 'to go about in search of sex'.[7] Closely related activities were 'ranging' or 'rangling' or 'intriguing with a variety of women'.[8]

A young unmarried Englishman, with a large fortune, spends but a small share of it on his common expenses; the greatest part is destined to his pleasures, that is to say, to the ladies.[9]

The rambling genre has its origins in texts published from the sixteenth century onwards, which delved further into the London underworld, pretending to be authentic and using sensational tales as their framework, but revealing no more than graphic detail. These texts, partly moralising, partly titillating, were aimed at 'Johnny Raws' from the country, and both tempted the reader with the excitement of urban life, but also warned against the corrupting influence and sophisticated criminals of the city. Such texts may be distinguished by their structure and take the form of 'spy' tales – journeys through the city.[10] Spy tales tell of various country gentlemen's initiations to the adventures of city life under the guidance of a streetwise urban relative, alert to the delights and entertainments, as well as the tricks and frauds, of the urban realm. The tradition continued into the eighteenth century, focusing on the seamy side of metropolitan life, with stories and pictures of crime, robbery and prostitution.[11]

The term ramble appeared alongside spy in the eighteenth century, and although the terms were often used in an interchangeable way, their emphasis differed slightly. Spy texts were fascinated with the darker aspects of urban life, while rambles were involved with excitement in the form of fun and pleasure. By the first decades of the nineteenth century, some publications continued to follow earlier models and focus on the detection and exposure of criminal codes, but a number of publications including *Real Life in London*,[12] Pierce Egan's *Life in London*,[13] William Heath's *Fashion and Folly*[14] and Bernard Blackmantle's *The English Spy*,[15] differed from the earlier texts in a number of ways.

Unlike the earlier, primarily scripted descriptions which included only a few black and white woodcuts, the new rambles were highly visual documents, with coloured lithographs, engravings and etchings. Instead of addressing themselves to the country visitor, these new rambles provided a place for urban dwellers to look at themselves. The 'look' of the urban explorer changed, from the secretive spy looking but not wanting to be looked at, to the fashionable rambler of the 1820s, a self-conscious man demanding to be visually appreciated. In the shift from the spy to the rambler, the importance of urban exploration and knowledge was retained, but the emphasis on the excitement of revealing secret activities was replaced by a new attention to fashion, display and spectacle. In the decade following the Napoleonic Wars, this attention to display coincided historically with the return of military men from Europe, especially Paris, bringing with them new French fashions and a flamboyant style of military dress. The early nineteenth-century rambler was a highly visible figure, proactive in his occupation of space.

> Our motto is be gay and free
> Make Love and Joy your choicest treasures
> Look on our book of glee
> And Ramble over scenes of Pleasure.[16]

For the rambler, mobility was a critical aspect of his masculinity and public urban identity. Structured around social and spatial contrasts, the ramble represents a culturally diverse journey ranging from high culture to popular culture, from grand interiors to dark streets. The most striking juxtapositions are between the east and the west, represented as two different class zones. From the seventeenth century onwards, the city and the eastern districts surrounding it were commercial and industrial zones, inhabited by the working class mostly in slums, including a large number of immigrants, most numerously the Irish. The west was populated by members of the aristocracy, nobility and wealthy bourgeois class who moved out of the city westwards to new residential squares, first to Covent Garden and Soho and later to St James and Piccadilly. In search of pleasure, the ramblers moved freely between the clubs, opera houses, theatres and arcades in the west of London and the places where 'real' life was to be found – the leisure spaces of the working class, from Covent Garden's Holy Land to the taverns of St. Giles and East Smithfield. The rambler's desire and ability to mix with a variety of social classes and experience both the west and east of the city represented an important part of his urban identity – his social and spatial mobility.

Through the pursuit of pleasure, rambling maps the city, both conceptually and physically. In traversing the city, looking in its open and its interior spaces for adventure and entertainment, the rambler redefines architectural spaces as spaces of social interactions, rather than as static objects. Examining the relation between the figures and spaces of the ramble enables us to explore the gendering of space through pleasurable leisure activities – consumption, exchange and display. In pursuit of pleasure, in constant motion, rambling represents the city as multiple and changing sites of desire.

The sites of ramble, the activity of rambling and the figure of the rambler, provide interesting objects of study for feminist architectural historians since by examining them we can develop our understanding of the gendering of space beyond the binary definitions offered by the separate spheres paradigm. Through the ramble we are able to demonstrate how public and private spheres co-exist and overlap, the boundaries defining them changing over time and in relation to activities and occupations. By looking at rambling, an urban movement which represents early nineteenth-century London as a series of gendered spaces, I argue that the gendering of space can be understood as a form of choreography, a series of performed movements between men and women, both real and ideal, material and metaphoric, which are constructed and represented through social relations of looking and moving – exchanging, consuming and displaying. Rambling represents gendered space as fluid and complex, varying according to time, specific urban location and the spatial patterning within buildings.

Exchange: cyprians as female ramblers

> We have already taken a promiscuous ramble from the West towards the East, and it has afforded some amusement; but our stock is abundant, and many objects of curiosity are still in view.[17]

The rambler's mobility represents an attempt to establish the public realm of the city as a place for men. The rambler's aim was to partake in a world of pleasure: heterosexual sexual pleasure. The pursuit of women was an important aspect of rambling. All the women the rambler encountered in the public spaces of the city were represented in terms of their sexuality and described as 'cyprians'. The word is defined as 'belonging to Cyprus, an island in the eastern Mediterranean, famous in ancient times for the worship of Aphrodite or Venus', goddess of love, as 'licentious, lewd', and, in the eighteenth and nineteenth centuries, 'applied to prostitutes'.[18] The term cyprian described women occupying public space as prostitutes, whether or not they were exchanging sex for financial benefit. Cyprians were stimuli to the ramble; the rambler's desire for, and pursuit of, these female sexual commodities defined his urban masculinity and heterosexuality.

Moving was also a defining feature of the cyprian. Cyprians were described as 'lady birds', having 'lightness and mobility of spirit' or 'energy of body and spirit'. The names of cyprians spotted by ramblers in the park corresponded to birds, such as the Sparrow Hawk and the White Crow.[19] Their mobility defined in terms lightness and flightiness referred to their moral constitution – their 'moral frailty' – as well as their ability to move. Movement for women held moral connotations. For example, although female magazines encouraged their readers to walk as a suitable form of female exercise, it was only under certain controlled conditions: moderately, in the early morning, with company. Walking in the public streets, especially lingering rather than hurrying, and wearing revealing or conspicuous clothes, were suggestive of a woman's immorality.[20]

The cyprian was an urban peripatetic – a nymph of the *pavé*.[21] Her mobility in the public places of the city was a cause of concern. Her link to the street, as streetwalker or nightwalker, associated her with the lowest class of prostitute. Whereas the movement of the rambler, his active engagement in the constant pursuit of pleasure, was celebrated as urban exploration, the mobility of the cyprian was represented as the cause of her eventual destruction. Her movement was transgressive, blurring the boundaries between public and private, suggesting the uncontrollability of women in the city. The cyprian body was perceived as disorderly, because as a moving female public body it flouted patriarchal rules for women's occupation of space.

Exchange: *maison close*

> I had not begun to exist save in my pretension to be a needed womb and mother for you. ... Participating in your economy, I did not know what I could have desired.[22]

Like a rambler, I 'went about' in pursuit of pleasure, but my pursuit involved knowing the urban past. Through the labyrinth of the British Library I pursued the rambler as he pursued pleasure in nineteenth-century London. Between historical evidence and critical theory, between past and present, city and self, I encountered various sites of methodological struggle where difficult questions of spatial and historical knowledge were raised. I was also offered tantalising and 'knowing' glimpses of the reciprocal relation between outer and inner worlds.

Meanwhile, politically and poetically, Luce Irigaray offered a way of mediating past and present, historical evidence and theoretical insight. Her concept of 'exchange' evoked a new way of theorising gender and space, one which both critiqued existing systems of patriarchy and offered new ways of re-thinking the relation between female subjects and spaces, reconceptualising the gendering of space.[23]

Belonging to a number of conceptual systems, exchange is caught up in a network of interlocking and interdependent relationships: language systems, patriarchal kinship systems, economic systems, philosophical systems.[24] In Irigaray's critique of exchange, the epistemological demarcations between one field of inquiry and another are deliberately blurred in order to show that in all these systems homogeneity is constituted by the exclusion of woman/women except as object/objects of exchange.[25]

In patriarchal relations of exchange, men are the subjects of exchange, whereas women are the objects of exchange. Men move through space, women are moved through space between men. Men own space and women as property, whereas women are owned as property, confined as and in space. For Irigaray, women's space is one chosen for them by men; women are owned as dwelling places for men, as wombs:

> You grant me space, you grant me my space. But in so doing you have always taken me away from my expanding place. What you intend for me is the place which is appropriate for the need you have of me. What you reveal to me is the place where you have positioned me, so that I remain available for your needs.[26]

Irigaray calls the spaces in which women are positioned 'the house of the male subject', 'a *maison close*', a 'House of Ill-Fame', a brothel, a closed house. Women are placed within prisons:

> Your body is my prison. But since you possess me from the inside, since you pierce inside my very skin, I cannot cover myself in skin again in order to return to the outside [...] Proprietor, your skin is hard. A body becomes a prison when it contracts into a whole. When it proclaims itself mine or thine. When a line is drawn around it, its territory mapped out.[27]

The boundaries drawn around women are closed and fixed, permanent and privileged, over other spaces. The boundaries men produce are solid walls.

> For them, walls are solid. Even those of their body. They have to rub or strike hard to pass from the one to the other.[28]

Women are doubly contained by men – men dwell within women's bodies, while housing or imprisoning women within the spaces of male language and exchange systems:

> He contains or envelopes her with walls while enveloping himself and his things with her flesh.[29]

Exchange: angels

> In order for [sexual] difference to be thought and lived, we have to recon-
> sider the whole problematic of space and time. [...] A change of epoch
> requires a mutation in the perception of space time, the inhabitation of
> place and of the envelopes of identity.[30]

But as well as critiquing existing forms of exchange and the confinement of
women within them, Irigaray is also able to theorise the movement of
women in emancipatory terms. Irigaray's work suggests ways of thinking
about a different female spatiality and subjectivity. Along with French feminist, Hélène Cixous, Irigaray has critiqued the work of Sigmund Freud and
Jacques Lacan, arguing that their constructions of self and subjectivity are
based on the male subject and male subjectivity.[31] Further, Irigaray has
argued that 'any theory of the subject' has always been appropriated by the
masculine; when women submit to such theories they either subject themselves to objectification by being female, or try to re-objectify themselves as
masculine subjects.[32] The female subject must instead be imagined from a
position of difference.

For Irigaray, there are three areas of questioning for thinking about the
space of the female subject: the way in which male philosophers have
constructed dwellings for themselves; the question of their ownership or
appropriation of female space, for example, nature and the cavern; and
possible re-conceptualisations which could provide new dwelling places for
women. For Irigaray, the topography of the male subject is conceptualised in
terms of reflection, space–time, dwelling, *différance* and *espacement*. In each
case the maternal body is used as a philosophical building material. Such
exploitation prevents women's accession to subjectivity. Irigaray argues that
women have their own topology – their own space–time, dwelling, *espacement* and reflection.[33] In answer to her own question, 'Where and how to
dwell?',[34] Irigaray's work presents new ways of configuring women's space
and time; in terms of the threshold, mucosity, *espacement*, the passage
between, the angel, air, singing and dancing.[35]

Irigaray aims to free women from a language governed by the presence of
the phallus, based on a syntax of has/has not, a symbolic language in which a
feminine presence cannot make itself known. This requires not merely the
reversal of the hierarchy of male and female but a challenge to the opposition
itself, by showing that the feminine and female sexuality exceed the complementary role that they have been assigned in the opposition male/female.
Where female sexuality is based on masculine parameters, for example,
masculine activity/feminine passivity, male presence/female lack, where the
penis is the only sexual organ assigned value, Irigaray argues instead for a
female libidinal economy, defined not as like/not like the phallus.

Irigaray's most common metaphor to re-think and construct the spatiality
of the female subject are the 'two lips'. Based metaphorically on the female

genitals, this alternative female vaginal symbolism has a different syntax of meaning, a symbolism based on two pairs of two lips – both oral and vaginal – which both auto-erotically challenge the unity of the phallus. From the phallic point of view the vagina may be a hole, or a flaw, but when viewed as a founding symbol, a new configuration of meaning can occur. Two lips allow space and time to be thought of together – the volume of the female subject changes through time. The 'one' of the male subject becomes 'two' constantly in touch with each other, not separated by negation, but connecting, interacting, merging, not unitary but diffuse, diversified, multiple, decentred, a threat to masculine discourse because of their fluidity and double role as inside and threshold:

> My lips are not opposed to generation. They keep the passage open.[36]

Two lips allow open-ness as well as closed-ness. One characteristic of women's sexual bodies is that they are not closed, they can be entered in the act of love, and when one is born one leaves them and passes across the threshold.

> Openness is not reflected, not mimed, not reproduced. Not even produced. Openness, a clearing, without surrounding walls. A Space, not demarcated not enclosed. Outside any possible symmetry or inversion ... Openness permits exchange, ensures movement, prevents saturation in possession or consumption.[37]

Indicating a passage in and out,[38] porous rather than solid, always partly open, mucus allows the passage of fluids.[39] Mucus is not a part object like the penis, it cannot be separated from the body, it is neither simply solid nor fluid, it has no fixed form. Mucus expands, but not in a shape; it is mobile and immobile, permanent and flowing, with multiple punctuations possible. Mucus is essential to exchange between the sexes; it corresponds to sexuality and to speech, and is related to air, to breathing, to singing and speaking.[40]

> Woman is neither open nor closed. She is indefinite, in-finite, form is never complete in her.[41]

Two lips, mucus and open-ness suggest an empathy between women and movement, a connection which patriarchal preoccupations with male property, ownership and containment do not allow. The figure of the angel who circulates as mediator is a far more emancipatory way of thinking about women and movement.[42] According to Irigaray, the angel poses an alternative to the phallus – the angel goes between and bridges.[43]

> the angel is that which unceasingly passes through the envelopes or

container(s), goes from one side to the other, reworking every deadline, changing very decision, thwarting all representation.[44]

Considering the cyprian as angel provides a way of celebrating a moving female figure as one who, rather than 'be moved' passively between men as an object of exchange, instead moves actively, bridging 'between' people and places in the city, and creating connections between women and movement. The angel relates to another of Irigaray's concerns about dwelling places – that women are nomadic.

Women are nomadic; their 'living house' should move with them.[45]

Consumption: bazaars as pleasure houses of consumption

A new kind of establishment for the shew and sale of goods in London has begun, and which by the Indians are called Bazaars, or collections of small shops in one space.[46]

The rambler's pursuit of pleasure through the city took him to clubs, theatres, drinking venues, assembly rooms, but in the early nineteenth century, no urban site offered more potential delights than the new luxury shopping venues, the exchanges, bazaars and arcades found to the west of Regent Street.[47] The new bazaars were like both Walter Benjamin's arcades, 'a city, indeed a world in miniature', and the world exhibitions, 'places of pilgrimage to the fetish Commodity'.[48] Physically, the English bazaar was a building of more than one storey, containing shopping stalls rented out to retailers of different trades, as well as picture galleries, indoor gardens and menageries. The 'bazaar' also evoked otherworldliness through the signifying qualities of the word itself – the exoticism of the 'unknown' East. Bazaars represented magical spaces of enchantment, sites of intoxication and desire, inspired by the enticing display of luxurious commodities – dresses, accessories, millinery – with satiation promised through their consumption.

The first London bazaar was the Soho Bazaar, a conversion of a warehouse by John Trotter in 1816. It occupied several houses on the north-west corner of Soho Square with counters on two floors. The Western Exchange was built in the same year at 10 Old Bond Street, adjoining the Burlington Arcade. In 1834 the Pantheon, an assembly room on Oxford Street, was converted to a bazaar and picture gallery, selling drapery, outfitting, accessories, children's clothes, books, sheet music, fancy goods and toys, with an aviary and conservatory for the sale of birds and plants. Other bazaars followed rapidly in Leicester Square, Newsman Street, Bond Street, James Street and the Strand.[49] By the 1830s they included the Royal London Bazaar, the Baker Street Bazaar, the Horse Bazaar and the Coach Bazaar or Pantechnicon at Moycombe Street in Belgravia.

Consumption: women and commodities

> It [The Soho Bazaar] consists of two large floors, in which upwards of 200 female dealers are daily occupied in the sale of almost every article of human consumption.[50]

Women were the main employees of the bazaars – 'the officiating priestesses of this great vanity-fair'. The Soho Bazaar, for example, was set up with the express purpose of providing work for women; it was a place where widows and orphans of army officers could sell items that they had made.[51] Of the 200 people working there, only two were men.[52] In these nascent spaces of commodity capitalism, it was essential to entrepreneurs, like Trotter, that profits were made. The presence of middle- and working-class women as consumers was fundamental to the success of the bazaar.

> The articles sold are almost exclusively pertaining to the dress and personal decoration of ladies and children; such as millinery, lace, gloves, jewellery etc.[53]

As spaces for women outside the home, such shopping spaces needed to be promoted as safe places. Bazaars were promoted as places of charity, where upper-class women sold wares to raise funds for orphans and other destitutes. In contemporary novels aimed at women readers, shopping venues were seen as respectable female zones.[54] In a period of rising evangelism, images of femininity and the female body were used to represent middle-class values of virtue and morality. In this developing value system, the women working in the bazaar operated as signs of exchange, representing, through their dress and demeanour, capitalist enterprises as pure:

> A plain and modest style of dress, on the part of the young females who serve at the stalls, is invariably insisted on, a matron being at hand to superintend the whole.[55]

Ideas of purity were also conjured up through architectural references. Bazaars were safe environments, well protected, usually under the management of one proprietor. They were physically secure, with safety features such as guards and lockable gates which promoted order and control. For example, the premises of the Pantheon were described as: 'large dry, commodious, well lighted, warmed, ventilated, and *properly watched*'.[56] These buildings were mono-functional, designed along strict and rational grids. With no hidden spaces or secret activities, everything in the bazaar was on display and in its place. In contrast to the surrounding unruly city, associated with danger and threat, emphasis was placed on order, both in the layout of the space itself and in the strict rules governing behaviour on the premises:

every stall must have its wares displayed by a particular hour in the morning, under penalty of a fine from the renter; the rent is paid day by day, and if the renter be ill, she has to pay for the services of a substitute, the substitute being such a one as is approved by the principals of the establishment.[57]

Of the many sites of desire mapped through the ramble, the bazaars formed an interesting locus for my encounter with early nineteenth-century London and my exploration of gender and space. On the one hand, the buying and selling of commodities was considered a respectable urban activity, but on the other, shopping venues were also connected with male sexual pursuit and female display. The oriental connotation of the term suggests sensuality and eroticism, and the rambling texts represented bazaars as places of intrigue.[58] For George Cruikshank the bazaar functioned solely as a place for arranging sexual exchanges and transactions.[59]

Consumption: women as commodities

> fashionable lounging places for the great and titled ones, and the places of assignation for supposed casual encounters[60]

Although women in the bazaar were engaged in the buying and selling of commodities, their active role as subjects and exchangers of commodities was never represented. Instead, these women were described passively, being sold or bought, in real and metaphoric terms. Women were described, first, as commodities and, second, in the same language as commodities. During the early nineteenth century, the word 'commodity' was commonly used to describe a woman's genital organs – a modest woman was a 'private commodity' and a prostitute was a 'public commodity'.[61] In rambling texts, in the bazaars, the same words, for example, 'piece' or 'article' both represented commodities and the female body-as-commodity:

> 'The Price of a Female Article in a bazaar': A young buck at Liverpool went into a bazaar, and leaning on the table stared a handsome young lady full in the face for some minutes. The lady, at last, holding up a fancy piece of goods, said 'Sir, if you are admiring *that* the price is ten shillings.' The reply was, 'No my dear, I am admiring you as the prettiest *piece* to be seen.' 'That alters the case, sir, the price of the *piece* you admire is one guinea.' A purchase was made to their mutual satisfaction.[62]

Described as articles or pieces, conflated with the commodities they were selling, the rambling tales also represented bazaar women as self-determining in their eagerness to display themselves for sale on the commodity market, in place of, or as well as, the commodities they were selling. Women were represented as active agents in the selling of themselves, in the commodification of their own bodies:

> Mr. Dick asked her rather impertinently, as she leant over the table – 'Do you mean, my lady, to offer yourself or the article for sale?' – 'Both', she answered. 'Some of my friends here can testify, that me and my *article* always go together.'[63]

Women's occupation of public space was indicative of their subversive sexuality; it was an act of transgression. In bazaars, exposed, unprotected and often in close physical relation to strange men, women's sexual reputations were open to lurid speculation. Particular kinds of commodities had strong links to the female body and sexual licentiousness. By spatial analogy, the 'snuff box' or 'reticule' served to represent female genitalia, often in terms of embellishment, such as an 'embroidered snuff box',[64] or a 'fine fancy gold worked reticule'.[65]

Consumption: women on the market

> The economy – in both the narrow and the broad sense – that is in place in our societies thus requires women to lend themselves to alienation in consumption, and to exchanges in which they do not participate, that men be exempt from being used and circulated like commodities.[66]

Irigaray's conception of woman-as-commodity is critical to understanding the gendering of space through consumption. In patriarchal capitalism, men are distinguished from women through their relationship to space – men move through space as subjects of exchange, whereas women are moved through space between men as sexual commodities. In patriarchal ideology, women can only be the property of men, and since relations of exchange can only function between property owners, that is between men, women can only be exchanged, they can only be commodities.

Irigaray's woman-as-commodity – the object of physical and metaphorical exchange among men – is a re-working of concepts of exchange and commodity as conceptualised in Marxist economics and structuralist anthropology.[67] For structuralist anthropologist, Lévi-Strauss, exchange is fundamental to all kinship structures in terms of the exchange of women. As objects and signs, women are both essential commodities in systems of exchange and also exchangeable signs in kinship systems.[68] Irigaray argues that by making commerce of women but not with them, the power relationships between men and women appear to be dependent on the relationships between men, thus reinforcing patriarchal social order. In his materialist analysis of the commodity, Marx makes a distinction between exchange and use value. The use value of a commodity is determined by physical properties, whereas when goods are produced for exchange in the market they are seen not only as articles of utility but as inherently valuable objects with special mystical properties.[69] Irigaray makes analogous use of Marxism, pointing out that women are feminine products of exchange within the masculine economy of patriarchy.

Will it be objected that this interpretation is analogical by nature? I accept the question, on condition that it be addressed also, and in the first place, to Marx's analysis of commodities. Did not Aristotle, a 'great thinker' according to Marx, determine the relation of form to matter by analogy with the relation between masculine and feminine? Returning to the question of the difference between the sexes would amount instead, then, to going back through analogism.[70]

Like the commodity in Marxist analysis, the female body as a commodity is divided into two irreconcilable 'bodies': utilitarian objects and bearers of value. Women have use and exchange value; they represent natural and social value. In Irigaray's symbolic order, women have three positions: the mother who represents pure use value; the virgin who represents pure exchange value; and the prostitute who represents both use and exchange value.[71] As different kinds of use and exchange values, these three female figures are associated with different kinds of space, the space of use or private property and the space of exchange or the market. The virgin is both the place and sign of exchange between men. As virgin, as natural exchange value, woman is on the market, but once violated, she is removed from exchange among men, relegated to the status of use value, and confined in private property. The mother is both the place and sign of use value. As mother, as natural use value, woman is taken off the market, excluded from exchange as private property. The prostitute does not fall into the binary opposition of use or exchange value, private property or market; once used she is not confined in and as private property; instead she remains on the market, both useful and exchangeable.[72]

Prostitution amounts to *usage that is exchanged*[73]

Display: scopophilia, the desire to look

All the worth-less elegance of dress and decoration are here displayed on the counters in gaudy profusion. ... The Bazaar, in a word, is a fashionable lounge for all those who have nothing to do except see and be seen.[74]

The importance of visual consumption, delight in the gaze and the exchange of looks, played a critical role in constructing the social space of the bazaars, or pleasure-house of commodity consumption. Scopophilia, what Freud called the desire to look, is stimulated by structures of voyeurism and narcissism, both of which derive pleasure in looking. Voyeurism is a controlling and distanced way of looking in which pleasure is derived from looking at a figure as an object. Narcissistic pleasure is produced by identification with the image and can be considered analogous to Lacan's mirror stage – just as a child forms his/her ego by identifying with the perfect mirror image, so the spectator derives pleasure from identification with the perfect image of themselves in others.

Laura Mulvey has argued that various kinds of visual pleasure are constructed through relations of sexual difference, structured by the gendered unconscious rather than the conscious. For example, in the work of Freud, the fear and anxiety of castration which arise in the boy child as a result of looking cause him to invent fetish objects to stand in for the mother's lack of phallus. Here looking is active and gendered masculine, being-looked-at is passive and feminised. This model of the male gaze and the female spectacle, although binary in nature and over-simplified, provides a useful starting point for thinking about the gendering of space through looking.[75] In the first instance, it positions the rambler as an active 'looking' male subject. Representations of the male gaze are integral to the construction of urban masculinity. The rambler's precedent, the London spy, is represented as a voyeur, and his successor, the Parisian *flâneur*, associated with a 'mobile, free, eroticized and avaricious gaze'.[76] Rambling is connected with visual pleasure, with narcissism and voyeurism, with the desire to look.

For the rambler, looking was connected to exploring and to knowing. For example, *Life in London* provided a 'complete cyclopedia' – a new kind of book for a new kind of city – a text which allowed readers to 'see life'.[77] By adopting a *'camera obscura'* view of the city, Egan's rambler became a voyeur, possessing 'the invaluable advantages of SEEING and not being seen'.[78] The *camera obscura* position allowed the viewer to gain visionary control, to frame the object like a picture. On a visit to a low-life tavern, a site of potential danger, the ramblers donned disguises which served to distance them from the scene in a voyeuristic manner.[79] On a visit to Newgate, the reality of the scene – prisoners preparing to die – was suppressed by adopting a panoramic and distancing view, tending towards a surveillant and categorising gaze.[80]

The rambler also demanded visual reciprocity. The rambler had a narcissistic body – one associated with its own surface – a surface which made social position apparent through body position and gesture, and the display of materials or ornaments.[81] Fashion played an essential role in the construction of male urban identity in the early nineteenth century. Rambling tales strongly stressed the difference between town and country through ways of dressing.[82] In the eighteenth century, court hierarchies of dressing had been rejected in favour of simple and practical styles, derived from the dress of the sporting country gentleman. The John Bull outfit consisted of everyday riding clothes – a top hat, a simple neckcloth, a small coat (cut away in the front), a waistcoat, breeches fitting into riding boots and a stick, later modified to suit urban lifestyles and a city aesthetic.[83] In *Life in London*, on arrival in the metropolis the country relative must first undergo an 'elegant metamorphose', discarding his 'rustic habit' for fashionable top-boots, white cord breeches, a green coat with brass buttons and a neat waist-coat.[84]

Display: bazaar beauties

> The Rambler in the public streets,
> Admires at everything he meets ...
> Ladies you'll find of every class,
> In shape, just like the hour glass ... [85]

Although 'looking' and 'being-looked-at' are, in certain cases, reciprocal positions which can both be adopted by one sex, psychoanalytic theories of the male gaze and the female spectacle tend to allow us to consider women only as looked-at objects on display. The cyprian body was the site of the ramblers' desire and gaze – an object of display in the public spaces in the city. Rambling texts represented female identity in terms of surface display.

A favourite haunt of ramblers, the *Rambler* magazine ran a series of monthly features entitled 'Bazaar Beauties', which undermined the moral aspirations of these venues, and exposed the real purpose of bazaars – as places for men to look at women. Such written descriptions served to reinforce the role of female employees as the site of desire in the bazaar. Rambling texts speculated on the improbable chastity of these demure matrons, and rather than female subjects represented them as objects for the projection of male lust, their bodies on display to men, in parts. Lady Agar Ellis was 'said to have the finest neck and shoulders of all the ladies who go to court, her lips are thick and pouting'; the Widow of Castlereagh had 'a noble Grecian face, and a remarkably small foot';[86] and Lady Francis F—e was 'greatly admired – but particularly her beautifully shaped arm, which she displays naked, nearly up to the shoulder'.[87]

> Lord P-t-h-m ... accosted the lovely and amiable Mistress Hughes, whose table was surrounded by fashionables, laying out their money for the attractions of her blue eyes and smiles, more than real principles of charity.[88]

In places of commodity consumption, as in other public spaces, the visibility of women also implied their sexual availability, whether through intrigue or through prostitution. The active display by prostitutes of their own bodies – in windows, on streets, and by adopting indecent attitudes, signs and invitations to attract the attention of passengers – suggested to the male viewer that any woman on display in the public realm was also available for visual, if not sexual, consumption.[89] Within the material place of the bazaar, women were located as the main attraction, at booths organised into easily traversed aisles, behind tables full of merchandise on display. In visual representations of bazaars, the objectifying function of the male gaze was reinforced by positioning women as the focus of the look within the space of the image. The heroine of Fanny Burney's *The Wanderer* notes the careful and exploitative positioning of women in retail spaces such as millinery shops:

images of advertisement in a manner that savours of genteel prostitution; the prettier girls are placed at the window to attract male customers and dalliers. The labour is treated as a frivolity, and the girls are being taught to sell themselves.[90]

Display: the vanity of the commodity

> woman must be nude because she is not situated, does not situate herself in her place. Her clothes, her makeup, and her jewels are the things with which she tries to create her container(s), her envelope(s). She cannot make use of the envelope that she is, and must create artificial ones.[91]

The displayed surface of the body is composed of a close relationship between clothes and the fleshy body. In the early nineteenth century, the issue of 'covering' was connected with a number of gendered themes around decency. A correct amount and kind of covering represented feminine decency in terms of honesty and modesty, whereas an incorrect covering represented indecency in terms of dishonesty and immodesty. Clothing was expected to be neither too revealing nor too obscuring of the body that lay beneath. To cover too little was immodest, to cover too much was dishonest. Both transgressions were connected with excess, extravagance and with prostitution. An excess of flesh represented exposure and wantonness, and an excess of clothing in the form of decoration represented artifice and vanity.

Strict rules governing the appropriate amount and kind of covering to be worn were recorded as 'fashion' in women's magazines.[92] Fashionable clothing for women of the upper classes in England in the first two decades of the nineteenth century was a highly minimal costume adopted from post-revolutionary Paris and inspired by the democratic politics of Greek culture. The gowns were full length, of a semi-transparent white fabric, worn with minimal undergarments and stockings. Sparse, revealing and *décolleté*, the waist was raised to draw attention to the breasts. The material was dampened so that it clung to the body like drapery, representing the body as a sculptural form.[93] But fear of French politics meant that by the end of the second decade of the nineteenth century, nakedness was connected with political radicalism. The exposure of the breast and the transparency of the gown were considered immoral.[94]

In rambles, cyprians were associated with surface value and considered to be kept for '*empty shew* than *real use*'.[95] In *Life in London*, the display of breasts by females in the street and in the theatre and assembly rooms represented them as cyprians.[96] Cyprians were also distinguished by the excessive display of gaudy dresses and decorative headwear and jewellery. Vanity, or concern with the surface – artifice – is a female problem: the vanity of the commodity.

> Woman's physical vanity, which compensates for her original sexual inferiority, is said to be caused by penis envy.[97]

Display: masquerade

> the duplicity of the veil's function … used to cover a lesser value and over-value the fetish [98]

If we take traditional models of psychoanalysis where the gaze is constructed through the development of the male subject, it is only possible for a female spectator 'to look' if she is identified with an active male, or to consider the construction of female identity in relation to being looked at. For Joan Rivière, woman *is* masquerade, the display or performance of femininity,[99] but for other feminists masquerade theorised this way is an alienated or false version of femininity.[100] Irigaray's work utilises the operations of masquerade and mimicry as conscious subversive, destabilising and defamiliarising strategies for flaunting spectacle and speech. Irigaray suggests that by deliberately assuming the feminine style assigned to them, women can uncover the mechanisms which exploit them.[101]

Irigaray's theory of 'mimicry' shows how, when working within a symbolic system with predetermined notions of feminine and masculine, where there is no theory of the female subject, women can seek to represent themselves through mimicking the system itself. It is a subversive act which seeks to expose the limitations of the binary oppositions of phallocentric discourse. Through imitation, a gap appears between the female subject herself and the feminine sexed identity she is imitating. Even when women represent themselves, their subjectivity involves a conception of themselves as objects and that 'operations of disguise, display and collaboration function in the creation of feminine subjectivities'.[102]

Removed from the everyday world of the city, and constructed as liminal zones where desires were played out, the sexual excitement of the bazaar for the rambler lay in the emphasis on the 'feminine' as screen for projecting fantasy. Using bazaars as pick-up zones or for setting up sexual liaisons of a clandestine, if not economic nature, the women who occupied these places were both chaste and lewd, prostitutes and non-prostitutes. It was the rambler's inability to decipher the 'true' sexual identity of a woman from her appearance which titillated. The frivolity and decorative function of many of the items for sale only served to heighten the sexual excitement by striking an analogy with the spatial tension of surface to depth. Ramblers enjoyed imagining how a demure exterior might indicate a suppressed wantonness:

> In a Bazaar good and evil are mingled together, there are hundreds of women of rank and fashion, who are known to be daughters of the game.[103]

The play of the form of the surface for its own sake is also perceived as problematic. Cyprians were believed to be motivated by 'allure',[104] 'principles of lust, idleness, or avarice'[105]. Their desire to 'dress up' above their class in order to

attract rich clients connected them with wearing deceitful coverings. Similarly, since their occupation could often not be distinguished through their surface appearance, cyprians' clothes also represented deceitfulness. Evidence that some cyprians, dress-lodgers, did not own their clothes but rented them from brothels,[106] and that others would pawn their clothes in hard times, substantiated suspicions concerning the dishonest quality of cyprian dress.[107] Irigaray's theory of mimicry suggests that such occasions of female deception might be reinterpreted in relation to a female subject actively engaged in constructing their own surface in order to confuse and distract the male viewer.

Similarly, in relation to emerging discourses around the threat of female presence in public space, male ambivalence placed emphasis on the looked-at nature of the surface, on the tension between display – what was being revealed – and secrecy – what remained hidden. Places occupied by women, such as the bow windows of shopping arcades, the boxes of the opera, carriages in the park, as well as stalls in bazaars, were represented as sites of intrigue and deceit. The fears concerning such 'deviant' spaces may also be interpreted by reconsidering the role of women as owners of space. Shops, boxes and carriages were often owned by women, a subversion of patriarchal codes concerning sex and property ownership. Such female visibility is a display of female property-owning status – a threat to patriarchal fears of women as property owners.

Epilogue: a powerful and seductive concept

This spatial story has told of the pursuit of pleasure, the rambler and the Cyprian, and the gendering of urban space. The ramble suggests a way of thinking about the gendering of space which, rather than the static binary of the separate spheres, is dynamic and follows men's pursuit of pleasure through early nineteenth-century London. But my own pursuit of pleasure, my pursuit of historical knowledge of the ramble, was mediated by my reading of Irigaray. Irigaray's work offered me 'a powerful and seductive concept', the exchange of women, a critical and imaginative feminist perspective on the gendering of space.[108] The 'exchange of women' suggests that men and women traverse space, but in different ways, according to their sex. Their positions and pathways, the spatial patterns composed between them, both materially and metaphorically, are choreographies of exchange, consumption, display, where men and women represent different relations of moving and looking – moving/being-moved and looking/being-looked-at. Men move and look, whereas women are objects to be looked at, exchangeable commodities, moved between men as objects and signs of exchange, as commodities and values.

The pursuit of historical knowledge operates through poignant forms of exchange – between theoretical and historical, between past and present, between city and self. The urban past, the city we seek to know, can only be known in relation to ourselves in the present. What we have is not an after-image of what has gone before, but a veiled view of what we are to become.

Myself, woman, womb, with grilled windows, veiled eyes. Tortuous streets, secret cells, labyrinths and more labyrinths.[109]

In writing the city, I am writing myself.

Notes

1 Aidan Andrew Dunn, *Vale Royal*, Uppingham: Goldmark, 1995, p. 9.
2 Michael de Certeau, 'Spatial Stories', in *The Practice of Everyday Life*, Berkeley, CA: University of California Press, 1988, pp. 115–22.
, 3 See *Strangely Familiar: Narratives of Architecture in the City* ed. Iain Borden, Joe Kerr, Alicia Pivaro and Jane Rendell, London: Routledge, 1995; and *Unknown City: Contesting Architecture and Social Space*, ed. Iain Borden, Joe Kerr, Jane Rendell and Alicia Pivaro, Cambridge MA: MIT Press, 1999.
4 Pierce Egan, *Life in London*, London: Sherwood, Neely and Jones, 1821. n.p.
5 *Oxford English Dictionary*, CD ROM, 2nd edition, 1989.
6 Nathaniel S. Wheaton, *A Journal of a Residence During Several Months in London*, Hartford: H. and F.J. Huntington, 1830, p. 119.
7 Eric Partridge, *A Dictionary of Slang and Unconventional English*, London: Routledge and Kegan Paul, 1964, p. 958.
8 Francis Grose, *A Classical Dictionary of the Vulgar Tongue*, London: S. Hooper, 1788, n.p.
9 M.D. Archenholz, *Picture of England*, Dublin: P. Byrne, 1791, p. 197.
10 The semi-narrative structure first appears in Edward Ward, *The London Spy*, London: J. Nutt and J. How, 1698–9.
11 See for example, R. King, *The Complete London Spy for the Present Year 1781*, London: Alex Hogg, 1781.
12 Amateur, *Real Life in London*, London: Jones and Co., 1821–2.
13 Egan *Life in London*.
14 William Heath, *Fashion and Folly: or the Buck's Pilgrimage*, London: William Sams, 1822.
15 Bernard Blackmantle, *The English Spy*, London: Sherwood, Jones and Co., 1825.
16 'Rambler in London', in *The Rambler*, 1824, v. 1, n. 1.
17 Amateur, *Real Life*, pp. 198–9.
18 *O. E. D.*; Partridge, *Dictionary of Slang*, p. 284.
19 Blackmantle, *The English Spy*, v. 2, 18–9.
20 *La Belle Assemblée*, London: J. Bell, 1806, July, p. 314.
21 George Smeeton, *Doings in London*, London: Smeeton, 1828.
22 Luce Irigaray, *Elemental Passions*, London, The Athlone Press, 1992, p. 61.
23 Irigaray, *The Speculum of the Other Woman*, Ithaca, NY: Cornell University Press, 1985; Irigaray, *This Sex Which is Not One*, Ithaca, NY: Cornell University Press, 1985; Irigaray, *Elemental Passions*; Irigaray, *An Ethics of Sexual Difference*, London: The Athlone Press, 1993; and Irigaray, *Je, Tu, Nous: Towards a Culture of Difference*, London: Routledge, 1993.
24 Margaret Whitford, *Luce Irigaray: Philosophy in the Feminine*, London: Routledge, 1991, p. 197.
25 Whitford, *Luce Irigaray*, p. 188.
26 Irigaray, *Elemental Passions*, p. 47.
27 Irigaray, *Elemental Passions*, pp. 14 and 17.
28 Irigaray, *Elemental Passions*, p. 67.
29 Irigaray, *An Ethics of Sexual Difference*, p. 11.
30 Quoted in Whitford, *Luce Irigaray*, p. 155.

31 See for example, Hélène Cixous, 'The Laugh of the Medusa', Elaine Marks and Isabelle de Courtivron (eds), *New French Feminisms: An Anthology*, London: Harvester, 1981, pp. 243–64, and Irigaray, 'When Our Lips Speak Together', *This Sex Which is Not One*, pp. 205–18.

32 Irigaray, 'Any Theory of the "Subject" has always been appropriated by the "Masculine"', *Speculum*, pp. 133–46.

33 Whitford, *Luce Irigaray*, p. 155.

34 Whitford, *Luce Irigaray*, p. 157.

35 Whitford, *Luce Irigaray*, p. 159.

36 Irigaray, *Elemental Passions*, p. 65.

37 Irigaray, *Elemental Passions*, p. 63.

38 Whitford, *Luce Irigaray*, p. 164.

39 Irigaray, *Elemental Passions*, p. 66.

40 Whitford, *Luce Irigaray*, p. 162.

41 Irigaray, *Speculum*, p. 229.

42 Irigaray, *An Ethics of Sexual Difference*, p. 15.

43 Whitford, *Luce Irigaray*, p. 163.

44 Irigaray, *An Ethics of Sexual Difference*, p. 15.

45 Whitford, *Luce Irigaray*, p. 165.

46 John Feltham, *The Picture of London*, London: Longman, Hurst, Rees, Orme and Brown, 1821, pp. 264–5.

47 For other places of commodity consumption see '"Industrious Females" and "Professional Beauties", or, "Fine Articles for Sale in the Burlington Arcade"', in *Strangely Familiar*, 1995, pp. 32–6; 'Subjective Space: A Feminist Architectural History of the Burlington Arcade', in *Desiring Practices: Gender, Architecture and the Inter-Disciplinary*, ed. Duncan McCorquodale, Katerina Ruedi and Sarah Wigglesworth, London: Blackdog Publishing, 1996, pp. 217–33; and 'Displaying Sexuality: Gendered Identities in the Early Nineteenth Century Street', in *Images of the Street: Representation, Experience, and Control in Public Space*, ed. Nick Fyfe, London: Routledge, 1998, pp. 75–91.

48 Walter Benjamin, 'Paris – Capital of the Nineteenth Century', in *Charles Baudelaire: A Lyric Poet in the Era of High Capitalism*, London: Verso, 1973, pp. 158 and 165.

49 *La Belle Assemblée*, April 1816, n.13, 191.

50 Feltham, *The Picture of London*, pp. 264–5.

51 Gary Dyer, 'The "Vanity Fair" of Nineteenth Century England: Commerce, Women and the East in the Ladies Bazaar', *Nineteenth Century Literature*, 1991, v. 46, n.2, 196–222.

52 Wheaton, *A Journal of a Residence*, pp. 189–90.

53 Knight's, *London*, 1851, quoted in Alison Adburgham, *Shops and Shopping 1800–1914*, London: George Allen and Unwin, 1964, p. 22.

54 Frances Burney, *Evelina*, London: Jones and Co., 1822.

55 Knight's, *London*, p. 22.

56 *The Gentleman's Magazine*, p. 272.

57 Knight's, *London*, p. 22.

58 *The Rambler*, 1828, v. 2, 27.

59 George Cruikshank, *A Bazaar*, London: J. Johnston, 1816.

60 Whittick's *Complete Book of Trades*, quoted in Adburgham, *Shopping in Style*, London: Thames and Hudson, 1979.

61 Grose, *A Classical Dictionary*; Grose, *Lexicon Balatronicum: A Dictionary of Buckish Slang, University Wit and Pickpocket Elegance*, London: C. Chappel, 1811; and Egan, *Grose's Classical Dictionary of the Vulgar Tongue*, London: Sherwood, Neely and Jones, 1823.

62 *The Rambler*, 1828, v.1, 251.

63 *The Rambler*, 1828, v. 2, 28.

64 *The Rambler*, 1828, v. 2, 27.
65 *The Rambler*, 1828, v. 2, 28.
66 Irigaray, *'This Sex'*, p. 186.
67 Irigaray, *'This Sex'*, pp. 170–91.
68 Claude Lévi-Strauss, *The Elementary Structures of Kinship*, Boston, MA: Beacon Press, 1969, p. 496.
69 Karl Marx, *Capital: The Process of Production of Capital*, Harmondsworth, Middlesex: Penguin, 1976, p. 126.
70 Irigaray, *'This Sex'*, p. 174, footnote 3.
71 Irigaray, *'This Sex'*, pp. 185–6.
72 Irigaray, *'This Sex'*, p. 186.
73 Irigaray, *'This Sex'*, p. 186.
74 Wheaton, *A Journal of a Residence*, pp. 189–90.
75 See for example, Laura Mulvey, 'Visual Pleasure and Narrative Cinema', in *Visual and Other Pleasure*, ed. Laura Mulvey, London: Macmillan, 1989, pp. 14–26.
76 See for example, Janet Wolff, 'The Invisible *Flâneuse*: Women and the Literature of Modernity', *Theory, Culture and Society*, 1985, v. 2, n. 3, pp. 36–46 and Griselda Pollock, *Vision and Difference: Femininity, Feminism and the Histories of Art*, London: Routledge, 1988, p. 79.
77 Egan, *Life in London*, pp. 23–4.
78 See chap. 2 entitled 'A Camera-Obscura View of the Metropolis, the Light and Shade attached to "seeing Life"' in Egan, *Life in London*, p. 18.
79 See 'TOM and JERRY *"masquerading it"* among the *cadgers* in the *Back Slums* in the Holy Land', in Egan, *Life in London*, p. 346.
80 Egan, *Life in London*, p. 282.
81 Arthur W. Frank, 'For a Sociology of the Body: An Analytic Overview', in *The Body: Social Process and Cultural Theory*, ed. Mike Featherstone, Mike Hepworth and Bryan S. Turner, London: Sage Publications, 1991, pp. 36–102, pp. 63 and 67, and Pierre Bourdieu, *Distinction: A Social Critique of the Judgement of Taste*, London: Routledge and Kegan Paul, 1984, p. 190.
82 Amateur, *Real Life in London*, v. 1, 102.
83 James Laver, *Dandies*, London: Weidenfeld and Nicolson, 1968, pp. 10 and 153.
84 Egan, *Life in London*, pp. 145–8.
85 *The Rambler*, March 1822, v. 1, n. 3, 109.
86 *The Rambler*, 1828, v. 2, 26.
87 *The Rambler*, 1828, v. 2, 101.
88 *The Rambler*, 1828, v. 2, 27.
89 Michael Ryan, *Prostitution in London*, London, 1839, p. 87.
90 Fanny Burney, *The Wanderer*, 1816, Oxford: Oxford University Press, 1991, p. 452.
91 Irigaray, *An Ethics of Sexual Difference*, p. 11.
92 *La Belle Assemblée*, July 1806, p. 231, and *La Belle Assemblée*, July 1809, p. 43.
93 *La Belle Assemblée*, February 1806, p. 64.
94 *La Belle Assemblée* (February 1806, pp. 16 and 20.
95 *The Rambler*, April 1822, v. 1, n. 4, 161.
96 Egan, *Life in London*, p. 173.
97 Irigaray, *Speculum*, p. 113.
98 Irigaray, *Speculum*, p. 116.
99 Joan Rivière, 'Womanliness as Masquerade', *International Journal of Psychoanalysis*, 1929, v. 10, pp. 303–13.
100 See, for example, Mary Ann Doane, 'Film and the Masquerade: Theorising the Female Spectator', *Screen*, September–October 1982, v. 23, ns. 2–4, pp. 74–87.
101 Irigaray, *Speculum*, pp. 113–17 and Irigaray, *This Sex Which is Not One*, p. 84.
102 Toril Moi, *Sexual/Textual Politics: Feminist Literary Theory*, London: Methuen, 1985, pp. 139–40.

103 *The Rambler*, 1828, v. 2, 100.

104 Mary Wilson, *The Whore's Catechism*, London: Sarah Brown, 1830, p. 76.

105 William Hale, *Considerations on the Causes and the Prevalence of Female Prostitution*, London: E. Justing, 1812, p. 4.

106 Amateur, *Real Life in London*, v. 1, 571.

107 Amateur, *Real in London*, v. 1, 566–7.

108 Gayle Rubin, 'The Traffic in Women: Notes on the "Political Economy" of Sex', 1975; reprinted in *Feminism and History*, ed. Joan W. Scott, Oxford: Oxford University Press, 1996, p. 118.

109 In her second diary, Anaïs Nin wrote of Fez that the image of the interior of the city was an image of her inner self. See Barbara Black Koltuv, *Weaving Woman: Essays in Feminine Psychology from the Notebooks of a Jungian Analyst*, Maine: Nicolas-Hays, 1990, p. 7.

9 Gay Paris

Trace and ruin

Adrian Rifkin

> Les formes de temps et d'espace seront, sauf expérience contraire, inventées et proposées à la praxis. Que l'imagination se déploie, non pas l'imaginaire qui permet la fuite et l'évasion, qui véhicule des idéologies, mais l'imaginaire qui s'investit dans *l'appropriation* (du temps, de l'espace, de la vie physiologique, du désir).[2]

In a radio interview some years ago Bernard Tschumi spoke of the Park of La Villette to the effect that he wanted it to resemble, in an entirely new way, the coexistences and conjunctions of the industrial city in all its classic densities. Without actually invoking Poe, Simmel or Benjamin his aspirations remapped their figurations of chance and shock, of speed and anomie, of intensity and *blasé* resignation.[3] To make his point Tschumi gave the instance of the park's running track, designed eventually to pass through the piano bar so that while the drinkers are to drink and the runners are to run around, sometimes they will change roles and places, and sometimes may watch or not watch each other run and drink.

Even as a version of the nightmare or epiphany of consumer blandness that is the (re)construction of the Paris of the *grands projets*, this seems pretty weak. I. M. Pei's entrance and shopping mall for the Louvre achieve much the same effect with a less self-conscious and ironic rhetoric of more obvious splendour, while the premature decay of the Opéra Bastille turns urban entropy towards a perverse sublimity. Thoroughly vapid, Tschumi's aspiration does little more than repeat the pitiful delusion that planning can ever fully coincide with the historicity that shapes it and that it will eventually frame, but which must always have been and be for ever more nothing more or less than its excess and its other. So Tschumi's park, neither as it was promised nor as it has as yet become, is barely more than Simmel's metropolis without the shock, channelling diversity down the walkways of consumer choice in an adventure playground of cultural excellence and canal rides, of gravel for *boules* and grass for football. Imagine that a field visit to La Villette were to be offered as a bonus for a group of urban anthropologists on holiday in EuroDisney, then they might discover that something has gone as badly wrong in the city as in its aseptic annexe, and in much the same way; with Disney, you get what you pay for; in La Villette, you get it anyway.

It might in itself seem strange that, while the model of the city quickened by Tschumi's discourse is one of which the allure was ever its capacity to incite a sense of the uncanny, then its postmodern consummation should either try so wholly to exclude the uncanny, or, like Disney, to represent it as just one amongst the many tricks of industrial entertainment. Yet if Freud's classic formulation of the *heimliche* and the *unheimliche* as wholly belonging to each other remains valid, then we have to think of the uncanny as the very circumstance of the quotidian.[4] For, as the bearer of everydayness's otherness to itself, it renders the everyday more or less supportable and opens it to a critical alterity. Planning and its technologies, as the ordering and representation of abstract property relations and the relations of power that attend them, necessarily set out to re-press the uncanny below or beside an access to the level of daily consciousness. And it is the suspended affect of this repression that renders spaces such as La Villette and the Carré du Louvre at once fatally attractive for the freedom from anxiety that they offer, and, for the same reason, utterly unbearable. Planning and postmodern intricacies in design theory conspire to close the pathways between the conscious and its unbeing in favour of an overweening hygiene, not least in their unworldly disregard for the production of the space of sex.

So let's get away from these grand schemata to more subtle microtechnologies of capital's incessant remaking of the urban web: in Paris, at least, the digicode is perhaps the most prevalent symptom of the reallocation of power and space that we call gentrification. There are few streets so humble that landlords and co-ops do not see the need to protect their threshold with a digicode. Not only has it progressively excluded the stroller and architectural connoisseur from the complex interiorities of the Parisian fabric, from its archaeologies and sometimes heterotopic caesurae, but it has radically restricted the once comfortably elided sites of sexual gratification. In the 'old days' cruising gay men could readily enough, their glances crossed and met and the instant accord made, seize on this heterotopic capacity of the doorway to make over its hinterland into that privacy within the almost private that we give the name of *public sex*. The twisting of a stairwell, the shelter of a lean-to, the convolution or disarticulation of an industrial courtyard, any of these, could momentarily become the uncanny site of the unspoken, unseen production of the aleatory poetic of urban encounter. A poetry, moreover, that stood in exquisite apposition to that of the stroller-connoisseur in a strange inversion of each other's manner. For if the stroller aimed to historicise the anomie of the street's façades, making an act of penetration so as to turn out the details of time's passage, the cruiser pulled this complexity into the synchronic configurations of a sexual identity, a coming out of time into a mode of the transitory-absolute. Uncanniness inhabits the sexual encounter in the slippage between the iterative character of cruising as such and the random, non-iterative nature of its fulfilment as the contingency of any given place that is not first and foremost a cruising ground.

This distinction or complementariness is important as a matter of being in the city. For while the stroller observes and records history in texts or snapshots, the cruiser becomes like it, or one of its effects. His pleasures are imprinted by historical morphologies, shaped by the materiality of places, so that their taking is a bodily practice of the history of space. Without leaving trace or record he, or his behaviour, thus becomes a trace quite unlike the stroller's tracings. Yet both, in their frustration and exclusion, now become an outcast of the city as prior to its reframing by the digicode. (Hence my use of the past tense in the preceding paragraph.)

It is difficult and probably even unnecessary to achieve sociological precision on this. After all, these matters are clear enough. That no one circulates with a dictionary of digicodes in their head. That the stroller who does not travel in an authorised group less and less has access to the courtyards and doorways of Paris, nowadays experiencing serendipity rather as a ready-made commodity, perhaps in those scholarly exhibitions of Pavillon de l'Arsenal.[5] That, as most of my friends in Paris vouch, there has been decline in the quantity and quality of street cruising outside the traditionally defined runs of the *quais*, the Tuileries, *pissoirs* or other fully determined fields of sexual encounter. And that all of this belongs to a larger plan. The great industrial semi-wastelands like the Passage du Bureau are covered with offices, schools, community centres and municipal housing. Not just the doorways and the courtyards that once lent their shelter to a chance encounter have been locked, but the bushes round Notre Dame fenced off, the central garden of the Boulevard Richard-Lenior made more familial, more of a place and less of a borderline.

This adds up to an ensemble of details that register a broader shift in the texture of Parisian public space from the intimate to the spectacular. The grand axis to La Défense is complete, and on its route to final fitting out, the Tuileries, that immemorial cruising way, is under 'restoration'. The Place de la Bastille is turned into a giant theatre set as the setting for a giant theatre, but the passages of the Faubourg-Saint Antoine are closed at night. This is not to say that outdoor cruising does not go on, that there are not still major spaces for public sex – the Canal, Bercy. Nor that new ones are not in the making wherever the city structure crumbles or turns into a construction site, wherever the *friche* (waste land) can be reinvented. But that the sexual outcome of a chance encounter just about anywhere in the city, that momentary and contingent gaying of a space, is more and more difficult to imagine and to accomplish. With this the secret sexual charge of the streets diminishes as an ideality of their everydayness. The great, barely spoken other of the heterosexual idea of the golden-hearted whore, gay men's practised freedom of the street, is displaced and restricted at the expense of the whole *imaginaire*.

And as this process of exclusion more or less coincides with that of gay liberation and of the final commercialisation of gay life and its efflorescence as the defining character as whole areas of the city, the Marais in Paris, Soho in London, Christopher Street in New York, Canal Street in Manchester, it collides with newly achieved freedoms in an untoward moment of overdetermination to produce the *interior* as the place for the memorisation and retracing of the street. And this is no longer a trace of one city's history but of the ways in which such behaviour has come into being in different cities, different national cultures, and their expectations of and fantasies about each other.

But before pursuing this path, let us step back to a crucial figuration of the uncanny in the modern city; for example, to Edgar Allen Poe's *Double assassinat dans la rue Morgue*, a text which has as much claim as any to the status of an origin. This is because it uses the confluence of orders and layers of coincidence that build up through the movements, flows and rumours of the city to congeal into the temporary figure of a truth, the resolution of the crime as a moment of delay and understanding. The narrator and his friend, Poe's detective, Dupin spend a shuttered life by daytime, blocking out the light and waiting only for the fall of real darkness to set out into a Paris that Poe himself never knew at all, but imagined as yielding its secrets only at a tangent to perception. A Paris which Charles Baudelaire, the translator of this story as I quote it, would recognise and recreate. In his paradigmatic poem of urban disquiet, *Le Cygne*, he condenses for ever more the aporia of imagining the unseeable object in all its over-present detail that Poe evoked in a Paris he had never seen:

> Alors nous nous échappions à travers les rues, bras dessus bras dessous, continuant la conversation du jour, rôdant au hasard jusqu'à une heure très avancée et cherchant à travers les lumières désordonnées et les ténèbres de la populeuse cité ces innombrables excitations spirituelles que l'étude paisible ne peut pas donner.[6]

In the few paragraphs of Dupin's and the narrator's night-time walk the great amateur detective reveals his powers of analysis in an astonishing account of the latter's train of thought. The explanation of Dupin's perspicacity turns around a moment when the narrator, pushed by a fruitseller, stumbles on a pile of cobblestones, 'un tas de pavés amoncelés dans un endroit où la voie est an réparation',[7] a vexation that releases the symptoms of half-conscious thoughts and which is assuaged only by a new, smoothly laid passage of wooden blocks. The conjunction of an ambulant salesman with the hazards of a city in repair and reconstruction; the provocation of a state of mind by a chance conjuncture: these invent and then recall the poet Baudelaire himself wandering through the ruins that are the construction site of Haussmann's Paris when he encounters the swan of his eponymous poem. For this poem is the crucial moment in his work in which *all* the inanimate signs of modernity finally transmute into allegory and the city fully signifies the plenary absence of the self. This is a Paris of the uncanny, of the upturned *pavé* that jolts you into the involuntary experience of alterity, on the borderlines between reason and fear or cleanliness and sleaze, the form of presentiment rather than any one feeling in itself.

But if this uncanny already has an unsettling pre-history, then it lies in Balzac's Paris of inexhaustible convolutions, in his *Illusions perdues* (1837) and *Splendeurs et misères des courtisanes* (1838), as the situation of love between two men, the criminal Vautrin and his protégé Lucien de Rubempré. The predominant drive of its literary and poetic succession is to transpose, abject and abstract

Balzac's gayed spatiality and its other, Baudelaire's emptiness, into a play of denotation which, in naming Paris as woman or as parts of woman, finally achieves a heterosexual normativity in which the gay appears as never more than the connoted accident that underlines its authority and truth. The world dwindling with the digicode is both the hidden substance of this old myth of Paris and the witness to its bad faith. The world rising with the digicode is both a denial and a repository of the whole ensemble.

Consider for a moment, then, the poetics of the sauna, in Paris, in the 1990s, if I tread first the streets to reach it, and then the slippery pathways that lie within. *IDM*, then, 4 Rue du Faubourg Montmartre, *fond de cour*. To turn from the bright, touristic Faubourg down into the classic *cité* of Louis-Philippe's time repeats the kitschy, old thrill of a transgression, a passage between two worlds that are fully visible to each other in the bright-blue blinds that shutter *IDM*'s first-floor windows in the fancy stonework of the epoch. Then half a dozen modern, clumsy concrete steps mount up to the entrance, and the heavy glass door reveals the cheerful, pretty *caissier*, the promise of any traditional, Parisian commerce. In the entrance a double perspective: to the right is the gym beyond a narrow bar, bright, well-equipped yet accessory, even if it gets some serious use. Between bar and gym are stairs down to the changing rooms, bare, functional, bright, unpleasant. To the left, a darker world of tiles, the sound of showers and jacuzzi bubbles, vapour, bodies passing in and out of half-glassed cubicles, the bright red flannel of their towels. Above, reached by no less than three separate staircases, are the corridors and cabins, a bustling warren of dark corners, dead-ends and smaller spiral stairs to more dead-ends and the video room. The space supposes a movement both restricted and endlessly free around its thin partitions, doors hanging now half-open, now closed to a rhythm of shifting bodies that defies all sense of repetition. Up, and again, and round and round the main assemblies of cabins, sandwiched between the corridors, a dull glow from the glass bricks under foot, time has no meaning other than which can be measured by the unmeasurable length of expectation. But down on the left, in front of the steam-room, the space contracts from the jacuzzi, showers and urinals, to a tight and darker funnel, night-time lighted in shades of orange or grey-blue that seem capable of infinite dimming before darkness: a double air-lock of reticulated glass veils the ultimate, shrouding mystery that is the steam itself, ensuring a strangely indifferent intimacy as clients squeeze by each other on their way in and out of this sightless room.

Or, in the *Univers*, Rue des Bons Enfants, up against the Palais Royal, thick, clear but heavily misted steam-room windows, oblong and body-height articulate a long, tiled wall, and stare out at the great central piazza of the hot-tub and video-projections. This plaza itself is surrounded by a maze of corridors and facilities that imitate now the bazaar, now the building site, and from the steam-room you can catch sight of the gazes, connections, hesitancies and decisions of the other men as they circulate.

Here, then, the sheets of glass are screens for the projection of fantasy rather than for its discipline or concealment, abetted by the cobalt lights which turn out to have changed from time to time, softly provoking shifts in perception. Beautifully articulated, the spatial relations between steam, hot-tub and showers ensure an environment of aural enjoyment as the door opens, and if you close your eyes it might be the Villa d'Este on an overcast and humid day in August, the almost cool tiles slippery to the back or shoulder. And, wandering to the right out of the steam, right again and left, a small lobby lit by the flickering of a video screen. Then a doorway to the total darkness of the maze, to the always partial acting out of the lurid yet faded projections on the monitor above the door, another passage like that from street to courtyard, from the glance and its fantasy to a moment of its materiality.

Now, here, at this moment and in this context, I insist on this time–space conjunction: the steam takes on its particular quality of being structured like a metaphor; a gasping flow of as-yet uncathected desire; a proto-spermal seepage; a mood of lonely autumn days in the great city, in the fine rain, the blue light of November at six in the evening, a synthesis of these different weathers yet an artificial foil to any in their inadequate naturalness. Slippage from metaphor; the muscles of a thigh tensing itself along the tiling ledge as a hand strays, appreciating the indentations of deep blue shadow, sensing and assessing the reactions to its movement; torsos brushing, not quite touching, or embracing against the window, shadows on neither side of the glass. It is indeed uncanny how much the city outside, or at least its memory, is present in this labyrinth, how a historically specific system of gestures is condensed out of a hecatomb of its previous embodiments, a Paris of lovers, of tenderly deferred desire and temporary meeting. Moreover, unlike Doisneau's famous *Kiss*, none of this is faked. For only such national symbols need faking, so rarely do they coincide with a sentiment that we might call popular, so crudely must they abject and eliminate all diversity.

But could I be idealising? Though this is for me quite as good as a really fine performance of Fauré, Maggie Teyte for example, the intensely sexual, white half-voice singing '*une vaste et tendre apaisement...*', I could do without the musak. The same cretinous late disco, with its overly insistent and controlling rhythm, is played in almost any gay establishment in the world, a reminder of that point in the late 1970s when the gay contribution to world culture was held to be dancing well. And probably the men too, were I to find out all of their origins, would turn out mainly to be tourists from Blackpool or Nova Scotia or Perth. Moreover the videos are nearly all American, with hardly one in twenty by France's own porno-maestro Cadinot. But then in his films you can see the condoms getting grubby. And that's a nicety of French gay culture not easily assimilated in these central palaces of Parisian and tourist pleasures, where the ideal of American beauty reigns as a more appropriate French ideal. (At a more off-centre location, such as the leather bar *Mec Zone*, only a kilometre but another world away towards Anvers, Cadinot is the order of the day.)

Yet, at the same time, even if the ensemble of movements through the corridors and darkrooms is much like that of any metropolitan street, purposive without apparent object, slow and speedy by turn, hesitant and directed, in that collective exaltation of individual will that is the determined, agentless practice of the city, the cadence is not just like Montréal. Montréal is more regardful, perhaps more friendly and deliberated. It is quite unlike Berlin with all its confounding directness. What Georg Simmel would call eccentricity, that is to say exacerbated individuality, is everywhere exhibited as style, a style of body, whether gym-built or used-up and ragged, a style of partial dress, of draping a towel, wearing street boots or holding a cigarette. Specific to Paris? Residually, and then only perhaps: a different range of relations to the body from what we would see in Chicago, more nervy, uneasy here than in Germany, more creatively edgy than in Australia, even though the boots or jockstraps issue from the same Korean production lines. The city is not the same, nor are its masquerades.

Upstairs at *IDM* the landing that connects the two blocks of cabins opens out into a three-sided room, some five metres square, high-ceilinged and framed by a narrow *pourtour* (walkway) supported at its corners by Corinthian columns. Early Haussmann, I would guess, a subsequent addition to the building of this one amongst many Restoration and Louis-Philippe *cités* that are characteristic of the ninth arrondissement. Men lounge on leatherette couches in the ruins of the Second Empire, against a copy of a David Hockney *Boy climbing out of a Pool* painting that, cut in three panels, serves to mask the windows. The *Key West*, near the Gare du Nord, has a similar disjunctive decor, though of a late Haussmannian or Third Republic design. Outlandishly marked by the inordinately high ceilings of the lower floors, the circulation seems rather ant-like. Of course, by the last floor the ceilings have lowered themselves some two metres and so has the sex, more tight clustering under the canopy of the roof spaces. And in the squat metal-barred kennels that must once have been the *chambres de bonne*, sexuality is superabundantly exposed in this sometime fantasmatic space of social difference and sexual repression. If *IDM* is Paris as a warren, as a contingent cluster of different kinds of space that touch each other and overlap, *Key West* is rather the vertical mode of social differentiation turned over exclusively to sex as the elaboration of personal tastes and preferences.

One historical problem with this *imaginaire* lies in its unresolved involvement with the *beau idéal* of sleaze. In the old days, the days before AIDS on the one hand and the generalization of gay lifestyle in the city centre on the other, the Parisian sauna was, with the very rare exception, quintessentially sleazy. From the *Grands Bains d'Odessa* to the *Hammam Voltaire*, it was not only dilapidated with age but its sociability framed and conditioned in the shadowy past of renunciation, concealment and self-negation. Furtiveness and decay went hand in hand, elaborating their own pleasure it is true, but ill at ease in a city of diminishing shadow and technological modernity. In the 1960s and 1970s the baths seemed like refugees from another epoch, like all those ageing groceries round *Les Halles*, after the pavilions had been pulled down, while the first establishments of the young generation had the same kind of peculiar feeling as the Louvre cleaned. The new sauna, despite and because of all its freedom, has lost the relation to the body that interwove the emotion of time-honoured repressions with outmoded and inefficient plumbing. It is hardly sleazy at all. On the contrary, it is pleonasm made material, unfolding an obsessive cleanliness, the endless flow of water and purifying steam; the odours of chlorox and disinfectant rather than those of sweat and bodies. Silent workers, usually African, move through the ever night-time corridors, cabins or labyrinths with torches, rubber gloves and pincers, removing paper towels, condoms, wrappers, wiping, disinfecting couches and floors. The resemblance to the cleaning of the touristic Paris of Chirac's mayoral administration, out there in the sunshine and the drizzle, is more than comic. Though in setting them side by side like this I do risk dallying with the concept of a 'total social fact'.

For one of the facts of the matter is that gay life as a complex social process is the outcome of many determinations. And one of its most elaborate ironies is that having always layered itself in the interstitial spaces of the city, the last few years of Parisian tourism and gentrification have forced it into the re-invention of the liminal, or places of a newly imagined liminality, even as the need to hide has never been less urgent. So if the baths from before they were gay-as-such displayed a deeply historic sleaze, this was cut by a different function, a dysfunctional or counter-hygienic element coded as the exotic movement of social and sexual transgression. And if today a hard won, relatively easy *jouissance* in one's identity undermines the sleazy and the abject, the circulation in the baths has become more one of an imaginary community than the old identification with oneself as other. Yet the fantasy of self-othering, which is necessarily denied by an identitarian politics of community, remains deeply significant and pleasurable in the historical sediment of being-gay. The signifier sleaze, so difficult to renounce, is re-leased to articulate an internal difference, now within the thing in itself rather than between it and other forms of sexuality. SM sex, leather and fetish now stand on the lonely and knife-edge angle between marginality and fashion to provide gay society with the most accessible image of its own potential for generating otherness, a process of differentiation worked through into the details of the new cruising grounds of Disney's Paris. Here, in the bars and the baths, this takes place within the fabric of a relatively old Paris, an oldness that might range from the medieval cellar to the basement of an early 1970s' apartment block. And it is here that we can find the streets not of a temporally older Paris, but of *Vieux Paris* itself, of myth.

As we have seen with *IDM* and *Key West*, the Haussmannian fabric creates modes of circulation that both enforce the inside/outside relation of old Paris and invite a quite specific scale of sexual comportments and displays; a demand to furnish the space and a demand to perform it too. Whether in the clean-cut establishment inserted in older buildings like the *Univers*, or in the cruising club *Docks*, sited in a disaffected, concrete-built sauna of the 1970s, or the four-storied, pre-Haussmannian *Arène* of the quai de l'Hôtel de Ville, once a restaurant and disco, the configuration tends to that of the lost street plan, and to stand in for the figure of a social complexity that now lends itself to sexual diversity as a practical metaphor. A metaphor above all for choice, the desire for an alluring agency that characterises the broader sexual politics of our moment. To move around any of these baths or clubs, where the bar often seems little more than an absolution for the hypertrophic labyrinth, is to navigate from the dungeon to the *chambre de bonne*, from the caged exhibition of the sexual spectacle to the fragile privacy of the *chiffonier*'s cabin. It is to oversee and to overhear, to be distant in the proximity of a narrow corridor or twisting stair, yet also close in a glance across the crowded bar. It is to stand in little groups, idly lounging, chatting, half regarding or half ignoring some offered spectacle. It matters little whether you do or do not watch in the end, for this spectacle at least has not been paid for, and will repeat itself soon and often. It is to rediscover the vaults and cellars of old Paris lit by an artificial moonlight, but as if they were streets lined with the housing of the poor, badly insulated and weakly lit, the noises of unknown domesticities penetrating the collective passage. Every now and then at the *Keller* (it was Foucault's place), the oldest of the leather bars, its state of disrepair is underscored afresh. Rougher-still wooden partitions succeed their already rough predecessor, held together by scaffolding, miming stocks and racks and street corners. The backroom is a building site that disintegrates in a cult sacred to the refusal of contemporaneity, new ruins crumbled in contrast to the rest of this gentrifying *quartier* that has now lost even its name to that of the estate agent generic of 'Bastille'. Nowhere else in Paris could you find so poignantly the experience of the city that flows from Poe to Baudelaire, from Francis Carco to Léo Malet or Jacques Réda.

Yet the circulation in the bars and baths that I have sketched barely figures as an encounter with the involuntary terror of uncanniness. If you stumble against an upturned flooring stone or slip along a tile, it is more likely to be into the man of your dreams than some dreaded presentiment, even though he and it might be one and the same. Rather, it conserves an ideal of the uncanny that has come to be utopian, and which, ironically, is likely to be still further displaced by a politics of gay space that brings us closer still to Tschumi's park. Some recent queer writing, that justly claims and insists upon the right to public sex against the post-AIDS puritanism that plagues the USA, nonetheless tends to do so on the terrain of a demand for recognition that also entails a conventional designer ethic. Thus in works like *Policing Public Sex: Queer Politics and the Future of AIDS Activism*, we find a design project for sex bar architecture that smooths out the rough and the makeshift, such as the cutting of holes through partitions, so that the furniture matches the desire for an absolute outness on the one hand and an absolute safety of use on the other.[8] None of this furniture, nor the spaces of circulation, are to mimic the effects of decay or, by metonymy, the residue of an historical abjection. This is not to say that the traditional bar either was or is purposively built; only that its purpose as a style of building traces a history of marginality, and often still does so in a locally rooted and specific *imaginaire*. You have only to compare the strange conflation of industry and outback in the vast warehouse spaces of Melbourne's *Club 80* with the utterly dissimilar configuration of not unlike materials into the intimate street corner of the *Keller* or the shantytown shacks of Berlin's *Scheune* to get a glimpse of the multiple possibilities of slippage within the same. Rather, it is to suggest that while the current, queer demand for a total moral visibility registers a social and ethical imperative, it also equivocally and necessarily plays out its objectives on the plane of dominant representations. Mistaken in its mode of militant self-affirmation, it offers gay identity for a more complete appropriation by the city of total regulation. In this sense the new, queer architecture, which actually corresponds more closely to the baths than to the leather bars, makes the same kind of claims for the configuration of the city as Tschumi has made for La Villette. Upon the issue of this complex of debates in France and its transmutation into practice will hang the result of this alternative; that the gay circulation of the city will persist as some kind of a relative other to Paris itself, despite the digicode; or that, in the likely case that Paris itself finally becomes no more than an annexe to Disneyland, the gay, now as Disney's French other, will have to rethink itself. That this, in turn, can be thought through the informal and commercial production of architectural space as sexual practice, signals that the very diversity Tschumi wants to bludgeon into life may yet only live without him.

Notes

1   This is a reworked version of an article commissioned for the *Australian Journal of French Studies*, vol. xxxv, no. 1, pp. 48–56. I am grateful to the editors for permission to re-use some of the materials here and especially to Jill Forbes for her suggestion that I write the essay and for inviting me to Melbourne. My thanks to Marq Smith for his reading of this text and to Simon Ofield for his sharing of so many ideas on gay space.

2   From Henri Lefebvre, *Le droit à la ville suivi d'Espace et politique* Paris, 1972, p. 117. 'Unless there be contrary indication, forms of time and space will be invented and proposed for practice. Let the imagination come into play, not the *imaginaire* that permits flight and evasion, which is the vehicle of ideologies, but *imaginaire* which invests itself in the *appropriation* (of time, of space, of physiological life, of desire).'

3   The bibliography for this piece is wide-ranging in the forms and periods of literature, and these are just a few indications. In the first place, there are the canonical city texts such as Georg Simmel. 'The Metropolis and Mental Life' [1903], in *Classic Essays on the Culture of Cities*, edited by Richard Sennet (New York, 1969), and Walter Benjamin, *Charles Baudelaire: A Lyric Poet in the Era of High Capitalism* (London, 1971). See especially his discussion of Edgar Allen Poe's 'Man in the Crowd', pp. 48–54. In terms of a specific scholarship of gay space, a fine and original generic model for discussion is to be found in Henning Bech's *When Men Meet* (Oxford, 1997), and my own conclusion here reflects some of his thinking. Also, see Henry Urbach, 'Spatial Rubbing: The Zone', an important essay on the Los Angeles cruise bar, the Zone, and close to my own approach, in *Sites*, no. 21 (1993). Another, more heteroclite model is the collection of essays *Queers in Space: Communities, Public Spaces, Sites of Resistance*, edited by Gordon Brent Ingram *et al.* See especially Jean-Ulrick Deser, 'Queer Space' and Maurice van Lieshout, 'Leather Nights in the Woods: Locating Male Homosexuality and Sadomasochism in a Dutch Highway Rest Area'. The French sociologists of gay life Rommel Mendes-Leite and Pierre-Olivier de Busscher have published a slim volume entitled *Back-rooms: microgéographic <<sexographique>> de deux back-rooms parisiennes* (Lille, 1997). In my view this disheartening essay yields nothing but pretentious, prim and evasive

namings of bar comportments, the whole justified by gesturing to the demands of AIDS education. Like van Lieshout, they deploy anthropologically correct concepts such as courtship, rather than the more general, Foucauldian notion of comportment that subtends my thinking. Frédéric Martel's much discussed *Le rose et le noir* (Paris, 1997), is deeply flawed both as a history of a sociability and a movement, while it is often well documented on histories of gay business, etc. My research is based on practice and conversations, vernacular discussion in the gay press, and the diaries of a close friend, Jean M., who has written copious pages for every day of the past 25 years of cruising in gay Paris and other cities. See also my 'The Poetics of Space Rewritten: From Renaud Camus to the Gay City Guide', in *Parisian Fields*, edited by Michael Sheringham (London, 1996).

4   Sigmund Freud, 'The "Uncanny" ', in *Studies in Parapsychology*, New York, 1963.

5   See, for example, Jean des Cars and Pierre Pinon, *Paris-Haussmann le pari d'Haussmann*, Paris, 1991, or Jean-Louis Cohen and André Lortie, *Des fortifs au périf*, Paris, 1992, for two excellent catalogues of these in fact wonderful exhibitions.

6   Poe, *Histoires Extraordinaires*, trans. Charles Baudelaire, preface by Julio Cortazar, Paris, 1988, pp. 52–53. This is my own re-translation. Poe's original being altogether another subject: 'And so we escaped arm in arm through the streets, continuing our daytime conversation, roving by chance until the early hours and seeking amongst the chaotic lights and shadows of the thronging city those innumerable excitations of the spirit that peaceful study cannot offer.'

7   'a pile of cobblestones heaped in a spot where the way is under repair ...'

8   *Policing Public Sex: Queer Politics and the Future of AIDS Activism*, ed. Dangerous Bedfellows, South End Press, 1996. See John Lindell, 'Public Space for Public Sex' and Allan Berubé, 'The History of Gay Bathhouses'.

Part IV

The representational metropolis

10 'Waiting, waiting': the hotel lobby, in the modern city[1]

Douglas Tallack

Figure 10.1 Edward Hopper, American painter (1882–1967), *Hotel Lobby*, 1943, oil
on canvas, 321/4 x 403/4 inches. IMA47.4

Source: Indianapolis Museum of Art, William Ray Adams Memorial Collection.

In the hotel lobbies of American film and literature one can meet (among many
others) Sam Spade and Philip Marlowe and their accomplices and adversaries; a
pair of hapless out-of-towners; Amory Blaine and, a few years later, Monroe
Stahr; Lolita and Humbert Humbert; Roger Thornley in pursuit of George
Kaplan from New York to Chicago; Emma McChesney; Hurstwood and Carrie;
Michael J. Fox as the concierge, Richard Gere's pretty woman, and the night-

clerk in the films and novel with those titles; and, perhaps most memorably, Benjamin Braddock waiting to meet Mrs Robinson.

With his eye for indiscriminate heterogeneity, it was Henry James who was among the first to speculate whether 'the hotel-spirit may not just *be* the American spirit most seeking and most finding itself'.[2] But it was left to Sinclair Lewis, in an obscure and obsessive novel called *Work of Art* (1934) which pursues a road not taken in his own life, to write the great American hotel-novel. *Work of Art* is the story of a practical man, Myron Weagle, whose driving ambition is to design and run a hotel as an epic work of art. When in Washington DC he has no time for the White House or the Capitol because he is too busy taking notes in lobbies. And in New York City, working at the Westward Ho!, he marvels at the lobby in words inspired by the trade journal, *Hotel Management*:

> two stories high, floored with pink marble, wainscoted with yellow marble, supported with pillars of marble pink and yellow and green and black. Above the wainscoting was a frieze ... showing the development of New York from the Dutch, through the English, Irish, and Jews, to the Italians.[3]

This is F. Scott Fitzgerald's *The Great Gatsby* but set in a hotel lobby, while other classic American themes are re-cast by Lewis as lobby dramas: as Myron goes West; as he returns to redecorate his hometown lobby, where he is briefly tempted by Modernist design; and, on his Great Tour, as he compares European and American hotel interiors, remarking that, on the whole, Bolshevism and Fascism produced a worse regime for the hotel worker than 'Capitalistic Democracy'. His Jamesian European tour is a 'passionate pilgrimage', during which he completes two volumes of his 'Hotel Project Notes' and concludes with the insight, 'Funny how many top-notch European hotels have toothpicks right on the table!'[4] The novel ends even more bizarrely, though with no apparent irony, when Myron's son persuades him to turn his attention from hotels to the new 'tourist camps', devoted to holidaymakers who had given up on railroad travel and taken to their cars. Although Myron hopes that tourists will not just pass through but will stay a few days at *his* camp, hotel-history tells us that these motels – as they would become – will not need lobbies. But *Work of Art* – like Frederick Jackson Turner's frontier thesis – refuses to become a tragedy.

No account could do justice to this variety and, in any case, there is a risk of losing all proportion – in the manner of Sinclair Lewis' hero – in merely accumulating examples. However, the surprising oscillation between the comic and the slightly disturbing in and across some of these examples of fictional hotel lobbies is marked enough to prompt an interpretation of this overlooked, though ubiquitous, modern space, beginning with the observation that when examples do come to mind they tend to do so not as specifically memorable spaces but as spaces associated with events and even stories. In James Donald's formulation of the relationship between the textual and the social, 'Space is less the already existing setting for … stories, than the production of space through that *taking place*, through the act of narration.'[5] Consequently, a starting definition of the hotel lobby might be that it is a space which *takes place* in narratives. And, here, Edmund Goulding's 1932 MGM treatment of Vicki Baum's novel *Grand Hotel*, published in German in 1929, provides a representative example of this 'taking place' of the hotel lobby in what can be termed the modern period; that is to say, in the broad period prior to John Portman's re-modelling of these spaces and Fredric Jameson's now canonic theorising of one of Portman's hotels. The stories of the five main characters in Goulding's film criss-cross the lobby in a succession of meetings, collisions, gazes and glances. There is constant foreground and background action as deals are struck, cons perpetrated and relationships instigated, developed and broken. Narratives are set in motion. A lowly employee of a powerful industrialist intends to spend all his savings on a final immersion in luxury before his terminal illness ends a humdrum life. But he comes unexpectedly into money, recovers his health and, in the final scene in the lobby, asks for his mail to be forwarded to the Grand Hotel, Paris, because he is blithely confident that there will be a Grand Hotel everywhere. He then leaves with the girl on his arm. Known initially as 'the stenographer', she enters the hotel lobby through the revolving doors near the beginning of the film to 'temp' for the powerful industrialist, but leaves it in the money. And yet all of this often comic activity, including that of the extras who populate this busy lobby, is framed spatially by the revolving doors and the elevators and framed verbally by the prologue intoned by a cynical war-wounded doctor and then repeated as an epigraph: 'Grand Hotel. People come and people go. Nothing changes.'[6] In a vaguely troubling way, the film is also regularly punctuated by the doctor asking at the desk whether a telegram, a letter or a message has come for him. And even the busy industrialist refers to himself as 'waiting, waiting' in the hotel lobby. It is this combination of movement and stasis, space and events, which suggests a reading of the hotel lobby as emblematic of certain aspects of modernity: broadly speaking, its routine yet kaleidoscopic, assembling and disassembling, comic and disturbing character. In the heterogeneous crowd of the lobby – as in that of the city – the familiar and unfamiliar, the homely and unhomely, mixture which Freud calls the uncanny is just about discernible, even in scenes in which the comic mode is dominant.

The intriguing architectonics of the hotel lobby have attracted the attention of two acute observers of modern life, working in different media. Some time between 1922 and 1925 the German cultural and film critic, Siegfried Kracauer, wrote an essay entitled 'The Hotel Lobby'. It was one of a number of short but telling analyses of contemporary German culture published in the feuilleton section of the *Frankfurter Zeitung*. The genre of the *feuilleton* specialised in the quotidian and, in an untheorised but compelling mixture of sociology and phenomenology, reported on arcades, cafés and music halls but also unemployment offices and the routine rather than the thrills of sporting events and syncopated dancing displays. In the manner of his teacher, Georg Simmel, and

his better-known contemporary, Walter Benjamin, the philosophical and socio-logical analyses written by Kracauer map the sphere of the quotidian and mark it out as part of the cultural landscape of modernity. What comes through in these short pieces is Kracauer's insistence that spaces such as the hotel lobby need to be subjected *to* critique but might also provide the perspective or distance required *by* critique, a concept which would be adumbrated more fully by Theodor Adorno, Max Horkheimer and other figures more central to the Frankfurt School than Kracauer.

Such high theory would probably have annoyed the determinedly anti-intellec-tual American artist, Edward Hopper. But he, like Kracauer, was fascinated by overlooked places: drug stores, automats, diners, and a variety of hotel settings, including the hotel lobby, the subject of a 1943 painting, entitled *Hotel Lobby* (see Fig. 10.1). This coincidence of interest centres on the way in which, for Kracauer and Hopper, the hotel lobby was part of the interior visual transformation of the modern city in Germany and the United States, specifically in the cities of New York and Berlin. It is quite fitting that Kracauer should have made for the United States when he was fleeing from Germany in the early 1940s because the hotel lobby is just one of a number of modern spaces which figure often, and in illumi-nating ways, in American popular culture, notably film and detective fiction. And just as Kracauer's essay is most insightful when he introduces occasional examples to make theoretical points so Hopper's interest in, and painting of, a bit of Americana offers theoretical knowledge, albeit differently presented.

The hotel lobby is a semi-public gateway to private places. There is a gate-keeper – the reception clerk; a route – typically, entry through a revolving door to the lobby; and – as often as not – a conspicuous crossing of the lobby to a reception desk and from there to the elevator. This ritual involves signing one's name and providing a minimum of personal history and even a rudimentary recent narrative of sorts. At this stage there is sometimes an element of fiction or storytelling, as in the excruciatingly embarrassing arrival of Nabokov's Humbert and Lolita at The Enchanted Hunters or Benjamin's prolonged efforts to book a room for himself and Mrs Robinson in *The Graduate*. This semi-public ritual, however honest or dishonest in parts, gives access to the bedrooms, the site of exaggeratedly private acts. The whole of Stephen Schneck's 1965 novel, *The Nightclerk*, is posited upon this ritual of access to the esoterically and even dangerous private realm of 'upstairs':

> The pseudonymous and transient tribes of Smith, Jones, Johns, Brown, White and Gray have left veracity no room on the page. Reality has been crowded off the register. Names are regularly changed to protect the guilty.[7]

And in smarter hotels than *The Nightclerk*'s Travelers Hotel in downtown San Francisco, the lower one's class and income the harder it is to get upstairs. On the other hand, the revolving door introduces an element of chance into one's entry into the lobby: would one spin to success or spin right on out of the hotel again?

In terms of a negotiation between the private and public spheres, hotel lobbies have regularly had a gender and class dimension to them. It was during the Gilded Age in the United States – when middle-class women moved more significantly into the public sphere – that the hotel lobby functioned as part of the discourse on the spatial boundaries of public and private; and began to rival the drawing-rooms and private libraries and gardens of Victorian fiction. William Dean Howells' novel, *A Hazard of New Fortunes* (1899), charts an intermediary stage in this social and fictional process. When Howells' characters Mr and Mrs March are contemplating a move from genteel Boston to cosmopolitan New York, they stay in 'a quiet hotel far down-town'. The clerk asks Mr March if Mrs March is with him 'and said then he supposed they would want their usual quarters; and in a moment they were domesticated in a far interior that seemed to have been waiting for them'.[8] While it acts as a refuge during their trying and challenging ventures into the city when apartment-hunting, even this halfway house momentarily tempts the Marches with the idea that they could also cut loose from their children and their familiar but staid past. A few years later, in Edna Ferba's Emma McChesney stories (for instance, *Roast Beef, Medium* of 1913), the lead character, a travelling saleswoman in the petticoat trade, goes from hotel to hotel. The way is prepared for the stenographer in *Grand Hotel* to make her way up the social ladder from the moment she enters the revolving doors of the lobby to the moment she leaves it on the nouveau-riche arm of the former lowly employee. The meeting places of characters such as these are the spatial analogues of the element of luck in the narratives of Horatio Alger; while in Hollywood's substitute for nineteenth-century popular fiction the lobby is transformed from a purposeless place into one which locks in to the purposive narrative of success without any need to draw on the resources of the work ethic. Work, when it takes place in the lobby, has an intangible feel to it and is barely distinguishable from not working. Significantly, *Grand Hotel* was released at the height of the Depression and the hotel loses both the decorum of the hotel in Vicki Baum's novel and also its sense of instability:

> In the corridor an electrician was kneeling on the floor, busied over some repair to the wires. Ever since they had had those powerful lights to illuminate the hotel frontage there had always been something going wrong with the overworked installation of the hotel.[9]

It was in the late 1920s and early 1930s that the great hotels in New York were built: the new Waldorf-Astoria, the Barbizon and the Carlyle. And built, it appeared, to survive the Depression. As Siegfried Kracauer remarks, from his not dissimilar Weimar perspective, 'spatial images are the dreams of society. Wherever the hieroglyphics of these images can be deciphered, one finds the basis of social reality.'[10]

The hotel lobby, then, is one of those revealing sites where the larger picture (a society's often static image of itself) and the local narrative come uneasily or (same difference) all-too-easily together. For while narrative might be needed for the hotel lobby to be memorable, the lobby, in its turn, spatialises narrative.

And this is one way in which ideology functions. Put more mundanely, change becomes merely the movement of a revolving door. When, in the early twenties, Scott and Zelda Fitzgerald were already suggesting that they might soon become frozen into their own image of frenetic immobility, they actually spun themselves into a state of dizziness – as children sometimes do – but, in their case, in the revolving doors of the Commodore on 42nd Street.[11]

As is apparent, even from these few instances, the hotel lobby's small contribution to the redefinition of class and gender was largely social and economic, rather than political. Because the lobby is semi-private and semi-public it does constitute – in Hannah Arendt's phase – a 'space … of appearance' but it lacks the political or civic significance which Arendt had in mind when using that phrase.[12] Indeed, the private/public amalgam of the commercially-owned hotel lobby might be less political than the private spaces of home or hotel bedroom for which feminism has at least given us a political language. And certainly it was not a place of politics for Victorian women. Instead, a common experience for a woman was to wait for a man in a lobby, rather than always wait for him at home. Or to make the hotel – as a semi-private transition to the fully public place of the street – a place of work, though in the emerging service sphere. At one end of the social scale there is a connection between hotels and prostitution. Mid-way, Emma McChesney strikes commercial deals in petticoats. While, at the other end of the scale, Lucius Boomer (who owned the Waldorf-Astoria) employed women as managers in his hotels because they brought a touch of home to his business.[13] Whether or not it decoratively draws upon the outside world for its designs, the lobby can be a haven, an upholstered substitute for the reality of the street. Henry James quite approved of the entrance to the Waldorf-Astoria because he thought it had a female quality to it – in contrast to the skyscraper.

Although the hotel lobby is a conduit and takes on its meanings in relation to the spheres which it links, it is also a place which some people do not pass through or immediately pass through. Instead, it becomes a place of waiting, even for those in a hurry. The lobby in *Grand Hotel* is very much a space filled with events, though sometimes the anticipated events do not happen or happen as part of a repeated pattern or are spatialised in the image of the revolving door. It is this peculiar limbo quality, rather than the notion of the lobby as a place of activity and social change which interests the lobby-watchers, Siegfried Kracauer and Edward Hopper. Kracauer founds his analysis of the hotel lobby upon a contrast between the lobby as an impersonal space, where strangers gather without knowing the host, and the community of the church:

> The typical characteristics of the *hotel lobby*, which appears repeatedly in detective novels, indicate that it is conceived as the inverted image of the house of God. It is a negative church … It is the setting for those who neither seek nor find the one who is always sought, and who are therefore guests in space as such – a space that encompasses them and has no function other than to encompass them.[14]

In contrast to the traditional community of the church and its participation in a drama of 'higher meaning', those who congregate in the hotel lobby are (in the title of another Kracauer essay) merely 'Those Who Wait'. In this interior space there is a peculiar way of being or – less portentously than Kracauer has it – of behaving. Figures in the street outside the lobby might be difficult to pin down in terms of definable pursuits simply because they cannot be tracked to their destinations or their destinations become enigmatic, as in Poe's parable of modernity, 'The Man of the Crowd'. Admittedly, the figures in a hotel lobby might also be difficult to define but this is more because they do not really inhabit a purposive space. For while the hotel lobby is a modern space which only fully came into existence after a travel and transportation revolution in the nineteenth century, it lacks the purpose of other modern interiors such as – and it is Kracauer's example – 'the conference room of a corporation'.[15] Of course, one *can* just wait in a boardroom or café or the foyer of a department store but the context makes all the difference.

Kracauer's 'The Hotel Lobby' is part of a study of the detective novel and, impressionistically at least, the hotel lobby does seem to appear 'repeatedly in detective novels'. Possibly, the very form of the novel changes when hotel lobbies appear. If pushed too far this could come out as an overblown hotel-lobby-theory-of-fiction, but there is something in the notion that (as Kracauer remarks of the detective novel) 'It is not the force of the event [the crime, however violent] which takes one's breath away but the opacity of the causal chain which determines the fact.'[16] Hotel lobbies are needed as sites of coincidence but also multiply those sites. For the post-domestic or post-communal novel (the kind of novel which supersedes *Mansfield Park* or *Middlemarch*, for instance), the hotel lobby is one kind of solution to the challenge posed in a society of travel when characters have to arrive someplace on their own or perhaps with just one other person; and that someplace should not necessarily – or at least not in a modern world – immediately assign them to a family or community structure. The hotel lobby exemplifies this problem, to which the detective novel with its gradually revealed emplotment of apparently anonymous characters is an exaggerated reaction. Moreover, the coincidences which occur in detective stories and in hotel lobbies are not 'psychological' but, as Kracauer claims, 'the distortion of a determination which operates as reality'.[17] Put a bit more glibly, if hotel lobbies did not exist they would have to be invented because sooner or later the coincidence will occur. That is to say, there is a logic to be revealed, a by-product of that quality of the fortuitous and the ephemeral which Baudelaire thought characterised urban modernity.

In the life of the hotel lobby, Kracauer continues, there is 'purposiveness' unaccompanied by 'any representation of a purpose'[18] and this insight supplies the most interesting, if oblique, link with the detective story. The lack of purposeful activity in the hotel lobby where the conventions of behaviour produce a fairly small number of possible scenarios is comparable with the formulaic quality in detective fiction. Yet there is a dynamic to be derived from 'waiting, waiting' because repetition can stimulate over-interpretation and the constructing of narratives out of seemingly static scenes. Hotel lobbies are spaces waiting to be given meaning by purposeful narratives and minimal signs of activity, the checking of a watch or a brief exchange of glances, stimulate a hermeneutics of suspicion, a preoccupation with the visual signs or clues which will turn banality into intrigue, routine into a plot. These visual clues are given off by a transient population who might well be here for a purpose yet seem, often, to be doing nothing but waiting. That is to say, the sense of just waiting – particularly if the lobby is windowless – stimulates a habitual 'just looking', albeit a looking which pretends to be disinterested, and a 'being-looked-at', which, again, involves some degree of dissimulation. When Dashiell Hammett's Sam Spade is planning a surveillance in the lobby of the St Mark hotel he says to Miss Wonderly: 'It'll help some if you either meet Thursby downstairs or let yourself be seen with him at some time.'[19]

As an interior, the lobby is differently spaced and paced from the street, in which flux and the rapid sequence of impressions create a certain kind of modern personality type: for Baudelaire the *flâneur* and for Georg Simmel the *blasé* metropolitan inhabitant. However, in spite of its challenges to identity, the street can accord a welcome anonymity, whereas the hotel lobby's anonymous population is subject to observation, if not exactly surveillance. Kracauer's metaphysics of the lobby bears upon the themes of surveillance but also loss and alienation played out in the downtown settings of the American tough detective story from Dashiell Hammett and Raymond Chandler onwards, a tradition with which there seems to have been cross-fertilisation with Edward Hopper's work. But, to recall an earlier observation, the peculiar space of looking of the hotel lobby also lends itself to comedy and in the most self-conscious of detective stories, there is a knowingness about the use of this location. Sometimes the private eye who has come to the lobby to observe can become the target, as in Hammett's *The Maltese Falcon* when Sam Spade exposes the inexperienced gumshoe, Wilmer, who is on a stake-out, to the attention of the house-detective in the lobby of the Hotel Belvedere:

> Sauntering, he crossed the lobby to the divan from which the elevators could be seen and sat down beside – not more than a foot from – the young man who was apparently reading a newspaper. ...
>
> Spade lighted his cigarette, leaned back comfortably on the divan, and spoke with good-natured carelessness: 'You'll have to talk to me before you're through, sonny – some of you will – and you can tell G. I said so.'
>
> The boy put his paper down quickly and faced Spade, staring at his necktie with bleak hazel eyes. ... 'Keep asking for it and you're going to get it,' he said, 'plenty'. ...
>
> Spade caught the attention of [Luke, the house-detective] ...
>
> 'What do you let these cheap gunmen hang out in your lobby for, with their tools bulging their clothes?' ...
>
> The boy looked like a schoolboy standing in front of them.
>
> Luke said: 'Well, if you don't want anything, beat it, and don't come back.'
> The boy said, 'I won't forget you guys,' and went out.[20]

In Chandler's 1943 novel, *The High Window*, the lobby of the Hotel Metropole in downtown Los Angeles is the secret yet exposed meeting place for Marlowe, who is also the narrator, and another amateur:

> A blond man in a brown suit, dark glasses and the now familiar hat came into the lobby and moved unobtrusively among the potted palms and the stucco arches to the cigar counter. He bought a package of cigarettes and broke it open standing there, using the time to lean his back against the counter and give the lobby the benefit of his eagle eye.
>
> He picked up his change and went over and sat down with his back to a pillar. He tipped his hat down over his dark glasses and seemed to go to sleep with an unlighted cigarette between his lips.
>
> I got up and wandered over and dropped into the chair beside him. I looked at him sideways. He didn't move. ...
>
> I struck a match and held the flame to his cigarette. 'Light?'
>
> 'Oh – thanks,' he said, very surprised. ... 'Haven't I seen you somewhere before?'
>
> 'Over on Dresden Avenue in Pasadena. This morning.'
>
> I could see his cheeks get pinker than they had been. He sighed.
>
> 'I must be lousy,' he said.
>
> 'Boy, you stink,' I agreed.
>
> 'Maybe it's the hat,' he said.[21]

While the hotel lobby is an interior and sometimes windowless space, it can, it would seem, produce a form of visual agoraphobia. The related motifs of visibility and observing are cinematically signalled in *Grand Hotel* by the startling view from above of concentric circles of balconies and, in the centre, the circular reception desk. As a response to this agoraphobic sensation, there are defences against being looked at. 'Faces disappear behind newspapers',[22] stoically so in the scene in the Belvedere in *The Maltese Falcon*. The hotel lobby is a place to meet others but also to avoid the look of others; a place of seeing and being seen – but also of reserve and, as such, lounging in a lobby qualifies as a paradigmatic urban experience as this has been defined by Simmel, Benjamin and Kracauer.

Edward Hopper's *Hotel Lobby* has an exposed feel to it, as though there is no respite from seeing and being seen. And yet it is an enclosed, windowless place. Defences, such as reading, are needed in case one becomes the object of looking; perhaps defences are needed as much in a busy lobby, such as that in *Grand Hotel*, as in Hopper's austere example, suggesting that there is not that much difference between the 'revolving' quality of the busy lobby in *Grand Hotel* and Hopper's sparsely populated lobby. It is as though Hopper's painting extracts the minimal but essential elements of the lobby: a few people who wait and who, in the main, do not communicate. Kracauer's words – which were not written with Hopper or *Grand Hotel* in mind – come close to expressing the outcome for those who inhabit these spaces. 'What is presented in the hotel lobby is the formal similarity of the figures, an equivalence that signifies not fulfilment but evacuation.'[23]

In one of the sketches which Hopper made for his painting and which – it seems reasonable to assume – was closer to the actual scene observed, there is an extra person to the left of the couple. The couple are talking or at least looking at each other and the man on the right is not reading, though he is not necessarily looking at the couple. But in the painting, Hopper edits out signs of communication and the people are separated in their chairs. As Kracauer archly remarks, in words which anticipate the damning tone of the opening of Adorno and Horkheimer's 1944 essay, 'The Culture Industry', 'in tasteful lounge chairs a civilization intent on rationalization comes to an end'.[24] In identifying the lobby's combination of boredom, distraction, alienation, displacement and the quality of someone looking, and in linking this modern space with the detective novel, Kracauer – but also Hopper in a different way – asserts a generalised knowledge which arises out of a specific site:

> The fact that the structure of the life presented in the detective novel is so typical indicates that the consciousness producing it is not an individual, coincidental one; at the same time, it shows that what has been singled out are the seemingly metaphysical characteristics. ... The composition of the detective novel transforms an ungraspable life into a translatable analogue of actual reality.

And:

> In the detective novel, proponents of that society and their functions give an account of themselves and divulge their hidden significance. ... the detective novel really thinks through to the end the society dominated by autonomous *Ratio*.[25]

In the way that Kracauer and Hopper present the hotel lobby it, like a church, is a space separated from the modern crowd in the street. Yet it is the inertness of the hotel lobby and the detective novel and *not* the higher community of 'the House of God' which holds Kracauer's attention and he goes so far as to theorise the relationship in question:

> Without being an artwork, the *detective novel* still shows civilised society its own face in a purer way than society is usually accustomed to seeing it. In the detective novel, proponents of that society and their function give an account of themselves and divulge their hidden significance.[26]

That is to say, the detective novel presents a pared-down reading of the structure and typology of modern society. Composition, even the formulaic composition of a detective story, gives the life experienced in such places as the hotel lobby a form of articulation. By the consistency with which he painted these modern places, Hopper, too, indicates that in them a peculiarly representative kind of life could be discerned. These are still Kracauer's words:

The more life is submerged, the more it needs the artwork, which unseals its withdrawnness and puts its pieces back in place.... The unity of the aesthetic construct, the manner in which it distributes the emphases and consolidates the event, gives a voice to the inexpressive world, gives meaning to the themes broached within it.[27]

It is the indeterminate character of the hotel lobby, neither fully public nor fully private, and both exposed and enclosed, which provokes comic and disturbing representations alike. The hotel lobby scene in *The Graduate* is a wonderful comedy of the visually exposed in which the open spaces of the lobby press upon Benjamin. He becomes the centre of attention – or so he feels. Conversely, in *Grand Hotel* the openness and activity of the lobby are circumscribed by the sense of nothing happening and of a compulsion to repeat this lack of activity. Hence 'waiting, waiting'. At such moments, what Freud memorably defines as 'the uncanny' can be experienced, that combination of the homely and the unhomely, the familiar and the unfamiliar.[28] The hotel in Stephen Schneck's *The Nightclerk* is just about recognisable as in the tradition of the Waldorf and the hotel in *Grand Hotel* but now falling into misuse and disuse:

> Down at the end of town, at the bottom of Market Street, the monstrous Travelers Hotel occupies a full city block ...
>
> Steeped in the heartbroken tradition of the thirties, the splendid, ruined lobby of the Travelers is hung with wreaths of stale cigar smoke. This lobby, a stage set that was meant to dazzle for a season, has been expecting the wrecker for ages.[29]

We meet the nightclerk sitting 'at the edge of that dim wasteland of a lobby' and, once adjusted to his perspective are introduced not simply to the uncanny quality which has surfaced in other fictional lobbies but explicitly to a modern space which has taken on distinctively *Modernist* dimensions:

> There are even some few person who have gone so far as to suspect that this hotel, confined neither to space nor time, has entrances and exits on every dimension. They would have it that there exist five, six, seven hotels, all called the Travelers ...
>
> If it were true, then no man could ever be certain that he had entered the correct hotel.[30]

But it is the Nightclerk's lobby which is truly unsettling, in the manner of Hopper's lobby and Freud's uncanny:

> the entire lobby of the Travelers Hotel, from unseen ceiling to the vague horizons that one *assumes* are walls of the lobby, the entire area was a matter of conjecture. Say that it was intuitively perceived, rather than visu-

ally defined. The sort of lobby where one found exactly what one thought he would find. And if those shapes were not built into the walls, well then, perhaps they weren't. Perhaps they were something else.[31]

In Hopper's *Hotel Lobby* it is less the surprise of discerning a fourth figure in the painting, a desk clerk in the right middle-ground, which creates unease than a gradual awareness of the odd angle from which the space is painted and from which we see it and, in seeing it, are drawn into the hotel lobby. Hopper's hotel lobby, like Siegfried Kracauer's, is 'the space does not refer beyond itself'.[32]

Notes

1 The present essay originally appeared in *The Irish Journal of American Studies* and is reprinted with the kind permission of the editors.
2 Henry James, *The American Scene*, Bloomington, IN: Indiana University Press, 1968, p. 102.
3 Sinclair Lewis, *Work of Art: A Novel*, London: Jonathan Cape, 1934, p. 177.
4 Lewis, *Work of Art*, pp. 318 and 316.
5 James Donald, 'This, Here, Now: Imagining the Modern City', in *Imagining Cities: Scripts, Signs, Memory*, ed. Sallie Westwood and John Williams, London: Routledge, 1997, p. 183.
6 *Grand Hotel*, directed by Edmund Goulding, USA, MGM, 1932.
7 Stephen Schneck, *The Nightclerk: Being his Perfectly True Confession*, London: Panther Books, 1986, p. 12.
8 William Dean Howells, *A Hazard of New Fortunes*, New York: Bantam Books, 1960, p. 30.
9 Vicki Baum, *Grand Hotel*, trans. Basil Creighton, London, Geoffrey Bles, 1930, p. 2.
10 Quoted in Anthony Vidler, 'Agoraphobia: Spatial Estrangement in Georg Simmel and Siegfried Kracauer', *New German Critique*, 54 (Fall 1991): 33.
11 See Peter Conrad, *The Art of the City: Views and Versions of New York*, New York: Oxford University Press, 1984, p. 188.
12 Hannah Arendt, *The Human Condition*, Chicago, IL: University of Chicago Press, 1958, p. 199.
13 See William Leach, *Land of Desire: Merchants, Power, and the Rise of a New American Culture*, New York: Vintage Books, 1994, pp. 132–3.
14 Siegfried Kracauer, 'The Mass Ornament', in *The Mass Ornament: Weimar Essays*, trans. and ed. Thomas Y. Levin, Cambridge, MA: Harvard University Press, 1995, pp. 175–6.
15 Kracauer, *The Mass Ornament*, pp. 176–7.
16 Quoted in David Frisby, *Fragments of Modernity: Theories of Modernity in the Work of Simmel, Kracauer and Benjamin*, London and Cambridge: Polity Press, 1985, pp. 130–1.
17 Quoted in Frisby, *Fragments of Modernity*, p. 132.
18 Kracauer, 'The Mass Ornament', p. 177.
19 Dashiell Hammett, *The Maltese Falcon*, Harmondsworth: Penguin Books, 1963, pp. 11.
20 Hammett, *The Maltese Falcon*, pp. 87 and 88.
21 *The Raymond Chandler Omnibus*, London: Book Club Associates, 1975, p. 350.
22 Kracauer, 'The Mass Ornament', p. 183.
23 Kracauer, 'The Mass Ornament', p. 179.
24 Kracauer, 'The Mass Ornament', p. 178.
25 Kracauer, 'The Mass Ornament', pp. 175 and 174.

26 Kracauer, 'The Mass Ornament', p. 174.
27 Kracauer, 'The Mass Ornament', p. 173.
28 Sigmund Freud, 'The "Uncanny"', in *The Pelican Freud Library*, vol. 14, translated under the general editorship of James Strachey, ed. Albert Dickson, Harmondsworth: Penguin Books, 1985, pp. 335–76. See, also, Anthony Vidler, *The Architectural Uncanny: Essays in the Modern Unhomely*, Cambridge, MA: MIT Press, 1992.
29 Schneck, *The Nightclerk*, pp. 12 and 15.
30 Schneck, *The Nightclerk*, pp. 13 and 14.
31 Schneck, *The Nightclerk*, pp. 15–16.
32 Kracauer, 'The Mass Ornament', p. 177. For a more detailed analysis of Hopper's *Hotel Lobby*, see Glyn Marshall, 'Edward Hopper: Visions of Modernity', unpublished paper, University of Nottingham, 1998.

11 Venice

Masking the real

Barry Curtis and Claire Pajaczkowska

Figure 11.1 Palazzo Querini-Stampalia, Venice.
Photograph by Natasha Chibireva.

Venice is both archetypal and exceptional. Its battle for survival and transfigura-
tion has transformed it into an icon of both the victory and fragility of culture.
Constructed on low-lying land in a lagoon, its imposing stone buildings rest on
a base of petrified wooden piles driven into the ground and hardened with time.
The city has frequently been seen by its visitors as both magical and as a
metaphor for the human work of sublimation which can transform raw materials
into complex and awe-inspiring works of culture. One consequence of the
transformations and juxtapositions which have generated the city is that its
meaning has become secured in the ambivalent logic of the unconscious where
opposites co-exist with only oblique reference to the real.

Mythic and archetypal themes serve to frame and mask the historical account of Venice's development. Writing about a city supposedly 'frozen in time' seems inappropriate in a collection of essays concerned with cities whose urbanity is essentially related to more recent transformations. 'La Serenissima' has become idealised for its resistance to change, its serenity and immemorial allegiance to the past. However, Venice has been subject to the shaping forces of history, even after the violation of its autonomy at the end of the eighteenth century. At the onset of a new millennium it can still function as a model for current and impending urban issues. Michael Sorkin has suggested of Los Angeles that it has become a city representative of a certain time, available for a certain kind of canonisation because it has taken on 'a kind of comforting stasis, destined to the historically unique'. Perhaps it is this fixity which has made it the appropriate locale for narratives of hubris and imminent disaster.[1] Venice has similarly been re-appropriated as a 'doomed city' but also as a megastructure, theme park, model for urban integrity, and city of ecological malpractice and cultural tourism.

Venice is an extreme city which by historical accident has achieved a degree of zoning unrealised by the most ardent Modernists. The separation of components of the collective city of the lagoon is comparable to the 'abstractions from the unities of ambiance discovered by psychogeographers in existing cities'[2] and the urban visions of the Situationists. The 'historic centre' which most people know as Venice is accompanied by 'pleasure zones' – the Lidos, the industrial complex of Marghera and the business, residential and recreational centre of Mestre, to which many Venetians have migrated. The historic islands of Venice are unusual in their preservation from most of the influences which have shaped the twentieth-century city. As a result of Venice's uniqueness and celebrity it is hard to encounter it without preconceptions.

All cities, as well as being material and localised objects, are compounds of expectations, myth and subjective observation. The self-conscious testing of experience against data is a fundamental component of travel writing and the tourist experience and is particularly notable in descriptions of Venice since the late Middle Ages. Visitors have been aware in a particularly acute way of its textuality. The 'explanation' of Venice offered here is, as the etymology of the term suggests, an unfolding of a 'map' – *ex planere* where the map is more a folded piece of material – tactile and sensuous – rather than an instrumental, two-dimensional triumph of cartography. It is an explanation of the celebrations of the city, as well as a negotiation of its contradictory histories.

From the early nineteenth century, Venice was a colony of world tourism and a home for tourist colonies. By then it was already a city understood to be in decline and inadequately defended against the adverse elements. The meanings which were elaborated around the experience of Venice involved narratives of decay and entropy. There were strong resistances to remedying this situation and in particular to allowing modernisation to intrude. In much of the literature, written by non-Venetians, there was a strong sense of it being a place better cared for by resident émigrés than by its native population. This ahistorical and universalising tendency persists in guidebooks and travel writing, which since the nineteenth century have tended to deplore signs of everyday modernisation.

The powerful fantasies associated with Venice as a place of decay, decadence, perversity and death were associated with Oriental, erotic and voyeuristic themes. Venice has always mediated between East and West. Like all hybrids it has been an anxiogenic object, prone to exoticisation. Since the early Renaissance the city has been associated with wealth, which is not only extraordinary but also testimony to extensive trade and aggressively pursued mercantile adventure. Although various estimates indicate that less than 5 per cent of the wealth of Venice remains *in situ*, the historic centre is still renowned as a palimpsest of treasures. But it was also a manufacturing city. At the height of its military and political power it was known for its productivity, particularly with respect to innovations in production line manufacture in the Arsenale and in the development of printing.

There is a reality which lies, in the words of a recent exhibition of vernacular architecture in Venice – 'behind the palaces' – both in the sense of the less spectacular, everyday aspects of historic Venetian life and the repressed recent history of the city. In the early years of the twentieth century Venice was still industrial. The 1913 edition of Baedecker describes it as: 'a shipbuilding, cotton spinning and iron working centre', incorporating a large number of factories and a considerable industrial proletariat. When the Austrians bombed Venice in 1915 they laid waste many workshops and factories. By then the museumisation of the city was sufficiently advanced for Marinetti to suggest that the Italians should have carried out the bombing themselves and that they should replace the Grand Canal with a motor route.

The sense of there being a 'hidden Venice' has operated in a number of ways. It suggests a reality beyond the grasp of casual tourists – a knowledge which at the deepest level is the preserve of Venetians themselves and in a more recondite way of the numerous émigrés, long-term tourists or property-owning foreigners. But this element of concealment is very much part of the myth of Venice. The 'mask' has played a central metaphoric role in constructing the city since at least the end of the eighteenth century. Georg Simmel, writing of Venice, suggested that it was a mask which hid reality whilst also revealing the absence of that reality. For Simmel, Venice presented dualities which could not be resolved. His deliberations on bridges and doors as differential correlations of separateness and unity has particular significance in a city where many of the hundreds of bridges end abruptly at a door. The suggestion that Venice is essentially ambivalent or that it lacks depth or core is common in the literature which seeks to describe and analyse it. Nietzsche's perception that Venice was 'one hundred profound solitudes' rather than a community provides testimony to the intense subjectivity which is so commonly brought to these judgements.

The more obvious association of the metaphorical term 'mask' is with the real masks which play a central role in Venetian carnivals and festivals, and which serve as ubiquitous souvenirs. In terms of representation, the mask is a fitting metaphor for the increasingly dominant tourist industry through which the majority of Venetians now make a living. Various processes of masking are understandably operative in concealing evidence of change, in the social history and everyday life of the city. This form of masking as façadism, of maintaining the façades of buildings regardless of what is going on behind them, is of course now a common conservationist preoccupation in historic centres,[3] but in Venice the very strict regulations on altering the outward appearance of buildings has led to some particularly discrepant, even surreal relationships between interior and exterior.

Venice was one of the first, and in many ways is still the paradigmatic tourist city of the West. It has been conceived over a long period in terms of paradox and dream. Its appeal lies in the oscillation between power and powerlessness, nature and culture, visibility and mystery. Its dreamlike quality arises from the unlikely proposition of building a huge Imperial city on water and the strange juxtapositions and condensations of experience which it offers.

The compact, edited quality of transition in Venice has become commonplace in theme parks and is increasingly informing the planning of city centres. Venice, restricted by its waterways and the need to reclaim land for building, maintains a dreamlike distillation of experience which must once have been more commonplace before the demands of transport and suburbanisation. There is virtually no 'dead' space or 'non-place' and the cramped format of the city provides juxtapositions and palimpsests which are experienced as 'unreal' in relation to the more gradual transitions offered by urban spaces which have been planned or zoned in the interests of motorised traffic.

I have tried to isolate some of the main tropes which have developed to explain and celebrate the unique quality of Venice:

Venice is often represented as 'excessive'. This theme is frequently located in descriptions of the richness of decoration and the crowded *mise en scène* of the city. It is related to a history of accumulation and display. Venice was renowned for ceremonial events which linked the civic with the spiritual. The physical space of the city was embellished and extended to accommodate progressively grander state rituals. Yi-Fu Tuan has referred to the Venice of the Renaissance as: 'a moral and aesthetic state'[4] which in the context of a neo-Platonist intellectual culture related external beauty to inner virtue. The spectacular and public nature of the events was intended to serve constitutional ends – to affirm a form of government and proclaim the relation between the Doge as representative of the state, the people and the environmental circumstances of the city. The mood of excessive expense, detail and scale is conspicuous in travellers' tales and tourist literature.

Venice is considered 'entropic'. From the earliest days of the Republic, maintaining the authority of the city depended on intelligence, diplomacy and the maintenance of a network of trade and political influence rather than the more normal Imperial strategy of conquering and possessing land. The decline of the Venetian Empire was attributable to the discovery of the New World and the consequent de-centring of the Mediterranean and its trade routes, but the fading of power was drawn out over centuries and formally concluded by

Napoleon's overthrow of the Republic. Venice was understood over a long period of time to be in a state of potential or imminent decline. The narrative of decadence was invested in the nineteenth century with various morbid associations. Venice's mood of decay has been a fictional theme which has continued to be realised throughout the twentieth century.

Venice has always been regarded as a place of 'mystery'. At the height of its power, the Venetian Republic relied to a unique extent on espionage and information. The State Archive contains rooms full of reports from ambassadors and agents employed to report on a range of issues at the courts of every European power. Credit ratings, inventions, the dates of sailings and state intelligence had great significance for the maintenance of individual and corporate power. The state was known to guard its own manufacturing secrets, often by sinister means and to maintain complex networks of surveillance on citizens and visitors. Representations of the secret places of the state, which were particularly associated with imprisonment and execution, became emblematic of masking and subterfuge. The dialectic relationship between Venice as a multicultural site for the exchange of commercial and cultural information and the dark side of concealment and remote manipulation persists in twentieth-century fictions.

The sense of theatricality which was managed by the state and is now a component of the tourist experience extends to the buildings in a number of ways. They rivalled and exceeded those of other major cities in terms of scale and grandeur and had to be constructed in ways which took into account the insubstantial land on which they were built. The façades can be likened to masquerades, concealing the fragility of the foundations, contributing to the perception of Venice as a theatrical set. In the later history of Venice the waning political power of the state threw into relief the constructedness of the public and private spectacle which remained a conspicuous part of Venetian life.

Venice has often been represented in terms of a paradox of microcosm and macrocosm. From the earliest years of the ascendancy of the Republic there was a widely noted discrepancy between the small island in the lagoon and the vast trading Empire which it administered. The relation between the extensive quality of Venice and the jewel-like detailing of the city is a trope of current tourist representations which display grand vistas but also try to capture the essence of the city through its characteristic details. Many commentators have also expressed a sense of the confusion of interior and exterior. Napoleon is said to have referred to St Mark's Square as Europe's grandest salon. Adrian Stokes observed that:

> the absence of a raised footway provides, as does the water, an unbroken horizontal plane from which a building grows … Hence an architecture is developed whose sides, on their lower levels, possess a familiarity that elsewhere is associated with indoor accoutrements, a banister rail or a mantelpiece.[5]

Venice has frequently been regarded as a place of inexhaustable density and complexity, but also as a place which has been endlessly described and explained. As early as 1494, Canon Pietro Casola, a visitor to Venice, wrote:

So much has been said, there appears nothing more to be said.

Henry James, writing almost exactly four centuries later, expressed what had become an often recorded anxiety:

There is nothing left to discover or describe.

As a visitor to Venice it is hardly possible not to be aware of the burden of historical information and mediation. There is something about the pervasive sense of loss and the impending sense of doom which stimulates a sense of closure and a corresponding need to experience and investigate. Many commentators of the last two centuries express this troubling relationship to a city which provokes curiosity whilst at the same time threatening to permit only repetitions of experience.

Venice has always been regarded as intermediate. It distinguished itself from rival maritime powers by its claims to be 'married to the sea' – in doing so the city identified itself in a particular way with the sea as trade route, battleground and defensive margin. Stokes has noted that moving within the circulation of canals in the city renders it 'a potent symbol of the mother'.[6] In Western eyes, Venice was always a renowned meeting place for different cultures and its own forms of cultural expression were hybrid and exotic. It was frequently represented as indeterminate in its relation to the East – partaking of some of the characteristics attributed to the Orient, whilst representing Italian and European culture. Venice was a bulwark of Christianity against the territorial and trading ambitions of the Muslim, although it maintained highly ambivalent relations with Byzantium. It is significant that the city owed its origins to the need to shelter from marauding invaders – developing its unique strengths as a result of vulnerability and negotiation. Underlying this sense of a miscegenated culture is a suggestion of sexual profligacy, an association with seduction and infection. The historical figure of Casanova embodies the expertise and promiscuity which is more generally associated with the city. Apollinaire's reference to Venice as 'the genitals of Europe' condenses its geographical position with a historic sense of sensuality and miscegenation. The city simultaneously embodied Orient and Occident in binarised and superimposed associations of oligarchy and democracy, timelessness and modernity, obscurity and visibility.

Venice has strong literary associations with death. Many representations of Venice which resonate in the popular imagination – including well-known works by Thomas Mann, Daphne du Maurier, Nicholas Roeg and Ian McEwan and its function as *mise en scène* for James Bond films – have dramatised the city as a locus for a powerful combinatory narratives of luxury, death and desire. There is an abundant literature which figures Venice as a place for mysterious

sexuality and concealed crimes. Psychoanalyst Hyatt-Williams has suggested that perverse fantasies circulate around a central unconscious fantasy of a dead child[7] – a haunting feature of du Maurier/Roeg's memorable film *Don't Look Now*. Certainly the city's economy has threatened the retention of young people and the average age of the population of the historic centre is now over 40, but at a more symbolic level these fantasies represent a culture whose regenerative powers have been compromised by perceived political impotence and a subjection to the voyeuristic and debilitating effects of tourism.

The relative stability of Venice over a long historical period (it remained autonomous for over 1000 years) has contributed to the complexity of its representations. Its reputation as a cruel and decadent place was cultivated by French historians in the late eighteenth century as a justification for Napoleon's assumption of power. In 1848 the short-lived Venetian Republic hired its own historian in an attempt to correct this constructed history. Politicians, among them Disraeli, commented on the similarities between Venetian and British history, although they were often at pains to point out that the British parliamentary system was superior and less likely to result in the entropic fate of Venice. William Thayer, an American historian, and Balzac both suggested that the decline of Venice could be considered a warning to the British.[8] Ruskin saw Venetian maritime power as an opportunity to claim continuities and analogies between Tyre and Britain but hoped that for the British Empire there would be a happier outcome.[9]

The Gothic imagination has always fantasised Venice as a place of concealed mystery. The young William Beckford recorded a visit to the Ducal Palace in the 1780s in which he was fascinated by the stone faces which he remembered as covering the walls.[10] Beckford's vision of the mysterious structures of the city was conditioned by his familiarity with the work of Piranesi. Piranesi, the son of a Venetian mason, trained in the city as an architect and engineer. Piranesi's widely disseminated engravings combined a mood of fear with ambiguous perspectives and indistinct spaces. Venice's romantic and hallucinatory nature was a key feature of its mediation in the nineteenth century. For Byron it was an occupied and enslaved place – a shadow and a ruin of its former glory; for Bonington it was picturesque and exotic. Turner saw it as a city uniquely merged with Nature. In the Romantic Period, Venice was regarded as a curiosity and an allegory. Ruskin provided a more historically and empirically detailed view which conceived of the city as an embodiment of natural laws containing fractal evidence of a lost harmony. Proust in his preface to a translation of Ruskin's 'Sesame and Lilies' saw San Marco as an exposition palace, interpreting Venice in the light of the latest forms of Parisian spectacle.

In the latter part of the nineteenth century a number of developments in transportation and organisation opened up Venice to more tourists. In 1846 a viaduct was built which enabled road traffic to reach the island. In 1857 the railway reached the historic centre with a station on the Grand Canal. In 1867 the first Cook's tour followed closely on the departure of the Austrian administration and a consequent weakening of the local economy. In 1871 the Mount Cenis tunnel was opened, making Italy more accessible to northern Europe. In the 1880s came the first 'vaporetti', reducing the cost of local transport. At the same time the Lido began to be developed as a tourist zone, significantly marked by the construction of the first great luxury hotel – 'The Excelsior' in 1898. By 1900, Venice had a population of 150,000 and three kilometres of docks. Factories on the island produced glass, tobacco, wood, leather, engineering products and cotton goods, and the tourist industry was well established.

At around the time of the Great War the areas around the lagoon began to be industrialised and there was a great deal of residential and industrial construction. The area of Santa Elena was added and reconstructions and additions were made to the historic centre. In the fascist period Santa Marta and the road bridge to Piazzale Roma were built. With an increasing concern for the maintenance of the commercial viability and prestige of Venice the Film Festival was inaugurated and the Carnevale was revived.

The traditional Christian festival of Carnival is associated with the beginning of the holiest season of the year with Easter Sunday as its most significant rite. It often coincided with Shrove Tuesday, a festivity which involved eating meat and rich foods which were to be renounced for Lent. As an event preceding the extended period of mourning at Easter and Holy Week, Carnival often took the form of a period of transgression. Bakhtin's[11] work has focused on the overturning of hierarchies through a system of manipulated signifiers. This manic festivity of the assumption of stolen identities found a particularly acute expression in the masked participants in the Venetian Carnevale where masking was overdetermined by a mythos of mystery and deception.

In the Carnevale the personae that are used as disguises in the contemporary festival are borrowed from the *Commedia dell'Arte* theatre, but there is a characteristic reduction to a cloak and a dark-coloured domino mask which conceals and highlights the eyes. The costume recapitulates the Venetian history of spying, but transforms the economic and political motives into a game of concealment, seduction and spectatorship. The Carnevale also rehearses and reconciles extremes signifying both the impassive rictus and the all-seeing capacity of the secret agent. During the period of the Republic there was a particular significance in the misuse of official ritual spaces. In a tourist culture the Carnevale increasingly is the lie that tells the truth about a city given over to recreation. It is significant that the souvenir shops which sell countless masks for tourists have increasingly taken the place of small shops serving the local community. In the eighteenth century the festivities could last for months, starting as early as 26 December. Revived under fascism they were restricted to a week, and revived again in 1979 Carnevale was more fully integrated into the tourist season.

The Western tradition of masks is derived from the theatre of Ancient Greece where the mask was used by actors to amplify the sound of the speaker's voice. From this practice is derived the word 'person': '*per sona*', the sound travelling through. The fascinating dialectic in the concept of persona was born of the alienation of the self behind the assumed identity of the theatrical character and its mask. In psychoanalytic terms this parallels the alienation of the self in the mirror at the moment at which an image of a unified self, or persona, is forged from the ego's attempt to merge with its ego ideal. In Lacanian terms, at the moment when there is a jubilant assumption of identity, there is a simultaneous ineradicable splitting with the psyche which motivates all subsequent attempts to consolidate it. In the Venice of the imaginary – the mask and the façade are founded on an unstable and dynamic elements – they function as emblematic appearances contributing to the mysteries of deception and ambivalence.

Venice's 'reality' has frequently been perceived as paradoxical and interstitial. Simmel commented on the city's lack of belonging to land or water, and other writers have referred to its illusory quality. Ruskin commented on the interchangeability of the city and its shadow, and James Morris evoked the city in terms of its illusory reflections. Venice has also been represented, more menacingly, as a maze or trap. Baudrillard among others has suggested that the configuration often leads to confrontations with others and the self. At least two artistic projects have exploited the complexity and circularity of Venice's routes. Ralph Rumney used it as the basis for a supposedly psychogeographic derive in 1957, commenting on the resulting photomontage:

> It is our thesis that cities should embody a built in play factor.
> We are studying here a play–environment relationship.[12]

Some years later Baudrillard commented on the 'assisted *dérive*'[13] of Sophie Calle (see also Chapter 3) which explored the effects of walking and following in Venice – that the city is effectively a closed circuit with no side exits.

Venice is 'dreamlike' partly because of the extraordinary concentration of urban texture. The retention of a medieval street pattern in conjunction with wide ceremonial piazza creates intense spatial contradictions. There are points of intersection which bring together strangely discrepant effects of light and shade, cramped spaces and open vistas. Venice has few 'transitional' spaces – and is marked by sudden juxtapositions. Freud's theory of 'condensation', first developed in *The Interpretation of Dreams* in 1900 describes how one idea stands at the point of intersection of several associative chains. Negotiating Venice produces analagous effects of combination and disruption. The '*capriccio*' – a genre of paintings which montages real and imaginary buildings – is a Venetian genre and it has become a frequently used representational form in the imagery of modern tourism. The editing out of transitional spaces contributes to the sense of unreal and dreamlike 'access' in a way that provides a similarly dense and arbitrary landscape to those experienced in dreams. This experiential richness which Modernism sought to consign to the disordered past is now conceived of as an essential aspect of urbanism.

Adrian Stokes was particularly fascinated by the ways in which the spatial illogic of Venice prompted reveries and associative deleria:

> Alive with trompe l'oeil deceits of perspective, odd foreshortenings, distortions and hallucinations.[14]

Stokes commented on the appearance of inversion produced by reflections seen in canals and the strange effects produced on buildings on occasions when the sea appeared lighter than the sky. He also noted that perceived inversion was an effect of an architectural style which featured unusually heavy bases and columns which do not express the carrying of weight. His reflections on Venice were characteristic of a sensibility which was able to translate the bad objects of decay, over-civilisation and excess into a fascination with surface and artifice. The enduring legacy of Venice is the plenitude of meanings it can generate. It has given birth to dozens of simulacra – various 'Venices of ... the north, the east, the west' – perhaps the most ambitious was recently constructed in the desert city of Las Vegas.

The tourist experience and the reconfiguring of cities to provide a meaningful pattern of sites – what John Urry has described as 'tourist geometry' – emphasise mobility and authorised points of view. Venice offers a particular kind of tourist experience. The population of the city has now been reduced to an estimated 75,000 and there are over 9,000,000 visitors a year.

In many respects, as the city becomes more disposed to tourism, it also becomes more inscrutable. It has been subject to similar kinds of virtualisation as other cities have undergone in recent years. Many of its palazzi, factories and warehouses are now used for purposes different from those originally intended – mostly to serve the trade in cultural tourism – as galleries, museums, offices and small workshops. One of the consequences of these adaptations is to disrupt and make strange the form/function and fitness relationships on which traditional uses and Modernist aspirations were, in their different ways, reliant.

Venice is often presented in tourist literature as a case of arrested development – a city at the end of its history – a city which has never completely separated itself from its origins in nature and is subject to the return of natural forces long repressed and resisted. To the Futurists, Venice was the most aggravated example of the museumisation of Italy – the antithesis of Modernism, over-refined, encrusted with ornaments and feminised by its association with serenity, deliquescence and passivity. For them the associations with death and impotence were an insult to their masculine and vital aspirations for Italian art and culture.

Deeply rooted in the past, Venice presented itself to the twentieth century as a palimpsest of memories and looted fragments. Like all memorials and ruins it provoked its visitors into speculating on origins and narratives. Each component of the densely packed urban milieu functions as a metaphor and mnemonic to produce phantom versions of the city – a phenomenon intensively explored by Italo Calvino in *Invisible Cities*.[15]

Venice's reputation for ritual and civic festivities has provided a number of inspirational prompts for tourism and regeneration. In the early years of Docklands a poster was displayed throughout London with the copy: 'Looks like Venice. Works like New York' – an appealing combination of the most magical and dynamic urban metaphors. Venetian building and planning had a particular relation to ritual needs and have enabled historic Venice to function as a model for postmodern urbanism. David Harvey made a claim for re-conceiving the city less in terms of system, function or organism and more in the form of celebration:

the organisation of spectacle and theatricality – achieved though an eclectic mixture of style, historical quotation, ornamentation and diversification of services.[16]

Venice has been invoked as a model particularly for regenerations of docklands and riversides. Spurred by a comparison of Manhattan waterfronts, Manfredo Tafuri claimed New York as 'an allegory of the Venice of modern times',[17] drawing on Nietzsche's claim that the city of lagoons is a foretaste of the city of the future 'as a system of solitudes' – a place where loss of identity is institutionalised:

> wherein the maximum formalism of its structures gives rise to a code of behaviour dominated by 'vanity' and 'comedy'.

Venice has become a complex and contradictory cultural icon capable of many interpretations. Its mystery lies largely in its extravagance, its fragility and endurance. In particular it is the model of city as artifice and has provoked many centuries in which the city has appeared as a model for contemplating the highly overdetermined relation between substance and appearance. Masquerade has been a particularly durable metaphor for describing the paradoxes involved. In architectural terms the tensions between form and structure, function and spectacle, embodied in the Venetian fabric, have generated a series of models for contemporary practice. As a city of lost integrity or a pioneering example of virtuality, Venice is still a quarry for the architectural imagination.

Notes

1 As Mike Davis has demonstrated in *Ecology of Fear: Los Angeles and the Imagination of Disaster*, London: Picador/Macmillan, 1998. Michael Sorkin's deliberations on Los Angeles in the essay: 'Explaining Los Angeles', in M. Sorkin, *Exquisite Corpe*, Cambridge, MA: MIT Press, 1991, pp. 48–. Sorkin makes the claim that: 'LA is probably the most mediated town in America, nearly unviewable save through the fictive scrim of its mythologizers.'
2 Simon Sadler's phrase in Simon Sadler, *The Situationist City*, Cambridge, MA: MIT Press, 1998, p. 139.
3 Martin Pawley has discussed this phenomenon as 'stealth building' in his book *Terminal Architecture*, Reaktion Books: London, 1998, pp. 135–7.
4 Yi-Fu Tuan, *Passing Strange and Wonderful: Aesthetics, Nature and Culture*, New York: Kodansha Globe, 1995, p. 193.
5 Adrian Stokes, *Venice: An Aspect of Art*, London: Faber, 1945, p. 16.
6 Stokes, *Venice: An Aspect of Art*, p. 7.
7 A. Hyatt -Williams, *Cruelty, Violence and Murder*, London: Karnak Books, 1998, p. 156.
8 The Venetian–British analogies are discussed at length in John Pemble, *Venice Rediscovered*, Oxford: Oxford University Press, 1995, pp. 98–109.
9 Manuel de Landa has pointed to another order of similarity between Venice and London – both functioning at different times, in the fourteenth and nineteenth centuries respectively, as 'gateway cities' which functioned at the core of the

European trade network. See Manuel de Landa, *A Thousand Years of Non Linear History*, New York: Zone Books, 1997, pp. 44–5.

10 Quoted in Richard Davenport-Hines, *Gothic: Four Hundred Years of Excess, Horror, Evil and Ruin*, London: Fourth Estate, 1998, pp. 203–4.

11 Mikhail Bakhtin, *Rabelais and his World*, Bloomington, IN: Indiana University Press, 1984 [1965].

12 Ralph Rumney, 'Psychogeographic Maps of Venice', in *An endless adventure... an endless passion ... an endless banquet: A Situationist Scrapbook*, ed. Iwona Blazwick, London and New York: ICA/Verso, 1989, pp. 45–9.

13 '*Derive*: experimental behavioural mode, linked directly to the conditions of urban society: technique for passing rapidly through varied environments. Also used, more specifically to denote a period of continuous practice of this research', is the definitioin supplied in Alan Woods, *The Map is Not the Territory*, Manchester: Manchester University Press, 2000.

14 Stokes, *Venice: An Aspect of Art*, p. 4.

15 Italo Calvino, *Invisible Cities*, trans. William Weaver, London: Vintage, 1997.

16 David Harvey, *The Condition of Post modernity*, Oxford: Blackwell, 1989, p. 93.

17 Manfredo Tafuri, *The Sphere and the Labyrinth*, Cambridge, MA: MIT Press, 1987, p. 291.

12 Benjamin's Moscow, Baudrillard's America[1]

Graeme Gilloch

My presentation will be devoid of all theory. In this fashion I hope to succeed in allowing the 'creatural' to speak for itself: inasmuch as I have succeeded in seizing and rendering this very new and disorienting language that echoes loudly through the resounding mask of an environment that has been totally transformed. I want to write a description of Moscow at the present moment in which 'all factuality is already theory' and which would thereby refrain from any deductive abstraction, from any prognostication, and even within certain limits, from any judgement.

(MD, p. 132)

This intriguing claim by Walter Benjamin is found in a letter to Martin Buber of 23 February 1927, a letter written a few weeks after Benjamin's return to Berlin following a two-month sojourn in the new Soviet capital and just prior to the completion of an essay on the city for Buber's journal, simply to be entitled 'Moscow'. As a statement of intent, I suggest that this passage provides the key to understanding the numerous and impressionistic city portraits composed in the mid to late 1920s, fragments which Benjamin termed *Denkbilder* ('thought-images').[2]

The *Denkbilder* are imagistic miniatures which seek to pioneer new modes of urban representation, ones which capture the fluid and fleeting character of metropolitan existence. The cityscape is not naively perused by the 'banal tourist' (OWS, p. 168) or the complacent, distracted *flâneur*. Rather, it is discerned and dissected by the critical and keen eye of the physiognomist *en passant*, so that it may subsequently be represented with the precision and plenitude of an urban photograph or film.[3] Benjamin seeks a tactile proximity with the urban environment. In a letter to Scholem from Rome/Florence (12 October–5 November 1924), he writes:

my inductive way of getting to know the topography of different places and seeking out every great structure in its own labyrinthine environment of banal, beautiful or wretched houses, takes up too much time and thus prevents me from actually studying the relevant books. Since I must dispense with that, I am left only with impressions of the architecture. But

I do come away with an excellent image of the topography of these places. The first and most important thing you have to do is feel your way through a city so that you can return to it with complete assurance.

(COR, p. 254)

Benjamin's city portraits are concerned with identifying and articulating the structuring principles of the cityscape as they manifest themselves in their particularity and concreteness within mundane urban life. The city is to be read and represented through the most specific and precise rendering of its minutiae: the trivial, the accidental, the neglected.

This attention to the micrological manifestations and traces of the everyday is fundamental. For Benjamin, abstraction is to be avoided at all costs. The theoretical grounding of the *Denkbilder* is paradoxically and precisely the abstention from theory, or a wilful resolution and dissolution of theory. Intrusive interpretation and overarching analysis – these are to be eschewed in favour of an approach which apparently permits the actual material 'to speak for itself'. The task of the writer is, through the selection and arrangement of elements, to 'show [*zeigen*]' (ARC, p. 460). Composed of a plethora of carefully gathered and juxtaposed concrete particulars, monadological fragments, the *Denkbilder* are kaleidoscopic representations, miniature mosaics, urban montages.[4] 'All factuality is already theory' – this then is not to be understood as the simplistic affirmation of a naive positivism, a 'wide-eyed presentation of mere facts' (Adorno in AP, p. 129) rendering the world 'just as it is', but as the principle guiding a technique of fragmentary construction and profane illumination.

Moscow poses a particular dilemma for Benjamin in this respect. On the one hand, he recognises that: 'Only he who, by decision, has made his dialectical peace with the world can grasp the concrete. But someone who wishes to decide "on the basis of facts" will find no basis in the facts' (OWS, p. 177). Benjamin admits wryly: 'the only real guarantee of a correct understanding is to have chosen your position before you come. In Russia, above all you can only see if you have already decided' (OWS, p. 177). On the other hand, such 'decisionism' also risks 'facile theorizing' (MD, p. 114). Benjamin remains critical of the preconceptions and prejudices which blind visiting European 'intellectuals' to the full 'scope of the Russian experience' (MD, p. 114). He notes: 'When one penetrates more deeply into the Russian situation, one no longer feels oneself immediately driven to the abstractions that so effortlessly come to the European's mind' (MD, p. 114). Indeed for Benjamin, the principal significance and 'most indisputable consequence' (MD, p. 114) of visiting Moscow lies not in superficial pronouncements on the Soviet system, but precisely in what one discovers about European culture and the European intellect. Benjamin writes:

However little one might still know of Russia, one learns to observe and judge Europe with a conscious awareness of what is taking place in Russia.

> This is the first thing that is incumbent on the attentive European in Russia. It is moreover precisely for this reason that a stay in Russia is so exact a touchstone for the foreign visitor. It obliges everybody to choose and carefully define his point of view.
>
> (OWS, p. 177)

Hence, the 'attentive European' refrains 'from any deductive abstraction, from any prognostication' and seeks instead to grasp the specificity and monadological significance of the quotidian fragments of Muscovite existence. Indeed, for Benjamin this concern with concretion and 'immediacy' has a particular resonance in Moscow, for it is precisely the diminution of distance, the promise of a new proximity and tactility, the realisation of revolutionary theory in the material domain, which are the hallmarks of experience in the new Russia.

The *leitmotifs* of his Moscow *Denkbild* are the notions of proximity and tactility. 'Moscow' registers the distinctive challenges and experiences encountered by the stranger who wishes to explore a city in perpetual flux and constant mobilisation, a city attuned to discordant and disconcerting rhythms. The newcomer to Moscow must abandon all lofty pretensions and immerse himself in the cityscape and its milling crowds, must 'feel' his way through the urban environment. There is no space to do otherwise. Benjamin notes that one cannot adopt the leisurely role of a 'grand seigneur promenading on the terrace of his mansion' (OWS, p. 178). Instead, to make progress along the overcrowded and peculiarly narrow pavements the pedestrian must devise a 'strategy of shoving and weaving', a distinctive 'loitering, serpentine gait' (OWS, p. 178). Moreover, one must master again 'the technique of achieving locomotion' (OWS, p. 178) since on the 'thick sheet ice of the streets walking has to be relearned' (OWS, p. 179).[5] Moscow is explored not in the guise of the indolent, independent *flâneur*, but from an unstable vantage point akin to that of the tottering child.

In the sleigh, too, the principal mode of transport of the city, Benjamin notes that 'You feel like a child gliding through the house on its little chair' (OWS, p. 191). This also involves a particular sense of intimacy:

> The passenger is not enthroned high up; he looks out on the same level as everyone else and brushes the passers-by with his sleeve. Even this is an incomparable experience for the sense of touch. Where Europeans, on their rapid journeys, enjoy superiority, dominance over the masses, the Muscovite in the little sleigh is closely mingled with people and things. No condescending gaze: a tender, swift brushing along stones, people and horses.
>
> (OWS, p. 191)

One is not *reduced* to being a child. Rather, for Benjamin, the child has a privileged proximity to, and a special tactile appreciation of, the urban setting. In the eyes of the child, the cityscape is subject to a process of 'enlargement'.

Moreover, to become a child in the city is to see it 'at first sight', with a gaze unencumbered by the tedium of familiarity and habit, with a heightened receptivity and acuity. In Moscow: 'The instant one arrives, the childhood stage begins' (OWS, p. 179). Nothing could be more precarious, nothing more precious.

It is, however, neither the ungainly pedestrian nor the gliding sleigh but rather the streetcar which provides Benjamin with the definitive monadological fragment in 'Moscow'.[6] Like walking, this, too, is 'a tactical experience' for the newcomer, a close encounter with the multitude. Boarding involves 'A tenacious barging and shoving', until the vehicle is 'overloaded to the point of bursting' (OWS, p. 190). It is an unpredictable journey. Unable to see through the windows of the tram, and unable to get out in any event because of the 'human wedge' (OWS, p. 191) barring the exit, one awaits a suitable moment to alight with the mass of fellow passengers, wherever that happens to be. Providing for collective, rather than individual, destinations, the streetcar ride is a 'mass phenomenon' (OWS, p. 191) in which one is even more 'closely mingled with people and things', in which individual solitude and self-determination are impossible.

To 'feel' one's way through a city – such navigation requires and valorises a familiarity and reciprocity with its jostling crowds, a proximity to its profusion of objects, an expectancy and excitement in its encounters and surprises. This sensitivity to, and privileging of, such public urban experiences may be seen as the antithesis of the haughty, insular bourgeois subject who, maintaining distance and shunning contact, hurries joylessly past. Here Moscow becomes the 'touchstone' by which the European, and in particular the German, cultural condition is illuminated.[7] Benjamin opens his Moscow *Denkbild* with the bold assertion: 'More quickly than Moscow, one gets to know Berlin through Moscow' (OWS, p. 177). Back in his native city, he notes: 'For someone who has arrived from Moscow, Berlin is a dead city. The people on the street seem desperately isolated, each one at a great distance from the next, alone in the midst of a broad stretch of street' (MD, pp. 113–14). In comparison to Moscow, 'Berlin is a deserted city' (OWS, p. 178), awash with 'unspeakable' (OWS, p. 178) luxury, a cityscape where the streets 'are like a freshly swept, empty racecourse on which a field of six-day cyclists hastens comfortlessly on' (OWS, p. 178). In Berlin, one no longer enjoys being 'closely mingled with people and things', but rather ominously senses that the 'Warmth is ebbing from things. The objects of daily use gently but insistently repel us' (OWS, p. 58).

Moreover, it is not only the Muscovite street and streetcar that are sites of enforced proximity: the former private and exclusive interior spaces of the city are also subject to the population of space and diminution of distance. 'Bolshevism has abolished private life', Benjamin declares with relief: 'Apartments that earlier accommodated single families in their five to eight rooms now often lodge eight' (OWS, p. 187). The bourgeois interior has been transformed into an 'army camp' in which 'each citizen is entitled by law to only thirteen square metres of living space' (OWS, p. 188). All comfort, all stifling 'cosiness' (OWS, p. 188) has been eradicated.

The hallowed resting places of bourgeois culture also have new occupants. Benjamin observes:

> nothing is more pleasantly surprising on a visit to Moscow's museums than to see how, singly or in groups, sometimes around a guide, children and workers move easily through these rooms. Nothing is to be seen of the forlornness of the few proletarians who dare to show themselves to the other visitors in our museums. In Russia the proletariat has really begun to take possession of bourgeois culture, whereas on such occasions in our own country they have the appearance of planning a burglary.
>
> (OWS, p. 183)

In the Tretiakov Gallery, Benjamin notes:

> Here the proletarian finds subjects from the history of his movement ... And the fact that such scenes are still painted entirely in the spirit of bourgeois art not only does no harm – it actually brings them closer to the public.
>
> (OWS, p. 184)

In the museum and gallery the masses have begun to appropriate works of art and thereby create a new intimacy with them. The work of art is no longer an object of solitary bourgeois contemplation but rather a didactic instrument and collective resource for 'the child or the proletarian who is educating himself' (OWS, p. 184). Painting in the 'bourgeois spirit' is transformed by reception in proletarian practice. Indeed, if, as Benjamin suggests in his 1925/6 fragment 'Traumkitsch', 'What we used to call art, begins at a distance of two metres away from the body' (SW2, p 4), then Muscovite proximity promises, if not the abolition of art, then certainly its radical reconceptualisation.[8]

For Benjamin, this transformation of the cultural sphere through proximity is decisive. In Moscow, there is no longer any space for the bourgeois subject, no longer any reverential distance in which bourgeois culture can weave its spell. While one witnesses the bourgeoisie being 'ground to pieces by the struggle between labour and capital' (OWS, p. 198) in the collapsing economies of Europe, in the Soviet capital the eradication of the bourgeois is already complete. 'In this,' Benjamin notes, 'Russia is ahead of Western development – but not as far ahead as is believed' (OWS, p. 198). As the site of a 'world-historical experiment' (OWS, p. 190), Moscow is characterised by a distinctively 'radical', indeed 'eccentric', modernity: it constitutes the as yet unfinished form of the 'future catastrophe' of the bourgeois subject.

Most importantly for Benjamin, in Moscow there is no longer any room for manoeuvre for the European bourgeois intellectual: with the demise of the bourgeois class, 'the free-lance writer must also disappear' (OWS, p. 198). This is fundamental for it is precisely the fate of the intellectual, the critic, which preoccupies Benjamin in 'Moscow'. When workers and children assume the role once enjoyed by the critic, when the position of the expert cultural intermediary is compressed by the diminution of distance, what becomes of the critic? For Benjamin, the redundant intellectual is re-functioned as 'a functionary, working in departments of censorship, justice, finance, and, if he survives, participating in work' (OWS pp. 198–9). The intellectual becomes a worker. This is a fitting fate. The 'mental means of production' and the 'material means' both fall under public ownership and are re-integrated.[9] The Soviet system no longer requires revolutionary theories and concepts, but tangible works. Theoreticians must become technicians. Benjamin writes:

> Now it is made clear to every Communist that the revolutionary work of the hour is not conflict, not civil war, but canal construction, electrification, and factory. The revolutionary nature of technology is emphasised ever more clearly.
>
> (OWS, p. 207)[10]

In constructing the Soviet system, achieving utopia, revolutionary ideas are to be given substance, to be realised through material practice. In Moscow, all theory must become factuality.

'Moscow' attests to the fatal future awaiting the *homme des lettres*. Benjamin's response to this is one of profound and typical ambivalence. On the one hand, the bankruptcy and despicable sham of the supposedly 'independent' European intellectual, in reality the creature of the moribund bourgeoisie, are abundantly clear to him.[11] For Benjamin, the 'fat books' (OWS, p. 63) spawned by the academy with their affected 'scholarly' stance' (COR, p. 281) have long relinquished any claim to intellectual integrity and insight.[12] In such circumstances, the immediate abolition of the European 'intellectual', far from being a source of regret, constitutes an overdue and merciful release.[13]

Hence, Benjamin notes enthusiastically: 'the entire scheme of existence of the western European intelligentsia is utterly impoverished in comparison to the countless constellations that offer themselves to an individual here in the space of a month' (MD, p. 72). Indeed, this is why the experience of Moscow is so 'incommensurable' (MD, p. 134)[14] for Benjamin, this is what makes the 'facile theorizing' of the European 'intellectual' so fatuous and contemptible, this is why it is incumbent on the 'attentive' visitor to 'refrain from any deductive abstraction, from any prognostication and even within certain limits, from any judgement'.[15] It is only in 'particularly small and disparate notes' (MD, p. 129) that one can presume 'to write something "comprehensive" about Moscow' (MD, p. 129). Hence, it is here that the fragmentary *Denkbild* form reveals itself as the only legitimate mode of discourse for the genuine contemporary thinker.

On the other hand, the role of the functionary, notwithstanding the promise of such 'countless constellations', still proves less enticing than that of the intellectual 'trail-blazer' (MD, p. 73), however 'impoverished'. Benjamin finds

Moscow educative, but not seductive. It is a 'touchstone' for the 'intelligent European', not a lodestone. On 1 February 1927, Benjamin bid a final farewell to Moscow and, having failed to make his 'dialectical peace with the world', returned to the 'Princely solitude, princely desolation' (OWS, p. 178) of the not-so-wild W.W. of Berlin.[16]

It is not as an intellectual functionary of the collective but rather as the self-styled 'Aeronautic missionary of the silent majorities' (A, p. 14) that Jean Baudrillard touches down in America. At first sight, a comparison between Benjamin's 1927 essay on Moscow and Baudrillard's 1986 travelogue of the United States seems an unpromising if not wholly improbable enterprise. However, there are a number of affinities and parallels which make such an exercise more than a perverse provocation: both writers understand their chosen destinations as the touchstones of contemporary and future cultural transformation, and cast a critical retrospective glance at the retarded cultural and intellectual condition of Europe;[17] both deploy a new vocabulary and conceptual repertoire which is more attuned to, and justified by, the radical otherness and exigencies of these disorienting new scenarios; both writers perceive themselves as anachronistic figures, as intellectuals in environments where such a role is already thoroughly obsolete; in both, this disconcerting recognition evokes a mixture of ironic delight and melancholic disquiet.

Whereas for Benjamin, the 'new Russia' is a precarious 'world-historical experiment',[18] for Baudrillard, America is, and has always been, nothing other than the fully formed prototypical community of the future, a 'utopia achieved' (A, p. 77).[19] In this highly ironic expression, Baudrillard claims that from the outset America, as a model society purpose-built according to eighteenth-century radical European political ideals, regarded itself as the immanent realisation of such utopian aspirations. Baudrillard states wryly that America is:

> built on the idea that it is the realisation of everything the others have dreamt of – justice, plenty, rule of law, wealth, freedom: it knows this, it believes in it, and in the end, the others have come to believe in it too.
>
> (A, p. 77)[20]

Founded as a utopian and modern order in opposition to the moribund and decadent cultures of Europe, America was and remains the materialisation of European hopes wholly beyond both the realities and the practical capacities of the Old World.[21] In America, utopia is an immanent principle rather than a transcendent goal. Americans prove themselves to be pragmatic utopians; we Europeans, by contrast:

> remain nostalgic utopians, agonizing over our ideals, but baulking ultimately at their realization, professing that everything is possible, but never that everything has been achieved. Yet that is what America asserts. Our problem is that our old goals – revolution, progress, freedom – will have evaporated before they were achieved, before they became reality. Hence

our melancholy ... We live in negativity and contradiction; they live in paradox (for a realized utopia is a paradox).

(A, pp. 78–9)

While this notion of America as a 'utopia achieved' is undoubtedly to be understood as a playful provocation (and one which fails to withstand serious scholarly scrutiny), for Baudrillard it is a necessary fiction to understand a culture which is itself only intelligible as 'fiction'.[22] America as a 'utopia achieved' underpins the two apparently contradictory key themes of his study: first, America as the original and only genuine site of modernity (America as a simulation, as the future); and, second, America as a non-culture of naive factuality and radical superficiality (America as a 'primitive' society, as a desert).[23] If, for Benjamin, Moscow is distinguished by the bizarre juxtaposition of the ideologically and culturally advanced Bolshevik and the stubbornly traditional 'Asiatic' modes of existence, an incongruity which generates 'an experience which, by Western standards, I discovered to be far more incommensurable than I had expected' (MD, p. 134), so, similarly, for Baudrillard the most modern social form and a wholly 'primitive' culture combine to create an incommensurable American condition which thoroughly exceeds and eludes the tired theoretical constructions of European social thought. The paradoxes of America are incomprehensible in terms of European 'negativity and contradiction', exposing thereby the limits of such thinking, adding to 'our melancholy'.

Baudrillard contends that, while based on a European imaginary, the 'utopia achieved' of America constituted the most decisive and radical break from the oppressive burdens of European history and tradition. He notes:

Octavio Paz is right when he argues that America was created in the hope of escaping from history, of building a utopia sheltered from history, and it has in part succeeded in that project, a project it is still pursuing today.

(A, p. 80)

Abandoning the venerable origins and painful historical progress of the Old World, America was brought into being as an original and already fully evolved model, not a reflection of Europe, but a simulation of its most radical antithesis, an 'artificial' paradise (A, p. 8).[24] This revolutionary moment of historical rupture is fundamental for Baudrillard: it is what makes America modern. He boldly asserts: 'it is, therefore, in America and nowhere else that modernity is original. We can only imitate it without being able to challenge it on its own home territory' (A, p. 81).

The experience of this radical disjuncture is what irrevocably separates modern America from contemporary, but always antiquated, Europe. Baudrillard insists:

The confrontation between America and Europe reveals not so much a *rapprochement* as a distortion, an unbridgeable rift. There isn't just a gap between us, but a whole chasm of modernity. You are born modern, you do not become so. And we have never become so. What strikes you immediately in Paris is that you are in the nineteenth century. Coming from Los Angeles you land back in the 1800s.

(A, p. 73)

More quickly than America, one gets to know Paris through America.[25]

In a witty cinematic metaphor Baudrillard notes: 'America is the original version of modernity. We are the dubbed or subtitled version' (A, p. 76). Europe is revealed as a pale imitation, a second-hand, indeed second-rate, version of American modernity. Here we see Baudrillard's notion of the precession of simulacra writ large on an international scale – the model/simulation (America) now takes precedence over and is superior to that from which it was formerly derived (Europe). Once a simulation of what a modern Europe might conceivably be, America, now the 'eccentric' (A, p. 81) centre of the world, is the model which an unmodern Europe will one day vainly seek to mimic. Baudrillard writes:

We shall never catch them up, and we shall never have their candour. We merely imitate them, parody them with a 50 year time lag, and we are not even successful at that. We do not have the spirit or the audacity for what might be called the zero degree of culture, the power of (un)culture.

(A, p. 78)

Condemned to copying the original and inherent modernity of America, 'We shall,' Baudrillard notes, '... never be modern in the proper sense of the term' (A, p. 81).

As the most modern society, America is also culturally the most 'primitive', that is, the most naive. Baudrillard writes:

Americans believe in facts, but not in facticity.[26] They do not know that facts are factitious, as their name suggests. It is in this belief in facts, in the total credibility of what is done or seen, in this pragmatic evidence of things, and an accompanying contempt for what may be called the play of appearances ... that the Americans are a true utopian society, in their religion of the *fait accompli*, in the naivety of their deductions, in their ignorance of the evil genius of things. You have to be utopian to think that in a human order, of whatever nature, things can be as simple as that.

(A, p. 85)

As a 'utopia achieved' America has never been concerned with theoretical speculation and analysis, but only with 'realizing concepts and materializing ideas' (A, p. 84).[27] This is what makes them modern, this is what makes them 'primitive'. In America, all theory is already factuality, all factuality already banality.[28] For Baudrillard: 'This is the land of the "just as it is"' (A, p. 28). In America 'there is no dissidence, no suspicion' (A, p. 85), only the blithe acceptance of the surface manifestation. There is an innocent faith that things are what they seem, no sense of the cunning duplicity of signs and objects.[29] Signs exhaust themselves in simple appearance, contain no secret meaning, indeed, no meaning at all. Baudrillard's comments on the utterly sincere, utterly insincere American smile are exemplary:

> Smile and others will smile back. Smile to show how transparent, how candid you are. Smile if you have nothing to say. Most of all, do not hide the fact you have nothing to say nor your total indifference to others. Let this emptiness, this profound indifference shine out spontaneously in your smile. Give your emptiness and indifference to others, light up your face with the zero degree of joy and pleasure, smile smile smile … Americans may have no identity, but they do have wonderful teeth … Reagan's credibility is exactly equal to his transparency and the nullity of his smile.
>
> (A, p. 34)[30]

Nothing is hidden, everything is already visible, crudely on display. America is a land of the perfectly superficial and the wholly transparent, of an 'obesity, saturation and overabundance' (A, p. 39) of signs and 'anorexic' absence of sense (A, p. 39), of a wanton cultural nullity and a brazenly paraded cultural nudity.[31] Nothing is left to the imagination. American (un)culture is obscene. Baudrillard notes:

> A miracle of obscenity that is genuinely American: a miracle of total availability, of the transparency of all functions in space, though this nonetheless remains unfathomable in its vastness and can only be exorcised by speed.
>
> (A, p. 8)

If, for Benjamin, the hallmarks of Moscow culture are the revolutionary diminution of distance and the creation of a new proximity, the distinctiveness of American (un)culture for Baudrillard lies precisely in the radical extension of distance and the endless expansion of space as pure surface, pure horizontality.[32] This is a culture to be crossed at speed, not contemplated at length. Baudrillard writes:

> I went in search of astral America, not social and cultural America, but the America of the empty absolute freedom of freeways, not the deep America of mores and mentalities, but the America of desert speed, of motels and mineral surfaces. I looked for it in the speed of the screenplay, in the indifferent reflex of television, in the film of days and nights projected across an empty space, the marvellous affectless succession of signs, images, faces and ritual acts on the road.
>
> (A, p. 5)

The central motif here is that of the desert. Baudrillard writes:

> The inhumanity of our ulterior, asocial, superficial world immediately finds
> its aesthetic form here, its ecstatic form. For the desert is simply that: an
> ecstatic critique of culture, an ecstatic form of disappearance.
>
> (A, p. 5)[33]

America is characterised by a 'radical absence of culture' (A, p. 86) in the
European sense, only banality, aridity, the impenetrability and transparency of crystalline surfaces.[34] In 'the deserts of meaninglessness' (A, p. 8) one finds only the
skeletal remains of culture, the bleached bones of the social, the 'anorexic ruins' of
modernity. 'The desert is everywhere, preserving insignificance' (A, p. 8).

Desertification, depthlessness[35] and disappearance – these characteristics
of American culture finds fullest expression in Baudrillard's description of the
horizontal sprawl of Los Angeles as 'an inhabited fragment of the desert' (A,
p. 53):

> No elevator or subway in Los Angeles. No verticality or underground, no
> intimacy or collectivity, no streets or facades, no centre or monuments: a
> fantastical space, a spectral and discontinuous succession of all the various
> functions, of all signs with no hierarchical ordering – an extravaganza of
> indifference, extravaganza of undifferentiated surfaces – the power of
> pure open space, the kind you find in deserts. The power of the desert
> form: it is the erasure of traces in the desert, of the signified of signs in
> the cities, of any psychology in bodies. An animal and metaphysical fasci-
> nation – the direct fascination of space, the immanent fascination of
> dryness and sterility.
>
> (A, p. 125).

In the American cityscape, as in the desert, there is nothing left to be read,
nothing to be remembered, only a 'Triumph of forgetting over memory, an
uncultivated, amnesiac intoxication' (A, p. 6) as one speeds through it. We are
at the 'vanishing point' (A, p. 1) of culture, a vanishing not *of* distance, but *into*
the distance. Baudrillard writes:

> It is here, therefore, that we should look for the ideal type of the end of
> culture. It is the American way of life, which we think naive or culturally
> worthless, which will provide us with a complete graphic representation of
> the end of our values.
>
> (A, p. 98)

It is not only America's modernity which Europe will imitate 50 years hence,
but also its cultural 'primitiveness', its obesity, anorexia and obscenity.
Baudrillard notes: 'Deep down, the US ... is the only remaining primitive
society. The fascinating thing is to travel through it as though it were the primi-

tive society of the future' (A, p. 7). As the original modern (un)culture, the authentic form of the inauthentic, as 'utopia achieved', America is nothing other than 'the finished form of the future catastrophe of the social' (A, p. 5).

'What figure does the man of letters cut' (OWS, p. 197) here amid the 'aesthetics of disappearance'[36] and the disappearance of aesthetics? American culture eludes the American mind. Lacking any sense of the irony of appearances, beguiled by the evil of transparency, Americans perceive this cultural void unambiguously 'just as it is'. In the ultimate simulation society, they themselves are part of the simulation and, assuming it as their vantage point, fail to discern it. The 'primitive' American lacks the reflexivity to notice their own primitiveness. In a 'utopia achieved' everything is decided in advance – this guarantees that one does not see. Baudrillard states: 'The Americans for their part, have no sense of simulation. They are themselves simulation in its most developed state, but they have no language to describe it, since they themselves are the model' (A, pp. 28–9). In the eyes of the American, all simulation, all factitiousness is already factuality. Hence, Baudrillard writes:

> No one is capable of analysing it, least of all the American intellectuals shut away on their campuses, dramatically cut off from the fabulous concrete mythology developing all around them.
>
> (A, p. 23)[37]

In the cultural desert, the American scholar becomes an endangered species, artificially preserved in remote and rarefied reservations. Sufficient erudition is imported to ensure the indigenous species flourishes, but this cross-fertilisation unfortunately makes them even less fitted for the surrounding habitat. They have no contact with local flora and fauna in 'an environment that has been totally transformed'. Baudrillard observes that:

> the American intellectual cannot understand his own culture because he is locked into an intellectual ghetto. His defensive style is to mimic European culture which is why there is such a great divide between the American intellectual and American culture.
>
> (BL, p. 135)[38]

The American intellectual lives with borrowed ideas on borrowed time.

Hence, Baudrillard notes: 'It may be that the truth of America can only be seen by a European, since he alone will discover here the perfect simulacrum' (A, p. 28). However, the European scholar is also prone to a myopia produced by hopelessly unmodern, hopelessly outmoded expectations and ideas.[39] Baudrillard writes:

> searching for works of art or sophisticated entertainment here has always seemed tiresome and out of place to me. A mark of cultural ethnocentrism. If it is lack of culture that is original, then it is the lack of culture

one should embrace. If the term taste has any meaning, then it commands us not to export our aesthetic demands to places where they do not belong.

(A, p. 101)

European theories and concepts have no place in, and no purchase on, the 'ultramodern' (A, p. 70) American condition. The 'future catastrophe of the social' reveals the obsolescence of the central categories of cultural analysis. Sociology, as a mapping, a simulation of the social, is unmasked as a feeble imposition and aging impostor. In America, all theory is already factitiousness. Baudrillard states:

> it will be noticed retrospectively that the concepts 'class', 'social relations', 'power', 'status' – and 'social' itself – all those too explicit concepts which are the glory of the legitimate sciences, have also only ever been muddled notions themselves, but notions upon which agreement has nevertheless been reached for mysterious ends: those of preserving a certain code of analysis.

(SS, pp. 4–5)

The desert is no place (a utopia) for sociologists – they might recognise themselves in its fossilised forms.

Baudrillard observes: 'We philosophise on the end of lots of things but it is here that they actually come to an end' (A, p. 98). In the 'perfect simulacrum' the European intellectual discovers the image of their own end. America is their fatal future – 'The intellectual has no future' (BL, p. 155). This recognition prompts a mischievously ironic and ambivalent response from Baudrillard. He observes: 'America is powerful and original; America is violent and abominable. We should not seek to deny either of these aspects, nor reconcile them' (A, p. 88). On the one hand, Baudrillard shares 'our melancholy', if only because there is 'no charm, no seduction in all this' (A, p. 124),[40] no promise. Banality is boring. On the other hand, while:

> there is no seduction ... there is an absolute fascination – the fascination of the very disappearance of all aesthetic and critical forms ... The fascination of the desert: immobility without desire. Of Los Angeles: insane circulation without desire. The end of aesthetics.

(A, p. 124)

The inanity, the vacuity, the emptiness of American non-culture, serve as antidotes to the obsessive introspection and supercilious sophistication of Europe. As a simulation, America may inevitably be a site of pretence, but it is free from 'prejudice and pretentiousness' (A, p. 93). It is not their primitiveness but 'our affectation which is ridiculous' (A, p. 93), our 'analyses which seem vulgar' (A, p. 102) our 'cultural pathos' which is 'sickly' (A, p. 100). America is the touchstone for the contemporary intellectual and, Baudrillard declares, 'I shall never forgive anyone who passes a condescending or contemptuous judgement on America' (CM, p. 209).

For Baudrillard, 'the mystery of American reality exceeds our fictions and our interpretations' (A, p. 98). One must refrain from European judgements and pioneer new languages and modes of representation which do justice to the 'originality' of America:[41] that is, images which capture the purity of surface, the thrill of speed, the breathtaking banality of it all.[42] This is precisely Baudrillard's purpose. He writes:

> Where others spend their time in libraries, I spend mine in the deserts and on the roads. Where they draw their material from the history of ideas, I draw mine from the life of the streets, the beauty of nature. This country is naive, so you have to be naive. ... My hunting grounds are the deserts, the mountains, Los Angeles, the freeways, the Safeways, the ghost towns, or the downtowns, not lectures at the university.
>
> (A, p. 63)

For Baudrillard, 'astral America' is only comprehensible as fiction, as image,[43] on screen: in the cinematic film,[44] on the ubiquitous television, and, most importantly, on that other screen of moving images, the car windscreen. He states unequivocally: 'The point is not to write the sociology or psychology of the car, the point is to drive. That way you learn more about this society than all academia could ever tell you' (A, p. 54). Appropriately, it is the combination of freeway and film that provides the opening to, and metarepresentation for, Baudrillard's study:

> Snapshots aren't enough. We'd need the whole film of the trip in real time, including the unbearable heat and the music. We'd have to replay it all from end to end at home in a darkened room, rediscover the magic of the freeways and the distance and the ice-cold alcohol in the desert and the speed and live it all again on the video at home in real time, not simply for the pleasure of remembering[45] but because the fascination of senseless repetition is already present in the abstraction of the journey. The unfolding of the desert is infinitely close to the timelessness of film ...
>
> (A, p. 1)

'Moscow' is a transient 'thought-image'; America is a 'real-time' road-movie. One does not 'feel' one's way through America, one drives without destination.[46] One is no longer 'closely mingled with people and things', but on collision course for the vanishing point. Nevertheless, a shared sensibility is evident: the sensitivity to the blinding light and deceptive silence of landscapes and cityscapes;[47] the scrupulous attention to micrological and monadological (Baudrillard uses the term 'holographic')[48] detail; and the privileging of the fleeting and momentary glimpsed *en passant*.

Accordingly, for Baudrillard, as for Benjamin, it is only in a plethora of fragments, the 'fractal' image, that one can perceive and present the experience of his or her odyssey. Fragmentation is a mimetic,[49] a tactical[50] and a methodological imperative, one that brings with it a particular puzzle. Baudrillard muses:

> For America, only one method: given a certain number of fragments, notes and stories collected over a given time, there must be a solution which integrates them all, including the most banal into a necessary whole, without adding or removing any: the very necessity which, beneath the surface, presided over their collection. Making the supposition that this is the only material and the best, because it is secretly ordered by the same thinking, and assuming that everything conceived as part of the same obsession has a meaning and that there must be a solution to the problem of reconstituting it. The work starts out from the certainty that everything is already there and it will be sufficient simply to find the key.
>
> (CM, p. 219)

In the collection of fragments 'everything is already there', all theory already present. What remains elusive is their inner logic, the principle for their editing and replaying.

But such fragments, such images are not naive. Indeed, the key came first. Fantastic, fictional, fragmentary, passionately imagistic,[51] superficial, depthless, meaningless, excessive, obese, anorexic, silent, absurd, incommensurable – America as pure modernity, pure simulation, pure hyperreality, pure paradox, is the ultimate materialisation,[52] the utopia achieved, of Baudrillard's own conceptual repertoire. Unlike Benjamin, Baudrillard most definitely chose his position before he went:

> All the themes that I first examined in my previous books suddenly appeared, in *America*, stretching out before me in concrete form. In a way, then, I finally left theory behind me and at the same time rediscovered all the questions and the enigmas that I had first posited conceptually. Everything there seemed significant to me, but at the same time everything also testified to the disappearance of all meaning.
>
> (BL, p. 135)

In this exact correspondence, this perfect simulation, America constitutes not the actual realization, but the fictional manifestation, and hence the immanent end, of Baudrillard's own theoretical enterprise. When all theory is already factitiousness, already fiction, already fatality, there is nothing for it to do except await the catastrophe it 'prefigures'.[53] All that remains for the intellectual is silence,[54] playfulness,[55] idleness.[56] Baudrillard, like America, is 'without hope' (A, p. 123).

Benjamin and Baudrillard are witnesses to the end of European bourgeois culture – in revolutionary Moscow in the radical absence of distance, in a profound tactility, in the abolition of the bourgeois subject; in astral America, in the unfathomable absence of depth, in a banal obscenity, in the catastrophe of the social. Both transformations promise a fatal future for the independent European intellectual. In Moscow, the cultural critic has no room for manoeuvre; in America, s/he tumbles into the abyss of surface. Deprived of distance, the critic vanishes into the collective as bureaucratic functionary. Deprived of depth, the intellectual holes up on campus or hits the road as fugitive. Where all factuality is already theory, where all theory is already factitiousness, there the intellectual is made redundant, becomes a sightseer, a reluctant, though not 'banal' tourist. The intellectual goes on precisely the kind of vacation ironically described by Baudrillard in *Cool Memories*:

> Holidays are in no sense an alternative to the congestion and bustle of work. Quite the contrary. People look to escape into an intensification of the conditions of ordinary life, into a deliberate aggravation of those conditions: further from nature, nearer to artifice, to abstraction to total pollution, to well above average levels of stress, pressure, concentration and monotony – this is the ideal of popular entertainment. No one is interested in overcoming alienation; the point is to plunge into it to the point of ecstasy. This is what holidays are for.
>
> (CM, pp. 69–70)[57]

Moscow and America are precisely such holiday destinations, vacation colonies[58] from which Benjamin and Baudrillard are only able to send home a few 'disparate notes', a few imagistic fragments specifically designed to survive the perils of travel: picture postcards from post-cultures. Wish you were here.

Notes

1 This paper was originally given at the Aesthetic Theory Seminar (on the theme 'Denkbild/Bilddenken') of the Nordic Summer University, Helsinki, 27th July 1999. It was first published in the anthology of the NSU entitled *Ruinøs Modernitet (Ruinous Modernity)*. I am very grateful for the provocative comments and stimulating ideas of the seminar group which enriched the paper enormously. In particular, I would like to thank Troels Degn Johansson, Erik Steinskog and Claus Krogholm Kristiansen for their thoughts and for permission to reproduce this paper here. I am also grateful to Tim Dant and Bernadette Boyle for their invaluable comments and suggestions.

2 Namely, 'Naples' (September/October 1924), 'Moscow' (December/January 1926–7), 'Weimar' (June 1928), 'Marseilles' and 'Hashish in Marseilles' (October 1928–January 1929), 'Paris, the City in the Mirror' (January 1929), 'San Gimignano' (published August 1929), 'North Sea' (a pen-picture of Bergen, completed on 15 August 1930).

3 Walking the labyrinthine streets of Moscow, Benjamin notes: 'The whole exciting sequence of topographical dummies ... could only be shown by a film' (OWS, p. 179).

4 With their emphasis on the proximity of phenomena, the tactile intimacy with them, concreteness, immediacy, the imagistic, and the juxtaposing of elements to create provocative incongruity and mutual illumination, the *Denkbilder* clearly anticipate

and encapsulate many of the methodological and formal innovations and properties of 'One-Way Street' and the 'Arcades Project'.

5 As we shall see, Benjamin is not alone in his concern with techniques for dealing with slippery surfaces.

6 Benjamin notes: 'the complete interpenetration of technological and primitive modes of life, this world-historical experiment in the new Russia, is illustrated in miniature by a streetcar ride' (OWS, p. 190).

7 Thus, 'Kaiserpanorama: A Tour of German Inflation', Benjamin's series of bitter reflections on the prevailing circumstances in ruinous Weimar Germany, constitutes the counterpoint to 'Moscow'. Composed as a result of a journey through Germany during 1923, and subsequently incorporated in the 'One-Way Street' collection, 'Kaiserpanorama' is Benjamin's Berlin *Denkbild*.

8 This theme clearly prefigures notions developed in Benjamin's famous 1935 essay 'The Work of Art in the Age of Mechanical Reproduction'. Here, the genuine work of art is characterised by its authenticity and uniqueness 'imbedded in the fabric of tradition' (ILL, p. 225). The work of art is distinguished by 'aura', a sense of awe in the presence of the original artefact, 'the unique phenomenon of distance, however close it may be' (ILL, p. 224). In the 'Work of Art' essay, it is the development and proliferation of new forms of technology and cultural reproduction, in particular film and photography, which precipitate the demise of aura and the possibilities of new collective cultural practices, ones in which the worker is elevated to the position of cultural critic (ILL, p. 242). In Moscow, European bourgeois aesthetic sensibilities and practices are similarly abolished as the workers and children of the Soviet capital take possession of the city's cultural spaces and objects, irrevocably rupture the traditions and contexts in which the authentic work of art exerted its power, and bridge the 'unique sense of distance' of the auratic artefact. Here, tactility, rather than reproducibility, leads to the eradication of aura.

9 Benjamin notes: 'there is no knowledge and no faculty that are not somehow appropriated by collective life and made to serve it' (OWS, p. 187).

10 This passage reiterates a view expressed by Asja Lacis in a conversation with Benjamin on 13 January 1927 (see MD, p. 82).

11 Benjamin scornfully writes: 'Again and again it has been shown that society's attachment to its familiar and long-since-forfeited life is so rigid as to nullify the genuinely human application of intellect, forethought, even in dire peril. So that in this society the picture of imbecility is complete: uncertainty, indeed perversion of vital instincts, and impotence, indeed, decay of the intellect. This is the condition of the entire German bourgeoisie' (OWS, p. 55).

12 Benjamin observes wryly: 'the book is, as the present mode of scholarly production demonstrates, an outdated mediation between two different filing systems. For everything that matters is to be found in the card box of the researcher who wrote it, and the scholar studying it assimilates it into his own card index' (OWS, p. 62). Hence, Benjamin adds: 'The typical work of modern scholarship is intended to be read like a catalogue' (OWS, p. 63).

13 In his 1934 essay 'The Author as Producer', Benjamin notes: 'the Soviet state does not, like Plato's Republic, propose to expel its writers, but it does ... propose to assign them tasks which will make it impossible for them to parade the richness of the creative personality, which has long been a myth and a fake, in new masterpieces' (UB, p. 97).

14 Benjamin notes that 'the country is isolated from the West less by frontiers and censorship than by the intensity of an existence that is beyond all comparison with Europe' (OWS, p. 198).

15 For Benjamin, it is 'only the more feeble and distracted' who take 'inimitable pleasure in conclusions, feeling themselves thereby given back to life' (OWS, p. 48).

16 In a letter to Scholem of 17 April 1931 Benjamin writes: 'Where is my production plant located? It is located (in this, too, I do not harbour the slightest illusions) in Berlin W., W.W. if you like' (Scholem 1982, p. 232).

17 This is despite Baudrillard's ironic claim that: 'In reality, you do not, as I had hoped, get any distance on Europe. You do not acquire a fresh angle on it. When you turn around it has quite simply disappeared' (A, p. 29).

18 In his letter to Buber he notes: 'Moscow as it appears at present reveals a full range of possibilities in schematic form; above all, the possibility that the Revolution might fail or succeed. In either case, something unforeseeable will result and its picture will be far different from any programmatic sketch one might draw of the future' (MD, p. 6).

19 Baudrillard suggests that this condition reached its apotheosis in the 1950s and is now being recycled in simulated form under the prevailing Reagan administration

20 Baudrillard states: 'America is neither dream nor reality. It is hyperreality. It is a hyperreality because it is a utopia which has behaved from the very beginning as though it were already achieved' (A, p. 28).

21 Baudrillard notes: 'What is thought in Europe becomes reality in America' (A, p. 84).

22 "What you have to do,' Baudrillard insists, 'is enter the fiction of America, enter America as fiction. It is, indeed, on this fictive basis that America dominates the world' (A, p. 29). See also A, p. 95.

23 Baudrillard writes: 'What is new in America is the clash of the first level (primitive and wild) and the "third" (the absolute simulacrum). There is no second level' (A, p. 104).

24 America is wholly artifical and therefore wholly modern. Baudrillard credits Baudelaire with the insight that 'the secret of true modernity was to be found in artifice' (A, p. 70).

25 Baudrillard observes: 'Europe can no longer be understood by starting out from Europe itself' (A, p. 98).

26 Given his view of the impossibility of deciding 'on the basis of facts', Benjamin, one may be relieved to learn, is no American.

27 Baudrillard notes: 'They build the real out of ideas. We transform the real into ideas, or into ideology. Here in America only what is produced or manifested has meaning; for us in Europe only what can be thought or concealed has meaning' (A, p. 84).

28 America is a land of 'mythic banality' (A, p. 95).

29 Baudrillard notes that America 'is naive and primitive; it knows nothing of the irony of concepts, nor the irony of seduction' (A, p. 97). It is perhaps appropriate that Baudrillard's American critics have failed to appreciate the ironic power of his observations. See, for example, Kellner (1989, pp. 168–73) and Vidich (1991).

30 Baudrillard precedes this with: 'they certainly smile at you here, though neither from courtesy, nor from an effort to charm. This smile signifies only the need to smile. It is a bit like the Cheshire Cat's grin: it continues to float on faces long after all emotion has disappeared' (A, p. 33).

31 Baudrillard notes: 'The emperor has no clothes; the facts are there before us' (A, p. 85).

32 Baudrillard notes the cramped conditions of Europe: 'It is the same with European cars. No one actually lives in them; there isn't enough space. The cities, too, do not have enough space' (A, p. 18). If, for Benjamin, Muscovites' are tipsy with time (OWS, p. 190), Americans are intoxicated with space.

33 Baudrillard is at pains to point out that, of course, the desert is wholly mediated by culture: 'the desert you pass through is like the set of a Western' (A, p. 56). The desert is, paradoxically, the image of a culturally mediated absence of culture.

34 Baudrillard states unequivocally: 'There is no culture here, no cultural discourse' (A, p. 100).

35 'Depth', Baudrillard informs us, 'isn't what it used to be' (CM, p. 6).

36 Baudrillard cites Paul Virilio's phrase here (A, p. 5).

37 See, for example, Baudrillard's comments on the deconcentration and disconnection of the Santa Cruz campus as the 'ideal cosy nook' (A, p. 44). Elsewhere he compares the campus to Disneyland (see CM3, p. 42).

38 Baudrillard emphasises this gulf when he notes: 'Before me a scholarly man, of European culture, head of a literary department in one of the great universities of the West. He speaks of it with bitterness, as do almost all his colleagues. Culture is not what it was and he has not the slightest regard for mass culture' (CM, p. 205).

39 By contrast, Baudrillard's perception has been irrevocably transformed by the American experience: 'When you come out of the Mojave, writes Banham, it is difficult to focus less than fifteen miles ahead of you. Your eye can no longer rest on objects that are near. It can no longer properly settle on things, and all the human or natural constructions that intercept your gaze seem irksome obstacles which merely corrupt the perfect reach of your vision. When you emerge from the desert, your eyes go on trying to create emptiness all around; in every inhabited area, every landscape they see desert beneath, like a watermark. It takes a long time to get back to a normal vision of things and you never succeed completely' (A, pp. 68–9).

40 Baudrillard notes there is no seduction in America, since 'seduction requires a secret' (A, p. 7).

41 Baudrillard states: 'If you approach this society with the nuances of moral, aesthetic, or critical judgement, you will miss its originality, which comes precisely from its defying judgement and pulling off a prodigious confusion of effects' (A, p. 67).

42 In America 'Culture is space, speed, cinema, technology. This culture is authentic, if anything can be said to be authentic' (A, p. 100).

43 As Baudrillard points out in a rather different context, here: 'Image alone counts' (A, p. 109)

44 Baudrillard writes: 'It is not the least of America's charms that even outside the movie theatres the whole country is cinematic. The desert you pass through is like the set of a Western, the city a screen of signs and formulas. ... The American city seems to have stepped out of the movies. To grasp its secret, you should not, then, begin with the city and move inwards to the screen; you should begin with the screen and move outwards to the city. It is there that cinema does not assume an exceptional form, but simply invests the streets and the entire town with a mythical atmosphere' (A, p. 56). In a later fragment he notes that here: 'The cinema has absorbed everything' (A, p. 69).

45 For him: 'Driving is a spectacular form of amnesia. Everything is to be discovered, everything to be obliterated' (A, p. 9).

46 Baudrillard notes: 'The further you travel the more you realize that the journey (destiny) is all that matters' (CM, p. 168).

47 Benjamin writes: 'Moscow in winter is a quiet city. The immense bustle on its streets takes place softly. This is because of the snow, but also because of the backwardness of the traffic' (OWS, p. 179). Baudrillard notes: 'The silence of the desert is a visual thing, too. A product of the gaze which stares out and finds nothing to reflect it' (A, p. 6).

48 Baudrillard observes: 'America is a giant hologram, in the sense that information concerning the whole is contained in each of its elements. Take the tiniest little place in the desert, any old street in a Mid-West town, a parking lot, a Californian house, a BurgerKing or a Studebaker, and you have the whole of the US – South, North, East or West' (A, p. 29).

49 Baudrillard insists: 'The book must break up so as to resemble the ever increasing number of extreme situations. It must break up to resemble the flashes of holograms' (CM, p. 116).

50 Baudrillard wittily observes: 'Another promise of fragments is that they alone will survive the catastrophe, the destruction of meaning and language, like the flies in the plane crash which are the only survivors because they are ultra-light. Like the flotsam in Poe's maelstrom: the lightest items sink the most slowly into the abyss. It is these one must hang on to' (CM3, p. 9).

51 Baudrillard notes the American 'passion for images' (A, p. 56).

52 America is home to '*the material fiction of the image*' (A, p. 57).

53 Baudrillard notes that 'Theory does not derive its legitimacy from established facts, but from future events. Its value is not in the past events it can illuminate, but in the shockwave of the events it prefigures' (CM, p. 215).

54 Baudrillard writes: 'If everything is perfect, language is useless' (CM, p. 84).

55 Baudrillard confesses: 'I play out the end of things' (BL, pp. 132–3).

56 Baudrillard concludes *Cool Memories* with: 'This journal is a subtle matrix of idleness' (CM, p. 234). Idleness is itself a 'fatal strategy' (CM2, p. 7) and the 'ideal condition for work' (CM2, p. 57).

57 Such a 'holiday' is an altogether more serious business than Turner's notion of 'cruising' suggests. See Rojek and Turner (eds) (1993), pp. 146–61. Turner describes 'cruising' as: 'a trivial exercise' (p. 152).

58 Benajmin notes that the low-rise architecture of Moscow 'gives it the appearance of a summer vaction colony' (MD, p. 17). Baudrillard describes America as a 'soft, resort-style civilization' (A, p. 31), one which 'irresistibly evokes the end of the world' (A, p. 31).

Primary texts and abbreviations

Baudrillard, Jean

A   Baudrillard, Jean (1988) *America*, trans. Chris Turner, London: Verso.

BL   Baudrillard, Jean (1993) *Baudrillard Live: Selected Interviews*, ed. Mike Gane, London: Routledge.

CM   Baudrillard, Jean (1990) *Cool Memories: 1980–1985*, trans. Chris Turner, London: Verso.

CM2   Baudrillard, Jean (1996) *Cool Memories II: 1987–1990*, trans. Chris Turner, Cambridge: Polity Press.

CM3   Baudrillard, Jean (1997) *Cool Memories III: Fragments 1990–1995*, trans. Chris Turner, London: Verso.

SS   Baudrillard, Jean (1983) *In the Shadow of the Silent Majorities*, New York: Semiotext(e).

Benjamin, Walter

AP   Taylor, Ronald (ed) (1980) *Aesthetics and Politics: Debates between Bloch, Lukacs, Brecht, Benjamin, Adorno*, trans. Ronald Taylor, London: Verso.

ARC   Benjamin, Walker (1999) *The Arcades Project*, ed. and trans. Howard Eiland and Kevin McLaughlin, Cambridge, MA: Belknap Press of Harvard University

COR   Benjamin, Walter (1994) *The Correspondence of Walter Benjamin*, ed. Gershom Scholem and Theodor Adorno, trans. Manfred and Evelyn Jacobson, Chicago and London: University of Chicago Press.

GS   Benjamin, Walter (1991) *Gesammelte Schriften*, ed. Rolf Tiedemann and Hermann Schweppenhäuser, *et al.*, Taschenbuch Ausgabe , Frankfurt a.M.: Suhrkamp Verlag,

ILL   Benjamin, Walter (1973) *Illuminations*, ed. Hannah Arendt, trans. Harry Zohn, London: Collins

MD   Benjamin, Walter (1986) *Moscow Diary*, ed. Gary Smith, trans. Richard Sieburth, Cambridge, MA and London: Harvard University Press.

OWS   Benjamin, Walter (1985) *One-Way Street and Other Writings*, trans. Edmund Jephcott and Kingsley Shorter, London: Verso.

SW2   Benjamin, Walker (1999) *Selected Writings*, vol. 2, ed. Marcus Bullock, Michael Jennings, *et al.*, Cambridge, MA: Harvard University Press.

UB   Benjamin, Walter (1983) *Understanding Brecht*, trans. Anna Bostock, London: Verso.

Other references

Buck-Morss, Susan (1989) *The Dialectics of Seeing: Walter Benjamin and the Arcades Project*, Cambridge, MA: MIT Press.

Gane, Mike (1991a) *Baudrillard's Bestiary: Baudrillard and Culture*, London: Routledge.

Gane, Mike (1991b) *Baudrillard: Critical and Fatal Theory*, London: Routledge.

Gilloch, Graeme (1996) *Myth and Metropolis: Walter Benjamin and the City*, Cambridge: Polity Press.

Gundersen, Roy and Dobson, Stephen (1996) *Baudrillard's Journey to America*, London: Minerva.

Kellner, Douglas (1989) *Jean Baudrillard: From Marxism to Postmodernism and Beyond*, Stanford, CA: Stanford, University Press.

Rojek, Chris and Turner, Bryan (eds) (1993) *Forget Baudrillard?*, London: Routledge.

Scholem, Gershom (1982) *Walter Benjamin: The Story of a Friendship*, London: Faber and Faber.

Vidich, Arthur (1991) 'Baudrillard's America: Lost in the Ultimate Simulacrum', *Theory, Culture and Society*, 8 (2) (May): 135–44.

Watt, Stephen (1991) 'Baudrillard's America (and Ours?): Image, Virus, Catastrophe', in *Modernity and Mass Culture*, ed. James Naremore and Patrick Brantlinger, Bloomington, IN: Indiana University Press, pp. 135–57.

13 Addressing the post-urban

Los Angeles, Las Vegas, New York[1]

Sarah Chaplin and Eric Holding

In this chapter, we will consider the way in which the contemporary city is being reconfigured as a result of current patterns of consumption, marketing practice, media coverage, tourism and life style choice. As Anthony King has argued in *Re-presenting Cities*,[2] increasingly the city figures in the social imaginary more as a representation than as material reality, understood through mediated urban experience and vicarious encounter and, in academia, constructed as a discourse.[3]

We will be articulating this reconfiguration through the concept of the 'post-urban'. The prefix 'post' implies that contemporary understanding of the concept of the urban has entered a critical self-aware stage, both historically and conceptually, with regard to the marketable status and image of the city. We wish to emphasise that this level of awareness of the processes operating culturally, socially and politically with respect to cities has not been brought about by scholarly research in the humanities alone, nor is it a result of the design decisions of architects and planners. It is largely through the actions of marketing executives, brand managers, political strategists, tourist board directors and financial analysts that this awareness has come about, and is now beginning to direct the way in which urban environments develop and communicate their respective identities.

In other words, *the post-urban city is not what it is, but what it is made out to be*. As such, the city has become part of the culture of the 30-second soundbite along with all other aspects of lived experience, and, like politicians, global cities are required to compete for airtime through cinema, television and print media for news coverage. This apparent desire to be noticed on the part of those promoting the city uses a variety of tactics, notably undertaking Olympic bids, Millennium projects, new tourist attractions and promoting the city as a film location,[4] a location for a world summit[5] or the setting of a newsworthy story.[6]

The post-urban is not, then, a synonym for the post-industrial or the post-modern, although it depends to some extent upon the work carried out by theorists of the post-industrial[7] and the post-modern,[8] in that we are treating these as related conceptualisations. In terms of other theorisations of the contemporary city, the post-urban is more than simply the culmination or amalgamation of key economic, socio-spatial or socio-political forces at work, such as de-industrialisation and de-urbanisation. It is an outcome of the combined effect produced by such forces of change as gentrification, globalisation, multi-culturism, cosmopolitanism and post-Fordism.

It will require considerable unpicking to trace the complex interdependent effects of all these forces. We have therefore chosen in this chapter to focus specifically on two active processes at work in the emergence of post-urban space, namely, McDonaldisation and Disneyfication, where both may now be observed to have gone well beyond affecting their respective corporate environ-ments, and we will show how they have come to affect and inform people's expectations and use of urban spaces.

Those responsible for re-working cities such as London and New York now need to supply a density of accessible experiences for local inhabitants and visit-ors alike, and are responding with intense, overdetermined, simulated spaces, 'dark rides', etc. This sets up what might be described as an urban feedback loop, whereby entertainment developers capitalise on the collective mental image of a place, creating a recognisable image of a particular city, which is often the same image that is used in the establishing shots at the start of Hollywood blockbuster films,[9] travel programmes or situation comedies, to supply a necessary context. The actual city then has to live up to its image, such that in being offered as an experience to be consumed it effectively re-consumes its own image, as with the present redevelopment of Times Square in New York or the new Trocadero Centre in London.

In other words, the post-urban occurs whenever there is a conscious re-investment if not in the city *per se*, then in some reified version of 'citiness'. This re-investment is not a purely financial initiative: we are not discussing the various drives towards economic urban regeneration, but the effects of the impulse *behind* such initiatives effectively to promote the city in new ways. In one sense, we are more interested in the consequences of an outward emotional re-investment in the city, than in the benefits of inward financial investment.

The term 'post-urban' has to our knowledge been used to characterise a latent urban condition by three other authors: Elizabeth Wilson,[10] Anthony Vidler,[11] and Paul Virilio.[12]

Wilson refers specifically to shopping malls, theme parks and airports as post-urban spaces, and concludes that with the consumerisation of space and the rise of white trash culture, 'intellectuals' are increasingly alienated from projects which engage with the populist re-development of the city centre, and that architects have retreated to working instead with the urban periphery, 'humbled by the failure of many of the major post-war planning initiatives'.[13]

Vidler's characterisation of the post-urban is less concerned than Wilson's with the rift between the producers and consumers of the urban environment, and is instead more ideologically totalising. Post-urbanism is a term which for him refers to the end of urbanism, affecting collective memory and generating a particular sensibility which he mostly evidences through films such as *Blue Velvet* and *Down by Law*, where 'the margins have entirely invaded the centre and disseminated its focus'.[14] He argues that associated with the post-urban is the end of liberal humanism, and 'a belief in the (naturally good) public realm'.[15] Vidler concludes that a post-urbanist world is more realistic than idealistic, offering more inclusivity than grand hope.

Vidler and Wilson's notions of the post-urban both predict the passing of modern tropes of city planning and either lament the ossification of city centres into romanticised museums or herald a grim future in which cities are without qualities. Whilst we concur with these broad delineations of the post-urban, it is not our intention here to mount a lament, or to judge the effects of the post-urban as manipulative, romantic or banal.

Virilio's vision of the post-urban emerges from his analysis of what he calls the 'overexposed city', in which perceptions of time and distance have been irrevocably altered by the intrusion of new communications technology, such that 'we have to approach the question of access to the City in a new manner. For example, does the Metropolis possess its own façade? At what moment does the city show its face?'[16]

Of the three, Virilio's oblique probing of the nature of the post-urban is perhaps the closest to our own viewpoint: his questions strike to the heart of a new visual and spatial analysis of the city. Witnessed from the vantage point of a North American suburb, downtown is a neat but feared clump on the horizon, rarely visited, frequently mythologised and increasingly usurped in favour of the out-of-town mall.[17] Virilio points out that the effect of this relationship to the city makes 'places interchangeable at will', and produces 'a strange topology ... hidden in the obviousness of televised images'.[18] Through this 'obviousness' the urban is reborn: a saturated 'day-glo' version of itself, its topology born of the cinematic cut rather than the architectonic juxtaposition.

Whilst we acknowledge that the post-urban also partly exemplifies Jean Baudrillard's notion of the simulacrum[19] and is partly a reflection of Umberto Eco's speculations on the hyperreal,[20] it is not productive to analyse the post-urban in these terms, since both theorisations, despite being rooted in a post-modern paradigm, carry overtones of a lament and seek to judge present circumstances negatively against some infinitely superior idealised version of the past. Rather, we wish to situate our notion of the post-urban beyond a Marxist or Baudrillardian critique of commodification, the Situationist exposé of the urban as spectacle or Eco's indictment of American taste. This is because we believe that people's relationships to spaces of commodification and hence to capitalism itself have changed. Specifically, Marx's notions of alienation and passivity in the face of urban experiences encountered under capitalism are somewhat anachronistic and do not account for the role leisure plays in everyday life. Marxism has provided the necessary critical purchase with which to examine society, but its basic premise focuses on identity as formed through production rather than through consumption, and treats the city as the site in which alienation through industrial work takes place. Since our purpose here is to show the city's reconfiguration as predominantly a space of consumption, we need to set such theories to one side in order to derive fresh insights about the post-urban.

Addressing the post-urban is for us an attempt to re-think the city in its latest guise. This is a project which both Fredric Jameson[21] and Marc Augé[22] have called for: a new cognitive mapping to provide a new relationship to space. However, in our terms of reference, a *post-urban* cognitive mapping demands a reconsideration not just of the *actual* circumstances of urban living, such as the problems of crime, security and surveillance which Virilio outlines. Rather, it is the effect of *virtual* circumstances which precipitates the post-urban. For example, more criminal offences are committed on Coronation Street than any other street in Britain. Likewise, more fictional shoot-outs take place in New York than any armed attacks in real life,[23] aided by the introduction of an office set up by the mayor of New York to encourage the use of New York as a location for filming. These fictional 'facts' contribute more powerfully to a contemporary cognitive mapping than do the real facts of urban living. Similarly, the post-urban is evident not in the debates about how to attain the targets set for residential accommodation in the new millennium, but in the fact that developers are building lofts from scratch now that loft-living has become so over-subscribed that there are simply no more warehouses left which are suitable for conversion.[24]

Thus it can be shown that soap operas, property brochures, public relations exercises, advertising campaigns, focus groups, financial incentives and the rhetoric of single-issue politics affect the identity of post-urban spaces far more than the well-intentioned social agendas of architects and planners still wedded to modernism. Among contemporary theorists, this situation is typically decried, and blamed for producing environmental mediocrity. Jameson states that culture has been commodified and commodities have become cultural, such that in the Marxist scheme of things there is no longer a clear distinction to be drawn between base and superstructure, since new media constitute the central focus of economic activity and can therefore no longer be evaluated against the old standards.[25]

To re-think the urban is therefore to pass beyond an oppositional Marxist schema and the persistence of polarised categories such as rural/urban, public/private, place/non-place, modern/traditional or real/virtual. These fixed formulations do little to extend our understanding of the built environment, and we need instead to address the particularities of each socio-cultural construction of meaning before we analyse the physical construction of a specific locale.

McDonaldisation and Disneyfication

Recently, the Spanish city of Bilbao joined the ranks of those cities where the marketing decision has been taken to employ the services of a high-profile world architect to create an international cultural landmark. This has gained Bilbao valuable column inches, increasing its 'visibility' and at the same time extending the brand of Guggenheim to radical new architectural dimensions with Gehry's shiny sculptural museum. In the process, Frank Gehry has become a representational commodity, his architecture an aspirational life style good, and this particular project an exercise in product placement, a 'contra' between Bilbao and the Guggenheim family, creating a franchise which journalists have called McGuggenheim.[26] The reference to McDonald's is pejorative, referring to the fact that art-accumulating dynasties like Guggenheim and Getty operate a kind of corporate imperialism, which goes well beyond the benevolent gesture of funding a public museum. Similarly, Gehry's links with the Disney Corporation have been deplored as being instrumental in extending the theme park typology beyond Walt's legitimate boundaries and into the heart of 'real' cities.[27]

The impact of McDonald's and Disney has interested a wide variety of cultural commentators in the post-war period, notably Louis Marin,[28] George Ritzer,[29] John Findlay,[30] and Charles Rutheiser,[31] who have discussed at length the way in which such corporate institutions affect people's relationship to the built environment. More broadly, the subject of theming has itself been examined with respect to American urban environments by Mark Gottdiener.[32] Influenced by the success of many theme parks, themed restaurants and other themed environments such as casinos, resort complexes and leisure amenities, many cities have turned to theming as a way of promoting and accentuating their USP (unique selling point), which is very often the history of the place itself, exploiting this local point of difference as a means of attracting foreign visitors.

McDonald's operates, as Ritzer's analysis has shown, through four main strategies: efficiency, predictability, calculability and control. He argues that these not only condition the way in which hamburgers are ordered, prepared, served and consumed, but have also come to prescribe behaviour in a variety of other contexts, even circumscribing experience by shaping consumer expectations of services, goods and places encountered in everyday life. McDonaldisation is the exorcising of risk from experience, from the point of view of both consumer and producer, and creates a dependency on cosy familiarity and a preference for 'known quantities'.

In a McDonaldised society, the consistently satisfactory is valued more highly than the occasionally remarkable experience. However, in eliminating the risk of the unpredictable in the quality, quantity and timing of food, the consumer must turn elsewhere in order to experience surprise or to regain an element of the unexpected. Often in anticipation of this need, which remains unfulfilled under the system of McDonaldisation, ostensibly risky encounters are themselves engineered to satiate the customer's desire for the adrenaline released in a potentially dangerous situation.

The post-urban effect in Hollywood and Las Vegas

This is the situation which presents itself at Universal Studios in Los Angeles, a theme park built on a former Hollywood backlot and containing rides themed on *Back to the Future*, *ET*, *Jurassic Park* and *Backdraft*, the latter two revolving around narratives in which a safe ride has unexpectedly gone 'out of control'. Universal Studios theme park has been extended to include CityWalk, designed by Jon Jerde Partnership as a single street of shops, restaurants and a cinema, and built on the crest of a hill, which functions as a connection between the car parking facilities and the main entrance to the theme park. People come to CityWalk to spend time eating or shopping prior to or after visiting Universal Studios, but also to visit the development as an event in its own right, particularly in the early evening, as there is ample parking and it feels safe but exciting.

CityWalk draws on two main typologies, the cinema and the city, and is a hybrid of both, combining their respective attributes and physically existing in a space between the two. Contiguous with the backlots within Universal Studios, it operates like a film set, being only one street deep, all fronts and no backs, a collection of façades against which people can feature in their own movies. It is also operating as an excerpt from a reified notion of city, mimicking urban qualities along its angled street lined with speciality franchises selling themed goods. As such it is a totally reified leisure space and represents a stage beyond the arcade and the interiorised shopping mall, in that it is both abstracted and removed from an urban context and yet strives to create one of its own. The ambiguities in relation to context reveal the moment where the hybridity of city and cinema comes into conflict: to be a piece of the city there should be continuity with the rest of Los Angeles; to be a piece of cinema there should be a radical separation from the real. This is resolved by naming the entire complex 'Universal City', which encompasses both the idea that this is in itself a city and also maintains its discontinuity with the rest of Los Angeles.

Norman Klein has commented on the extent to which CityWalk is a 'scripted space' *par excellence*,[33] that is, a space which excludes, directs, supervises, constructs and orchestrates use. This act of scripting sets up CityWalk as a trailer, gesturing towards both city and cinema. As a trailer to a film, CityWalk acts as a preview, offering edited highlights, which have been collapsed together in soundbite style into a series of intense fragments, creating anticipation and desire for the actual film/city. It thereby precedes both the Universal Studios theme park experience at one end, and the multiplex cinema showing actual movies at the other end. As a trailer to the city, CityWalk could be seen to preview the emerging identity of the post-urban city, but this is achieved in such a way that CityWalk actually trails *behind* the city, following its lead, using its devices, attempting to capture its 'essence', which it can achieve only in a reified form.[34]

The reified quality of the post-urban city is like the experience of dining in a fast-food restaurant in terms of risk assessment, such that tourists and investment companies alike weigh up what it has to offer against a standardised list of ideal ingredients: Opera House, IMAX Theatre, Aquarium, waterfront restaurants, urban parks, historic precincts, significant retail developments, high-quality living accommodation, etc. Promotional leaflets produced by the

Figure 13.1 CityWalk, Universal Studios, Los Angeles
(credit: S. Chaplin/E. Holding)

marketing department of a city's tourist board list these leisure opportunities as highlights within a recommended tourist itinerary, and City Break brochures in travel agents list them as features of each package to a major capital city. This in turn creates the need for a sustainable array of attractions which are unique to each individual destination, and sets up a focus which often places the aspirations of the tourist above the needs of the local inhabitant. Measures are then introduced (following the classic marketing procedure of analysis, planning, implementation and control laid out by Kotler),[35] for crowd control, funnelling and shepherding groups for their own safety, but also to even out the distribution of visitors.[36]

This technique has been achieved via an innovative architectural solution in the downtown part of Las Vegas (see Fig. 13.2) adjacent to the train station, in another project by Jon Jerde, which turned Fremont Street into

Figure 13.2   Fremont Street, Las Vegas
(credit: S. Chaplin/E. Holding)

'the Fremont Street Experience'. Fremont Street was the first part of Las Vegas to be built, but by the early 1990s older casinos like the Horseshoe and the Golden Nugget had become increasingly shabby and sleazy as competition from the larger casinos along the Strip took trade away. This was a matter of concern to the Las Vegas city authority, which was losing tax revenue to the Strip, which lay outside the city limits, under the jurisdiction of the State of Nevada.

Jon Jerde was called in to appraise the situation, and decided it would not be enough just to pedestrianise the downtown area, it would have to be turned into an 'Experience'. To this end, Fremont Street was roofed over, collectivising the individual casinos, and making the street into a virtual interior. Norman Klein refers to this as 'malling' the space. As dusk falls the spectacle begins: all the older neon signs are turned off in an instant, and the barrel vault roof starts to perform. Instead of a floor show, millions of lights provide a 'ceiling show' which is electronic, pre-programmed, timetabled and viewed like cinema showings. Following the four traits of McDonaldisation, this is predictable, calculable, efficient and controllable. It brings large numbers of people, who might otherwise have stayed in their hotel-casinos farther up the Strip, to frequent the casinos on the street, and through the spaced timing of shows, supplies – like traffic lights – controlled pulses of gamblers to the casinos, which have not after all moved away from their primary purpose.

Thus Jerde's architectural intervention in its performative state momentarily unites the downtown environment, another variation of the way in which the post-urban city adopts the tactics of the cinema and invents a more extreme form of spectacle in order to compete. In terms of its theming, since this is a piece of theatre controlled by software, it is not a fixed structural effect: the themes of 'shows' can change to suit themes of the moment. Shows currently play on well-worn patriotic themes, with flags and cheerleaders, the Wild West, etc., but with lights capable of rendering any colour and any pattern, operating like the individual pixels on a computer screen, the visual opportunities are unlimited. Such changes also serve to increase sales of merchandise sold at the Fremont Street Experience store.

The effects of Disney can also clearly be detected in the Fremont Street Experience, and at casinos elsewhere, where 'musak', merchandising, 'cartoon-ified' maps, and the sense of a reduction of scale combine to make people relax and enjoy their urban encounter, and create an atmosphere which perhaps masks the real danger of losing a lot of money gambling. A walk down the Strip is similar to a walk down Disneyland's Main Street, with theatrical events along its length designed to entertain and lure people into the different casinos. When Venturi, Scott Brown and Izenour visited with their students in the early 1970s, Las Vegas was a city of adult entertainment, nocturnal in habit, to be seen from a car. By the end of the 1970s, the market for gambling alone was saturated, and Las Vegas had to reinvent itself as a resort aimed more at family- and pedestrian-oriented, daytime event-based entertainment. As a result, forecourt car parks have been replaced with roller coasters, volcanoes, pirate ships, steamboats, pyramids and lately, simulacra of entire cities: representations of New York, Paris and Venice have already been built (see Figs 13.3, 13.4 and 13.5).

The NewYork NewYork casino complex has been billed as the 'Greatest city in Las Vegas', and occupies a corner site on the Strip, opposite the MGM casino. NewYork NewYork presents people who may never go to the real New York with the image they carry round of Manhattan, one encountered first via television and film, or constructed from a number of classic postcard views of major sights, such as the Brooklyn Bridge, the Statue of Liberty, the Empire State building, the Chrysler Building, the Whitney Museum and the World Trade Centre. NewYork NewYork thereby acquires the status of the collective mental image of the real city, built up as a condensed series of establishing shots. It is the soundbite culture again, in which the representation is based upon other inferred representations in a complex series of cultural overlays.

NewYork NewYork is concerned, however, not with emulating or mimicking the real city, but with fashioning another form of 'trailer' or taster: it enables people to pre-experience the real New York (see Fig. 13.6), or to recall, via edited highlights/prompts, their own previous visit to New York. It presents a sanitised version of Manhattan, with fake refuse bins and graffiti, operating as a hermetic, security-conscious environment.

Figure 13.3   The Venetian Hotel-Casino, Las Vegas.
(credit: S. Chaplin/E. Holding)

The post-urban effect in New York and London

Those responsible for marketing the real New York, in response to the McDonaldising, Disneyfying tendencies which seek to reproduce the Big Apple elsewhere without the bruised bits, have now taken steps to reverse the relatively poor image of those same bruised parts of town. 'Business Improvement Districts' have been introduced in some places, where refuse collection is privatised and 'zero tolerance' imposed,[37] and in the area around 42nd Street and Times Square a complete redevelopment programme is underway called '42nd Street Now!'. Signs to 42nd Street now have a second sign saying 'New 42nd Street'. All the peepshows have been moved out, but some of the signs advertising them have been left in order to give a more 'authentic' feel. The development team included New York architect Robert Stern, who claimed that 'We're after vulgar heterogeneity. The goal is not a themed simulacrum of honky-tonk diversity, but the real thing.'[38] Stern employed six main design principles, displayed in the 42nd Street promotional office:

Figure 13.4 The Paris Hotel-Casino, Las Vegas.
(credit: S. Chaplin/E. Holding)

1   Layering of different styles/eras of architecture and signage.
2   Use of '*unplanning*' – where design co-ordination and consistent planning between individual tenants are expressly prohibited.
3   Contradiction and surprise – achieved by fierce competition between tenants for attention-seeking aesthetics and products.
4   Vivid around-the-clock pedestrian experience, enhanced by a broad variety of commercial activities – widely visible through glazed façades both at street level and above.
5   Emphasis on visual anchors at both ends of the block that by means of extravagant signage or brilliant architecture create dazzling gateways to the rejuvenated strip and mark it as a special place within the city.
6   In the long tradition of Times Square and 42nd Street as a visual experience like no other, the use of aesthetic elements not only as parts of larger architectural and commercial agendas, but as compelling tourist attractions in their own right.

Figure 13.5   New York, New York
(credit: S. Chaplin/E. Holding)

'Unplanning' is a major concept in the context of discussions about the post-urban, and represents an approach which could be described as 'post-urban design'. This works to alter the basis upon which urban developments are normally conceived and reverses the principles of visual harmony and spatial unity to achieve a new form of post-*laissez-faire* urbanism. The accidental juxtapositions of style and the lack of design coherence along a street façade becomes a desired effect. By applying these new principles, Stern's realisation of 'the real thing' is in effect nevertheless a representation of 42nd Street-ness, operating the four principles of McDonaldisation, efficiency, predictability, calculability and control, under the guise of a loose set of planning principles. This is not to say that it is inauthentic, and every effort has been made by Stern's office to analyse the quintessential 'New York-ness' of the signage, etc. It is, rather, an example of the 'new authenticity' which Koolhaas refers to,[39] part of an iterative cycle of intertextual referencing between the city and its image, whose goal is to create the 'citiest city', where the throbbing heart of the capital is momentarily and simultaneously glimpsed on screen and 'for real', self-consciously designed to maximise its seductive potential.

In London, the equivalent space to Times Square is of course Piccadilly Circus – the 'citiest bit' of London – where 'contradiction and surprise' are supplied by the London Pavilion and the Trocadero. In urban design terms, these figure as rebuilt historicist façades, containing high-tech tourist attrac-

Figure 13.6   Real New York
(credit: S. Chaplin/E. Holding)

tions such as the recently opened Segaworld, with a quantity of tourist shops and 'things to do' when visiting the city at ground floor level. Deyan Sudjic has commented that 'The Trocadero is what passes for the public space at the heart of London in the 1990s … a stealth bomber of a space, all but invisible behind its carefully preserved Edwardian facades. And equally invisible on the mental maps of most Londoners.'[40] Times Square and Piccadilly Circus function as spaces for gatherings and celebrations, not so much by virtue of being centrally located, but because of the presence of vast TV screens which relay words and images, maintaining the importance and reputation of the physical urban space by including a virtual sense of elsewhere.

This demonstrates a point of convergence with Las Vegas: to mark the start of 1997, the demolition of an old casino, the Hacienda, was televised as part of the New Year celebrations, timed to detonate at 9 pm Las Vegas time, so as to coincide with the clock striking midnight in Times Square, where it was shown on the giant TV screen.[41] Just as Las Vegas theatricalises even those moments of its own destruction, so New York capitalises on such events by (televised) association, asserting its relative importance compared to Las Vegas through a scheduling decision based on the larger concentration of crowds and television viewers. Both cities have to employ their own brand of special effects to rival the spectacular digital effects which Hollywood can now produce, in order to attract live crowds downtown.

Conclusion

Addressing the post-urban involves two projects: first, the search for a new system of classifying experience in cities of the developed world, and, second, a new understanding of the factors affecting the development of the built environment. This requires a new methodology, in which ethnographic research merges with market research, where concepts developed within the discourses of retailing and marketing are appropriated.[42] These reveal a characterisation of life at the begining of the twenty-first century which is different from the typical depictions of civilisation in decline which emerge whenever spaces of consumption are compared to ideal cities. Addressing the post-urban also involves reorganising and re-mapping categories of taste, to produce a spatial continuation of the work begun by Pierre Bourdieu.[43]

A post-urban experience blends past and present, real and virtual, public and private in ever-more complex scenarios. Rather than dismissing these new experiences as wilful acts of corporatism, it is first necessary to examine their status as spaces of consumption: Guy Debord famously said that 'Everything that was once lived has passed to representation.'[44] The results of the latest exit poll from the city-as-theme-park indicate that 'everything that was once only a representation is now lived'.

References

1 This chapter was first presented as a lecture, 'Addressing the Post-Urban', at the *morphe* conference, Deakin University, Australia, in July 1997.
2 Anthony King (ed.), *Re-presenting Cities*, London, 1996.
3 There are now Masters courses at several universities in the UK on City Management/Marketing European Cities.
4 A 'typical' street in Southwark has been listed in 1997 because it is often used by the film industry.
5 Such as the 1997 environment summit in Kyoto.
6 Witness the way in which the trials of O.J. Simpson and Louise Woodward drew attention to Los Angeles and Boston.
7 See H.V. Savitch, *Post-industrial Cities: Politics and Planning in New York, Paris and London*, Princeton, NJ, 1988; Margaret Rose, *The Post-Modern and the Post-Industrial*, Cambridge, 1991.
8 See David Harvey, *The Condition of Post-Modernity*, Oxford: Blackwell, 1989; Nan Ellin, *Postmodern Urbanism*, Oxford, 1996, Sophie Watson and Katherine Gibson (eds), *Postmodern Cities and Spaces*, Oxford, 1995.
9 Creating what Giuliana Bruno has called 'CinéCities', David B. Clarke, *The Cinematic City*, London, 1997, p. 46.
10 Elizabeth Wilson, 'The Rhetoric of Urban Space', *New Left Review* 209 (1995): 146–60.
11 Anthony Vidler, 'Post-urbanism', in *The Architectural Uncanny: Essays in the Modern Unhomely*, Cambridge, MA: MIT Press, 1992, pp. 177–86.
12 Paul Virilio, 'The Overexposed City', *The Lost Dimension*, trans. Daniel Moshenberg, Paris, 1991.
13 Wilson, 'The Rhetoric of Urban Space', p. 159.
14 Vidler, 'Post-urbanism', p. 186.
15 Vidler, 'Post-urbanism', p. 186.
16 Virilio, 'The Overexposed City', p. 12.

17 Postcards of the 'Mall of America' in West Bloomington, the biggest mall in the USA, show downtown Minneapolis somewhere far-off in the background as comparatively insignificant.

18 Virilio, 'The Overexposed City', p. 18.

19 Jean Baudrillard, *Simulations*, trans. P. Foss, P. Patton and P. Beitchman, New York: Semiotext(e), 1983.

20 Umberto Eco, 'Travels in Hyperreality', *Faith in Fakes*, London, 1986.

21 Fredric Jameson, 'Cognitive Mapping', in *Marxism and the Interpretation of Culture*, ed. C. Nelson and L. Grossberg, New York, 1988.

22 Marc Augé, *Non-Places: Introduction to an Anthropology of Supermodernity*, London, 1995.

23 In the film *Falling Down*, set in LA, children encounter the main character D-Fens with a gun, and assume he is an actor in a film (which of course he is), and show him how to shoot with it, because they have seen it in movies.

24 Sharon Zukin, *Landscapes of Power*, Berkeley, CA, 1992.

25 Fredric Jameson, 'Postmodernism and Consumer Society', in *Postmodern Culture*, ed. Hal Foster, London, 1985, pp. 111–25.

26 Editorial, *Architecture Today*, October 1997.

27 Mike Davis, *City of Quartz. Excavating the Future in Los Angeles*, Pimlico: London, 1990, p. 81. In Britain there is concern that Disney will take over plans for the Millennium Dome in Greenwich, while in Times Square Disney has expressed an interest in becoming a key player in the redevelopment plans.

28 Louis Marin, *Utopics: Spatial Play*, London, 1984.

29 George Ritzer, *The McDonaldization of Society*, rev. edn, California, 1996.

30 John Findlay, *Magic Lands: Western Cityscapes and American Culture after 1940*, Berkeley, CA, 1992.

31 Charles Rutheiser, *Imagineering Atlanta*, London, 1996.

32 Mark Gottdiener, *The Theming of America*, Oxford, 1997.

33 Norman Klein, 'Scripted Space: the Consumer-built City', in *Consuming Architecture, Architectural Design*, ed. Sarah Chaplin and Eric Holding, John Wiley and Sons, vol. 68, no. 1/2, Jan./Feb. 1998.

34 Interestingly, Rem Koolhaas has now been asked to work on the master plan for Universal City, and is at the same time preparing plans for the city of Hanoi in Cambodia. In this scenario, the question of which is leading the way forward and what is the model for what inevitably arises. Koolhaas himself is beginning to talk of a 'new authenticity', especially with respect to Asia, an authenticity born of what he calls a 'Photoshop paradigm' of urbanism, which for him represents one of the new software tools responsible for facilitating the easy digital reconfiguring of the city's image and its new existence as a physical entity.

35 P. Kotler and G. Armstrong, *Marketing: An Introduction*, 3rd edn, London, 1988.

36 The London-based Space Syntax Laboratory was involved in proposals to control crowds flocking to Trafalgar Square for Millennium celebrations.

37 Discussed in M. Christine Boyer, *Cybercities*, Cambridge, MA, 1996.

38 Quoted by Diller and Scofidio, 'Soft Sell', *City Speculations*, ed. Patricia Phillips, Princeton, NJ, 1996, p. 29.

39 Rem Koolhaas, lecture at the Royal Academy, London, June 1997.

40 Deyan Sudjic, 'Variations on a Theme Park', *The Guardian*, 5 September 1996, p. 6.

41 This event took place on December 31st 1996, Las Vegas.

42 See Stephen Brown, *Postmodern Marketing*, London, 1995.

43 Pierre Bourdieu, *Distinction*, London, 1984.

44 Guy Debord, *Society of the Spectacle*, London, 1987.

Part V
The filmic metropolis

14 'The Problem of London', or, how to explore the moods of the city

Steve Pile

> Like dream images, urban objects, relics of the last century, were hieroglyphic clues to a forgotten past.
>
> (Buck-Morss, 1989, p. 39)

Introduction, in which urban objects become clues

We know it's London. The opening shot precisely frames Tower Bridge; Tower Bridge, in turn, perfectly frames the flowing river. Between the towers of the bridge, we can just about see something – a ship of some sort – moving upstream, towards us. Unmistakably, this is London. One building is enough to tell us it is so. As it would be with Sydney's Opera House, or Paris' Eiffel Tower, or Kuala Lumpur's Petronas Towers. Sometimes, a fragment is enough of a clue. As if the iconic architecture wasn't enough to tell us where in the world we are, almost before we've had time to settle, the title of Patrick Keiller's (1993) film appears in bold white letters against a black background:

London

On this cue, the narrator enigmatically, wearily intones: 'It is a journey to the end of the world'. And, in this way, we are placed at the intersection of many stories; stories with beginnings, specific ends and a curious return (to the 'heart of darkness'?). In part, this short chapter is about these journeys through London; journeys that are, we can say, emblematic of city life in the way they mark particular trajectories in space and time. But the film is directed towards a deeper problem in city life, and this has to do with London itself: how to explore the experiences of the city, how to evoke its moods? The problem is, *partly*, that London – like any city – has too many experiences and too many moods; *partly*, that many of these experiences appear to be wholly absent, secret, invisible, hidden, intangible, tacit, forgotten, unfathomable; and, *partly*, that experiences of the city are at their sharpest at the point of disappearance, already dissipated by the time a story about them can be told. The focus of this chapter is on a particular experiment in the problem of cities; an experiment which might be described in general terms as psychogeographical; an experiment which is, in this case, on film.

It may sound like an artificial move to describe Keiller's film as psychogeo-graphical, but Keiller – through the narrator – sets the movie up as a research project, carefully grounded in various intellectual traditions. It is not far-fetched, moreover, to say that Keiller is conducting a series of experiments in the study of London. Here, I will tease out the film's connections to the psychogeography of the Situationist International. There are other traditions of thought too, but I will not go into these (but see also Daniels, 1995). By concentrating on the psychogeography of the film, it is possible to discern some of the spatial practices that underlie (what we might call) the hieroglyphic space of the city. In particular, we can see the city's cross-cutting and overlapping geographies and the ways in which these are constitutive of the city. With this in mind, it is possible to say something about the way this film explores the city and its distinctive cityness.

Film theorists have argued that film – in both its movie and photographic forms – is in particular sympathy with the city (Bruno, 1993). For Benjamin, for example, it is no accident that the technology of film arises at the same time as the experience of modernity and the modern city. This experience, for him, has something to do with the vast number of things that are going on in cities – the perpetual, and ever-faster, circulation of things: 'things' such as people, goods, money, ideas. With all this movement, the city becomes dreamlike – a proces-sion of ghostly figures, as in a dream; it becomes something to be decoded, like a dream (see also Frisby, chapter 1; Pile, 2000). In his writings on Berlin, Kracauer put it this way:

> An understanding of this city depends on an ability to decipher the dream-like images it generates … its contradictions and contrasts, its toughness, its openness, its juxtapositions and simultaneity, its lustre.
>
> (Kracauer, 1987, p. 41)

Photographs, then, seem able to capture the bizarre juxtapositions and strange coincidences that the modern city offers to the observer. Further, film can also *move* between places, capturing simultaneities and connections that are, in many ways, 'at a distance': for example, by cutting between one event and another; or, by moving backwards or forwards in time; or, by panning or zooming, in or out. Film appears to capture the 'flow of life' of the city, but it is in fact a patchwork of time spaces, stitched together into a seemingly seamless sequence (Kracauer, 1960). I am interested in how Keiller's film seeks to stitch together the time–spaces – the bits and pieces – of the city. In part, this is because he seems to slow the city down, rather than attempt to follow its intensities and (faster) speed, its tensions, its surre-alism. Paradoxically, it is this very slowing down that enables us to see and to hear, to experience, something of the speed and intensity of the city, with its forgotten pasts, its secret presents, its openness, its sheer quantity, its indif-ference, its irreducible antagonisms, its surfaces, its brilliance, its colour saturation.

In the next section, I will describe some elements of Keiller's film. Then, I will turn to some of the (psychogeographical) ideas that underpin its construction. However, describing the film and teasing out its psychogeographies are not 'merely descriptive' – for I will focus on those moments when the filmic space of the movie is spliced with the 'hieroglyphic spaces' of London.

London's hieroglyphics

The narrator has returned to London at the request of Robinson. We never see the narrator nor know his name. And we only ever hear about Robinson through the narrator, who sets the scene:

> Dirty old blighty. Economically backward, bizarre, a catalogue of modern miseries, with its fake traditions, its Irish war, its militarism, its silly old judges, its hatred of intellectuals, its ill-health and bad food, its sexual repression, its hypocrisy and racism, and its indolence – it's so exotic, so home made.

The date is the 11 January 1992 (timing is all important). Background: Robinson, we are informed, is an 'auto-didact' teaching in Fine Art and Architecture at the University of Barking. More background: Robinson reads Montaigne; Montaigne, we are told, lived in London for a while, like many exiled French writers, such as Mallarmé, Apollinaire (who was born in Rome), Rimbaud and (oddly, since he never lived in England) Baudelaire. Robinson is studying these writers.

Robinson – in keeping with the sentiment of his studies – is also an enthusiastic *flâneur*, though (paradoxically) he doesn't go out much. Going out is too much for him. A visit to a supermarket, for example, evokes a sense of overwhelming poignancy because it reminds Robinson of all the journeys abroad that he no longer feels able to make. In keeping with this intellectual tradition of experiencing and narrating the city, Robinson is committed to a project in which he will attempt to grasp London's mode of feeling, its atmosphere, its forgotten pasts. But he cannot do it alone. And so, the narrator has come to the aid of his indisposed friend.

This film is a story of journeys, nonetheless. But more than this, it is a deliberate exploration of the city. In many ways, the film can be seen as a set of excursions across London much like those in Iain Sinclair's book *Lights Out for the Territory* (1997; see also Pile, forthcoming). In Sinclair's work, the journeys have varying, and seemingly perverse, logics. They are experiments in the possibility of understanding the city differently. Indeed, they are attempts to map the mood of the city by walking across it. Sinclair describes his project this way:

> Walking is the best way to explore and exploit the city; the changes, shifts, breaks in the cloud helmet, movement of light on water. Drifting purposefully is the recommended mode, tramping asphalted earth in alert reverie,

allowing the fiction of an underlying pattern to reveal itself... noticing *everything*. Alignments of telephone kiosks, maps made from the moss on the slopes of Victorian sepulchres, collections of prostitutes' cards, torn and defaced promotional bills for cancelled events at York Hall, visits to the homes of dead writers, bronze casts on war memorials, plaster dogs, beer mats, concentrations of used condoms, the crystalline patterns of glass shards surrounding an imploded BMW quarter-light window ... Walking, moving across a retreating townscape, stitches it all together: the illicit cocktail of bodily exhaustion and a raging carbon monoxide high.

(1997, p. 4)

For Sinclair, this practice of walking is a twist on an older (and much written about) style of walking: *flânerie* (see Tester, 1994; see also Rendell, chapter 8). Keiller's film undoubtedly owes a debt to these spatial practices of experiencing the city: practices that are found in the poetry of Baudelaire, that were fuelled by the writings of Walter Benjamin (1973, 1978), and that are kept alive by diverse practitioners (some known as cosmonauts) in contemporary London. More than walking, this urban spatial practice is an attempt to notice the overlooked, to examine the detail of the city to find its hidden secrets, to trace out alternative histories. For example, at a certain point, Keiller's film takes time to notice the fast-disappearing neo-Georgian telephone boxes. At the time, London telephone companies were replacing these because they were hard to clean and expensive to repair when vandalised. The smell of urine was being replaced by the smell of disinfectant. Robinson, the narrator tells us, is characteristically nostalgic about the whole thing; something was being permanently lost from public life.

Nevertheless, the neo-Georgian boxes have had an after-life. Some have survived, probably because they are so much a part of the distinctive look and feel (and smell) of London's streets. Postcards of London still show these telephone boxes. Thus, fragments – such as these telephone boxes – become metonyms for the city as a whole. In these fragments, then, are found something of the attributes and affects of the city itself. Further, such fragments become the hieroglyphic spaces of the city, requiring both collection and deciphering. The first task, as it had been for Benjamin, is to catalogue these fragments, as if collecting postcards from far-off lands (see Gilloch, chapter 12). Much as Sinclair 'notices everything' on his excursions across the city, Robinson (the narrator tells us) 'is preparing his own series of postcards of contemporary London'.

In keeping with this project, Keiller's film is seemingly comprised of lingering middle-distance shots (there are only three moving shots in the film, only one of which is noticeable), often without the voice of the narrator, when we are left listening to the silence of the music and ambient sound. But these postcards do not seem to stitch the city together (as Sinclair would have it), but instead they frame it, slow it down, enticing us to look at the city with different eyes. In part, the city 'doesn't add up' because the narrator's observations often jar against the postcards we see; the commentary seems to be coming from someplace else. As importantly, by giving us the time to look at the spaces of the city, other aspects of the physicality of the city become apparent: its motion, its duration, its endurance, its persistence ... and its passing. While similar in many respects to Sinclair's book, Keiller's film has its own atmosphere – a melancholic sense of a lost past pervades his film. The narrator is informative:

> The failure of the English revolution, said Robinson, is all around us: in the Westminster constitution, in Ireland, and poisoning English attitudes ... Everywhere we went, there was an atmosphere of conspiracy and intrigue.

And the film silently shows us MI6's monumental building in Vauxhall (the British Government still has not officially acknowledged the existence of MI6, despite 007, despite continued revelations: see Pile, 2001). London remains an alchemy of tacit power and possibilities for an alternative present. Failed experiments in the history of the city can be discovered in its neglected spaces. Thus, the narrator reveals Robinson's objective:

> He was searching for the location of a memory. A vivid recollection of a street of small factories backing onto a canal [voiced over shots of waste land in Wapping, East London] but they no longer exist ... And he has adopted the neighbourhood as a site for exercises in psychic landscaping, drifting and free association.

For me, it is tempting to stop at this point to reflect on the significance of 'psychic landscaping, drifting and free association', but I will wait to do this until the next section. For now, let us continue with the narrative:

> He seemed to be attempting to travel through time. [This is voiced over a prolonged shot of wooden cargo palettes burning, possibly/probably as a 'memory' of the Guy Fawkes night, seen later in the film.]

To travel through time is also to travel through space: in the labyrinth of the city, the journeys take place in time and space. Travelling, more precisely, is about moving in time–space: to find a memory, one also needs to locate it; to find its location is also to search out its past. By travelling in time–space, it is possible to see the ways that it might have been. This means more than simply decoding the space of the city as it is; it means placing the hieroglyphic spaces of the city into the flow of history once more, re-establishing their connections to other places. The derelict land once contained a street, backing onto factories. By evoking this space–time, the urban waste lands generated by the economic recessions of the late 1970s and 1980s are no longer simply about emptiness, nor about their absence of history, their absence of anything going on; they are now haunted by ghosts that say how it might have been, if it had kept its people, its jobs ... The journey is a deliberate attempt to experience the geography of the city differently. The film, thus, becomes a chronicle of Robinson's alternative time-and-spaces of London:

> He [Robinson] has asked me to accompany him on a series of journeys, each prompted by an aspect of his project. The first is to be a pilgrimage to the sources of English Romanticism. On March the 10th, we set out for Strawberry Hill, the house of Horace Walpole, but were disturbed by events on Wandsworth Common; the bomb had gone off at 7.10 that morning.

There are to be a series of expeditions, but many are overtaken by unexpected events; events created – we might say – by the city. Let us reflect on this. The aim of the journey is consistent with Romanticism itself: to see oneself from the outside, to see oneself as part of a romance. The film involves itself in the romance of origins and traditions. But this 'mode of feeling' is undone by 'the event'. The bomb detonates and rips through the romance. And the narrative is diverted into a consideration of a not-so-post colonial war and politics. Detonated into history, the bomb provokes a reflection on Londoners' capacity to forget history – such as events in Ireland and the long-standing bombing campaign in London itself.

If the film is a pilgrimage, it is less about reaching a source or a destination (the arrival at a place already known), than about the discoveries, frustrations and diversions of the city. As the journeys are embarked on and undertaken, they trace out specific geographies and histories of the city; geographies that are cross-cut by other geographies and other histories. In this film, we can discern some characteristically urban experiences. In part, these experiences have been engendered by 'the event' and 'the detour' – the ways in which the city amalgamates histories and geographies, bringing them together into some form of relation by co-presence. These histories and geographies are imaginatively reconstructed using certain techniques, which we have seen referred to as 'exercises in psychic landscaping, drifting and free association'. It is this that gives us an explicit link to the spatial practice of psychogeography. These exercises become ways of understanding the dream-like quality of cities: its juxtapositions and simultaneities, its connections and openness. The city, however, is not entirely open: its hieroglyphics need to be deciphered *in situ* (in situations).

Only particular paths are, and can be, taken in the city: the city is a rat-run of everyday practices (much as de Certeau would have us believe). Nevertheless, we also have to recognise that the specificity of journeys and experiments undertaken in Keiller's film, *London*, represents only a particular experience of the city. While we might agree (a little uncomfortably, since these are also parodies) with Robinson as he rants and rails against suburban Conservative governments and their attacks on the city and its freedoms, the film shows little political concern for domestic or working lives (outside the narrow confines of 'The University'), or even with the more intimate social and cultural life in the city, except in the abstract. This film is a profoundly detached and solitary encounter, located exclusively in public spaces (even when it is 'indoors'). To this extent, at least, it is straightforward to claim and demonstrate that the film explores a profoundly male and academic, white and middle-class, experience. Such criticisms are easy to make, and easy to extend. Even so, it might be possible to glimpse something about city life in the fragments of this film: it would be a pity to look at the moon and see only the craters. Looking elsewhere, we might find psychogeographies of the city.

Psychogeographies of the city

If there is 'the problem of London', then what is it?

> We are bored in the city, there is no longer any Temple of the Sun ... We are bored in the city, we really have to strain to still discover mysteries on the sidewalk billboards, the latest state of humour and poetry ...
>
> (Gilles Ivain [Ivan Chtcheglov], 1953, p. 14)

Ivain then lists some billboard captions. And some places: buildings on streets, something he has noticed, something strange, perhaps a memory, something 'without music and without geography' (1953, p. 14), and something that you cannot see: 'it does not exist' (ibid., p. 14). He continues:

> All cities are geological; you cannot take three steps without encountering ghosts bearing all the prestige of their legends. We move within a *closed* landscape whose landmarks constantly draw us toward the past. Certain *shifting* angles, certain *receding* perspectives, allow us to glimpse original conceptions of space, but this vision remains fragmentary.
>
> (Ibid., pp. 14–15)

A new formulation of city life would have to attend to the fragments, the pasts, the ghosts, the magic of the city. It might be clear that Keiller's *London* bears some of the mode of feeling of Ivain's analysis of the city, especially in its sense of a closed landscape, its mourning for something lost, its shifting angles of perception, its collection of fragments – and, most of all, a sense that the city can be explored through even its tiniest details, or in its surface appearance:

> Robinson believed that, if he looked at it hard enough, he could cause the surfaces of the city to reveal to him the molecular basis of historical events and, in this way, he hoped to see into the future.

In these works (by Keiller, Sinclair and Ivain), it is possible to see an argument about the essential (an unfashionable word nowadays) nature of the city. Since film is a series of postcards of the city, we (the audience) are asked to (really) look at the city: to see beyond its surfaces. Even so, we can observe that only specific surfaces – through which we are meant to understand the connections between the tiny events that comprise history – are presented to us. The landscape of the city is framed and, in this way, made into a closed landscape. But I do not think in any of these works that these are closed landscapes in the sense that they are isolated or framed by impermeable boundaries. Instead, we get a sense of the multiple and overlapping (hi)stories and geographies that 'make up' the cityscape. As we sit and watch the cityscape, buses, people, time crosses in front of us, following many different paths and trajectories. In Keiller's film, the gateposts are bearers of memories, of the sounds of children. They are due to be knocked down – to become the ghosts that Ivain talks of. The ghosts of the city haunt everyday life, but they are also confined by their haunts. The city, in these imaginations, is both closed and open: constituted by its openness, its porosity, its plasticity.

Postcards tell us about this characteristic of urban space: it is not that space is completely malleable. Buildings cannot simply or easily be torn down and others put in their place. But as we watch the movement, we become aware that what appears to be absolutely still is in fact actually moving, located in a particular rhythm of time–space. If you watch the surfaces of the city, then you can see that they are comprised of multiple time–space rhythms (to extend slightly Lefebvre's analysis of the city, see Kofman and Lebas, 1996; see also, Pryke, 1999). To this extent, it might be possible to discern the many futures of the city; the patterns of historical events, beyond the surface.

This way of seeing is not simply visual, seen only by the eyes. It involves the intelligences and sensations of the body, for sure, which are *also* experienced through the eyes (that is, this visuality is not disembodied). And, paradoxically, this becomes much clearer once you slow down and take the time to assess the changing moods of the city: high-rise blocks glimmering in the warm red light of evening, a street's ghosts come to life in the monochromatic light of the moon, skyscrapers awake to a cold crisp bright blue dawn, and people visibly wilt under a full-on too-fucking-hot I-should-be-on-a-beach sun. These time–spaces are sometimes linear, pressing forward in the rush towards a never-yet-achieved modernity, sometimes circular as times come back, as seasons turn, as ghosts fail to learn from the mistakes of the past, as never-ever realised futures lurk in the shadows of the city.

Maybe all this is stuff and nonsense, though. These works are evocative of something, but what? Of ghosts and dreams? Of pasts and futures? Of dust and death? But these aren't the only things going on in the city: where are the domestic and the domesticated stories? Nowhere. These stories are possible too. Behind the postcards, we can see the writings that tell other kinds of stories – family romances, perhaps: 'Weather awful'; 'Wish you were here'. Behind the surfaces, perhaps we can also make out other (hi)stories of the city. It is the porosity of these urban spaces that evokes *both* the multiplicity of stories *and also* the many time–spaces of the city, only some of which are allowed to become real. Others become ghosts; others remain dreams. It is in these other possibilities that we can begin to sense something of impassioned city life. Staring straight into the mirage of the modern city, other writers have attempted to apprehend the vicissitudes of urban experiences.

Like Keiller's Robinson, and like Gilles Ivain, Guy Debord believed practical experiments need to be conducted into city life. For Debord (1955, 1956), these experiments would constitute new urban practices and could be broadly described as *psychogeography*. In Debord's repertoire, it was the *dérive* that occupied centre stage. But when Robinson talks of psychic landscaping and free association, I hear in the background the noise of a psychodynamic understanding of the city that psychogeography only whispers. For psychic landscaping and free association might lead us to consider other ways of understanding the moods of the city: moods that are felt before there are words to describe them; moods that cannot be directly spoken, nor ever can be. Let us start, though, with psychogeography.

Debord describes psychogeography as a mode of observation. Interestingly, the term seems to have originated in a colonial encounter (a fact little commented on). Debord attests that the term was suggested by an illiterate Kabyle sometime in 1953. The Kabyle, of course, inhabited part of Algeria and were the subject of anthropological research by people like Pierre Bourdieu, but they were also implicated in an ever-more bloody post-colonial war, in which notable intellectuals like Jean-Paul Sartre and Frantz Fanon were becoming more and more deeply involved (in very different ways). Guy Debord's citation, therefore, is not an innocent act – it would be deliberately scandalous.

Psychogeography was meant to scandalise in other ways too: its intention, to provoke a crisis in happiness. In part, this was to be achieved by delineating the human experiences of urban landscapes, showing where they seemed – but failed – to meet desire. At the heart of this idea is a sense that city life, modernity, call it what you will, had led desire up a cul-de-sac, where it was promised satisfaction, but in fact met a dead-end. Psychogeography was directed towards turning (*détournment*) life into an 'excitive form' (Debord, 1955, p. 19). It would do this by flooding life with unrealisable desire – like demanding drinks that actually did quench your thirst, instead of making you thirstier – in this respect, desire and dreams of fulfilment were revolutionary, if they could be released. But there was something in the boredom, alienation and oblivion of city life that prevented desire from being articulated. Perhaps this had something to do with the changing ambience and moods of the city.

For Debord, the city was divided into distinct atmospheric zones, with distinct ambiences (and micro-climates). It was the task of psychogeography to map out these 'modes of feeling'. Debord thought that these zones could be identified using a specific spatial practice: the *dérive*, or drifting. It is this idea that Keiller and Sinclair deploy and extend in their use, respectively, of the journey and the excursion. Thus, walking across the city would be used as a way of assessing the impact of the urban environment on human experiences. Sensations of repellence, sadness, appeal, pleasure, would be mapped into places. (Note: this is neither simply an abstract intellectual exercise nor a purely visual practice.) Debord, and the early psychogeographers, recognised that there would not only be a diversity of sensations, but also that there would be contradictions. Urban space is nothing if not paradoxical; the question was how to get at these experiences of the city.

Experiments in drifting, psychic landscaping and free association

For Debord *inter alia*, mapping the paradoxes of the city involves the production of alternative cartographic techniques (see Pinder, 1996): the city is not spread out and summarised in symbols, not flattened and squared off. Instead, this map-making is a tactic for finding out about the relationship between experience and built form: the journey is a means to discover the geography of experience; by reversing the flow of the argument, we can also say that geography is a technique in the making of new maps. Cutting maps up to produce space differently, using maps from different places to get around, were essential tactics of psychogeography – precisely because they logic-chopped the rationally planned city, the city of boredom and oblivion. In order to map the city, new ways of moving through the city would be needed. One such technique was the *dérive*, or *drifting*. Drifting was not simply a random activity, but a deliberate attempt to think of spaces and spatiality different: to create situations in which space as currently produced becomes absurd.

Thus, the *dérive* is

> a technique of transient passage through varied ambiences. The *dérive* entails playful–constructive behaviour and awareness of psychogeographical effects … from the *dérive* point of view cities have a psychogeographical relief, with constant currents, fixed points and vortexes which strongly discourage entry into or exit from certain zones.
>
> (Debord, 1956, p. 22)

Paradoxically, moving through the city would demonstrate the *settled formations of power* in the city (see Allen, 1999): the places where access is denied – from the gates of government institutions, to military sites, to buildings for spies, to private houses. The porous city is more closed than open – porous because of what it filters out and because it channels through specific veins, rather than because it flows free and lets everything through. The freedoms of the city appear to be constantly under attack in the modern city, constantly circumscribed, constantly surveilled – often enough in the name of freedom, service and protection.

Psychogeography, then, as practised by the Situationist International and also by Keiller and Sinclair, is the study of direct experience of the environment – the city – on human emotions. The *dérive* is a technique through which these emotions are to be registered and experienced. *Détournment* is practice that turns existing settled formations of production (of space, of the city, of commodities, of life) towards something else. This turning does not mean there is a destination. Instead, it instigates a search for points of departure.

Fine. So, psychogeographers survey the city, taking notes on the atmosphere, ambience, mood, mode of feeling, at any given place. They are also attuned to the power relations that underlie these experiences. Now, I can't help but observe that all this can be astonishingly boring – ironically, given that boredom is seen as the enemy of the revolution: 'Boredom is Counter-Revolutionary', the Situationist International slogans shouted. Even so, the sheer quantity of observations can overwhelm the observer with a sense of abstraction from the very moods that are supposedly being discovered or described. A sense of detachment pervades these spatial practices. But maybe there is something (about the experience of the city) in this too. The city, pre-eminently, is unquantifiable: there are too many things to list, too many experiences; too many relations of power, too many resistances, to really get a grip on what is underlying it all – and this is why the surface of the city never reveals the molecular basis of anything.

Instead, the city is *turned* into a series of interlocking paradoxes in which we feel movement and fixity, in which we sense linear and cyclical time, in which space is continuous and fragmented. The rebus of the city lies in its shifting perspectives, in the way it shifts our perceptions. In this urbanised space, we can no longer expect to find one answer, nor one dream, nor decode the hieroglyph as if it pointed to only one meaning. Instead, these experiments are the first step in a sense of the multiplicity of cities that overlap, pass by one another, that cross, get crossed and get cross. This 'mode of feeling' is necessarily indifferent to quantity, necessarily provoked to emotion by the city, even before those emotions are understood or articulated.

The problem of London. In Keiller's film, the viewer sits back and enjoys the opportunity to view the city undistracted, smoothly mirroring experiences of the city in which people refuse to be distracted by the city's many and obvious distractions. In slowing down time, by reducing the quantity of the city, the film allows urban space to be seen – as if for the first time. Even so, paradoxically, London becomes abstract: its 'modes of feeling' are linked back into specific traditions, rather than moods and feelings. The film is an exercise in *drifting* – a deliberate attempt to assess the ambience of the city by putting space together in a counter-intuitive way, through the artifice of looking for (false?) origins and traditions. But let us think some more about the other techniques invoked by Robinson: what of psychic landscaping and free association?

There is a *psychic landscaping* of the city, but it remains out there, rather than evoking the 'out there' closest in. The cityscapes remain in the middle distance, framed by the edges of the camera's unblinking eye; an exterior mapping of conscious thoughts, written (as it were) on the front of the postcard. Psychic landscaping simultaneously through the mind and through the body might offer other ways of imagining the landscapes of cityness, of evoking the physicalities of the city through the mind and body. In this sense, cityscapes would not be exterior to the mind or body, nor available only as an *object* of reflection. It would be thought through, experienced in place, in situations. Then there is *free association*, but the chains of thought in the film often end with a romance, a connection to a particular literary tradition. Romance is everywhere, but it is not everything. Free associations might lead to other trains of thought (as Freud would have it: Pile, 1998). The film has odd moments: snowdrops, the moon, rain, all appear. Different markers of time-and-space. A nature that is associated with the city, somehow. Perhaps there is something else here: the freedom of association. The freedoms of the city lie in their capacity to make free associations, between people, between things, between people-and-things. Yet thoughts remain curiously chained to particular kinds of imagination. At the point of its discovery, it seems, the city disappears.

Conclusion, in which the clues disappear ... and reappear

> The true identity of London, he [Robinson] said, is in its absence. As a city, it no longer exists. In this alone, it is truly modern. London was the first metropolis to disappear.

Modernity, we are told, melts everything solid into air. The spatial practice of psychogeography, also, can make the city disappear. I have suggested throughout this chapter that only particular experiences are gleaned through psychogeographical practices and presented in the writings. More than this, the attendance to specific kinds of mythologies might also lead to the layering of a particular ambience over the mood of the city: an atmosphere that you already knew in advance of the experiment. It may seem strange, since it looks as if I am resorting to an argument I have just claimed to be inadequate in important respects, but these writings do show that there are more ghosts and dreams in the city than it would at first appear. Ghosts and dreams pervade the city. It is not by seeing the city as a fixed space or as a space of perpetual (speeding up) motion that we will catch sight of these ghosts and dreams.

It is only through spatial practices which trace out the city, which map-make it, that the experiences of haunting and of desire can be discerned. If the ramble, the stroll, the walk and the *dérive* are a beginning, they are only a beginning. The city is urgently calling out for new spatial practices – if only because the city has now become almost too small and nearly too big to sense properly. It will be through an understanding of the multiplicity of time–spaces that we will understand the actual disappearance of the city. Disappeared because they have forgotten the dreams on which they were built. Disappeared because of the ghosts of the past that have not been exorcised. Disappeared because clues to other experiences of the city have been overlooked (and this is as true of Keiller's movie – and this chapter – as anything else). Cities have become hieroglyphic spaces in the sense that they have become a language that 'we' have forgotten how to speak and write: an interlocking set of picture puzzles from a lost time-and-space. But it is not the forgotten past that concerns me, it is the lost futures that can no longer be articulated.

London does not exist – any more than anywhere else – until we make it.

Acknowledgements

I would like to thank Neil Leach and Jenny Robinson for their comments on an earlier draft and to Jane's Addiction and Morcheeba for providing the soundtrack.

References

Allen, J. (1999) 'Cities of Power and Influence: Settled Formations', in *Unsettling Cities: Movement/Settlement*, ed. J. Allen, D. Massey and M. Pryke, London: The Open University/Routledge, pp. 181–218.

Benjamin, W. (1973) *Charles Baudelaire: A Lyric Poet in the Era of High Capitalism*, London: Verso, 1997.

Benjamin, W. (1978) *One Way Street and Other Writings*, London: Verso, 1985.

Bruno, G. (1993) *Streetwalking on a Ruined Map: Cultural Theory and the City Films of Elvira Notari*, Princeton, NJ: Princeton University Press.

Buck-Morss, S. (1989) *The Dialectics of Seeing: Walter Benjamin and the Arcades Project*, Cambridge, MA: MIT Press.

Daniels, S. (1995) 'Paris Envy: Patrick Keiller's *London*', *History Workshop Journal* 40: 220–2.

Debord, G. (1955) 'Introduction to a Critique of Urban Geography', in *Theory of the Dérive and Other Situationist Writings on the City*, ed. L. Andreotti and X. Costa, Barcelona: Museu d'Art Contemporani de Barcelona and ACTAR, 1996, pp. 18–21.

—— (1956) 'Theory of the Dérive', in *Theory of the Dérive and Other Situationist Writings on the City*, ed. L. Andreotti and X. Costa, Barcelona: Museu d'Art Contemporani de Barcelona and ACTAR, 1996, pp. 22–7.

de Certeau, M. (1984) *The Practice of Everyday Life*, Berkeley, CA: University of California Press.

Frisby, D., chap. 1, this volume.

Gilloch, G., chap. 12, this volume.

Ivain, G. (1953) 'Formulary for a New Urbanism', in *Theory of the Dérive and Other Situationist Writings on the City*, ed. L. Andreotti and X. Costa, Barcelona: Museu d'Art Contemporani de Barcelona and ACTAR, 1996, pp. 14–17.

Kofman, E. and Lebas, E. (eds) (1996) *Writing on Cities: Henri Lefebvre*, Oxford: Basil Blackwell.

Kracauer, S. (1960) *Theory of Film: The Redemption of Physical Reality*, Princeton, NJ: Princeton University Press.

Kracauer, S. (1987) *Strassen in Berlin und Anderswo*, Berlin: Das Arsenal; trans. Allan Cochrane, in 'Reimagining Berlin: world city, national capital or ordinary place?', ed. A. Cochrane and A. Jonas, *European Urban and Regional Studies*, 6 (2) (1999): 145–64.

Pile, S. (1998) 'Freud, Dreams and Imaginative Geographies', in *Freud 2000*, ed. A Elliott, Cambridge: Polity Press, pp. 204–34.

Pile, S. (2000) 'Sleepwalking in the Modern City: Walter Benjamin and Sigmund Freud in the World of Dreams', in *Blackwell Companion to Urban Studies*, ed. Gary Bridge and Sophie Watson, Oxford: Basil Blackwell, pp. 75–86.

Pile, S. (2001) 'The Un(known)City… or, an urban geography of what lies buried below the surface', in *The Unknown City*. ed. Iain Borden, Joe Kerr, Alicia Pivaro and Jane Rendell, Cambridge, MA: MIT Press, pp. 262–79.

Pile, S. (forthcoming) 'Telling Streets: Spaces of Memory and Forgetting', in *Temporalities: Autobiography in a Postmodern Age*, ed. J. Campbell and J. Harbord, Manchester: Manchester University Press.

Pinder, D. (1996) 'Subverting Cartography: The Situationists and Maps of the City', *Environment and Planning A*, 28 (3): 405–27.

Pryke, M. (1999) 'City Rhythms: Neo-liberalism and the Developing World', in *Unsettling Cities: Movement/Settlement*, ed. J. Allen, D. Massey and M. Pryke, London: The Open University/Routledge, pp. 229–60.

Rendell, J., chap. 8, this volume.

Sinclair, I. (1997) *Lights Out for the Territory*, London: Granta.

Tester, K. (ed.) (1994) *The Flâneur*, London: Routledge.

15 *Playtime*

'Tativille' and Paris

Iain Borden

Jean-Luc Godard's classic film *Alphaville* (1965), is the canonic portrayal of the dystopian state and its mechanistic city. Shot on location in Paris,[1] *Alphaville* depicts a world of disembodied computerised voices, flashing signals, directive arrows, tall towers, dark streets and fluorescent interiors; as a sign announces, it is an urbanism of 'silence, logic security, prudence'.

This correlation of modernism and the state was common in the 1950s and 1960s, and provides much of the context for the second of Jacques Tati's films to feature his famous invention, Monsieur Hulot. In *Mon Oncle*, (1958, production design Henri Schmitt), the Chaplinesque Hulot lives stooped under the eaves of a ramshackle tenement building of *vieux* Saint-Maur, in a fast-disappearing France replete with market, mischievous boys, chattering residents, cafés and horse-drawn carts. It is dirty, haphazard, old. By contrast, Hulot's sister Mme Arpel and husband occupy a different, highly bourgeois part of town (filmed in Créteil), with flat-roofed house, geometric garden, streamlined car, industrialised gadgets and suburban routines. It is hygienic, planned, modern.

Hulot moves between these two worlds, separated by a decrepit stone wall and newly-laid road. Not for him, though, the new Saint-Maur of modern school, chic restaurants, speeding traffic, plastic flowers ('flowers that last'), clean factories and rectilinear apartments; despite the improving efforts of his relatives, Hulot continually returns to old Saint-Maur by cyclomoteur. In the Arpels' eyes, Hulot is an embarrassing under-achiever unable to find his place in modernised France, and to be kept away from their son, Gérard.[2]

One might expect *Playtime* (1967, production design Eugène Roman), Tati's third film with Hulot, to exhibit similar preoccupations regarding the alienating nature of the modern city. To shoot *Playtime*, in 1964 Tati constructed a giant set on wasteland near Vincennes outside Paris, a 162,000 sq ft down-scaled pseudo-city that ate up 65,000 cubic yards of concrete, 42,300 sq ft of plastic, 342,000 sq ft of timber and 12,600 sq ft of glass.[3] It was quickly nicknamed 'Tativille'.[4] As Tati himself described it, the set was 'the real star of the film',[5] displaying a Paris comprised almost entirely of rectilinear glass, steel and concrete architecture, directly based on the Esso building at La Défense (1963) and implicitly on Lever House (1952) in New York.[6] Resolutely modern, Tativille is stripped of the history, memory, colours, dirt, nature, family relatives and other aspects of old France still visible in *Mon Oncle*, a city in which Hulot bumbles around from faltering business errand to unrequited *amour*. Unsurprisingly, given this setting, *Playtime* is commonly interpreted as an assault on modernism, a more playful counterpart to *Alphaville*.

However, it was not modernist architecture in itself which Tati found repellent. As he stated, '[i]f I had been against modern architecture I would have shown the most ugly buildings'. Instead, Tati made Tativille 'so that no architect could say anything against it. I took the finest I could. These buildings are beautiful.'[7] Similarly, when accused of attacking modern kitchens while many had none at all, Tati retorted that he was not criticising kitchens *per se*, only consumerist society.[8] He in fact reserves his most scathing critiques for cultural aspects of modern individuals; for example, when Hulot is waiting for his business appointment with M. Giffard, it is the haughty portraits of male executives hung high on the walls which define the ideology of the space, while Hulot has fun with the rest of the props.[9]

In this light, Tati's films are not so much 'shots *at* modern architecture',[10] as Andrea Kahn states, but shots *within* modern architecture. Furthermore, I contend, they are overtly positive attempts to reassert the poetic aspects of modern lives latent within modernist urbanism. In short, Tati's films help unlock the experiential and comic potential of modern architecture.

In many ways Tati's ambivalence towards modernism mirrored debates being conducted within contemporary French political and intellectual thought in reaction to the immense modernisation and Americanisation of post-war France then underway. On the one hand, Guy Debord, the Situationist International, Henri Lefebvre and other members of the Left viewed contemporary urban development with disdain, particularly for its tendency to create a modern city of images, a 'zero degree architecture' formulated as the 'space of blank sheets of paper, drawing-boards, plans, sections, elevations, scale models, geometrical projections'.[11] On the other hand, they were also concerned with reasserting the irrational, passionate, performed and contested elements of city life. As Lefebvre puts it, influenced by his arguments with Sartre and phenomenological existentialism:

> One truly gets the impression that every shape in space, every spatial plane, constitutes a mirror and produces a mirage effect; that within each body the rest of the world is reflected, and referred back to, in an ever-renewed to-and-fro of reciprocal reflection, an interplay of shifting colours, lights and forms.[12]

In essence, Lefebvre postulates that architecture as spatial Other can act as a way of knowing and producing oneself. This is why, perhaps, Tati engages so much with architecture – it represents a way in which one might come to grips with the urban environment and modernity as a whole.

Just how this might occur is revealed, for example, in an incident in *Mon*

Oncle. While in the Arpels' kitchen, Hulot drops a water jug – much to his surprise, it does not break but bounces. Hulot then proceeds, typically, to bounce the jug from increasingly greater heights. It is this process which Tati emphasises in *Playtime*. Whereas in *Mon Oncle* Hulot always leaves the modern suburb, retreating to old Saint-Maur, in *Playtime* he accepts the modern city and begins to play within it.

Comic democracy

Playtime, as is often noted, is in the tradition of Charlie Chaplin's *Modern Times* (1936), critiquing urban rationalism through the mode of comedy, wherein a seemingly hopeless character triumphs at the end. Certainly there are parallels between Hulot and Chaplin, and not only between the filmic characters; Tati himself, as with Chaplin, spent many years in the music hall as a mime-actor before making his first film, playing parts like a boxer, fisherman or horse-rider.[13] But where Chaplin's creation is clownish, actively disruptive of the regimented institutions and pompous individuals he encounters, Tati's is far more passive yet pervasive. He is called Monsieur Hulot, but we never learn his first name; he is recognised in the street, but also mistaken for others just as others are mistaken for him; he is usually ignored. He is frequently filmed by the long-shot lens, and rarely in a close-up. In *Playtime*, Hulot is not the 'star' of the movie, merely the most apparent of many characters; he is the just-another-nobody with whom we all partially identify. Hulot is each and every one of us, central yet peripheral to the city.

To Hulot, 'the son of the air and of the wind',[14] life simply happens as he circulates around town, occasionally provoking disorder (as when a Hulot look-alike causes Giffard to bash his nose into a glass door), but generally just creating fun from within. For example, in *Les vacances de monsieur Hulot* (1953), the first of Tati's Hulot films, an earnest male suitor impresses on the bored-looking Martine that 'it is the duty of the politically-conscious woman to play a more important role in exposing the decadence of the middle cl ...', while Hulot, searching for a ping-pong ball, is unknowingly disrupting two card games, later leading to volatile allegations of cheating. There is, then, a politics here, but not as overt assertion, for in Tati's films it is the dispersed nature of the humour which provides critical and hence radical qualities. This is an everyday humour of 'comic democracy',[15] where everyone has a right to be silly and ridiculous, to have fun and laugh.

The same is true of Tati's comic critique of architecture. Whereas Tati described his intentions as being simply to bring 'a little smile'[16] to modernist architecture, this is not wholly benign humour. This becomes clear from another of his statements, that he was trying 'to give more truth to the comic character'.[17] On the one hand this 'truth' means the right of Hulot-like characters to exist in architecture. On the other hand, the reverse is also true, wherein architecture and the city are given the right to a comic mode – a lighter and more humorous way of experience quite distinct from art-gallery reverence. If architecture is everywhere around us, so too, necessarily, is humour. Thus although *Playtime* is stuffed full of gags, most are dispersed quietly throughout the film, and often rely on acute observation from the audience (as, for example, when two nuns' hats flap in time). Ever-present, Tati's humorous moments suggest that all architectural scenes, whether in Tativille or the street outside, have such comic potential, if only we should pay enough attention to realise this much.

The way in which we are encouraged to do this is through the figure of Hulot, who is at once instigator and observer of comic potential in the modern city. Although Hulot's name was possibly derived from an architect of Tati's acquaintance, it is also close to the French *la hulotte* for tawny owl. Hulot is then like an owl, redolent of sagacity while comical in appearance. This association is underlined, in *Mon Oncle*, when Hulot visits his sister's house in the night, only to be confronted by the owl-like visage of the twin porthole windows (and the French for porthole is *hublot*), lit up like all-seeing eyes in which the Arpels' heads swivel like pupils.

The question is, how does this wise yet comic owl come to operate in the modern world? What encounters does Hulot undertake, and with what aspects of modern architecture?

Materiality

One facet of modern architecture made explicit in *Playtime* is a tendency toward homogeneity. Thus the opening scene is in the Aéroport de Paris at Orly, but the setting is initially unclear – a hospital perhaps? – for an attendant cleans the spotless floor, a nurse attends to a baby, nuns stroll around, and a married couple fuss over the husband's sore throat. The same space subsequently re-appears as a city-centre office, divided into identical cellular spaces: open-topped squares with pale green walls, blank metal exteriors and handleless doors. Outside, Paris is puzzlingly absent of its historic buildings. 'Where', asks a tourist, 'are the monuments?' Furthermore, *Playtime* insinuates, all cities are like this, and travel advertisements for London, Hawaii, Mexico and Stockholm all depict exactly the same modernist building. Such standardisation also works across scales, as when an artfully juxtaposed radio and building display the same proportions, styling and lighting.

The idea of abstract space – homogenised, infinite, uniform, ubiquitous – is emphasised by Tati's occasional use of the ceiling as a foil to the floor, and vice-versa. For example, the long office passage down which Giffard walks to greet Hulot is shot in single-point perspective, the corridor being a perfect vanishing square. Outside shots often have the same effect, notably the clear dawn sky outside the Royal Garden restaurant which exactly mirrors the blue pavement. As Robin Evans noted in his analysis of the Barcelona Pavilion, 'pressing architectural space between two horizontal sheets' like this tends to emphasise flatness, universality, order.[18]

Yet although Tati had reservations about the standardisation of architecture

– he disliked the 'blandness and uniformity of the new cities'[19] and the 'big buildings' which obliterated children's playgrounds and other spaces of silliness[20] – this was not his primary target. In short, although not necessarily wanting modernist architecture everywhere, given that it was so prevalent, Tati uses *Playtime* to explores its comic and pleasurable potential.

Above all, that potential lies in glass. Glass is everywhere in *Playtime*. There are glass doors, glass walls, glass roofs, glass partitions, glass counters, glass tables, glass spectacles, glass glasses. We have glass boundaries, barriers, shelters, entrances and surfaces. Consequently, *Playtime* is a paean to the comedy of transparency. Simple events include one workman asking another for a light, but the glass panel between them, at first invisible but suddenly revealed to the audience, means they have to move to an open doorway. In a more complicated comment, *Playtime* often enacts a complex game with reflections. When Hulot and Giffard keep missing each other, Hulot thinks that he spots Giffard in the glass-walled building opposite. In fact, Giffard is a few metres to his left, and it is Giffard's reflection that Hulot misinterprets. This whole gag is predicated on glass being occasionally entirely transparent and, at other times, only partially transparent due to obscuring reflectivity. As this demonstrates, transparency is not about seeing everything but seeing something under particular conditions. In this sense, glass structures our very way of seeing the world; in *Playtime*, architecture acts as a frame, simultaneously enabling and restricting what we can view.

Illusory transparency is another twist of Tativille, where the idea that one can always walk through an opening is rudely denied, as when Giffard collides with the glass door. On one level this is a gag of mime artist, but it is also more profound. Glass and its transparency carry epistemological properties, wherein sight is deemed to produce knowledge and mastery of its object. Tativille at once acknowledges and repudiates that epistemo-visual system, for when Giffard collides with the glass he is confronted not only with the physicality of the glass but also with the limits of his ability to see and control the object he seeks (Hulot).

Whatever the visual construction, it is the humour of a mundane yet meaningful interaction that is most important. Thus in *Mon Oncle*, the doorman of Rington's restaurant mimics the closure of the automated glass doors with a slow turn of his head. In *Playtime*, after the glass doorway to the Royal Garden has been broken, the doorman continues his task by holding the golden doorknob in his hand, swinging his stiff-limbed arm away from the guests as they arrive and depart (significantly it is Hulot who does this first, not deliberately, but accidentally and hence comically). Modern architecture, having been erased, is made present once again within the comic action of the human body.

In another, more fantastical translation of glass, female American tourists in their bus are reflected in the window of a nearby building. When a window cleaner swivels the glass to gain more reach, the women apparently swing through the air as if on a fair-ground ride, sighing with delight. At this moment, Tati asks us to believe that the women are weightless, transposed from corporeal matter into the nothingness of a mirror image.

At other times, Tati does the opposite and makes explicit film's operation as a structure of viewing. For example, when outside of the Giffard/Schneider apartment block, we watch two families watching television and apparently watching each other – here, with the exception of ourselves as spectators, all the participants are unaware of what is going on. This is a complex visual mechanism, which simultaneously notes yet denies the standard American-Hollywood assumption that the pleasure of cinematic looking should be based on a voyeuristic gaze.[21] We do observe the subdued erotic potential between the characters, as when Mme Giffard appears to watch M. Schneider undress, but ultimately the humour comes from the way that these characters are revealed to us; we laugh at the absurdity of our frontal gaze, constrained by the elevation view to see something falsely.

Soundscape

If materiality in Tativille deals with the immateriality of glass and space, it also involves sound, for *Playtime* not only has a visual landscape but also a highly sophisticated aural landscape, a *paysage sonore*.[22]

Film, even 'silent' film accompanied by music and live interpretation, has always been an auditory production.[23] In *Playtime*, this is sound of a very particular kind. Tati combines music (by Francis Lemarque, James Campbell and David Stein) with multi-language dialogue (much of it barely comprehensible), and closely microphoned details that are frequently foregrounded on the aural stage. By contrast, there is little of the background, obfuscating rumble of the city. As such, *Playtime*'s soundscape, originally recorded by sound director Jacques Maumont onto five stereophonic tracks, bears comparison with *musique concrète*. Originally pioneered by French sound technician Pierre Schaeffer and taken up by composers like Karlheinz Stockhausen, who worked on his seminal *Etude* in Paris in the early 1950s, concrete music offers an urbanised construction variously composed from 'real' and synthesised sounds, white noise, feedback, chance operations and improvised performances.[24]

The composition that results in *Playtime* has no real keynote (a base-tone against which other sounds are modulated) other than the babbling dialogue of different European languages. Yet, as with concrete music, what may first seem like chaos is in *Playtime* a highly ordered composition. The low ambient level renders a resolutely hi-fi rather than lo-fi quality, in which distinct sounds and, hence, social as well as aural, effects are identifiable.

The most obvious sound in *Playtime* is that which gives identity to people. Footsteps, opening doors and other actions are all carefully recorded to generate a sonic presence for each individual – in *Les vacances*, for example, it is Hulot's rambunctiously misfiring car that first announces his arrival. Above all, in *Playtime* there is the dialogue – not the quick-fire repartee, logical conversation or argued suspense of conventional films, but a continual yet frequently unintelligible set of phrases and exchanges, often conducted in more than one language. As Michel Chion notes, the effect is like European beaches, where sun-worshippers from countless countries create an international mixture, all curiously estranged from each other.[25]

Sound also gives identity to particular spaces. In the opening scene, it is the languid pronouncements of flight information, quickly followed by the roar of jets, that first define it as an airport. Similarly, throughout the events set in Giffard's office building, the stern mood of the architecture is subtly augmented by barely audible electronic humming and buzzes.

At other times, it is the separation of space which is emphasised. For example, when outside the Giffard/Schneider apartment building, we are aware from movements and gesticulations that the residents are speaking and that the television is on, while we hear nothing except for the occasional passing car. Sound, or its absence, divides one space (apartment interior) from another (street exterior), while this very separation simultaneously highlights the *visual* connection of the two, and hence to question what is inside and out, private and public. In a yet more complex variant, sound at once identifies, separates and unifies the different parts of Tativille. Notably, the female announcer first heard in the airport is also evident in the Salon des Arts Ménagers and hotel foyer, thus telling us we are in a particular kind of building while emphasising homogeneity across these spaces.

If space can be demarcated by sound, it can also be intensified. For example, echo is often cited by phenomenologists as a measurement of architectural space, yielding a sense of size and scale. However, such formulations tend to stress the 'timeless task of architecture' to provide a structure between the universality of its space-types – the ruin, cave, cavern, house – and the equally universal subject, man.[26] By contrast, echo is almost entirely absent from Tativille, where sound stresses the very specificity of space and person that phenomenology tends to erase. In the office waiting room scene, it is Hulot who fidgets and rustles, makes rushes of air as he sits down on modern chairs and squeaks as he moves across the hard floor. As a result, the waiting room becomes more like a waiting room, and Hulot more like a person waiting.

Implicit here is an important aspect of soundscapes: that it is not just sound itself – the sound event – which re-works architecture, but the way people perceive sound, the *auditory* event. Whereas vision tends to place us at the margin of a space, where we notice only what happens in front of our eyes, sound tends to place us at the centre, where we become more aware of what is happening all around. In addition, sounds tends to makes us more participatory – a condition noted by a range of urban commentators, from geographer Paul Rodaway[27] to architectural theorist Juhani Pallasmaa:

> Sight makes us solitary, whereas hearing creates a sense of connection and solidarity ... We stare alone at the suspense of the circus, but the burst of applause after the relaxation of suspense unites us to the crowd.[28]

For example, towards the start of *Playtime*, Hulot, while high up on a building terrace, is attracted by two 'sound signals', a car horn and police whistle. Here the visual regime of architecture is disrupted by a noise that does not conform to what can be seen, encouraging Hulot to do something different: he looks downward to street level, where Barbara (the main female character, later befriended by Hulot) and her fellow tourists are arriving at the same building. And although Hulot and Barbara do not meet, remaining unaware of each other, the sound signal nonetheless joins them momentarily. Here, sound is subversive, flowing outside the bounded visual system imposed by architecture, causing people to do things and to open possibilities.

The effect, particularly as the aural city often changes more rapidly than the visual city, is to impose a different rhythm onto the visual and physical rhythm of the city, leading in turn to layering, interweaving and discontinuity, as when sound transgresses barriers. For example, when a cockerel crows at dawn outside the Royal Garden, this is a soundmark, an aural landmark, used to denote a shared conception of community, in this case rural France. A cockerel in the heart of Tativille is then an absurd intrusion of the countryside into the city, challenging the boundary between urban and rural.

As this suggests, *Playtime*'s treatment of sound is not entirely logical, and often when observing Tativille we clearly hear distant things as if they were nearby. At other times, steps and other sounds conflict with what is seen on the screen; in one airport shot, several different people walk along, including a man delivering flowers, none of which corresponds to some curiously sucking footsteps that dominate the soundstage, only to fade away for no apparent reason.

Sometimes this illogicality of sound occurs within a soundfield (the sound made by a single source), as when the door in which Barbara sees a reflection of the Eiffel Tower emits a wholly inappropriate low-pitched and muted boom. In a more spatialised example, when Giffard advances along the corridor towards the waiting Hulot, his footsteps get louder, yet only after fluctuating in volume; while their rhythm stays constant, reaffirming the presence of a human body; their varying loudness challenges both position of the body and the length, linearity and aural qualities of the passage. Tati here disrupts the dialectic of sight and sound, oscillating sound while allowing visual information to proceed linearly. One rhythm is out of synchronisation with another.

At other times the discontinuity is within a soundscape (formed by a multiplicity of different soundfields). For example, Tati often switches levels in two or more speakers' dialogue, making one suddenly much louder (an effect achieved by post-synchronising the dialogue and recording it very close up[29]). Alternatively several people can be clearly heard, but only as a mumble, with odd phrases floating to the foreground; snatches of conversation like 'I feel at home everywhere I go', 'I hope my daughter writes', 'Do you remember the guide in Amsterdam?' are all audible in one scene, but without any connecting interaction. Meaningless in context, these are what Chion calls these 'memory burps',[30] aural fragments of other lives and histories that bubble onto the surface of Tativille, recalling Walter Benjamin's assertion that '[t]he past can be seized only as an image which flashes up at the instant when it can be recognized and is never seen again'.[31] Sound is one way in which other worlds and other lives infiltrate Tativille.

Because the logic of Tativille's soundscape is frequently disrupted, it has to be reconfigured by the audience. One part of this operation is to consciously realise that all sounds are sounds of action. For a person, the sound comes from speaking to someone, walking on something, sitting on a chair. For a thing, sound comes from a chair being moved, a floor being walked upon, an engine running. Thus in the waiting room scene, Hulot's body acts as a mediator between the chairs, flooring and the room volume, a process revealed to us by a sequence of sounds.[32] Tati's obsession with immobile sounds – sounds which do not track across the screen – emphasises this effect; rather than a movement, they emphasise a particular place and source. Everything, as Chion notes, is a *grelot*, a small bell that we hang up to notify presence. Sound is hooked on to something.[33]

The movement of sound in Tativille is mostly compositional, where one sound interacts with another. For example, in the waiting room, Hulot's foot-steps, brushes, gusts and scrapes are punctuated by periods of silence. Furthermore, these sounds are juxtaposed with the other man also waiting, who, in contrast to the erratic Hulot, precisely opens his briefcase, extracts a document and pen, makes notes, and then replaces his accoutrements, creating a highly detailed series of noises that runs: brush, crick, zip, sniff, brush, flick, click, tap, click, clap, zip, sniff, steps [and exit].

The rhythms of sound in Tativille formulate a poetic composition of dialogue, footsteps, scrapes, clashes and quietude. Furthermore, these are rhythms which conjoin with other rhythms in the film – visual, comedic, narra-tive, spatial – to create a complex rhythm-world where each element has its own life yet also feeds off all others. This soundscape is a cumulative, mutating and experiential entity, requiring people for its production and reception.

This is not, therefore, a soundscape in the manner of a comprehensive street map. Not is it a set of objects, where sound events exist in their own right. Rather than just reading the city by looking at, Tativille suggests a sonorous engagement between people and architecture; along with being *spectators* of architecture we could also recover the auditory aspects of architecture, becoming its *audience* (from the Latin *audire*: to hear). Tativille indicates how we might do this, and so learn to participate in the *musique concrète* of the city.

Bodies and questions

There is little body-to-body contact in Tati's films. Beyond the occasional embrace and dance, there is almost no slapstick or dramatic action, still less sweaty sex. This does not mean bodies are unimportant, just that their interac-tion tends to be less with other human bodies and more with the body of architecture.

At the start, *Playtime* sets up a very passive human body through two kinds of herd, one female with American tourists led by a male guide, the other male with businessmen led by a female guide. These are docile bodies, transported with minimal effort to a realm of rationalised decisions and snapshots (at one point, Barbara takes a photograph because a friend, reading the guidebook, tells her to). Similarly, while wandering around the cellular office maze, Hulot views a receptionist head-on, her body strangely unreal through Dalek-like containment within a glass booth. When he sees her again from a different vantage point, she still faces him directly. (In fact, the booth has simply rotated through 90°, thus causing Hulot's perplexity.) *Mon Oncle* makes a similar play on the robotic body, as when Gérard rushes into the house, crying 'Mother, mother, look!', only to find an automated vacuum cleaner has replaced her and is slowly traversing the floor.

Yet although *Mon Oncle* and *Playtime* make such comments on the inactive body, Tati also counters passivity through a series of comic visualisations. *Playtime*'s 70 mm format allows Tati to depict each character in full-length, and also to edit down that full-length form whenever desired. This is most explicit when he shows a male travel agent behind a long horizontal counter, moving rapidly from one customer to another, with only his upper body in view. In a subsequent view from behind, visible beneath a raised screen, the reverse is true, and we see only the man's disembodied legs as they scuttle back and forth on a tri-castored chair. This a gag about vision but also about the human body – we laugh not just because we can see his legs, but because of what these legs *do*, moving speedily crab-like between moments of precise stopping and starting. Modern architecture is a necessary prerequisite (the smooth floor surface allows movement, the modernist screen and front counter provide conditions of transparency and opacity), but it is only through engagement with the body that its comic potential is realised.

Some of the delicate touches in *Playtime* may arise from Tati's frequent use of an amateur cast – for example, Barbara is played by Barbara Dennek, a German neighbour of Tati's, while the other women were American army wives in Paris, shown wearing their own clothes and choice of flowered hats.[34] The most visible of bodies in *Playtime* is, however, a highly trained one, that of Hulot, played by Tati himself, and clearly drawing on his previous experiences as a mime artist. In describing this quixotic character, one can do no better than Chion's summary:

> The usual image, Hulot's identikit portrait, shows him to be tall, with pipe in mouth, in too-short trousers which reveal striped socks. Always proper, however, whether Hulot is in a suit or sports dress; whether he wears a bow tie or open collar, a too-short raincoat or a summer jacket. He often raises his hat courteously, and is armed with an umbrella. His walk is unique: first, he advances with big determined strides, as if moved by a decision of which he says nothing; but then a hesitation-waltz comes to complicate his approaching steps. He is never really at rest; even when he does not move, it is as if he were always going somewhere – a true human turntable. His expression can't be defined ... there is an air of something about Hulot, but we never quite know what.[35]

As this suggests, although incongruous in appearance, it is not Hulot's physicality in itself which is the source of his comedy, but, as Lefebvre notes of Chaplin, 'in the relation of this body to something else: a social relation with the material world and the social world'.[36] How then does Hulot operate in Tativille?

Vision is commonly considered to be a passive mode of engagement, wherein the experiencing subject maintains a physical and psychological distance from the object. Often, the viewer's body is static, rendering the object into a two-dimensional picture, and if the subject moves it is to gather more of these distant views, like a tourist with a camera. Similarly, the experience of architecture is also considered to be increasingly passive and visual – 'architecture of our time is turning into the retinal art of the eye'[37] – to the detriment of other senses and thoughts.

However, viewing architecture does not have to be passively constrained to matters of observation, the viewer questioning the object by allowing it to be reproduced through their own body. As Lefebvre notes:

> Architecture produces living bodies, each with its own distinctive traits. The animating principle of such a body, its presence, is neither visible nor legible as such, nor is it the object of any discourse, for it reproduces itself within those who *use* the space in question, within their lived experience. Of that experience the tourist, the passive spectator, can grasp but a pale shadow.[38]

Hulot performs this task consistently, most explicitly by asking *questions* of Tativille. Here is an indicative list:

- *Where do I wait?* – Before entering, Hulot cautiously inspects the office waiting room proffered to him, then uncertainly paces up and down before sitting down.
- *Which is inside and which is outside?* – While in the waiting room, a shot from behind shows Hulot staring out through the massive glass wall into the street, where he appears to be stood.
- *What is this material?* – Hulot touches the furniture in the waiting room, unsure of its fabrication. He tests the firmness and grip of the floor with his foot. He remains unconvinced.
- *Where should I go to?* – After waiting for some time, Hulot is sent after Giffard. Hulot quickly loses his way. He inspects a floor plan. This does not help.
- *How do I get up there?* – Hulot accidentally finds himself in the office lift. He travels up and down, not knowing where he is going.
- *Where am I?* – Ejected from the lift, Hulot is lost. He touches a chair, the same kind as in the waiting room, wondering if he is back there. He is not.
- *How do I get over there?* – From above, Hulot spies Giffard in the gridded and partitioned ground floor. Once down below Hulot cannot orient himself. He fails to find Giffard.

- *How do I get out?* – Hulot cannot leave the Schneider/Giffard apartment block as he cannot locate the door-release button. He remains locked in the hallway, hidden in the dark.

Although these questions are decidedly experiential, dealing largely with questions of perception and movement, Hulot's body challenges the authority of architecture to control movement and vision. As a result, other questions less phenomenal and more social in character are implicitly posed:

- *Why live predominantly in the internal, domestic realm?* – In *Mon Oncle*, Hulot is hardly ever at home. In *Playtime*, he operates peripatetically between office, restaurant, street and other people's residences. If Hulot's body is a 'human turntable', his trajectory is invariably centrifugal and outward.
- *What gender is this space?* – Although there are female-dominated domiciles and male-dominated offices in Tati's films, there are also signs of gender and sexual ambiguity. While *Les vacances* contains several jokes concerning the male gaze upon the female body, *Playtime*'s camera rarely lingers on any body, male or female. Similarly, the spaces visited tend not to be intimate ones. In *Mon Oncle*, we never see the Arpels' upstairs bedrooms. In *Playtime*, Hulot has no discernible residence, and meets Barbara not in her hotel room but in one of many spaces inbetween public and private – the exhibition, the restaurant, the street. Theirs is a world not wholly gender- or sexually-specific. Significantly, we also have no idea where either of them come from or go to outside of the film's 24-hour setting, and in this sense *Playtime* is very different to the typical gendered spatial-narrative of a Hollywood film, where the feminine home and institution of marriage frequently provides opening and closure.[39] Hulot establishes no space of feminine safety, nor sphere of masculinist, testosterone-fuelled adventure.
- Hulot challenges the authority of buildings and building managers to dictate behaviour – Giffard, self-importantly busy at his office cannot prevent Hulot from wandering off. So who has authority over this space? As M. Arpel remarks in *Mon Oncle* of Hulot's apparent disregard for their house and behavioural codes: 'Maybe he doesn't like it here. Oh no, no, no. It's the limit. This house, who paid for it? It's my work, my efforts. His uncle. Maybe he wants to take my place. I wouldn't be surprised. Is that it? Is that it?'[40]
- Hulot and his fellow characters challenge the dominion of the architectural profession – struggling with innumerable snagging problems on the opening night of the Royal Garden, the bow-tied architect tries to sneak off. Without the presence of a masterful professional, the revellers improvise their own, more decadent atmosphere and circumscribed territories. The question now posed is: who controls the Royal Garden, the architect, *maître d'hôtel* or restaurant users?

- *What information am I given?* – In the office building, the executive committee room has no external markings to signify its importance. Hulot, naturally, bursts in. Here, the information provided by the differentiation of spaces, doors and signage is inadequate. A building plan, akin to a circuit diagram and seen by Hulot prominently displayed in the lift, is similarly ineffective.
- *What payment is due?* – In *Mon Oncle*, M. Arpel's not-so-subtle payment to the violinist in Rington's restaurant contrasts with Hulot's attempt to pay (politely declined) for a boisterous 'taxi-ride' in the horse-drawn cart. In *Playtime*, when the paid jazz band stops performing, Barbara plays the piano while another guest sings traditional French songs. The implication is clear: not only are comedy and revelry important, so they should not, perhaps necessarily, be commodified.
- *What are the race politics of this place?* – A black male is immediately turned away from the Royal Garden, perhaps because of his red-and-white striped cap and casual dress, but more likely because of his skin colour. He is, however, allowed entry once it becomes clear that he is one of the restaurant musicians.

These are not oppositional or wholly destructive questions. Hulot may shatter the glass door of the Royal Garden, but that is an accident. In *Trafic* (1971), the fourth and last of Tati's Hulot films, there is a multiple road accident but, significantly, no one suffers any serious injury. Instead, Hulot interrogates the possibilities of modern architecture by gentle actions like gingerly sitting, timidly peering, hesitantly pacing and a generally indifferent going-about of his own business.

If Hulot does not try to entirely reconstruct architecture, so, in *Playtime*, he expects that architecture should not reconstruct Hulot. His body counters abstract space and, in Lefebvre's words, 'will not allow itself to be dismembered without a protest, or to be divided into fragments, deprived of its rhythms, reduced to its catalogued needs, to images and specialisations'.[41] Hulot may, like everyone else, conform to some of the micro-directions of the city, in *Mon Oncle* dutifully following the circuitous path and stepping stones across the Arpel's garden (the house was a ridiculous stage-set, designed by Jacques Tati and Jacques Lagrange as a collage of images clipped from architectural magazines[42]), or, in *Playtime* obeying a shop's designated exit. However, in the bigger picture Hulot goes more or less where he will, untroubled by the city's larger instructions.

This raises a second mode by which the passivity of vision can be rendered more active. Together with his inquisition of architecture, Hulot also moves through it, restlessly and without tiring. His is a body of legs, and little else. And as Chion notes, even when he is static, Hulot gives the impression of moving in his thoughts, the ultimate Baroque individual, quite in keeping with August Schmarsow's understanding of architectural space.

> We cannot express its relation to ourselves in any other way than by imagining that we are in motion, measuring the length, width and depth, or by

attributing to the static lines, surfaces, and volumes the movement that our eyes and our kinesthetic sensations suggest to us, even though we survey the dimensions while standing still.[43]

In *Playtime*, Hulot constructs a spatial circuit, a moving body that cannot be controlled. Others, similarly, have the same right. Barbara, even though a tourist, is free to shop, dress, dine and dance, free to meet with a strange Frenchman in a strange city, free to exchange pleasantries and accept gifts, and free also to depart. By the end of the film, the arrows which were at first obeyed are now disregarded, Tativille's inhabitants having learned to pursue their own instincts and paths; when a drunken reveller exits the Royal Garden uncertainly, only to tilt his head upwards, see the coiled restaurant insignia on canopy above and spin back inside, it is less the logo than alcoholic reverie which propels him. The architecture of the city becomes not a maze but a stage of possibilities on which the characters move, allowing without determining their desires and directions (Barbara's and Hulot's paths intersect several times before they finally meet). All of this is done with walls, doors, windows and roads, with words and glances, with actions, intimations, crossings and encounters. Everything is an exchange, a connection between people and spaces.

And it is worth noting here that Tati, as in much early cinema, pastes details across the screen while giving camera and spectator time to scan this surface (a technique heightened by the 70 mm format).[44] To direct attention, Tati often places a character at stage front, back to the audience and looking inward. In such constructions, the audience takes up the same position and so becomes part of the watching process – apart from yet within the space of the movie. More generally, however, Tati simply invites the audience to inspect the film for their own point of entry. Furthermore, the audience is frequently asked to participate in the construction of the scene. For example, when Hulot leaves the Schneider residence, the camera pans away. When it returns, Hulot is still stuck in the hallway. The humour produced results both from Hulot's inability to get out, and from the audience's realisation that we had originally missed this possibility. Through humour, we too join in with the possibilities of Tativille.

Architecture, therefore, depends as much upon experiencing subjects, the vectors they trace, the perception they have, as it does upon architectural materiality or architects' intentions. Architecture is not unimportant – far from it, for it is only because of specific constructions that engagement with architecture can occur, all bound up within the aleatory nature of the city. Body meets body, maybe.

Dancing partners

The architectural questions identified above are inquisitive rather than demanding. Hulot is uncertainty and charm confronting a society of which he is at once part and not part. Yet if that confrontation is normally gentle, at other times it is more conflictual.

In *Playtime*, the ability of architecture and its devices to function as intended is set up at the Salon des Arts Ménagers, where the American women experience the best of modern design: a vacuum cleaner with headlights for seeing under furniture, spectacles with tilt-up lenses to allow eye make-up to be applied, and office doors that make no sound ('Slam Your Doors in Golden Silence').

In the end, however, this modern world gets out of hand. When the women, together with other guests, go to a dinner-dance at the Royal Garden, a plethora of errors are revealed. The barman cannot serve, as the canopy is too low. The serving hatch is too small for the speciality of the house, the *Turbot à la royal*. Tiles on the dance floor stick to the soles of passing waiters. The Royal Garden crown motifs on the chairs make marks on the backs of the guests. The air conditioning alternates between chillingly cold and unbearably hot. Lights explode. A section of the ceiling collapses (caused, of course, by a well-meaning Hulot).

But even here the diners re-assert themselves. The barman dodges between the canopy slats. The *Turbot à la royal* is passed sideways through the hatch. The high temperature becomes an excuse to drink and be merry. As the night wears on the diners metamorphise into party revellers, the air filled with the exotic sounds of wild jazz and the dance-floor packed with exuberantly gyrating couples (Hulot even dances with Barbara, albeit accidentally and politely). The effect, in contrast to the meek disorder normally created by Hulot, is a full-blown reversal of the ordered modern city. All hell breaks loose. However, this deranged carnival has limits – the revellers are in fact quite organised, as, for example, when the crown mark becomes the pretext by which the crass American Schultz admits or rejects 'guests' to his club-within-a-club.

Other worlds

If the characters are careful to control their own territories, so Tati maintains tight hold on every other aspect of Tativille. In particular, *Playtime* follows another modernist principle by suppressing the past. When Barbara tries to take a picture of an old lady and traditional flower stall, ('That's really Paris!'), she is constantly frustrated by a succession of modern-looking passers-by, including a pair of Americanised rock'n' roll teenagers. Yet despite the intensity of Tativille's modernity the old Paris is there nonetheless, often as reflected glimpses of the Arc de Triomphe and Eiffel Tower, which are also imprinted on the scarf Hulot buys for Barbara ('Oh look, there's Sacré-Cœur'). Thus, in his extraordinary specification of high modernism, Tati still allows other worlds of historical monuments (glass reflections), popular songs (at the Royal Garden), countryside (the cockerel) and market traditions (flower stalls) to leak in. Tativille-Paris is one Paris-world among many others, where there is always another presence and an outside.

These other worlds find their way into *Playtime* in a number of surprising ways, especially late in the film when the intersection between modernism and characters has fully developed. Tativille here becomes a fantasy world, where the everyday experience of modern architecture is jacked up to the level of illusion, as when the women are reflected into a fairground ride, or when a heavily traf-ficked roundabout becomes a merry-go-round, replete with organ music, vertically oscillating passengers and cars, and interchanging riders. Similarly, road-side lamp-posts appear to Barbara as if flowers on the end of elegantly curved stalks; she has received a small sprig of flowers from Hulot, and thus an amorous gesture has psychologically transformed the city into a place of height-ened beauty and pleasure.

At the very end of *Playtime*, and in contrast to the common chase sequence and/or boy-gets-girl denouement of comic films, Barbara leaves Tativille while Hulot returns to his own life. We too, as audience, are returned to the world we inhabit, somehow changed by our temporary absence.

Suffering itself is denied, and this denial is put on display. In this fictitious negation we reach the limits of art. On leaving the darkness of the cinema, we rediscover the same world as before, it closes around us again. And yet the comic event has taken place, and we feel decontaminated, returned to normality, purified somehow, and stronger.[45]

Modernity

Tativille is not a place apart, but a parallel world where city life is turned up a notch on the dial. Just as Brecht's epic theatre sought its basic model in the traffic accident and the street corner,[46] so in *Playtime* Tati set out to portray everyday life just as it was. He was delighted when a 14-year-old young man remarked that when he left the movie theatre, the street outside had exactly the same architecture, people and behaviour.[47] In this respect, Tati was once again working in an old cinematic tradition, where pre-narrative films recorded not only important historical events like coronations and state funerals but also everyday street scenes, workplaces and leisure.[48]

After *Les vacances*, Hulot was described by French film critic André Bazin as someone who seemed 'not to dare to wholly exist',[49] while in *Mon Oncle*, Hulot is cast spatially and socially apart from the bourgeois modernism of his relatives. In *Playtime*, however, Hulot has moved on within the modern world, existing no longer apart from but through the city, perhaps even being the very hesitant birth of the new metropolitan individual, 'bursting forth in all his beauty and undeniable authenticity', who revels in the pleasures and opportuni-ties of the city.[50]

What does this mean for modernism today? While there is a renewed interest in modernism, as architecture from Norman Foster to Claudio Silvestrin, retro-furniture designs from Bertoia to Panton, restaurants and shops from Wagamama to Ikea, and magazines from *The Architectural Review* to *Elle Decoration, Living etc* and *Wallpaper**,[51] too often this modernism is constrained to matters of visualisation, forms and surfaces. Hence the phenome-nologist counter-reactions of those like Stephen Holl and Juhani Pallasmaa, who call for 'movement between the absolutes of architectural intention and the indefinite urban assemblage' and for 'an understanding of alternative ways of moving through cities'.[52] *Playtime* shows how this might happen, as a modernism of friendships, amusement, pleasure and gentle love. This is a place of reflections, visions, utterances, noises, rhythms, journeys, exchanges – a place of modern and material delights. Kristin Ross, studying post-war French culture, identified in Tati's films an architectural world that 'tended to dictate to people their gestures and movements'.[53] But what I see in *Playtime* is a myriad of possibilities and pleasures.

Acknowledgment

This article has benefited greatly from seminar discussions with students of the Masters in Architectural History programme at the Bartlett, University College London. I am particularly grateful to Léonard Hamburger and Jung Hee Lee. A shorter version of this essay first appeared as Iain Borden, 'Material Sounds: Jacques Tati and Modern Architecture', *Architectural Design (AD)*, special issue on 'Architecture and Film, II'.

Notes

1 Anthony Esthope 'Cinécities in the Sixties', in *The Cinematic City*, ed. David B. Clarke, London: Routledge, 1997, pp. 134–5.
2 Gérard is called Jimmy in the English language version of *Mon Oncle*.
3 Lucy Fischer, *Home Ludens; An Analysis of Four Films by Jacques Tati*, PhD thesis, New York University, 1978, cited in Andrea Kahn, 'Playtime with Architects', *Design Book Review*, no. 24 (Spring) (1992): 23.
4 The set is visible in *Cours du Soir*, a short film by Nicolas Ribowski about the making of *Playtime*.
5 Quoted in François Penz, 'Architecture in the Films of Jacques Tati', in *Cinema and Architecture: Méliès, Mallet-Stevens, Multimedia*, ed. François Penz and Maureen Thomas, London: British Film Institute, 1997, p. 64.
6 Penz, 'Architecture in the Films of Jacques Tati', p. 65.
7 J.A. Fieschi and J. Narboni, 'Le Champ large', interview with Jacques Tati, *Les cahiers du cinéma*, no. 199 (March) (1968).
8 Freddy Bruache, *Le cinéma français des années 60*, Paris: Five Continents, 1987, pp. 17–18, cited in Léonard Hamburger, 'Jacques Tati, Witness of Modernism', course essay, MSc Architectural History, The Bartlett, University College London, 1997.
9 One of the faces is that of the company chairman, previously seen being anxiously questioned by reporters in the opening airport scene.
10 Kahn, 'Playtime with Architects', p. 22.
11 Henri Lefebvre, 'Notes on the New Town', *Introduction to Modernity: Twelve Preludes, September 1959 – May 1961*, Oxford: Blackwell, 1995, pp. 116–31; Henri Lefebvre, *The Production of Space*, Oxford: Blackwell, 1991, p. 200.
12 Lefebvre, *The Production of Space*, p. 183.
13 Michel Chion, *The Films of Jacques Tati*, Toronto: Guernica, 1997, p. 167.
14 Jacques Kermabon, *Les vacances de monsieur Hulot*, Crisnée: Yellow Now, 1988, quoted in Hamburger, 'Jacques Tati, Witness of Modernism'.
15 Chion, *The Films of Jacques Tati*, pp. 20–40. Chion is following here Jonathan Rosenbaum.

16 Fieschi and Narboni, 'Le Champ large'.
17 André Bazin and François Truffaut, 'Entretien avec Jacques Tati', *Les cahiers du cinéma*, no. 83 (May) (1958), quoted in Chion, *The Films of Jacques Tati*, p. 23.
18 Robin Evans, 'Mies van der Rohe's Paradoxical Symmetries', In *Translations from Drawing to Building and Other Essays*, London: Architectural Association/AA Documents 2, 1997, pp. 249–54 and 258–61.
19 Bazin and Truffaut, 'Entretien avec Jacques Tati', quoted in Penz, 'Architecture in the Films of Jacques Tati', p. 63.
20 Jacques Tati, interview, Armand J. Cauliez, *Jacques Tati*, Paris: Seghers, 1962, cited in Hamburger, 'Jacques Tati, Witness of Modernism'.
21 Laura Mulvey, 'Visual Pleasure and Narrative Cinema', *Visual and Other Pleasures*, London: Macmillan, 1989, pp. 14–26.
22 *Le paysage sonore*, along with some of the other terminology in this section, is borrowed from Paul Rodaway, 'Auditory Geographies', *Sensuous Geographies: Body, Sense and Place*, London: Routledge, 1994, pp. 82–113, and, in particular, Rodaway's discussion of the work of R.M. Schafer.
23 Norman King, 'The Sound of Silents', in *Silent Film*, ed. Richard Abel, London: Athlone Press, 1999, pp. 31–44.
24 Joe Staines and Jonathan Buckley (eds) *Classical Music*, 2nd edn, London: Rough Guides, 1998, pp. 398–402.
25 Chion, *The Films of Jacques Tati*, p. 65.
26 Juhani Pallasmaa, 'An Architecture of the Seven Senses', in 'Questions of Perception: Phenomenology of Architecture', ed. Steven Holl, Juhani Pallasmaa and Alberto Pérez-Gómez, special issue of *A + U* (*Architecture and Urbanism*) (July) (1994), pp. 30–1 and 37.
27 Rodaway, *Sensuous Geographies*, p. 102.
28 Pallasmaa, 'Architecture of the Seven Senses', p. 31.
29 Chion, *The Films of Jacques Tati*, p. 140; and Penz, 'Architecture in the Films of Jacques Tati', p. 66.
30 Chion, *The Films of Jacques Tati*, p. 59
31 Walter Benjamin, 'Theses on the Philosophy of History', *Illuminations*, New York: Schocken Books, 1969, p. 255.
32 Jung Hee Lee, '*Playtime* by Jacques Tati', course essay, MSc Architectural History, The Bartlett, University College London, 1997.
33 Chion, *The Films of Jacques Tati*, pp. 128–9.
34 Hamburger, 'Jacques Tati, Witness of Modernism'.
35 Chion, *The Films of Jacques Tati*, p. 42.
36 Henri Lefebvre, *Critique of Everyday Life. Volume 1: Introduction*, London: Verso, 1991, p. 10.
37 Pallasmaa, 'Architecture of the Seven Senses', p. 29.
38 Lefebvre, *Production of Space*, p. 137.
39 See, for example, the discussion of the gendered narrative of the Western film genre in Laura Mulvey, 'Pandora: Topographies of the Mask and Curiosity', in *Sexuality and Space*, ed. Beatriz Colomina, New York: Princeton Architectural Press, 1992, pp. 55–6.
40 Quotation based on the English language version of *Mon Oncle*.
41 Henri Lefebvre, *The Survival of Capitalism: Reproduction of the Relations of Production*, New York: St. Martin's Press, 1976, p. 89.
42 Jacques Tati, *Journal des Monuments Historiques*, 1985, cited in Penz, 'Architecture in the Films of Jacques Tati', p. 64.
43 August Schmarsow, 'The Essence of Architectural Creation', in *Empathy, Form and Space: Problems in German Aesthetics, 1873–1893*, ed. Harry Francis Mallgrave and Eleftherios Ikonomou, Santa Monica: Getty Center for the History of Art and the Humanities, 1994, p. 291.

44 Chion, *The Films of Jacques Tati*, p. 28; and M. Christine Boyer, *The City of Collective Memory: Its Historical Imagery and Architectural Entertainments*, Cambridge, MA: MIT Press, 1994, pp. 317–18.

45 Lefebvre, *Critique of Everyday Life*, p. 13. Lefebvre is speaking of the effect of Chaplin's film.

46 Bertol Brecht, 'The Street Scene', In *Brecht on Theatre*, ed. J. Willett, London: Methuen, 1978, p. 126, and cited in Lefebvre, *Critique of Everyday Life*, p. 14.

47 Jacques Tati, interview, *Les cahiers du cinéma*, no. 303 (September) (1979), cited in Hamburger, 'Jacques Tati, Witness of Modernism'.

48 Boyer, *The City of Collective Memory*, p. 363.

49 André Bazin, *Qu'est-ce le cinéma*, Paris: Éditions du Cerf, 1975, p. 43, quoted in Chion, *The Films of Jacques Tati*, p. 48.

50 Lefebvre, *Critique of Everyday Life*, p. 64.

51 See, in particular, *Modernism and Modernization in Architecture*, ed. Helen Castle, London: Academy Editions, 1999.

52 Steven Holl, Juhani Pallasmaa and Alberto Pérez-Gómez, 'Phenomenal Zones', in Holl, Pallasmaa and Pérez-Gómez, 'Questions of Perception: Phenomenology of Architecture', p. 55.

53 Kristin Ross, *Fast Cars, Clean Bodies: Decolonization and the Reordering of French Culture*, Cambridge, MA: MIT Press, 1995, p. 5.

16 *Blade Runner*
'Ridleyville' and Los Angeles

Peter Wollen

In his book, *City of Quartz*[1], which first came out in 1990, Mike Davis categorised *Blade Runner* as noir revival, setting it in the context of an ongoing struggle between utopians and dystopians for control over the representation of Los Angeles. The chapter in which he briefly comments on the film is titled, 'Sunshine or Noir', and recounts the contrasting histories of boosterism and its pessimistic alter-ego, the 'nightmare anti-myth of noir', which between them shaped Los Angeles' divided vision of itself.

Two years later, in 1992, the year of the '*Director's Cut*', Mike Davis was more precise – he now took issue with what was already the dominant academics' view of the film – a postmodern classic – and categorised it as simply 'another edition of the core modernist vision' of the city as either Ville Radieuse or Monster Manhattan. Essentially, he now argued, *Blade Runner* provides us with what is 'recognizably the same vista of urban gigantism that Fritz Lang celebrated in Metropolis'. He dismisses the 'teeming Ginza' aspects of *Blade Runner*, the 'Noir', the 'high-tech plumbing retrofitted to street-level urban decay' as 'overlay', texturing on top of the basic Metropolis core. Los Angeles, he points out, is not the same as Gotham City or Metropolis. It is not a Wellsian city, but an endless un-spectacular vista of 'great unbroken plains of ageing bungalows, dingbats and ranch-style houses'.

Of course, he is right about this. Philip K. Dick's novel, *Do Androids Dream Of Electric Sheep?*,[2] from which *Blade Runner* was adapted, is set in San Francisco. The first screenwriter, Hampton Fancher, very soon changed the location to Los Angeles and there it stayed. However, the director, Ridley Scott, once appointed, moulded the film to his own vision, steering it through several rewrites from a second screenwriter, David Peoples. He was never deeply committed to the Los Angeles setting. His main inspiration was, indeed, New York, as Mike Davis surmised. He also thought about setting the film in either Los Angeles or Atlanta. But, in the end, he decided to stick with Los Angeles, largely because the decision to film in the Bradbury Building identified the location in an unmistakable way. Once this decision was taken, he then went on to shoot the opening sequence, portraying an unmistakable Los Angeles, as seen from Terminal Island, looking north towards downtown across a smoke-belching industrial landscape, a caricature version of the refineries and cat-crackers of Torrance and El Segundo.

It would be a mistake, however, to see *Blade Runner* as simply exchanging New York for Los Angeles. In reality, it provides an image of a generic world city, rather than any one particular conurbation. It is a conceptual montage of many different urban phenomena, drawn from a variety of sources. The main exterior set for the film, christened 'Ridleyville' by those working on it, was built on the classic old New York Street on the Warner Brothers lot, where scenes from *The Big Sleep* and *The Maltese Falcon* had been shot nearly forty years before. To this was added elements from contemporary New York, from London, Tokyo, Hong Kong and Milan. The overall look of the set was inspired by futurist illustration – Moebius' work for *Heavy Metal* and Syd Mead's for *The Sentinel*. Ridley Scott also refers to Hogarth's 'Gin Lane' prints of eighteenth-century London as an important source. Essentially Scott, Mead and the others were constructing a composite world city, which incorporated a number of different features of contemporary cities extrapolated into the future, to 2019.

The topography of world cities is well known by now. There is a postmodern downtown (a 'citadel' as Mike Davies dubs it) where corporate headquarters and financial nerve centres are clustered together, instantly linked to outposts around the world by satellite, fibre optics and data compression. This is the command and control centre for key sectors of the global economy. Around the hub, there is a dense environment of refurbished industrial spaces (for loft living), restaurants (for ethnic eating), cultural centres and art museums (for the upmarket *flâneur*), designer boutiques (for prestige shopping) and luxury hotels (with easy access to the international airport). These are all there in *Blade Runner*, except for the art museums and the opera houses. Nearby there are the humming hives of a range of specialised just-in-time service industries – suppliers, subcontractors, bankers, lawyers, accountants, PR people, advertisers, publishers, architects, and their retinues of researchers, software experts, drug dealers, visual designers and niche marketing consultants. Hurrying and scurrying, in the shadows, on the sidewalk, at the lunch-counters, in the public transit system, are the low-paid immigrant workers and, just a cut above them in status and salary, the part-time and free-lance cultural workers – the immigrants and ethnic minorities who work in the restaurant kitchens; the installation artists and off-Broadway actors who work as the restaurant waiters.

Los Angeles has many crucial elements of this model, but it does not quite fit all the necessary specifications. To begin with, Los Angeles is weak on banks and corporate headquarters. It doesn't have a serious stock exchange. There are too many mini-centres. The art museums and luxury stores are scattered all over the city. The Getty, Los Angeles' nearest equivalent to the Tyrell Corporation, with its view out to Catalina Island, is located somewhere on Highway 405. Lacma is on the old Miracle Mile, halfway down the Wilshire corridor. The Norton Simon is in Pasadena. The Gehry Music Center is endlessly delayed. You can tell there is something missing just by glancing at the silhouette of downtown, if you can see it through the smog. This is not New York or London or Tokyo. Los Angeles has not undergone the same massive change that has transformed other cities. In many ways, it maintains elements of the mythic city of Chandler and Nathanael West and Aldous Huxley, presences still to be felt in *Blade Runner*.

Los Angeles is a second-tier world city, like Miami or Singapore or São Paulo. But, in one respect, it is a paramount global centre. It is the undisputed capital of the world's entertainment industry, dominating both New York and Chicago, far out-reaching London, Bombay and Hong Kong. Los Angeles provides the metaphors which model our imaginative perception of the world and it does so in ways which reflect its own carefully cultivated civic narcissism. Ridley Scott's *Blade Runner* was not an instant commercial success. The modest amount of money it eventually made came from secondary or tertiary markets – Japan, video stores, TV rights, the *Director's Cut*. But it has been an immense cultural success in updating the noir image of Los Angeles into the next millennium. Its impact can be discerned both in a series of subsequent films and in the cultural shockwaves it sent through the futurist imaginary.

The idea of the world city as command-and-control centre for global capitalism, one of an archipelago or Hanseatic League of such cities circling the globe, housing transnational corporate headquarters, their business services, transnational institutions and telecommunications and information processing centres, goes back to John Friedmann's essay of 1986, 'The World City Hypothesis', postdating Ridley Scott by four years. Manuel Castells' *The Informational City*[3] followed in 1989; Saskia Sassen's *The Global City: London, New York, Tokyo*[4] in 1991. The economic model postulated by these books brought together elements from Wallenstein's concept of the global system with elements, it has to be admitted, of McLuhan's earlier idea of the global village. Sharon Zukin, from *Loft Living* onwards,[5] played an important part, as did theories of postmodernism developed in other fields and introduced to urban studies by Ed Soja and Fredric Jameson. It was in the shadow of postmodernism that Giuliana Bruno wrote her seminal study of *Blade Runner*, 'Ramble City', published in the art journal, *October*, in 1987.[6]

In this context, I would like to discuss three aspects of *Blade Runner* which I believe should be seen as crucial to our understanding of the world city, in a number of interconnected ways. First, the Tyrell Corporation; second, the replicant; and third, City-Speak. The Tyrell pyramid is the central and dominating building in Blade Runner, supposedly one mile high like Frank Lloyd Wright's notorious and never-realised skyscraper project. It is the headquarters, not simply of a transnational corporation, but of one which operates off-world, in space. The Corporation, rather than the political elite, is the centre of power in the city, and, through its manufacturing interests, is presumably responsible for the massive pollution which poisons the city's air and causes the climatic transformation which brings endless downpours of acid rain to fall upon the city. It is also responsible for the manufacture of replicants as slave labour and for the sharp social polarisation between elite and underclass. Hampton Fancher, the original screenwriter is explicit about this: '*Blade Runner* was always meant to be cautionary. For instance, BR was shot during the dawn of Reaganism. And I was flabbergasted by Ronald Reagan and everything he stood for. So the cruel politics portrayed in the film were my rebuttal of Reaganism, in a sense.'

The Tyrell Corporation is already, I think, somewhat anachronistic as a symbol of 'globalisation', because it represents manufacturing rather than financial capital. Nonetheless, manufacturing remains the foundation of the new capitalist order, despite the hegemonic role played by banks and the other FIRE sectors (Finance, Insurance, Real Estate). Manufacturing did not become truly 'global' until the 1970s when, as Alain Lipietz pointed out, in his 1982 essay 'Towards Global Fordism', manufacturing in the periphery accelerated much faster than in the core – more than three times faster in Bangladesh, Kenya, Yemen, Indonesia, Lesotho, Thailand, Nigeria, Ecuador, Tunisia, South Korea, Malaysia, Algeria, Hong Kong and Singapore. Essentially a new international division of labour was created during this period. At the same time, multinational corporations continued to remain dominant, the top thousand companies controlling over three-quarters of world manufacturing output. This expansion, moreover, was financed by borrowing on the international money market, rather than by domestic accumulation.

Its corporate headquarters, the Tyrell pyramid, with its Sant'Elia elevators copied from the Bonaventure Hotel, also invokes pre-Columbian architecture, a style which shaped Los Angeles during the 1920s through the designs of Robert Stacy-Judd, Francisco Mujica and, of course, Frank Lloyd Wright, whose Ennis House, drawing on Mayan temples, is explicitly used in the film. The pyramid, moreover, is also the site of death and entombment. Right up to the point of shooting, the script of *Blade Runner* contained a scene in which the 'Tyrell' killed by Batty is revealed to be a fake. The real Tyrell is preserved in a cryonic chamber in the heart of the pyramid, waiting for a cure to be found for his incurable disease. Thus global capitalism is represented as a culture of death, artificially preserved beyond its time. Plainly, there is no building closely resembling the Tyrell pyramid in Los Angeles today, but that is hardly the point. Like *Who Framed Roger Rabbit?*, a film much more closely based on the history of the city, *Blade Runner* works as allegory, in both story and visual dimensions. The Tyrell pyramid represents the global power of the Corporation as well as its location in Los Angeles and the death drive which sustains it. It also contributes to the image of city as spectacle, optical rather than tactile, to use Walter Benjamin's terms – a city to be looked at rather than lived in.

The replicants manufactured by the Tyrell Corporation are intended for use off-world, in the Colonisation Defence Program, for political homicide, for handling nuclear materials, and so on. They are part of the infrastructure of an industrial complex which involves both ruthless economic exploitation, colonial expansion into undeveloped territories and tight paramilitary control. There are also references in the film to the exploitation of Antarctica and the Oceans, logical areas of expansion for a predatory capitalist system. The replicants themselves are not simply industrial products but products with built-in obsolescence, like the automobiles Vance Packard wrote about in the 1950s. As Hampton Fancher put it: 'So the idea from the beginning was that Tyrell had

purposefully built in this breakdown so people would have to buy a new replicant every few years. He did that to keep his commerce running.'

The replicants, however, are customised in ways which Detroit never
managed to achieve. In *Blade Runner*, we are dealing with a post-Fordist rather
than a classically Fordist economy, to use the concepts developed by Lipietz and
Aglietta, an economy in which assembly lines have become, so to speak, 'intelligent' and can tailor their products unit by unit within a spectrum. Moreover, as
we know from the 'Eye Works' scene in the film, production of important
elements, such as eyes, is subcontracted out to small specialised workshops, run
on a craft rather than an industrial basis. 'Ridleyville' is presumably full of such
'out-source' workshops, alongside the animoid suppliers, noodle bars and
nightspots. Similarly, Sebastian, the toy-maker, is a freelance genetic engineer,
who has both a research & design relationship with Tyrell and a small craft business of his own as a luxury toy maker.

Most of the academic discussion of replicants in *Blade Runner* takes off from a
postmodern discourse on originals, copies and simulations or from a neo-Lacanian
interest in the psychology of sophisticated robots. In both cases, it is a discourse of
identity and difference, whether this is looked at philosophically or psychologically, whether in terms of ontological decidability or Oedipalised subjectivity. The
origins of these *topoi* are to be found in Philip K. Dick's original book, where the
issues, however, are explicitly political – capitalism destroys the realm of nature
and sets out to replace it with a world of manufactured goods, animoids as images
and commodities rather than as living creatures – a vision distinctly similar to Guy
Debord's concept of the 'Society of the Spectacle'[7] and one which therefore
reflects directly on Los Angeles, as capital city of the Spectacle. Or, as Manuel De
Landa might have described it, in his book, *A Thousand Years of Non-Linear
history*, we could see the replicants as signs of either the 'mineralization' of the
proletariat itself, if we see them in terms of microchip implant technology, or of a
long-term biological mutation as genetic engineering changes the realm of nature
into that of culture, biology into technology.[8]

At first sight, the principal characters of *Blade Runner* seem to be classical
figures of modernity – the replicant rebel is the outlaw dandy, a kind of
Nietzschean aesthete who is also the leader of a slave rebellion, while Deckard is
the working stiff, the plebeian who just gets on with the job. Both of them
despise the master of Metropolis, the ruler of the Tyrell Corporation, but they
take very different paths. But there are also significant differences between
Ridley Scott's film and that by Fritz Lang. In the character of Tyrell, the Master
is submerged into the figure of Rotwang, the evil magician and automaton
maker, creating a much more negative vision of the Master, no longer capable
of redemption. In Lang's *Metropolis*, the slaves are presented as a mass rather
than as individuals, transformed from mindless drudges into a mindless mob,
whereas the replicants in *Blade Runner* are intelligent individuals, an outlaw
elite. Deckard, who is the counterpart to the Master's son, is far from a wide-
eyed innocent – instead he is the typically world-weary protagonist of noir. Nor
is there any final reconciliation between Deckard and the replicants, although

there is mutual esteem, springing from Deckard's suspicion (and ours) that he is really one of them, a renegade replicant rather than a blade runner.

In *Blade Runner*, the drama is no longer between the proletarian mass-man and the gilded youth. There is no proletariat – or, if there is, it is off-world. In the city, there is only what we have come to call an underclass, mingled with a plethora of small-time peddlers and service providers, on the one hand, and a lone, single figure at the apex, a situation typical of contemporary postmodernity rather than the classic modernity of Weimar Germany. Perhaps, at this point, it is worth saying a few words about the question of 'postmodernism'. In a recent study, Perry Anderson proposes that postmodernity in the arts is really split between two trends, one which 'adjusts or appeals to the spectacular', the other which 'seeks to elude or refuse it'. The replicants, it seems to me, are both figures of the spectacular, especially in their deaths, but also renegades who seek to revenge themselves upon it. The same paradox marks the film as a whole – it is both an explicitly spectacular production, with its astonishing sets and stunning effects, and, at the same time, an implicit critique of the spectacle as a culture of death. It is clearly a product of the image industry and yet intellectually detached from it. It appeals to our fascination with postmodernity, while distancing itself from it. Again, this ambiguity probably reflects the underlying legacy of Philip K. Dick, the master of the dystopian 'trip', who consistently swings in his own work between euphoria and paranoia. In Dick's fiction, too, there is a consistent interpenetration of the public and the private, the world as outside force and the world as inner vision. It is as if the two poles of postmodernity – the global and the local, or the public rhetoric of advertising and the private world of fantasy – have become hopelessly entangled.

In the film (or, more accurately, in the *Director's Cut*) it is Gaff, Deckard's rival, played by Edward James Olmos, who appears to have access to the Blade Runner's dreams, as suggested by his poisoned gift of a dream image – an origami unicorn – at the very end of the film, thus raising the question of privacy. This is an issue with which we are all now much more familiar than we were when *Blade Runner* first came out, due to the way in which we seem to sense that our personal computer files are somehow part of our own identity, external to our body, of course, yet still as private as our bodily memory itself. Edward James Olmos was also, it seems, responsible for the use of 'City-Speak' as a polyglot street jargon, incorporating words from many different languages – Spanish, French, Chinese, German, Hungarian and Japanese. Olmos recounts how he 'went to the Berlitz School of Languages in Los Angeles, translated all these different bits and pieces of Gaff's original dialogue into fragments of foreign tongues and learned how to properly pronounce them. I also added some translated dialogue I'd made up myself. All that was a bitch and a half, but it really added to Gaff's character.'

It did more than that. It pinpointed the importance of language, as opposed to visual design, in defining the nature of the world city, as well as the nature of identity in the city. There are four categories of language spoken in *Blade*

Runner – there is English, the 'standard' language, used as a lingua franca; there are a number of vernacular languages, such as Chinese or Spanish; there is the code-switching sub-creole of City-Speak; and finally there is the hyper-language of computers. The Esper, the talking computer network which we see in use in Deckard's apartment and in a display of 'Incept tapes', was conceived as a system run by the police. 'Originally it was going to be everywhere – inside cars, out on the sidewalk, everywhere. But they got whittled down during rewrites until the Esper made only two appearances.' Similarly cars were to travel on an intelligent highway, a road with a mind of its own, exchanging information with vehicles through a sensor and controlling their path, flow and speed.

These languages each have their own socio-cultural context. English is 'unmarked', but besides being an interlingua, it is both the language of the elite and the language used in public or official situations by the police and by corporations. It is also, of course, the language implanted in replicants. Vernacular languages are used within ethnic groups, who are represented as members of an underclass of petty entrepreneurs, casual labourers and 'street people'. City-Speak is an *ad hoc* contact language, not far removed from a pidgin. Esper is a specialised network which is available only to a privileged elite who have private access to advanced communications technology. This linguistic landscape is one which reflects a sharply hierarchical system with a multitude of immigrant communities at the bottom. At the same time, the presence of a private communications network, while explicitly supporting the power of the local ruling elite, also implies that it has the global or (transglobal) reach characteristic of a world city. It is both a whirlpool, sucking immigrants in from the periphery, and a hub, controlling the periphery. By 1990 Los Angeles was already the North American urban region with the highest proportion of foreign-born residents (27 per cent, as opposed to New York's 20 per cent and Chicago's 11). At the same time, it had become increasingly bipolar, as wealth was re-distributed from rich to poor. The distribution of wealth thus parallels the distribution of linguistic skills between a technocratic lingua franca and a vernacular proto-creole, the germs of which we already see in the World Wide Web and the hubbub of the urban street.

In fact, the 'future metropolis' of *Blade Runner*, located in the year 2019, is surprisingly plausible as an extrapolation from trends which were dimly perceived in 1982 but have since become quite clear and the subject of considerable academic study. Underlying this type of city are a series of what we might call 'stratified mobility zones' (SMZs) – mobility of capital, mobility of elites and mobility of labour. Back in the 1950s, Marshall McLuhan's mentor, Harold Innis, noted that speed of communications favoured centralised power. Speed of global communications favours centralised global power, and this creates the conditions for the growth of world cities with specific social, demographic, cultural, spatial, architectural and linguistic characteristics. In this respect, *Blade Runner* was indeed premonitory on many different levels.

Credit for this must go to its writers (official and unofficial), to Ridley Scott, for his fanatical interest in the creation of a richly detailed environment, full of metaphoric meaning, and also to Syd Mead, who had previously worked in both the automobile and electronics industries as a 'futurist', giving visual form to his visions of feasible hardware set in a complete future environment. The city *Blade Runner* portrays is not precisely Los Angeles. In a way, it is both the city which Los Angeles wishes to be, perceived in boosterish, optimistic terms from the vantage-point of an elite, and that which it fears it will become, looked at in noir, pessimistic terms from the point of view of its critics and its immigrant and underclass population, numerically much greater but politically, of course, much weaker. Mike Davis is right in seeing it as an extension of the Fordist city of New York-Metropolis, but it is a New York which has been privatised, retrofitted and 'noir-ified'. The privatisation and retrofitting are both typical of the transition from Fordism to post-Fordism. The 'noir-ification' represents a new postmodern phase in a long-standing tradition of radical cultural critique, nurtured in Los Angeles itself.

This is not the same as a radical political critique – Fancher, obviously, is a left-liberal interested in ecology, but it was Ridley Scott, whom Fancher characterises as politically conservative, who describes the power of the Tyrell Corporation as 'patriarchal'. It is, however, a long tradition in Los Angeles, going back, as Mike Davis has chronicled, to Nathanael West (a favourite of Philip K. Dick), to Aldous Huxley (the great pioneer of prophetic science fiction), to Raymond Chandler and Dashiel Hammett (models for the creators of Deckard). In this sense, *Blade Runner* is certainly a Los Angeles movie, set in a great local tradition, a critique drawing on West and Chandler. At the same time, it has a global relevance and a global reach, of the kind Hollywood has long enjoyed, but not yet Los Angeles. It reflects both the vision of Los Angeles as a future world city and the unsustainable dystopia which that would involve.

Notes

1   Mike Davis, *City of Quartz: Excavating the Future in Los Angeles*, London and New York: Verso, 1990.
2   Philip K. Dick, *Do Androids Dream Of Electric Sheep?*, London: Rapp & Whiting, 1969.
3   Manuel Castells, *The Informational City: Information Technology, Economic Restructuring, and the Urban-Regional Process*, Oxford: Basil Blackwell, 1989.
4   Saskia Sassen, *The Global City: London, New York, Tokyo*, Princeton, NJ and Oxford: Princeton University Press, 1991.
5   Sharon Zukin, *Loft Living: Culture and Capital in Urban Change*, New Brunswick, NJ: Rutgers University Press, 1989.
6   Giuliana Bruno, 'Ramble City', *October*, 1987.
7   Guy Debord, *La Société du Spectacle*, Paris: Editions Gallimard, 1992.
8   Manuel de Landa, *A Thousand Years of Non-linear History*, New York: Zone Books, 1997.

Part VI
The economic metropolis

17 French *bidonvilles* around 1960s Paris

Urbanism and individual initiatives

Mireille Rosello

The word '*bidonville*' is the French equivalent of the English word 'shanty-town'. It was first used in Morocco in the 1950s, during the French protectorate, to refer to poor neighbourhoods where the roofs of makeshift houses had been cut out of metallic fuel containers ('*bidons*'), but between the 1950s and sometimes as late as the 1970s, the word *bidonville* became quite commonplace in the *metropole*, where thousands and thousands of immigrant workers, responding to a growing demand for cheap labour, found it impossible to have access to decent accommodation. In the 1960s, a generalised housing shortage due to the destruction of properties during the war and to the rapid growth of urban populations was compounded by their arrival. As a result, *bidonvilles* appeared all over France.

The greatest concentration was around Paris, especially in Champigny where almost 10,000 Portuguese migrants congregated, and in Nanterre where similar numbers of Algerian workers and their families survived in appalling conditions.[1] These maps, made by the Ministry of the Interior in 1966, give official and therefore probably conservative accounts of the situation. They are also abstract and quiet figurations which do not convey the miserable conditions of families who, for decades, typically lived in crumbling shacks, without water, without electricity, without proper streets, without sewage or rubbish collection.

Images exist of what people looked like when they had to live in a shanty-town. They are striking, sensationalist, heart-rending. We might think, at first, that they are more generous than maps because they scrutinise and therefore take into account human suffering instead of transforming it into statistics. On the other hand, it is perhaps easier to forget that such images are no more inno-cently humanitarian than administrative maps are neutrally scientific.[2] *Bidonvilles*, everybody agreed, were a problem. But the consensus disappeared when decisions had to be made, when policies had to be imagined and then implemented, when solutions had to be proposed.

Cities, towns and neighbourhoods have often been compared to texts. Like texts, they have many different readers with different interpretations, different reactions, different possible gestures of identification. *Bidonvilles*, like other urban phenomena, were the object of many conflictual readings that resulted in drastically different representations. And those representations, in turn, justified certain practices both inside and outside the *bidonville*. Like texts whose readers can be public or private, professional critics or anonymous commuters who finish a novel on the train, *bidonvilles* were interpreted very differently by readers whose voices were not equally heard, were not equally powerful. Perhaps not so paradoxically, in the presence of *bidonvilles* the most popular grids of interpretation were constructed by outsiders who may well have been incapable of surviving in the space they were quite competent at describing. When I say 'competent', I am not suggesting that they were providing an accurate description, nor that their reading was systematically irrelevant or incorrect. Rather, I am arguing that their competence could be measured by their ability to construct a narrative that sounded plausible to the general public and, eventually, to decision-makers, whether or not it was an adequate representation of the reality of the *bidonville*.

Certain types of reading influenced the existence, evolution and eventual destruction of *bidonvilles*. Such narratives were heard not only because their authors were relatively powerful, but because they were attractively totalising, centralising. They provided descriptions that could easily be read as explanations and therefore as solutions to what was unanimously identified as a disgrace. What I would like to suggest is that it is not so easy to define what constitutes a socially and politically desirable reading of the *bidonville* even if it is now possible, with hindsight, to point out that some readings were less neurotic than others. It is clear that some earlier interpretations were plainly inaccurate. In view of recent testimonies, we can provide less stereotypical interpretations. Still, I would like to show that neither incorrect nor correct deciphering necessarily leads to appropriate urban decisions. As Alexander Gelley explains: 'The city as text; its uses and practices as forms of reading, of operating such a text – we encounter this figure repeatedly, in works of literature, of criticism, and also of what may be classified as "urban disciplines" But we have not yet determined what it is we are looking for in a "city text", what kind of use (whether operational, hermeneutic, or cognitive) might be gained from such an investigation'.[3]

Before the recent publication of autobiographical texts by adults who grew up in *bidonvilles* and who are now old enough to testify to their experiences,[4] the traditional reading of *bidonvilles* came from the outside, from journalists, from politicians and from people who lived close by.[5] And regardless of the outsiders' political positioning (whether they blamed immigrant workers or whether, at the other end of the spectrum, they felt responsible and wished to help them out of their predicament), most tended to jump to the same conclusions. Ultimately, their readings of the *bidonville's* urban structure were mutually reinforcing and a sort of intertextual familiarity was slowly created by the repetition of the same stereotypes.

Both sympathetic and hostile readings analysed the *bidonville* as an enclave of chaos in the midst of organised planning, atypical pockets of disorder that contrasted with the imaginary perfection and visible straightforwardness of

Haussmannian boulevards. Forgetting that France as a whole was far from having solved its housing crisis, analysts perceived *bidonvilles* as an exception to the rule. The generally accepted phantasm was that *bidonvilles* were a space ruled by chance and haphazardness, where shacks were erected at random, one next to another. Literally as well as symbolically, *bidonvilles* were doomed to inexistence: they were not mapped out, and they were not on the map. Inexistence coexisted with perceived shapelessness: due to the lack of proper roads and infrastructure, mud, that intermediary element between the fluid and the solid, was both the very real enemy with which the inhabitants of the *bidonvilles* had to live and the symbol of a soft, spongy, ambiguous interstitial space which outsiders identified with filth. *Bidonvilles* were spineless.[6] Neither rurals nor townies, its inhabitants were mocked because their shoes made them look like displaced peasants who muddied the floors of supposedly more civilised, urban, bourgeois buses and rooms.[7] As in the case of nineteenth-century slums, images of housing rubbed off on the inhabitants, who were forced to live without sewage and in the midst of rats. They ended up being associated with the diseases they had to fight against, and they were compared to rats ('raton' is a particularly violent anti-Arab insult in France and anti-Arab violence is often called a 'ratonnade'). Lack of hygiene invited moral condemnation.[8]

Reading the *bidonville* as a helplessly chaotic assemblage of planks and metal had a direct result: it was imagined that such chaos could not be improved in any way whatsoever and that the only solution was total destruction. Powerful readings led to the idea that only one solution was viable: the complete and immediate eradication of *bidonvilles*. *Bidonvilles* were eventually bulldozed to make place for prestigious state buildings such as *préfectures* or a university in Nanterre. Only images and text remain. Unfortunately, it took decades for the policies to be implemented, and, while they lived in *bidonvilles* for sometimes as long as twenty years, whole populations were persecuted by the radical belief that only total destruction was acceptable because they were denied any agency in the matter of the evolution of their environment. They were treated as a sort of natural emanation of the mud.

The desire to see them disappear from the political and urban landscape seems to have generated a type of reaction akin to magic thinking: there was nothing more important than the complete erasure of *bidonvilles*. This included making them less visible, hiding them behind smokescreens of words and physical barriers: fences and walls were built, bulldozers piled up earth to create artificial hills that compounded the inhabitants' serious drainage problems but successfully hid unsightly *bidonvilles* from richer neighbourhoods. At the time, even comedians made fun of the operations. An even crueller strategy was used to stop any evolution: repairs and improvements were made illegal.

Former inhabitants of the *bidonville*s often talk about their fear of the so-called Brigade Z, a special team of policemen whose job was to inspect the *bidonvilles* and to make sure that no construction was taking place. The official reason was that the *bidonville* was not to be allowed to sprawl any more than it already had. In practice, this meant that the Brigade Z were commissioned vandals: their duty was to destroy everything that looked new or recent in the *bidonville*: 'We used to call them the "thug brigade" because it was their job to destroy our shacks.'[9] Whenever one of the families from the *bidonvilles* tried to improve their miserable huts, the Brigade Z would intervene and pull everything down. If people tried to fix their roofs, to repair a wall, to dig a hole in order to build rudimentary toilets, the Brigade Z would break into houses and destroy the individual's work. Their role was to curb the supposedly spontaneous growth of the *bidonville* but, because there was nothing spontaneous about the attempts made by the families to control humidity, leaks and the lack of hygiene, the Brigade Z ironically contributed to the perpetuation of the worst aspects of the *bidonville*. They participated in the creation of the stereotypical image they were seemingly fighting against. The common-sense idea that such poverty should disappear led to a devastating contradiction: people who lived in the *bidonvilles* could do nothing to fight against the most extreme forms of destitution. The Brigade Z was the logical emanation not of *bidonvilles* but rather of the contradictory attitude of the authorities towards them.

Their intransigence was greeted with a determined barrage of oppositional practices which, in a sense, constituted a different urban proposal: the *bidonville could* be improved. Lamenting the losing battle against the mud-invaded communal space, one witness remembers: 'Most of us are employed in the building industry. It would be easy to have access to trucks ... If we had our way, we would have proper streets here, nice clean streets.'[10] Transformations and alterations were constantly attempted, but instead of being celebrated as small victories against a grim reality, as evidence of individual initiatives, they fell into the category of fraudulent activities that had to be carried out in secret.

> So people made do. Some bribed the cops, others had ideas. I remember this guy who did not want to send his children to the public orphanage. He decided to make his shack a little bigger while his wife was pregnant. He built another shack inside his own and little by little, he pushed it outside, a few inches every week, like the lid of a can. He managed to gain one more metre.[11]

The slow evolution of *bidonvilles* towards more basic comfort was thus thwarted by the practical implementation of policies that spoke in the name of more comfort, more hygiene, more modern standards of living. At the time, no one seems to have noticed that the level of skills needed to survive under such conditions contradicted the very label of 'unskilled labour' attached to the immigrants. Perhaps people who did not live in *bidonvilles* never stopped to wonder whether they would know enough about building to erect the most rudimentary shelter for their family if they ever had to. The inhabitants of *bidonvilles* were forced to master a number of skills that are normally distributed among a large number of professions, and they were also being asked to deploy extra levels of ingenuity to overcome obstacles that administration added to their predicament: 'The *bidonville* was invented in an office,' concludes another witness (Lefort, p. 59).

In retrospect, the miserable shacks were not so much a symbolic portrait of the inhabitants' resignation nor even of their powerlessnes and poverty as an image of the corruption and contradictions rampant in the administrative strategies they had to contend with. The fact that *bidonvilles* existed at all testified not only to the immigrants' determination and will to live but also to their faith in their own creative resources. Somehow they knew that they would resort to the necessary ruses to bypass the extra hurdles placed in their way by *ad hoc* regulations that gave them no other choice than systematically to break the law. Charles Baudelaire and Walter Benjamin equated nineteenth-century Paris with the '*flâneur*'; later Georg Simmel suggested that new cities would replace the '*flâneur*' with the '*blasé*' type. But no cultural critic or poet of the *bidonville* ever stopped to consider that the typical *bidonville* inhabitant was another type of urban dweller, the '*débrouilleur*'. '*Débrouille*' is the art of making do. Its principle belongs to the type of activity that Michel de Certeau calls 'tactics', that is, forms of practice adopted by people who are aware that they have no territory recognised by the authorities as their own.[12] Paradoxically, while the middle class tended to react to '*débrouille*' with contempt and pity, in the 1960s and 1970s theoreticians and artists were re-appropriating many of the principles implicit in the practice of 'making do' and celebrating the creativity of recycling. It was apparently quite possible to live with that contradiction.

Of course, the practice of 'making do' came at a phenomenal cost for its practitioners because it necessitated adhering to the official image: immigrants lived in filth. Talking about people who repaired their shacks from the inside to avoid being noticed by the Brigade Z, Lefort writes: 'Other guys would repair the walls at night with cement and they would quickly dirty them with mud.'[13] The *bidonville* must be dirty. If it became less dirty, it had to be destroyed. In other words, the only guarantee of survival was to correspond to the most caricatural stereotype: the Arab who presumably liked to live in the mud.

A more optimistic reading would argue that the Brigade Z was a high price to pay for good intentions: if *bidonvilles* were not allowed to proliferate, people would leave earlier, presumably to be 'integrated' – they would have access to 'normal' housing conditions. But underlying assumptions about immigrants were already inscribed in the planning of supposedly suitable accommodation, and unexplored prejudices often resulted in a two-tier level of hypocrisy: the idea was to reject potential cultural differences, to enforce assimilation and integration into French culture, but at the same time, when housing projects were designed with immigrants in mind, they were a parody of what was considered acceptable for Europeans. Before being relocated to the brand-new high-rises that mushroomed on the outskirts of French cities in the 1960s and 1970s, immigrants first had to put up with so-called 'cités de transit',[14] which were conceived as a temporary solution, halfway houses that would ostensibly teach immigrants how to cope with modern facilities but which, in reality, placed them in ghettos.

A deeply cynical interpretation would be that the Brigade Z was the tip of a political iceberg: they acted out the real and unavowable logic of administrators who claimed that *bidonvilles* should disappear for humanitarian reasons but who would probably have been relieved to see its population disappear at the same time. The Brigade Z, whose work was to destroy without having any authority to propose anything else, was a caricature of the first measures taken by the state which kept trying to expropriate without being quite clear on what to replace the *bidonville* with. In 1964, when what would later be known as 'the Debré law' was discussed in the National Assembly, critics pointed out that the only clear element of the plan was the expropriation aspect: after the land had been repossessed by Prefects, no one knew which administration was supposed to carry out the rest of the relocation plan (Lallaoui, p. 71).

The solution envisaged by the state always involved an element of 'back to square one', a 'starting from scratch', which was profoundly utopian, profoundly unrealistic and also profoundly cruel to populations that had to deal with the consequences of abstract reasoning about good urban planning after being abandoned to their fates for decades. *Bidonvilles* were eradicated by bulldozers so that, for people who had lived there, the net result was more or less forced displacement, and at times increased segregation in the 'cités de transit'.

> We soon realised that they had put us there to separate us from the French. On one side, there is an empty lot, on the other one, a paper mill; at the back, the Seine and in front, the barracks of the riot police. The French don't dare come visit. They are scared and call our cité 'Alger la Blanche'.[15]

In the 1960s, dominated by utopian dreams of 'Radiant Cities', no-one suggested that, at the end of the day, piecemeal individual initiatives might be at least as desirable as the infuriating practices of the Brigade Z: constant promises followed by insanely long delays, and even the construction of low-cost, inadequate temporary housing that would soon replicate the very problems that it was meant to solve. Slow improvement and the evolution from *bidonville* to *ville* were never envisaged as a plausible solution and erroneous readings of the *bidonvilles* thus had disastrous results: the lack of decent housing, experienced by the inhabitants as a constant struggle against precarious physical conditions, was compounded by a radical lack of social and symbolic recognition on the part of the authorities. Officially, it was almost possible to make the *bidonville* disappear. For instance, the definition of the 'address' had to be completely reinvented: although some mail was distributed, postal services were unreliable and the principle of the individual mail box was replaced by centralised 'numbers' (sometimes attached to a café or a shop whose owners had the responsibility for dispatching the letters they received). The notion of an individual address further disintegrated when conflict with the administration occurred. Mr Ali, one of the witnesses quoted by Lallaoui, says: 'The police say that the *bidonville* is not a legal residence, so we are homeless, we don't have an address.'[16] The symbolic and legal lack of recognition was in bad faith but it created, as well as matched, the distressing absence of accommodation, of roots, of legitimate identity.

As time went by, however, it slowly became more and more obvious, first to decision-makers (including architects) and then to the general public, that the reading of *bidonvilles* as chaotic spaces of anarchy populated by either born delinquents or hapless victims was completely inaccurate. The inhabitants of *bidonvilles* had specific skills, they engaged in specific urban practices. They also had their own interpretation of the situation, but in the 1960s they were not primarily concerned with convincing others that their reading was the correct one. The energy required to decipher their environment was not deployed in rhetoric but in the translation of their mental narrative into tactics. Survival on a daily basis required that sacrifice. For example, while people lived in *bidonvilles*, inventing practical solutions to the problem of carrying water from the rare pumps to the shacks was probably more important than public relations operations. Besides, immigrant manual workers had no time, they were ghettoised and ostracised and often they could neither read nor write French. When the Algeria War started, they were isolated even more and treated as suspicious enemies within. During and after the Algerian War, all North Africans (including Moroccans and Tunisians) were deemed guilty by association and were under constant suspicion of terrorism or collusion with the FNL.[17] It is difficult to imagine a situation less conducive to the publication of personal accounts.

New readings have emerged, however, since the children who grew up in *bidonvilles* have come of age. Historians and sociologists have by now revised their narratives so that, in the past few years, a new collective discourse has gradually emerged that seeks to correct the original set of images and stereotypes and to replace them with what is perceived as a more accurate interpretation of *bidonvilles*. A sudden upsurge of interest has suddenly turned *bidonvilles* into a legitimate object of study among social scientists, and several collections addressed to the general public have been launched.[18] To be fair, minority voices among architects had already tried to propose different readings. For example, Serge Santelli and Isabelle Herpin produced commendably atypical work when they took the time to make a map of Nanterre's *bidonvilles*.[19] They even went as far as reading the structure of the miserable shack as a replica of typical North African houses. According to them, economic interpretations of and an exclusive focus on poverty cannot explain the grid of *bidonvilles*, and mask important organising principles: they see *bidonvilles* as a copy of typical Arab towns (Santelli, p. 188). Sayad and Dupuy concur: 'The bidonville is not chaotic; or rather it is chaotic only to those who don't have the key to its organization, who cannot understand the grammar of the text inscribed in the ground.'[20]

Santelli and Herpin's map was one of the very first revisions of the *bidonville* that refused the chaos theory. When they published their first analysis, a failed yet hegemonic reading perceived *bidonvilles* as disorder and anarchy, lack of organisation. If Santelli's chart had corresponded to the dominant discourse, other practices would undoubtedly have prevailed. Instead of referring to such complex structures as *bidonvilles*, instead of perceiving Nanterre as a pathological urban disease, other formulations could have become commonplace. Since then, for example, Yves Lacoste has suggested that the word *bidonville* is improper and that it would be more precise to talk about 'forms of spontaneous urban growth', even if it is clear that no urban development is either completely controlled or completely spontaneous.[21]

The replacement of earlier, neurotically paranoid readings of *bidonvilles* as contagious chaos is also due to the increasing literary activity of second-generation immigrants looking back on their past. Adults who grew up in *bidonvilles* can now paint quite a different picture from the inside (although such narratives are often relayed by a powerful European mediator). In recent autobiographical accounts, the *bidonville* is presented as a site of hyperactive, spontaneous urbanisation where very specific activities are valorised, taught, exchanged. Building, repairing, fixing, recycling are forever going on, on a micro but intensive scale. It is worth noting that such direct control over the physicality of the environment completely disappeared when families relocated to apartments where every need had supposedly been predicted and anticipated. Unlike the high-rise estates that were about to be built as an answer to the housing shortage that plagued French people and immigrants alike, *bidonvilles* also functioned as genuine neighbourhoods with commercial activities: Lefort remembers that 'People who lived in *bidonvilles* were well organised. There were shops: groceries, hairdressers, butchers, tailors, shoemakers and of course, cafés.'[22] Again, paradoxically, the presence of shopkeepers is what would be missing from the endless rows of monotonous H.L.M. buildings.[23] Sayad and Dupuy also point out that shops played the role of social cement:

> Besides their strictly technical functions, shops have a structuring effect. Groceries and cafés open very early, catering for workers on a night shift and for those who make a very early start.[24]

Once we recognise the high level of organisation inside the *bidonville*, different readings start forming interestingly divergent layers of interpretation: for example, the absence of running water can be documented by photographers who take sad pictures of children in rags waiting in the mud for their turn at the pump, or written as a comic episode in Azouz Begag's autobiographical *Le gone du Chaâba*[25] or even analysed as the origin of an example of parallel economy. Water was bought and sold inside the *bidonville*, a type of trade which Europeans had been familiar with until the nineteenth century but which their collective memory had obviously hastened to forget.[26]

Similarly, although it is commonly assumed that shacks are built on illegal terrain and have therefore no commercial value, Benaïcha points out that a whole parallel property system had developed within the *bidonville* community. Houses were bought, rented and sold and verbal agreements were as binding as any written documents although such transactions obviously remained invisible to the administration. 'Everyone owns his own shack. The sale agreement is oral. No written contract exists. And the only guarantee is the verbal agreement'.[27] But, he says elsewhere, 'here, the word is the Law.'[28]

This second reading of the *bidonville* is thus poles apart from the first one: here, the image of disgusting shapelessness is replaced by a vision of structure and order: 'Our shantytown constitutes a genuine micro-State.'[29] I would not want to argue, however, that if this second reading had prevailed, perfect solutions would have immediately been available. Even better readings can lead to undesirable practices. Of course, only if this second reading is kept in mind can one understand some surprising reactions: in *Le gone du Chaâba*, Azouz Begag explains that when his family had the opportunity to move out of the *bidonville*, the father resisted to the bitter end. Only if we understand that he was about to lose his precarious identity as the leader of the *bidonville* community can one empathise with his sense of loss and fear of the unknown. Dominant discourse would have used the father's incomprehensible refusal as evidence that immigrants as a whole were not ready to embrace progress. If we take into account the intense activity and tight social structure of the *bidonville*, it is easier to understand that its inhabitants did have something to lose by moving out of their painfully constructed 'micro-State'.

On the other hand, one dangerous temptation lies within this second reading: by focusing on the creativity, energy and determination of the *bidonville* community, we may unduly valorise tactics and practices that were imposed on the inhabitants of the poorest neighbourhoods. Admiration for a newly discovered structure can aestheticise poverty and idealise a constant struggle against the environment. As incredible as it may seem, there were still some *bidonvilles* left in Marseilles in 1991. And an article in *Le Monde Diplomatique* pointed out that there seemed to be a direct correlation between the survival of some *bidonvilles* and the fact they were very quiet and unproblematic neighbourhoods. In a sense, they suffered from this good reputation: they were not political irritants so no drastic measure was ever taken. The same journalist also wonders about the effect that visits of endless teams of researchers had on the morale of the museified inhabitants of the last French *bidonvilles*.[30]

A recognition of the complex organisation of *bidonvilles* is a welcome move away from an exclusively economic and sensationalist analysis but it should not be replaced by total blindness. Nor should it preclude an ethical appreciation of the tactics adopted as survival mechanisms. A potential danger of the second reading is to overestimate the cohesion of the *bidonville* community or rather to confuse cohesion with ideal equality. If governmental humanitarian discourses were often tainted with hypocrisy, the humanitarian fallacy also extended to the picture of perfect solidarity between immigrants. The second reading may be creating another stereotype.

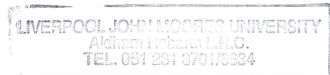

> We should not underestimate the role played by the owners of cafés, bars, hotels, apartments, who claimed to be generously concerned with the welfare of their brothers, and who were eventually dubbed 'sleep merchants.' They acted with authority, like landlords or landowners, and they are responsible for the building of the first shacks.[31]

The opposition between order and chaos cannot be simply superimposed over binarisms such as good and evil.[32] Similarly, the 'very ancient art of making do' as de Certeau puts it, is not a set of ethics (de Certeau, p. 30). It is not to be celebrated in principle. Sometimes, 'making do' meant that people from North Africa exploited people from North Africa.

Rather, what I was suggesting is that it is no longer possible to adopt a one-sided reading of the *bidonvilles*: they were always ambivalent spaces and the difficulty is to find a viewpoint that eschews both a racist amalgamation between the inhabitants and their housing conditions and the temptation to glorify the immigrants' capacity to survive under conditions that we would find unacceptable in the name of a sort of paternalistic admiration for what 'these people' can endure, for their ingenuity, for their courage.

The main difference in approach between the inhabitants of the *bidonvilles* and the authorities was a question of strategy and a philosophy: the former were reformist pessimists who did not envisage any radical short-term solution to their predicament and opted for slow and steady micro improvements. Their considerable ingenuity and *savoir-faire* were put at the service of their will to survive. Their efforts testify to a tremendous desire to improve their living conditions, to reach standards of which they were perfectly aware. Their values in terms of housing made them the same as those who treated them as radical others.

The authorities, on the other hand, were radicals and optimists verging on utopists. Radicals because they advocated change on a massive scale: they expected nothing less than the complete eradication of *bidonvilles*. They wanted to start from scratch and did not want to take responsibility for having allowed spontaneous urban growth to intervene. It was a utopian belief in the *tabula rasa*.

Reformist pessimism had, of course, one major drawback: it would take a very long time to transform *bidonvilles* into acceptable neighbourhoods and it could not be achieved without some centralised planning and the agreement of the authorities. But people believed they could have done it. Radical optimism had one major argument on its side: its ambition. But the total eradication of poverty is a utopian project that often becomes totalitarian because it does not take into account human memory and time. In its tempting simplicity, it refuses to acknowledge that a workable neighbourhood does not get built as one whole pre-packaged project. Moreover, it would have been commendable if, precisely, it had not taken so long to implement. But a radical strategy that takes twenty years to be finalised is no longer radical. In twenty years, was it really not possible to transform *bidonvilles* from the inside, like the Argonauts' ship?

Acknowledgement

Thank you to Wendy Michallat for her reading of the first draft.

Notes

1 See Abdelmalek Sayad and Eliane Dupuy's *Un Nanterre Algérien, terre de bidonvilles*, Paris: Editions Autrement, 1995, and Marie-Christine Volovitch-Tavares's *Portugais à Champigny, le temps des baraques*, Paris: Editions Autrement, collection: 'Français d'ailleurs, peuples d'ici', 1995.

2 See the strange commentary made by Sayad and Dupuy under a picture reproduced in their book: the photograph shows a young child inside a miserable shack and the authors interpret: 'Un regard d'enfant qui se passe de tout commentaire' ['A child's gaze that needs no comment'] (Sayad and Dupuy, *Un Nanterre Algérien, terre de bidonvilles*, p. 67). Isn't it precisely illusory to replace the relativity and subjectivity of texts and narratives with images because we assume that the image 'speaks for itself', that it make analysis redundant and useless? When journalists took pictures of children and later published them, some of the children resented the intrusion and were infuriated by the loss of control over their image. It took years for them to be able to publish their own commentaries.

3 Alexandre Gelley, 'City Texts: Representation, Semiology, Urbanism', in *Politics, Theory, and Contemporary Culture*, ed. Mark Poster, New York: Columbia University Press, 1993, pp. 237–60 (p. 240). For an analysis of the relationship between inhabitants and institutions, dwelling and governmental policies, see Christian Bachmann and Nicole Leguennec, *Violences urbaines: ascension et chute des classes moyennes à travers cinquante ans de la politique de la ville*, Paris: Albin Michel, 1996.

4 See Azouz Begag, *Le gone du Chaâba*, Paris: Seuil, 1986; Monique Hervo and Marie-Ange Charras, *Bidonvilles*, Paris: Maspéro, 1971; Brahim Benaïcha, *Vivre au paradis: d'une oasis à un bidonville*, Paris: Desclée de Brouwer, 1992; and Mehdi Lallaoui, *Du bidonville au HLM*, Paris: Syros, 1993.

5 Even more recently, novels published by French or Francophone writers have provided complex fictional accounts of the passage from shantytowns to postmodern cities. See especially *Les honneurs perdus* by Camerounian Calixthe Beyala, Paris: Albin Michel, 1997 and *Poisson d'or* by Jean-Marie Le Clézio, Paris: Gallimard, 1997. Both narratives focus on *bidonvilles* in an African context.

6 See Michel Laronde's analysis of the opposition between hard and soft. 'The world of soft urbanism is temporary and it corresponds to the transient mode of living adopted by the bidonville in the process of acclimation into another culture' ['Temporaire, le monde de l'Urbanisme mou correspond au mode d'être transitoire qu'assume le bidonville dans le schéma d'acclimation à une autre culture' (Laronde, *Autour du roman beur*, Paris: L'Harmattan, 1993, pp. 99–102). Housing projects symbolise the victory of the hard.

7 See Mehdi Lallaoui's *Du bidonville au HLM*, Paris: Syros, 1993, p. 50 and François Lefort's *Du bidonville à l'expulsion*, Paris: C.I.E.M, 1980, p. 56.

8 See Elizabeth Wilson's analysis of nineteenth-century London, 'Cesspool City', in *The Sphinx in the City: Urban Life, the Control of Disorder, and Women*, Berkeley, Los Angeles and Oxford: University of California Press, 1991, p. 37.

9 'Nous on les appelait la brigade des casseurs parce que c'était leur boulot de défoncer nos bicoques' (Lefort, *Du bidonville à l'expulsion*, p. 67).

10 'Beaucoup sont dans le bâtiment. C'est facile pour eux d'avoir un camion ... Si on nous laissait faire, on aurait de véritables rues ici ..., bien propres et tout' (Sayad and Dupuy, *Un Nanterre Algérien, terre de bidonvilles*, p. 97).

11 'Alors les gens se démerdaient, certains payaient cher les flics, d'autres avaient des idées. Je me souviens qu'un mec ne voulait pas envoyer ses enfants à l'Assistance Publique, il a décidé d'agrandir sa bicoque pendant que sa femme était enceinte. Il a construit une autre baraque à l'intérieur de sa baraque et petit à petit, il la faisait glisser dehors de dix centimètres par semaine, comme le couvercle d'une boîte, il a gagné un mètre' (Lefort, *Du bidonville à l'expulsion*, p. 72).

12 'Thus a North African living in Paris or Roubaix (France) insinuates into the system imposed on him by the construction of a low-income housing development or of the French language the ways of "dwelling" (in a house or a language) peculiar to his native Kabylia. He superimposes them and, by that combination, creates for himself a space in which he can find ways of using the constraining order of the place or of the language. Without leaving the place where he has no choice but to live and which lays down its law for him, he establishes within it a degree of plurality and creativity. By an art of being in between, he draws unexpected results from his situation' (Michel de Certeau, *The Practice of Everyday Life*, trans. Steven Rendall, Berkeley, CA: University of California Press, 1984, p. 30).

13 'D'autres mecs réparaient les murs la nuit avec du ciment et ils les salissaient vite avec de la boue' (Lefort, *Du bidonville à l'expulsion*, p. 72).

14 Transitional housing projects.

15 'On a vite compris qu'on nous avait mis là pour nous séparer des Français. D'un côté, on a un terrain vague; de l'autre, une usine de papier; derrière, la Seine et devant, une caserne de C.R.S. Les Français osent pas venir chez nous, ils ont peur et ils appellent notre cité: "Alger la Blanche" (Lefort, *Du bidonville à l'expulsion*, p. 101)'

16 'la police dit qu'au bidonville c'est pas un domicile fixe, c'est-à-dire qu'on est à la rue, quoi. On n'a pas de domicile' (quoted in Lallaoui, *Du bidonville au HLM*, p. 51)

17 Front National de Libération (the party fighting for the independence of Algeria).

18 See the collection called 'Français d'ailleurs, peuple d'ici: Les lieux de mémoire de l'immigration en France' [The French from elsewhere, a people here and now: the Realms of Memory of Immigration in France'] published by Autrement in Paris in the 1990s.

19 See Serge Santelli, 'Des Bidonvilles à Nanterre', in *Les Traversées de Paris: Deux siècles de révolutions dans la ville*, ed. Pierre Pinon, Paris: Editions du Moniteur, 1989, pp. 187–93.

20 'Le bidonville n'est pas un chaos; ou plutôt il n'est qu'un chaos que pour ceux qui n'en ont pas la clé, qui ne peuvent pas saisir la grammaire inscrite au sol' (Sayad and Dupuy, *Un Nanterre Algérien, terre de bidonvilles*, p. 105).

21 'formes de croissance urbaine spontanée' (Yves Lacoste, 'Bidonville', *Encyclopedia Universalis*. Paris: Editions Universalis, vol. 4, p. 104, column a).

22 'Les gens du bidonville étaient tout à fait organisés. Il y avait des magasins: épiciers, coiffeurs, bouchers, couturiers et cordonniers et bien sûr des cafés' (quoted in Lallaoui, *Du bidonville au HLM*, p. 55).

23 H.L.M. stands for 'Habitations à loyer modéré' (low rent accommodation).

24 'Outre leur fonction proprement technique, les commerces ont un effet structurant. L'ouverture fort matinale des épiceries et des cafés satisfait les ouvriers qui travaillent en équipe de nuit et ceux qui commencent très tôt le matin' (Sayad and Dupuy, *Un Nanterre Algérien, terre de bidonvilles*, p. 80).

25 A 'gone' is a slang word used in the region of Lyons to refer to children. 'Chaâba' was the name of a *bidonville* in the suburbs of Lyons. The title means, approximately, *Bidonville Kid*.

26 On the difficulties encountered by the urban working classes in the nineteenth century, see *The Sphinx in the City*: 'Even to obtain drinking water was often a major undertaking. The eventual provision of a supply of fresh drinking water and the

construction of sewage systems in the major towns of Britain were magnificent achievements. Yet, in the 1850s Sir John Simon, in his annual reports as Physician to the City of London, and George Godwin, in his magazine *The Builder*, were still describing the provision of water in the metropolis and other large towns – or rather, the lack of it – in horrific terms. Water was provided in casks. These, filled once or twice a week, were often located near dustbins or refuse, a potent source of contamination. Many families and individuals had no vessels for water in their rooms. John Simon described water butts made of decayed wood, filled three times a week' (Wilson, p. 36). It is only in the late 1960s that social housing was routinely equipped with bathrooms.

27 'Chacun est propriétaire de sa baraque. L'acte de vente est oral. Il n'y a aucun écrit. Et la seule garantie est celle de la parole donnée' (Benaïcha, *Vivre au paradis*, p. 43).

28 'Ici la parole a force de loi' (Benaïcha, *Vivre au paradis*, p. 24).

29 'Notre bidonville constitue un vrai mini-Etat' (Benaïcha, *Vivre au paradis*, p. 39).

30 Magali Cavanaggia, 'Marseille, quartiers nord: misère et solidarité dans les vieux bidonvilles', *Le Monde Diplomatique*, May (1991): 8.

31 'On n'insistera jamais assez sur le rôle joué, sous couvert de solidarité et de générosité, voire de fraternité, par ces tenanciers de café, de bars, d'hôtels, meublés et garnis, que l'on a fini par désigner sous le nom de "marchands de sommeil". Agissant avec autorité, comme des maîtres de céans, ils sont au départ de l'édification des premières baraques' (Sayad and Dupuy, *Un Nanterre Algérien, terre de bidonvilles*, p. 23).

32 The urbanist wants 'to impose a material institution upon a human collectivity in order to augment its well being and also, not incidentally, to make humanity better, but better according to a plan – the plan, precisely, of the new edifice or city – "the radiant city" (Le Corbusier), "the living city" (Frank Loyd Wright)' (Gelley, 'City Texts: Representation, Semiology, Urbanism', p. 244).

18 Pl(a)ys of marginality
Transmigrants in Paris

Doina Petrescu

Each culture proliferates on its margins.[1]

Mapping marginal phenomena in the context of contemporary theories of space is no longer a marginal undertaking. All that remains marginal are the methodologies, the paths and the rhythms that one can adopt within this undertaking.

This chapter proposes strategies and tactics to practice transmigration between concepts of 'margin' and 'marginality', at the intersection of language, politics and space.[2] We will follow active margins that allow new dynamics in society and that invent new spatial patterns and forms of mobility, interrogating the boundaries both between contemporary economies, policies and institutions and between the social remains of the earlier division of Europe.

Marginality and transmigration, their politics and poetics, are a matter of both playing and plying in this chapter. We take risks, we challenge, we speed. Yet, the whole idea of an association between 'marginality' and 'transmigration' prompts us to rethink the concept of 'marginality' through notions of 'movement' and 'mobility'. Once it has been traversed by movement, 'marginality' – the concept, the phenomenon – is redefined.

The Oas country is a region located in northern Romania, close to the frontier with Ukraine and Hungary. Since the fall of the Iron Curtain in 1989, many inhabitants of this region have started to leave their villages and migrate with their families to the West. They have invented a particular practice of migration which supposes a project of leaving and returning and establishes a rhythm of exchange between the village of origin and the country of immigration, based on periods of several months. For these Romanian peasants, the transmigrational practice functions within an ancient vocabulary of mobility: it is a substitute for the traditional practice of transhumance, which characterises the pastoral economy of the Romanian mountain regions. Transhumance is a phenomenon of migration of people and animals between different places which is regulated by seasonal cycles and specific economic logics and dynamics.

In contemporary social practices, 'transmigration' is a direct substitute for 'transhumance'. It has kept the *trans-*, the 'beyond', and has lost the 'earth', the 'humus'. What is important in transmigrational practices is the movement, the dynamics, and not the place. The modern transmigrants exchange not only places but states and nations, social and economical systems, codes, laws and languages as well.

Modern sociology has borrowed the term from religion. Transmigration comes from *transmigrare*: 'to emigrate from country to country' as the soul that 'passes from body to body'. A 'spirit without body', a *ghost*, a *host*, a *hostile*: that is a transmigrant. Sometimes *ghosts*, sometimes *hosts*, Romanian transmigrants exploit Western hospitality and haunt the political refugee systems throughout Europe, especially in the big cities such as Vienna, Paris, London and Rome.

They constitute a new sociological category that functions within a double social identity and a double economic activity. Peasant-hawkers, they still retain their homes in Romania but periodically leave for the West in order to obtain the status of 'SDF' ('person of no fixed abode'). They are emigrating, in other words, through their very *desire for marginality*. By completing an application for political asylum, they exploit this mechanism while keeping their family links in Romania: in the French case, social assistance currently amounts to 1200F/month. This is therefore a new class belonging to both archaic and new socio-economical structures that succeeds and exceeds the simple communist–capitalist political division, a mutating structure corresponding to the transnational realities of contemporary Europe.

Their exchanges function within a phenomenological rule that oscillates between stability and instability, hostility and hospitality, visibility and invisibility, appearance and disappearance. The logic of making themselves invisible during their Western season is doubled by a logic of ostentatious display during the Eastern part of the cycle. While they are in their villages, they show off their social and economic standing through their accumulated possessions. In the West, they prefer to remain invisible to authorities and administrations and to live illegally in the interstices of the city.[3]

This article proposes a cartography of the nomadic life styles of these 'transmigrants' whose current tactics and strategies, one can imagine, will soon be discovered, denounced and eradicated. As Paul Virilio has noticed, we belong to an epoch whose aesthetics are those 'of disappearance'. This chapter tries to map out some aspects of the socio-political value of this 'disappearing', of what is happening, what is appearing on the verge of 'disappearance'.

How does habitation take place within an invisible condition? What lines are necessary to map a life structured in mobility?

Lines

> As individuals and groups we are made of lines which are very diverse in nature.
>
> (Gilles Deleuze in the opening to his discussion to 'Politics')[4]

In order to speak about politics, Deleuze speaks about lines. *Lines* offer a metaphor that is abstract and complex enough to map the entire social field, to trace its shapes, its borders and its becomings. They can map the way 'life always proceeds at several rhythms and at several speeds'.[5] They map individual cracks and collective breaks within the segmentation and heterogeneity of power. *Lines* are always attached to geopolitics. Countries, too, are made out of lines. The lines of frontiers belong to conventions, codes and rules, and not to *relations*.

Transmigrants are the products of border lines. They cross them, make them porous, mocking their political seriousness. But at the same time, they depend on them, as they are always attracted by what is on the other side. Codes and rules demand to be flaunted in the same way that frontiers demand to be crossed, their deviations and detours creating another kind of line.

According to François Deligny,[6] 'The *detour* seems to come out of a certain idea that "the straight kind" exists. When one says *line* one thinks implicitly of *straight* and *right*.'[7]

Transmigrants ask for 'rights of detour'. The mapping of their practices should be made out of detours and deviations. From frontier to frontier, from periphery to periphery, from squat to squat, the lines of transmigration are always tangled with detours.

Deligny has proposed a particular way of mapping the daily patterns of behaviour of autistic children. His cartography traces customary lines and fluid lines, where the child curls up, finds something, slaps his hands, hums a tune, retraces his steps, and then makes 'meandering lines', *lignes d'erre*.

> a *chevêtre* [an 'entangled curl'] is similar to a detour as long as the necessity, the cause of this detour escapes our knowing. The term of 'chevêtre' desig-nates the fact that there is *something there that attracts* a perfusion of *lignes d'erre*.[8]

A map of Europe should exist which is crossed over by *meandering lines* that go around and around, making detours and deviations from country to country, looking for that 'something that … attracts'. This map should contain entangled customary lines, supple lines and curls indicating other kinds of social behaviour, economic and political opportunities other than 'straight' ones; 'lines of flight' should be an important landmark on such a map .

Deleuze defines the 'line of flight', *ligne de fuite*, not only as a simple line, but as the very force that maintains a tangle of lines: lines of escape, vanishing lines.

> There is a third type of line, even stranger still, as if something were carrying us away, through our segments but also across our thresholds; toward an unknown destination, neither foreseeable nor pre-existent.[9]

'I came here in *flight*'; said a transmigrant, referring to the illegal way he had crossed the frontiers of several countries on his way to France. 'And then, I will be repatriated', which means, in terms of French immigration legislation: a flight ticket with financial assistance for reinstatement in the country of origin consisting of approx. 1000F.

A new kind of logic reveals this repatriation, this 'going back home', as the real purpose of initial departure. Nothing happens other than a detour, a curl, a delay, a 'supplement'. This 'curling' logic transforms impedimenta into paths, obstacles into purposes, conflicts into alliances, policies of rejection into politics of welcoming, 'bad end' into 'happy end'.

How to use, to market a *line of flight*? – this is the main aim of the transmigrant condition. Transmigrants have invented a new market product that is migration itself, the double crossing of a frontier, the transversion, the movement by detour, the pure displacement of a person from one country to another and back again.

Analogical mapping and diagrams of life

The politics for managing such a quantity of entangled 'lines' have to remain close to the *diagram*. To remain 'diagrammatic' is to keep the possibility of community where it is impossible. For the destiny of an individual or a group, the *diagram* is the profitable 'passage through catastrophe'. Deleuze speaks about the diagram in the context of Francis Bacon's painting and notices that 'the diagram is chaos, a catastrophe, but also a germ of order or rhythm'.[10]

For transmigrants, 'losing all', 'leaving all', is not a tragedy but a *strategy*. Playing as if all is lost is therefore putting oneself in a state of diagram, in a 'state of factual possibility', as Deleuze says.[11] It is changing the 'impossible' into a 'state of possibility'.

'How have you got here?' 'I crossed over the garden', he replies mockingly. In this logic, the garden of the family house can be topologicaly extended to reach Paris, like 'the mouth', in some portraits of Bacon, that can go from one corner of the face to the other.[12] According to Deleuze:

> The diagram is therefore the operative totality of insignificant and non-representative, lines and zones, traits and spots.'[13]

A community is not made up exclusively of 'individual lines' but integrates equally 'insignificant and non-representative' *zones*, *lines* and *spots* of places and things with which individuals cohabit and operate diagrammatically in the practice of everyday life. The language of the diagram is *analogical*, according to Deleuze. Here we will tease out the idea of a possible coalescence between *analogy* and *diagram*.

It is the notion of modulation (and not that of sameness) that is generally apt to make us understand the nature of the analogical language or the diagram 'modulation' that functions in the analogical synthesisers: as an addition of 'intensive subtractions'.[14]

The notions of 'subtraction' and 'intensivity' can be associated with 'marginality'. *Marginality* may function as a *modulator* within the social field. Transmigrants respect codes and conventions so long as they can be modulated. They can make their own 'intensive subtractions' and transport them elsewhere. They practise a 'relational' way of doing inside a 'conventional' way of thinking.

For the transmigrant the *analogy* is not simply a way of doing but also a policy. Operating from thing to thing, person to person, situation to situation, a policy-based on *analogy* is more appropriate to marginality, than a policy based on codes and norms. 'Know how', tricks and lucky finds are related by ways of proximity.

Analogical thought works by 'correspondence' not by 'comparison'. As a form of imaginative insight, it recognises the familiar in the unfamiliar. The transmigrant reading of the landscape of the alien city keeps the 'familiar' at the other end of the rope. Romanian transmigrants have adopted a practice of squatting in abandoned houses in the proximity of the 'La Défense' district, the main business area in Paris, called 'La Grande Arche' or 'the great granary'. The main square of the district is called 'the *vague* field', as the place where they rub shoulders with tourists and bankers during the week and play football on Sundays. This particular way of naming things and places shows how the alienating logic of a financial metropolis can be absorbed and re-appropriated at the level of a village, in the same way that language can be condensed into jokes and puns.[15]

Moreover, the configuration of the native village, the order of streets and houses is topologically reproduced in the house in which they squat. Proximities and family relationships regulate the occupation of rooms. Previous proximities transport already existing habits and familiarities and modulate their intimate conditions within the promiscuity of the squat. The intimate, the private and the collective coalesce and overlap. One room acts as the dwelling place for several families and fulfils two main functions: it is both bedroom and dining room. Within these conditions the definition of the intimate is continually being renegotiated. And making love? 'We manage somehow ...'

The whole creative, poetic potential of the *analogy* lies in finding possible correspondences and connections between 'incompatible modes of otherness'. Making subtractions, additions, mixtures and compressing alterities constitute the inner logic of the squat. The word 'squat' is itself a transmigrant: it comes from the Old French *esquatir*: 'to flatten', takes on new meanings in English and returns to Modern French bearing these new meanings. *Esquatir* comes originally from the Latin *decogo, cogere*: 'to compel', 'to bring about by force', 'to condense, to contract'.[16]

Analogy allows us to handle concepts 'not at home' in any category. The transfer from familiar to unfamiliar lands us in an 'equivocal region', one of compressions and intensities situated inbetween prescriptive rules and laws.[17] We should not confuse *analogy* with established identity or isomorphism. When combined together, the prefix *ana* and the noun *logos* etymologically mean 'according to the same kind of way'. The equivocal region of the 'same kind of way', is that of similarities, affinities and approximations.

Transmigrants use imitations to approximate whatever is unattainable. Imitation – *mimesis* – as one knows from the animal world, is a form of adaptability. They live in the metropolis as in a village and in the village as in a metropolis. In Certeze – one of the villages in the Oas country – most peasants speak '*à la française*' and live a 'bourgeoise' existence.

But this imitation works both ways. In the West they feign 'poverty' and 'lack', in the East they feign 'opulence' and 'excess'; in the metropolis, they affect their 'disappearance', in the village, they show off their 'appearance'. 'Let's put in an extra window. Everyone will think that we have an extra bedroom' – so runs a conversation between a peasant and his architect.

A culture of *simulation* based on the 'representation of objects through analogic models which are easier to study and exploit' is a culture of opportunism and profit. Simulating a pattern, multiplying it, selling it, is always more profitable that the pattern itself.

Tactics

Transmigrants belong more to 'space' than to a specific 'place'.

According to de Certeau:

> The law of the 'proper' rules in the place; the elements taken into consideration are beside one another, each situated in its own 'proper' and distinct location, a location it defines. A place is thus an instantaneous configuration of positions. It implies an indication of stability. A space exists when one takes into consideration vectors of direction, velocities, and time variable ... In contradiction to the place, it has thus none of the univocality or stability of a 'proper'.[18]

There is no such thing as a 'proper' space, just as there is no 'proper' time. Yet, 'space' and 'time' can be invested and exploited by everyone. Everything is a question of tactics.

> Tactics are procedures that gain validity in relation to the pertinence they lend to time, to the circumstances which the precise instant of an intervention transforms into a favourable situation, to the rapidity of the movements that change the organisation of space, to the relations among successive moments in an action, to the possible intersections of duration and heterogeneous rhythms, etc.[19]

The transmigrants' profit margin is based on the management of time between completion of an application for political asylum and repatriation. All requests for asylum are automatically rejected but they are meant to be rejected, a calculation made from the very beginning. Transmigrants do not want to stay. The request for asylum is nothing but a device to obtain time. During this period, transmigrants receive financial assistance from the French government, social assistance from the Red Cross and a social status that allows them to sell 'news-papers of the marginal'. Their tactics consist, in this case, in literally creating a delay and making profit from it. Their inventiveness consists of working on time, with time, against time, rendering time capable of performing and of asso-ciating the self-timing of bureaucratic administrative systems with the speed of ruthless financial profit motive.

Enjoying time, putting space into play

> We have nothing but time, which is the privilege of those who have no resi-dence.
>
> (Guy Debord, quoting Baltasar Gracian, 'The Society of Spectacle')[20]

Debord speaks about 'time-merchandise', 'time as exchange value', 'deval-orised' or 'pseudo-valorised' time. Transmigrants – Situationists by definition – reconsider the value of time, enjoy its liquid qualities, its economic and spectac-ular aspects.

> In the moving space of the game and its freely chosen variations of rules, the autonomy of the place is to be found again, not by the necessity of an exclusive attachment to the ground, but by returning back to the reality of the journey and understanding life as a journey[21]

Transmigrants know how to take advantage of time, how to live productively out of their mobility, how to invent economic games and to put into play their spaces and their lives.

Transmigration is an *enjoyment of time*, a playing with space.

Plying with space. Plying travels. Plying for money. Plying with residence. Plying between places. Playing with plies [folds] of time.

In several European languages 'pl' is the diphthong which initiates 'pleasure'.

Power and pleasure

Transmigration is for social space what 'pleasure' is for the 'text'.

According to Barthes:

> Pleasure is neither an element of the text, nor a naive residue; it does not depend on the logic of understanding and sensation; it is a drift, something that is both revolutionary and asocial and can not be taken in charge by any

collectivity, mentality, or idiolecte. Something neutral? One can easily see that the pleasure of the text is scandalous: not because it is amoral, but because it is atopical.[22]

Atopical by definition, transmigrants scandalise by their practices. They are revolutionary in the sense of the Situationists, because while avoiding being 'consumers of products' they make themselves consumers of 'social and civic opportunities'. And for the same reason, they are equally asocial because they profit from the rules of democratic society. Revolutionary, they reverse and recycle the legislation according to their own social reality: they subvert the illegal into the legal. Asocial, they take advantage of the social, its defects, its slowness.

Lying belongs to the *art of the ruse*. In their practice of lying, they often recycle, into a democratic context, tactics and tricks inherited from their experience of resisting the totalitarian ideology: 'double thinking', 'cunning' and 'trickeries' are redeployed. They resist, in a sense, all authority and power. They know how to trick 'order' by an 'art'. A tactic is determined by the absence of power, just as a strategy is based on the conditions of power.

The absence of power allows invention and ruse which always belong to the weak.[23]

Jokes

The practice of transmigration is close to what Freud calls 'the technique of *Witz*' – the technique of *jokes* – and to the forms taken by 'the return of the repressed' within the field of an order: verbal economy and condensation, double meaning and misinterpretations, displacements and alliterations, multiple uses of the same material, etc.

They abuse laws and rules, and they subvert and undermine. For example, they use over and over again for different people, eventually in different countries, the same model of application for political asylum, which allows them to claim benefits several times over. In Paris they live in squats, but in their village they live in huge villas.

Like *analogy*, *Witz* makes connections between the heterogeneous. Moreover, it condenses them, combines them or conjoins them, most often by a form of misconnection, that prompts laughter in the listener and even in the one who is speaking.[24] But the procedures of the transmigrant do not bring a smile to the face of the administrative authorities: it reveals their bureaucratic impotence and slowness.

Witz, 'comedy' and 'humour' are, for Freud, forms of libidinal economy. Economic profit is the declared purpose of the transmigrant. If the 'dreamwork' is an individual production, *Witz* is a social production. It can only exist through the community, by an 'economic necessity of the third', by hawking, by transmigration.

The technique of *Witz* consists of juxtaposing different elements in order to produce a sudden flash casting the traditional in a novel and striking new light. De Certeau speaks about the art of 'pulling tricks' and 'taking order by surprise'.[25] 'Cross-cuts, fragments, cracks and lucky strikes in the framework of a system', these are the transmigrants' ways of operating as practical equivalents of *Witz*. But instead of linguistic products they attack laws and policies.

In 'The Pleasure of the Text', Barthes speaks about 'a subtle subversion':

> that one that is not directly interested in destruction, dodges the paradigm and seeks for another term: a third term, that is not, however, a term of synthesis, but an eccentric, incredible term. An example? Bataille, maybe, who thwarted the idealistic term by an unexpected materialism, where take places the vice, the devotion, the play, the impossible eroticism, etc. Thus, Bataille does not oppose modesty to sexual liberty but to ... *laughter*.[26]

To the serious idealism of Western democracy, Romanian transmigrants oppose what Barthes calls 'an unexpected materialism': the 'base materialism' of a good Bataille-like burst of laughter that shakes the good manners of the established system of welcoming and exchange.

'Unexpected materialism' as well as 'laughter' do not belong to the dialectical materialism of the Marxist–Leninist ideology but rather to the 'base materialism' of Bataille that was already operating during the communist period, within that ideology. The same 'base materialism' proves to be good enough to undermine the 'idealistic materialism' of Western capitalism. It is a 'base materialism' with a *double use value*.

A *double use value*

Speaking about materialism, Bataille emphasises:

> There exists a *high use* to which metaphysical idealism has devoted the rationalistic humanism, and there exists a *base use*.[27]

There exists *a refined use of marginality* – the mediatic use that belongs sometimes to political staff or groups of intellectuals practising it in order to comfort their proper ideological narcissism – and there exists also *a base use of marginality*, that is 'pretending to be marginal', taking advantage of marginality, treating marginality as a profitable condition.

Marginality is, in this case, an active condition which puts into question the centralised politics and demands for recognition of a new model of marginality and a new type of migrant. This migrant aims to emigrate and be repatriated, has a double activity in initiating financial mobility and hawking creative economies within multiple interactions between the place of origin and the place of immigration. Transmigrants transform *marginality* into *liminarity*.

Liminal marginality

Transmigrants know that in order to transgress one has to expose the limits, enclosures, barriers. They literally develop a whole economy of threshold. By making an inventory of thresholds, 'places of passage' in the city, they can completely re-map the space of the city and locate a network of invisible economic values corresponding to their own market system.

To install itself, to literally exploit the space of the threshold, *the liminarity* of a city – the most uncertain passage, the most critical, the most rapid, the most impossible to occupy and invest – this means also to invent 'the market opportunity' for this type of space: to sell something 'without value', something worth 'nothing at all' – as 'the newspaper of the marginal' – and to save money.

To undermine an economy of charity through an economy of capital, to exploit the 'gift', to develop an *economy of benefit* from an *economy of the gift* is to deconstruct the social democratic ethics that contemporary democracy inherited from the Christian tradition by insolent, liberal tactics and diversions. The phenomenological quality of the threshold that maintains being *sous le coup*, 'under the hit', while experiencing its ontological and physical fragility, proves to have a market value.

Transmigrants are good phenomenologists and dreamers. Within these tedious times, they are able to see marginality as a promising condition. *Marginality* is maybe for society what 'dream' is for 'thinking'. And the dream, as Freud says, 'doesn't think, doesn't reckon, and doesn't generally make statements, but keeps transforming'.[28]

Notes

1   Michel de Certeau, *Culture au pluriel*, Paris: Editions du Seuil, 1993 [my trans.].
2   This chapter was initially a conference paper in *Art Demanding Community Conference*, which was held at Westminster University of London, February 1998. It still bears the mark of an attempt to communicate within such a context.
    I am very grateful to Jennifer Bloomer and Alain Chiaradia for their sensitive commentaries and suggestions on previous versions of this chapter. For most of the information that I am using in the text, I have to thank the generosity of the sociologist Dana Diminescu who kindly let me borrow from her studies and stuff. Patricia Boinest Potter was of a great help in revising my English translation.
3   For example, in the Parisian periphery, they are squatting in abandoned houses (at St. Cloud, Suresnes, Puteaux, Courbevoie, Val-de-Fontennay, Cergy, Poissy, etc. ...), they are living in tunnels, caravans, under the railway tracks, in tents, cemeteries of cars, abandoned trucks or trash-improvised huts.
4   Gilles Deleuze and Claire Parnet, *On the Line*, Semiotext(e) Foreign Agents Series, 1983, p. 69.
5   Deleuze and Parnet, *On the Line*, p. 72.
6   François Deligny is a French psychoanalyst who has studied the behaviour of the autistic children. Both de Certeau and Deleuze invoked him in their texts. By adopting an unorthodox methodology with his practice of psychoanalysis, Deligny placed himself, in a way, on the margins of this discipline.
7   François Deligny, *Les enfants et le silence*, Paris: Editions Galilée, 1980, p. 19.
8   Deligny, *Les enfants et le silence*, p. 20.
9   Deleuze and Parnet, *On the Line*, pp. 70–1.

10 Gilles Deleuze, *Logique de la Sensation*, I, Paris Editions de la Différence 1981, p. 67 [my trans.].

11 Deleuze, *Logique de la Sensation*, p. 66.

12 Bacon, quoted by Deleuze in note 1, *Logique de la Sensation* I, pp. 65–6.

13 Deleuze, note 1, *Logique de la Sensation* I, p. 66.

14 Deleuze, note 1, *Logique de la Sensation* I, p. 76

15 See Sigmund Freud, *Jokes and their Relation to the Unconscious*, trans. J. Strachey, *The Standard Edition of the Complete Psychological Works of Sigmund Freud*, London: Hogarth Press.

16 squat *v. , adj., &n. -v.* 1. *intr.* a. crouch with the hams resting on the back of the heels. b. sit on the ground etc. with the knees drawn up and the heels close to or touching the hams. 2. tr. put (a person) into a squatting position. 3. intr. colloq. sit down. 4. a. act as a squatter. b. tr. occupy a buildings a squatter. 5. intr. (of an animal) crouch close to the ground. *-adj.* 1. (of a person) short and thick, dumpy. 2. in a squatting posture *-n.* 1. a squatting posture. 2. a. a place occupied by a squatter or squatters. b. being a squatter (*Oxford Dictionary*).

17 For more details on analogy as an 'equivocal region' see Ralph McIverny, *Studies in Analogy*, The Hague: Martinus Nijhoff, 1968, p. 82.

18 Michel de Certeau, *The Practice of Everyday Life*, trans. Steven Rendall, Berkeley, CA: University of California Press, 1988, p. 117.

19 De Certeau, *The Practice of Everyday Life*, pp. 38–9.

20 Guy Debord, *La Société du Spectacle*, Paris: Editions Gallimard, 1992, p. 147 [my trans.].

21 Debord, *La Société du Spectacle*, p. 178.

22 Roland Barthes, 'Le plaisir du texte', in *Oevres Complètes II*, Paris: Editions du Seuil, 1994, p. 1505 [my trans.].

23 Cf. de Certeau, *The Practice of Everyday Life*, p. 37.

24 Cf. Sigmund Freud, *Jokes and their Relation to the Unconscious*.

25 De Certeau, *The Practice of Everyday Life*, pp. 37–8.

26 Barthes, 'Le plaisir du texte', p. 1522.

27 Georges Bataille, 'Le bas-matérialisme et la gnose', in *OC I*, Paris: Editions Gallimard, p. 221 [my trans.].

28 Cf. Sigmund Freud, *The Interpretation of Dreams*, trans. James Strachey, London: Penguin, p. 650.

19 The capsular city

Lieven de Cauter

The capsular civilization has been anticipated for years in Los Angeles, where there have been speculations about it by several experiments with indoor biospheres in American deserts.

(René Boomkens)[1]

I

far from being a 'natural' system, as some apologists have tried to argue, historical capitalism is a patently absurd one.

(Immanuel Wallerstein)[2]

Capitalism today is omnipresent to such a degree that it tends to become invisible.[3] The word capitalism has disappeared from public discourse. Whosoever still uses it soon incurs an odium; it is like a public secret and hence a taboo. This is not only just another example of a policy of euphemisms ('free-market economy' sounds so much more appealing), but also points to a new phase in the evolution. The capitalism of the *New World Order* is not *late capitalism* – there is nothing late about it – but a *transcendental capitalism*. Transcendental means: without an opposite term, an all-inclusive condition of possibility, the most central concept in meaning as well as in scale. Without an opposite term: there seems to be no alternative for capitalism; no real alternative, not even a thinkable one. Capitalism with some social corrections is the best we can come up with. But precisely that socially corrected type of capitalism is being undermined by the globalisation of the economy.[4] All-inclusive condition of possibility: one can no longer understand our world without taking capitalism as a starting point, an axiom. Nothing is thinkable any longer without the input of capital, not even culture. Hence in scale and content it is ultimately the most central notion in our world.

Yet the transcendental aspect of capitalism is at the same time always deceptive. The transcendental illusion of capitalism consists in the fact, as is the case in any system, that it is natural, unavoidable and infinite. This deception has, say, since the fall of the Berlin Wall and the collapse of the Eastern bloc, consolidated itself to become second nature. Despite this, capitalism is and remains a historical system, which originated around 1500 (early capitalism), acquired its classical industrial shape in the nineteenth century (high capitalism) and came to full bloom in the second half of the twentieth century. It can be defined as follows: (1) it is a social system within which the stake and the impulse are the accumulation of capital, infinite accumulation as a goal in itself; (2) there is a relation of dominance between a centre and a periphery; and (3) this dominance is sometimes the cause, sometimes the effect, and often both at the same time, of an unequal trade between centre and periphery that makes 'profit', and hence the accumulation, possible.[5]

A consequence of this binary structure of capitalism is that there will never be a 'global village'. There will always be a centre and a periphery, an inside and an outside. As soon as the asymmetry becomes too small, the periphery needs to be repositioned (which is called 'de-location' from the point of view of production, or the 'exploring of new markets' from the point of view of distribution). As soon as the asymmetry becomes too big, however, the system may waver. The eruptions and social revolt from the past prove this. But transcendental capitalism seems to have become meta-stable: it no longer wavers, it has grown resistant to crises. An inevitable consequence, however, of too great an inequality is the rise of structures aimed at the defence of the interior against the exterior.

II

the petrochemical age is basically anti-urban.

(Richard Plunz)[6]

Capitalism has produced the metropolis, as a centre of power, trade, production and distribution. Though claims about the end of the city seem frequent enough, the metropolis is, in long-term historiography, very young. Around the start of the nineteenth century Paris and London were still small cities. New York did not exist. Los Angeles was not even on the map. One could divide the history of the modern metropolis into three eras: the steam age, the petrochemical age and the micro-electronic age (or emblematically: the train, the automobile and the Web). In the steam age the city became the metropolis. The first industrial revolution, with the demographic growth in its wake, turned Paris as well as London into metropolitan cities. According to Richard Plunz, a professor in urban planning at Columbia University, a shift takes place in America around the 1930s: whereas the major part of the population up until then lived in the cities, an intense process of suburbanisation was triggered. Plunz believes the consumption society would not have been possible without suburbanisation and de-urbanisation.[7] 'Each man his own car' (Henry Ford's slogan) has little appeal to an urban population. The massive and at the same time individualised consumption presupposed a conscious de-urbanisation (the house as a machine of comfort, the mall as a drive-in distribution). Plunz terms it a conspiracy against the city. An analogous suburbanisation has occurred in Europe, albeit a less extreme one. One cannot deny, however, that here also has the ancient metropolis changed in a very substantial manner. In its transition from the industrial to the post-industrial, from the petrochemical to the micro-electronic age, the (historical) centre has been either abandoned (as a marginal zone for migrants and bohemians) or re-invented for tourists and day trippers, and the inhabitants of the city become tourists in their own city.[8] There are two basic models: *Disneyfication* of the centre accompanied by a *Bronxification* of the periphery (with Paris as an example), or the implosion of the centre accompanied by the spread of the infi-nite suburbs (with Los Angeles as a model). Each city is in its difficult transition from the post-industrial age, simultaneously confronted by both options. They are not even options, but often results of the lack thereof. They may even be sides of the same coin: both are based on enclosure. The tourist zone as well as the ghetto can, beyond a certain threshold, become '*no go* areas' for most inhabitants of the city. The micro-electronic age will complete the sub- and de-surbanisation which started in the previous era. One can live anywhere, as long as one is connected to the networks. Thus originates the a-geographical city.[9] The final phase of the inhabited world then is the post-urban zone. This is not only the fact for America and South-East-Asia, but it is probably also the future of Europe. The Benelux for instance is on its way to becoming a post-urban zone, with amusement park-like historical centres as remnants of a past era, functioning as tourist hot spots in a generic network of spread-out building density, motorways and fibre optics cables. The new constellation is termed Cyburbia, the network city, the carpet metropolis or the generic city.

III

The characteristic feature of transcendental capitalism consists in its 'generic' aspect. The term generic is mostly used for products without a brand. But more generally it means that every product (varying from a Coke bottle to a restau-rant or building) is not an individual in itself, but an instance of a *corporate identity*, of its brand, its kind. It is therefore not 'particular', but 'generic', liter-ally: belonging to a 'sort' (genus). According to Sorkin, who introduced the term *generic urbanism*,[10] and Koolhaas, who invented the even apter term *generic city*, the city also is becoming 'generalised', in the way that airports are the same everywhere: without an identity, without a centre, without a history.[11] Koolhaas attempts, in his own partly ironic, partly cynical way, to see the liber-ating potential of this type of city. It is, however, a network city, a technological city, and mainly a city thoroughly governed by the logic of capitalism. Or to put it even more sharply: without capitalism the generic is incomprehensible. It is produced by the logic and by the aesthetics of multinationals. The generic city is the city in the age of transcendental capitalism. The unstoppable rise of the chains (shopping chains, hotel chains, fast-food chains, restaurant chains, etc.) – that is the generic. It has been coined 'McDonaldisation' or 'Hilton-culture'.

In its transition from the industrial to the post-industrial phase, the city is forced to find a new face, through history, culture, local colour, tourism. The many projects developed for waterfronts are symptomatic of this transition. Every city wants to be Mediterranean. The generic city is (and Sorkin and Koolhaas agree on this) a city of simulations: history is staged in reinvented historical quarters. The de-dramatisation of space in the post-urban zone, by means of urban sprawl and random, indifferent juxtaposition of motorways, housing and commercial 'emergency-architecture', and the re-staging of urban locations in historical centres, are deeply connected processes. At the same time, however, (post)modernity, especially for office-buildings and such like, is still being mass-produced. The city as a theme park reproduces generic history as well as generic modernity.

IV

The in transit condition is becoming universal.

(Rem Koolhaas)[12]

Travel light, Travel Hugo … Life's a journey.
(slogan for a perfume for young people by Hugo Boss)

The generic embodies the phantasm of weightlessness and mobility in the artificial paradises of consumption, where people sample a *personal identity* based on *corporate material*. It is the *fata Morgana* of universal tourism, the everlasting transit from hotspot to hotspot. Everything happens seamlessly and smoothly due to the ideological smoothness of the *sampling*, the *anything goes*, the *cool look* of *design and lifestyle magazines*. It is the interior of our social system: the commodity fetishism (from Marx to Benjamin and Adorno), the society of spectacle (Debord), the hyperreality (Baudrillard), etc. Yet a point of view from the exterior becomes more and more necessary. Next to growing mobility and consumption there is the fact that the world is becoming an increasingly dual one. Is there a causal relation between the two? Can the increase in consumption only be sustained by rejecting part of the world population? In the wake of the neo-liberal movement of withdrawal and the shrinking of the welfare state, the separation between rich and poor, inside and outside, is becoming stricter. The rampant demographic growth and migration seem to be simply overruling the system. More and more the Second, Third and Fourth Worlds have to be kept outside the First World in a heavy-handed way.

A society of mobility is unthinkable without omnipresent control. Whereas the disciplinary society was based on interiorisation, the control society functions externally: through militarisation of the urban space.[13] The technological devices, however, with their soft, almost invisible thresholds, do not suffice. The simultaneously archaic and hypermodern 'primal fact' of architecture and urbanism of the twenty-first century will be: the fence, the wall, the gate, the stronghold.

Because a separation of worlds never works, and the populations of the Second, Third and Fourth Worlds are spreading out and are by now everywhere, the First World is no longer a homogeneous empire with relatively homogeneous territory, but an archipelago of fortresses and strongholds.[14] Transport becomes to an increasing degree the transit between controlled and closed-off zones. The generic city is obsessed by closing-off, safety and control.[15] One can appropriately term this 'the cellular city', and even 'capsular civilisation'.[16]

V

> The capsule is cyborg architecture. Man, machine and space build a new organic body which transcends confrontation. … it creates an environment in itself. … A device which has become a living space in itself in the sense that man cannot hope to live elsewhere, is a capsule. And signs of such development are beginning to appear around us.
>
> (Kisho Kurokawa, 1969)[17]

Capsule architecture[18] is the architecture of the generic city. The capsule is a device which creates an artificial *ambience*, which minimises communication with the 'outside' by forming its own time–space, a closed-off (artificial) environment. All means of transport are, and this is the origin of the metaphor, capsules: the train, the automobile, the airplane, and obviously the space capsule. These are real capsules. There are, however, also virtual capsules, such as a screen, a Walkman, a mobile phone. The omnipresence of screens (television screens, computer screens, but also the windscreens of cars function, as Virilio tells us,[19] as screens) is a part of the 'capsularisation'. One could go so far as to say that each screen creates its own time–space, be it a virtual one or not. A book might be an ancient model of virtual capsules. The ancient and the hypermodern always meet again. Next to micro-capsules such as mobile phones, there are macro-capsules, such as closed-off buildings or fenced zones.

Indeed, architecture and even urban design become capsular as well: the airport, the mall, the theme park, the gated community. The hype concerning mobility, the network, the boundlessness, the smoothness, functions on the basis of these capsules. Capsules are at the same time also engines of simulation: they generate the simulation of the public sphere. The typical example is the television. In the case of architecture, the postmodern atrium is the prototype of capsularisation. It is external space simulated within, a sealed-off piazza.[20] The capsule abolishes the public sphere. Cocooning, the hypertrophy of the private sphere, is another symptom of capsularisation. Most capsules are mass-produced and hence essentially generic (such as automobiles). But the capsule architecture also tends to the generic, or, sometimes even worse, to a generic originality (catchy images, design). Besides all its other functions, the capsule has a constant side effect that guarantees its political relevance and efficiency: it induces a specific kind of numbness. Capsule architecture is ostrich policy.

VI

In the capsule everyday life is sucked in as in a vacuum cleaner. Designer Jon Jerde wrote about his 'Universal CityWalk', an exotic but closed-off city promenade (close to the Universal Film Studios) with among other things models of buildings to be seen elsewhere in Los Angeles if only one could go there: 'The only things kept out of this simulation are real poverty, crime and unplanned spontaneity.'[21] Where fear and fantasy construct artificial biospheres, the everyday is abolished. The 'ecology of fear' (militarisation) and of violence (by 'Bronxification') on the one hand, and the 'ecology of fantasy' ('Disneyfication') on the other, both repress the everyday in a very efficient manner.[22] The everyday is unconscious. As soon as a certain emphatic presence arises (by control and/or simulation), it disappears. This explains the unreal atmosphere of malls, theme parks, airports. And it does work: there is no unplanned spontaneity in Disneyland. One hardly ever sees signs of real enthusiasm, only the planned, short cheers after the ride, which die out quickly in the rows of disciplined queuing. Spontaneous happiness only seems to exist in commercials. And in the gestures of Disney characters in parades. Yet a parade always has a military parade as its model. Disneyland is as much a machine of discipline as it is a machine of amusement.[23] And everything, truly everything there is generic. The amusement park (and the city as a theme park as well) is a controlled, closed-off, generic zone. Hence the everyday probably offers no way out, no alternative to minimise and thus normalise the extremes of militarisation and Disneyfication.

VII

> nous devons nous attendre non seulement à de nouveaux camps, mais aussi à des définitions normatives de l'inscription de la vie dans la cité plus neuves et plus délirantes. Le camp qui est maintenant solidement installé en elle est le nouveau *nomos* biopolitique de la planète.
>
> (Giorgio Agamben)[24]

When sketching the history of the city from a bird's-eye view, the first thing appearing in the landscape is a fortified city. Whoever lived in the city, was considered a citizen (or in other words: whoever lived in the 'bourg', was 'bourgeois'). This type of fortified city, however, soon expanded out of its walls under the pressure of modernity (more specifically the pressure of capitalism, industrial and demographic growth). The bulwark became a boulevard. The Roman roads came into use again and were rebuilt into what would soon become the network of stone roads and later of motorways, and even later still simply the Network. But some bulwarks survived: the national frontiers. Since capitalism claims it does not function well with frontiers, constantly growing entities without inner frontiers have been created and are still being created: ultimately the mirage of the *global village*. For the moment, however, one gigantic wall still stands. It is usually invisible and causes no problems for us citizens. We can freely enter or exit ('freely' of course after due checks – more and more city gates from the past have been replaced by the gates of airports). It does, however, cause problems for the non-citizens. Sometimes the wall is visible in its full obscenity: a barbed wire indicates the border of the United States with Mexico, the Spanish enclaves on Moroccan territory are at this very moment being fenced with barbed wire as well. The New World Order has its own Iron Curtain: it separates the North from the South, Atlantic Megalocity from the barren outside. *Fortress Europe* is not a metaphor: Europe is a stronghold with walls and water surrounding it. This wall runs through every country in Europe. In Belgium it is for example the barbed wire around Steenokkerzeel (the camp is called 127b). Whosoever is on the other side of the wall has no rights, for only 'the human rights and rights of the citizen' exist. There is no legal version of human rights: human rights are not laws. Whosoever is not a citizen (that is, lives outside of the stronghold) is in fact without rights. This means that they may treated in any manner.[25]

In the light of the generic city as a city without a centre, the statement in CIAM's 'A Short Outline of the Core' from 1951 acquires a prophetic undertone: 'If new towns are built without a core they will never become more than camps'.[26] Is it possible to consider the evacuation of the public space and the trance, the calmness of the generic city Koolhaas mentions, in correlation with the camp as a paradigm? According to the Italian philosopher Giorgio Agamben this is apparently the case. Agamben claims that more and more people drop out of the statute of social life (*bios*) into the statute of mere life (*zoē*). In this mere life they are without rights and hence are outlaws. It is governed by the logic of the camp. The camp is not a prison, is not a legal institution, but is a territory outside of the law, an enclave in and mainly outside of society, an extra-territorial inlet, where no law is valid. Hence anything can happen there, even the unimaginable, not so much by human cruelty or the barbarity of an ideological indoctrination, but because of the juridical structure of the camp itself. Transit zones also are extra-territorial (and hence tax free). 'Closed refugee centres' are potential camps. But ghettos and *containment zones*, such as Skid Row in Los Angeles, also are starting to look like camps.[27] Perhaps Agamben is right, despite appearing to exaggerate grossly, when he states that the concentration camp is the paradigm of present day bio-politics, not the city.[28] The expanding refugee problem is on a geopolitical scale the only argument for the assumption that the *in transit condition* is becoming a universal one. The question Koolhaas takes as a starting point should definitely be taken seriously: what does the city look like when starting to resemble an airport? When one considers the airport as a whole, meaning not only its lobbies and lounges, its catering services, cargo firms and tour operators, but also the transit camps which are part of it, one can see the true face of the generic city.[29]

VIII

> We do indeed now live in fortress cities brutally divided into 'fortified cells'
> of affluence and 'places of terror' where police battle the criminalized poor.
>
> (Mike Davis)[30]

The *gated communities* and the detention camps for illegal refugees mirror one
another. The counterpart of the fortress is the camp. The former is a machine of
exclusion, the latter a machine of inclusion. Similar is the relation between the
tourist zone and the ghetto, the CityWalk and the containment zone. Or in other
words: no mall without a wall. The hype concerning the abolishment of frontiers
is but a sham. The World Wide Web, mobility and the boom in communication
are in direct proportion to capsularisation. The one is not conceivable without the
other. The famous globalisation is at the same time a re-delimitation of territories.
Transcendental capitalism cannot function without camps and capsules because it
is still based on the accumulation of capital through the unequal trade between
centre and periphery, and because this contrast is presently clearer than ever. To
put it more directly: our society cannot exist without barbed wire. The new Iron
Curtain in Ceuta and Melilla, subsidised by the European Community, proves
this. A newspaper reported in mid-August 1998:

> Spain wants to put into use its newest line of defense against the rush of
> African immigrants earlier than planned. The frontier barricades around the
> enclave cities of Melilla and Ceuta on the northern coast of Morocco, the
> construction of which started in March, 'has to be impenetrable by
> October already', official spokespersons confirmed on Wednesday. The
> double line of steel and barbed wire near Melilla, which has already been
> nicknamed 'the Berlin Wall', is equipped along a distance of 12 kilometers
> with 70 cameras, light towers, sensors and watch posts. Near Ceuta a
> similar wall is being built ... The Spanish frontier police is aware that the
> new defense lines will only result in immigration seeking other ways in. ...
> This is an important source of revenue for the Moroccan and Spanish
> mafias, who transport them across the Strait of Gibraltar in shoddy little
> boats. They often go down at sea ... and the bodies of the drowned immi-
> grants wash ashore on the beaches. It is estimated that this year already a
> thousand illegal immigrants have died in that manner.[31]

IX

Some day a historian in a distant future will discuss our age as one of the most
obscene ones in world history: that of the *capsular civilisation*. Why? Because
the level of technology and production stands out sharper than ever against the
systematic, uncompromising exclusion of a major, and still increasing, part of
mankind. The full awareness of this fact is shattering. 'We did not know', we
will say to the historian of the future, but s/he will condemn us.

Notes

1 René Boomkens, *Een drempelwereld. Moderne ervaring en stedelijke openbaarheid*, Rotterdam: Nai Uitgevers, 1998, p. 316. The theses put forward here have haunted me for quite some time now. They have been copied out as a result of the publishing of Boomkens' book (at the demand of the journal *Krisis*). They are the result of a lingering meditation on Koolhaas's essay on the generic city, but their direct context consists of the building and completion of the wall in Ceuta and Melilla, two Spanish enclaves on Moroccan territory, in the course of 1998, and most of all the death of a 26-year-old so-called illegal immigrant, Semira Adamu. After staying for quite some time in the Belgian detention camp 127b at Steenokkerzeel, she was killed on Sept. 22nd 1998 during the sixth attempt to put her on a plane back to Nigeria. Her protest consisted of singing. She was suffocated with a cushion. This text is dedicated to her memory.

2 Immanuel Wallerstein, *Historical Capitalism*, New York: Verso, 1994 [1984], p. 40.

3 See also Koen Gisen, 'Lifestyle en Transcendentaal kapitalisme' (a conversation with Lieven De Cauter and John King), in *Victoria*, driemaandelijks magazine van theater Victoria, Gent, Sept.–Dec. 1998.

4 See, for example, Ricardo Petrella, 'De klippen van de mondialisering', in *De Witte Raaf*, no. 75, Sept.–Dec. 1998, pp. 1–4.

5 Wallerstein, *Historical Capitalism*, pp. 13ff. See also Fernand Braudel, *La dynamique du capitalisme*, Paris: Flammarion, 1985.

6 Véronique Patteeuw, 'The Conspiracy against the City, Lieven De Cauter in conversation with Richard Plunz', in *Een stad in Beweging/ Une ville en mouvement/a Moving city*, Brussels: Studio Open City, 1998, p. 230.

7 'The consumer society and suburbanisation go hand in hand', see Patteeuw, 'The Conspiracy against the City', p. 230.

8 A beautiful description and analysis of the Universal CityWalk in Los Angeles is to be found in René Boomkens, *Een drempelwereld*, p. 316., pp. 343ff.

9 Michael Sorkin, 'Introduction', in *Variations on a Theme Park: The New American City and the End of Public Space*, ed. Sorkin, New York: Hill and Wang, 1992, p. XI.

10 Sorkin, 'Introduction', p. XII.

11 Rem Koolhaas, 'The Generic City', in *S, M, L, XL*, ed. Rem Koolhaas and Bruce Mau and Office for Metropolitan Architecture, Rotterdam; 010 Publishers, 1995. For a critique of this apology of the generic city, see Lieven de Cauter, 'The Flight Forward of Rem Koolhaas', *Archis*, 4 (1998).

12 Koolhaas, 'The Generic City', p. 1252.

13 Mike Davis, 'Fortress Los Angeles: The Militarization of Urban Space', in *Variations on a Theme Park*, ed. Sorkin. See also Mike Davis, *City of Quartz: Excavating the Future in Los Angeles*, New York: Verso, 1990 (repr. London: Pimlico, 1998) and Davis, *The Ecology of Fear*, New York: Metropolitan Books, 1998.

14 See Davis, *City of Quartz* and *The Ecology of Fear*; see also Boomkens, *Een drempelwereld*, p. 337.

15 As Sorkin and his co-authors emphasise, see Sorkin, *Variations on a Theme Park*.

16 Boomkens, *Een drempelwereld*, pp. 316 and 346.

17 Kisho Kurokawa, 'Capsule Deceleration', in *Metabolism in Architecture*, 1977 [1969], pp. 75–6.

18 The term was introduced in 1969 by Kurokawa, one of the young Japanese metabolists. See Kurokawa, 'Capsule Deceleration'.

19 Paul Virilio, 'La dromoscopie', in *L'horizon négatif: essay de dromoscopie*, Paris: Editions Galilée.

20 It is no coincidence that Sorkin as well as Koolhaas, however divergent their conclusions from their analyses of the new city, consider the atrium as a prototype of the simulated public sphere of the postmodern city.

21 Boomkens, *Een drempelwereld*, p. 343.

22 The expression 'Ecology of fear' was introduced by Mike Davis, the expression 'ecology of fantasy' by Margaret Crawford (Boomkens, *Een drempelwereld*, pp. 347, 351). About the understanding of the casual in urbanism and architecture, see Dieter De Clercq, *Het ontwrichten(de) van het alledaagse*, unpublished PhD, Leuven, 1998.

23 See also Michael Sorkin, 'See you in Disneyland', in *Variations on a Theme Park*, ed. Sorkin, pp. 205ff.

24 'We should not only expect new camps, but also new and delirious definitions of the inscription of life in the community. The camp which has established itself within it is the new bio-political standard of the planet', trans. Giorgio Agamben, 'Que ce qu'un camp?', in *Moyens sans fins: Notes sur la politique*, Paris: Payot/Rivages, 1995, p. 56.

25 The case of Semira Adamu, the numerous maltreatments she had to suffer during attempted expulsions and renewed imprisonments in camp 127b, and finally her death during the sixth attempt, offer tragic evidence of this. See Jan Hagel, 'Het Nieuwe Ijzeren Gordijn', column in *De Standaard*, 2nd September 98, in Lieven De Cauter, 'We zullen Steenokkerzeel als Jericho omsingelen', *De Standaard*, 24 September 1998.

26 'A Short Outline of the Core: Extracts from Statements Prepared during the 8th Congress of CIAM', in *The Heart of the City: Towards Humanisation of Urban Life*, ed. J. Tyrwhitt, J.L. Sert and E.N. Roger, Nendeln: Kraus Reprint, 1979, p. 165.

27 Davis, 'Fortress Los Angeles', p. 164; passim.

28 Giorgio Agamben, *Homo Sacer: Le Pouvoir Souverain et la Vie Nue*, Paris: Editions du Seuil, 1997, p. 195; passim.

29 See de Cauter, 'The Flight Forward of Rem Koolhaas'.

30 Davis, 'Fortress Los Angeles', p. 155.

31 *De Standaard*, 13 August 1998.

20 Media-polis/media-city

Constantin Petcou

Extra-territoriality

In the April 1997 issue of *Le Figaro économie*, a short note informs us that 'in order to rely on sponsors like Budweiser, the Stade de France could benefit from "extra-territorial" privilege'.

Strictly speaking, juridic 'extra-territoriality' will probably remain a 'privilege' and an exception for a long time to come. It concerns only very particular cases, like those of embassies, which fall under a juridical or political status other than that of the country in which they are actually located. This displacement is often the source of certain conflicts with the juridical or political context in that the latter functions according to different criteria.

Paradoxically, we are witnessing today a general explosion of different situations which, we could say, manifest all the characteristics of a form of cultural, economic, social and political 'extra-territoriality'. These ambiguous situations still remain attached to a 'juridic territoriality', while often relying on extra-territoriality as the 'juridical void' present in these new situations.

Recent phenomena, such as the development of multinational corporations, the internationalisation of money laundering circuits, ever more powerful movements affirming all types of minority groups and the existence of complex satellite networks used for military espionage, to name but a few well-known developments, have at least one thing in common: a strong sense of extra-territoriality in their functioning.

If the term 'extra-territoriality' is used exclusively today in the juridical world as a 'juridical fiction', and only for a very limited number of situations, the above-mentioned phenomena also seem to function as situations of 'extra-territoriality' and are actually quite representative of our contemporary world.

In their complex and penetrating study of the capitalist world,[1] Deleuze and Guattari used the paradigm of territoriality as one of the key tools for understanding the 'social machine', its general evolution and its actual state. In order to explain social changes and processes, they define two terms which always function in tandem: de-territorialisation and re-territorialisation. Their philosophical vision synthesises semiotic, anthropological and psychoanalytical research, describing three major stages or forms in the metamorphoses of the social machine according to their specific type of territoriality.

Capitalism, the most recent of these three forms, is described as a

> modern immanent machine, which consists in decoding the flows on the
> full body of capital-money: it has realised the immanence, it has rendered
> concrete the abstract as such and has naturalised the artificial, replacing the
> territorial codes and the despotic overcoding with an axiomatic of decoded
> flows, and a regulation of these flows; it effects the second great movement
> of deterritorialisation, but this time because it doesn't allow any part of the
> codes and overcodes to subsist.[2]

In the second volume of their *Capitalism and Schizophrenia*, Deleuze and
Guattari point out that 'the absolute deterritorialisation implies a "deterritorial-
ising element" and a "deterritorialised element"'.[3]

For Deleuze and Guattari de-territorialisation and re-territorialisation can be
represented as either fairly stable states – such as 'the imperial machine', which
is the second form of the 'social machine' – or as the two successive movements
in a process directed towards the territorialities or neo-territorialities imposed
by a de-territorialising element.

More recent phenomena, such as those mentioned above, fit into another
type of 'social machine' for which the contradictory relationship between two
identities is less significant, even if it is always present in the beginning. The
significant character of these new phenomena resides in their tendency to avoid
conflictual relationships and their ability to find new situations, and to invent or
to re-define the very presence of a 'unique' identity. This 'identity' evolves
within an empty context, lacking any presence other than itself, free of reference
and territoriality. We call this context 'extra-territoriality'.

The metropolis and extra-territoriality

What can be said about the context of Peter Eisenman's houses? Almost
nothing. This, apparently, is the wish of the architect himself, who did not take
the context into account in his famous axonometric sketches. These houses, we
could say, find themselves incorporated in an extra-territorial situation or extra-
contextual framework. This is also the case for Rietvield's Villa Schröder, for
Piano and Rogers' Centre Beaubourg, for the recent Fukuoka's housing
complex coordinated by Isozaki, as well as for an enormous number of other
buildings, significant or otherwise.

If totalitarian urbanism is a de-territorialising urbanism, where buildings
and the constructions of power are the de-territorialising elements of a deterritorialised city,[4] the postmodern metropolis has been built in a 'free' and
'anarchic' spirit of "extra-territoriality"'. This is the case for most major
American metropolises, as well as for some Asian cities. In these metropolitan
contexts, 'extra-territoriality' is becoming the new rule of social, economic,
cultural and political 'contextualism'.

In this form of 'extra-territoriality', relationships that usually evolve in neigh-

bourhoods are reduced to a minimum. Anonymity is becoming a type of generalised presence within the city. This sort of extra-contextual anonymity is not
restricted to the domain of architecture: analogous phenomena are at work in
communications networks and in the marketplace, to such an extent that even
the obligatory '*Made in …*' does not express much anymore. Most often, this
label marks only the 'prestigious' place where parts, coming from anywhere in
the world, are assembled. We are, in many cases, faced with this form of pack-
aging territorialisation, which no longer corresponds to anything since it has
been replaced by extra-territorialised transnational organisations.

Beyond the existing built environment and the world of artifacts, 'extra-
territoriality' manifests itself more obviously within contemporary cultural
production. Its fictional character imposes itself on most of the mass 'cultural
products': the television series *X-Files*, or films such as *Star Wars*, to name but
two examples.

The development of multiple new forms of 'life in common' – which have
replaced the 'standard model' of the traditional family – as for example the
married couples who travel separately most of the time and meet briefly only
within the family space, or heterosexual and homosexual free couples, or single
parent families, etc. – reflect the same extra-territorial tendency.[5]

Post-war capitalist civilisation has developed and democratised its leisure
activities; the sheer scale of amusement parks like Disneyland and the incredible
development of a worldwide touristic industry show a growing interest and a
pressing need for 'popular' extra-territoriality. If, in the beginning, the main
attraction of the industrialised city was the promise of greater freedom, and
hence, of greater territorialisation, today it is the mirage of extra-territoriality
and the 'night life condition' which attracts people to life in big cities. The
metropolitan nightlife is in a way the very symbol of our contemporary extra-
territorialised civilisation.

Multi-territoriality

Nevertheless, a recurrent example concerning the so-called 'ideal contemporary
habitat' is to be noticed: the situation of someone living in some anonymous
village while connected, through the new telecommunications networks, to his
or her professional framework and circle of friends, etc. This example illustrates
in a way the existence of two main directions of extra-territorialisation: one
towards an anonymous 'local' and the other towards an abstract 'global'. The
advantage of this situation is due to the paradoxical mix of small- and large-scale
'extra-territoriality'. These two tendencies coincide in many cases of extra-
territoriality. Nobody can deny today the increasing influence of cyber-culture
and the new media on the extra-territorial tendency of our civilisation.

On the other hand, there still remain certain institutions whose existence is
founded on frameworks of territorialisation: the state, the Church and other
major traditional communities constantly impose a territorial framework on
their own traditions in order to maintain their survival. We should also note the

existence of diverse categories of people who still suffer from a loss of territoriality. Cases range from the so-called communities 'at risk' and the business executives who are constrained by their work to travel permanently, to the homeless. This lack of territoriality demonstrates the still important necessity of maintaining a 'reserve of territoriality' within current social practices. But the real stakes, however, are now on the side of extra-territoriality.

Furthermore, it should be underlined that even if extra-territoriality were to remain open to the emergence of other types of territoriality, what might result, in the end, would probably be a multi-territorial civilisation.

Copy/paste: referentiality

Many recent music video directors have opted to use double or multiple imagery to represent singers performing in the same space and with identical or slightly different gestures in order to mark their simulacral autonomy. The result is that these singers appear as neither 'real' nor copy, but as an image of an image, an infinite self-multiplication of images for which the referent, the original, is replaced by a mediatised self.

We live in a society which strangely resembles these music video clips. Through the innumerable mediatic layers added on to the generalised extra-territoriality of the contemporary society, it has become almost impossible to identify the actors, the networks, the decision makers, the products or even the multinational institutions.[6] Their referentiality is lost beneath countless layers of representation and mediatisation.

Phenomena such as the digital revolution in the media, or the possibility of perfectly simulating everything, replacing any kind of referent and creating spectres without any referent, have generated a society of multiple mutations. One can see evidence of this in a plethora of industrial and cultural objects, within urban agglomerations and metropolitan contexts. Today, as Lyotard notes, we have the capacity to simulate even matter itself. He writes:

> what has been developed from this is a certain form of schizophrenia in our ways of representing and an increasing hegemony of the media: the coverage of the event is thereby confounded with the event itself. There is a feeling that there is no exterior reality, no Other than the representation itself. ... Simulacra, never the thing itself. Between them and ourselves, the veil of analogy. Even further the filter of digitalisation ..., the digital images allow us to go beyond and surpass the referent itself (the matter of representation) even if their process of fabrication remains sometimes attached to means of realist representation.[7]

As many recent examples have demonstrated, even the most concrete conflictual situations today have to pass through some mediatic threshold. In this process it is practically impossible to verify the concordance between the mediatic data and their referent – 'real' data; this is certainly the case with political and economic conflicts and many other types of conflictual situations which affect society today.[8]

Lyotard notes that this modification of our relationship to referentiality has permitted many breakthroughs and advances, especially in science. Quoting A. Koyré, he remarks that 'our new physics are constituted without any reference to sensible experience'.[9] Yet, taking Peter Eisenman's architecture as an example, Lyotard adds that one should consider more and more today that:

> it is not the building 'per se' which serves as reference in the architectural drawing, but rather the architect's plan, elevation and section which must be 'seen' as participating in the process of building. The notion of reference within the realm of architecture is inverted. The building thereby represents its representation on paper.[10]

But, while Lyotard notes these interesting developments, Baudrillard strongly denounces the 'liquidation' of the referent through simulation. According to him 'it is rather a question of substituting signs of the real for the real itself'.[11] And, furthermore, this system of mediation is no more than a 'gigantic simulacrum – not unreal, but a simulacrum nonetheless, which never exchanges again for what is real, but exchanges in itself, participating in an uninterrupted circuit without reference or circumference'.[12]

Reactions to such a loss of referentiality are very diverse, and demonstrate the complex character and the contradictory and unpredictable potential ramifications of such a referential crisis.[13]

Media-polis:[14] anabolic practices

In the 1940s, Orson Welles managed to generate a state of general panic in the United States with his radio broadcast of a 'live' invasion of Martians. He used, in an unusual and masterful way, an 'augmented rhetoric' along with the typical effects and codes of the radio broadcasting. In a very coherent manner, Welles used, for the first time in a radio programme, noises hitherto used only in live transmissions or in many sites transmission, thereby creating a product with an undeniable 'effect of reality'.

Today, advertising campaigns employ techniques of image and sound that would enable them to represent food products, for example, as more appetising than they actually are, and generally to create sensations even more striking than those of reality. This type of representation has colonised all forms of traditional and new media, and captivates the public by its 'more real than the real' and its 'more beautiful than it really is' qualities – its 'hyperreal effect'.

In analysing the signs produced by this 'hyperreal effect' in the context of the three principal types of signs introduced by Peirce's sign theory – signs differentiated by a more or less direct relationship between the signifier and signified – we can distinguish a type of sign which is characteristic of a signifier that overwhelms its referent. Beyond the symbol – the Peircian sign embodying the most conventional relationship between signifier and signified – we would here define a new type of sign, which is dominated by its signifier, and sometimes even reducible to it, producing thereby an increased sense of hyperreality. If the symbol is a sign which always conjoins two terms in equilibrium, the signified and signifier, we can imagine a type of sign which consists in an immeasurably amplified signifier. We call this the *anabolising* sign.[15]

Whether we live in an urban or rural environment we exist today in a world-wide milieu, manipulated and marked by the media through signs, most of which are anabolising signs. Political or institutional discourses, advertisements, tourist brochures, press campaigns for sports or cultural events, and media in general, envelop us within a semiotic anabolising milieu. Still further, this discursive anabolising milieu generates a form of contemporary generalised rhetoric.

Media-city:[16] catabolic society

This new discursive context remains anonymous for much of the time. We cannot say, in most cases, who or what is behind such and such a slogan, opinion poll, public report or piece of scientific information. The messages are transmitted continuously but their senders remain 'out-of-context'. We are thus faced with a mediatic scene whose discourses are 'off-screen'. This is apparently an imposed condition, due to the extra-territorial condition of our metropolitan global milieu.

We have therefore evolved from an ancient society organised around the image of power – a secular or sacred power which attempts to impose its discourse and thereby re-territorialise society – to a heterogeneous metropolitan and chaotic context haunted by a multitude of discursive fragments which attempt to redefine and reproduce as well as possible the desires and aspirations of its public. If, in totalitarian societies, the repressive forces of the political police control private communications in order to eradicate any individual attempt to think freely and 'territorialisingly', by contrast, in a metropolitan society all institutions try to find out and reveal, by whatever means, our very desires and most intimate dreams, and then offer them up for sale. One such example is the utilisation of contemporary means of communication, the Internet included, as highly sophisticated tools for learning about and controlling tastes, interests and social interactions; all this without any warning whatsoever. Electronic cultural spying is most of the time installed 'by default' in our systems of communication. This process of the erasure and replacement of social actors with robotised systems, whose sole goal is to sell back to us our own image, generates a diluted society – a society which represents itself through what I call *catabolic signifiers*.[17]

We are faced today with the ever-growing manipulation of reality through technologies of simulation, with the capacity to copy/paste/modify our symbols, images, discourses, signs and living matter *ad infinitum*, to bring about, in other words, a form of generalised cloning.

We are faced today with a catabolic and extra-territorial society which produces an amplified and anabolic discursive milieu.

Within the strangeness of this new milieu, the only kind of referentiality which still remains 'verifiable' is our very own personal identity. But this last 'refuge' is itself not secure: this milieu changes us continually by imposing its laws. We are asked to act more and more as 'catabolic and extra-territorial persons who produce an amplified and anabolic discursive milieu'. Without limiting ourselves to a simple 'referential illusion', in the case of teritorialities, or to a 'biographical illusion', in the case of catabolic identities – to refer to the concepts introduced by Barthes and Bourdieu – all that remains is the possibility of constructing, as free subjects, our own subjectivities as an expression of our true and authentic identities.

Yet, we must recognise, along with Michel Serres, that existence itself could have a double nature: parallel to the Heideggerian vision of being – *Dasein*, 'being-there' – there could be a second nature, which coincides with the virtual. This nature is revealed by the etymology of the word 'existence' itself, which comes from the Latin *ex-sistere* : 'being-placed-outside-of'.

This double nature could be perceived as both beneficial and dynamic. Within such a context, the metropolis could be seen at the same time as a territorialising and an extra-territorialising milieu.

Notes

1 Gilles Deleuze and Félix Guattari, *L'Anti-Oedipe: Capitalisme et schizophrénie*, Paris: Editions de Minuit, 1972.
2 Deleuze and Guattari, *Anti-Oedipus*, trans. R. Hurley, M. Seem and H. Lane, Minneapolis, MN: University of Minnesota Press, 1977.
3 Deleuze and Guattari, *A Thousand Plateaus*, trans. B. Massumi, Minneapolis, MN: University of Minnesota Press, 1987.
4 Constantin Petcou, 'Totalitarian City', in *Architecture and Revolution*, ed. Neil Leach, London and New York: Routledge, 1999.
5 It should be pointed out here that our term 'extra-territoriality' is close to what Foucault defined, in a 1967 conference, as *heterotopias*. Along with utopias, heterotopias 'have the curious property of being in relationship with all other emplacements but on such a mode that they suspend, neutralize or inverse the very ensemble of relationships'. Examples of *heterotopias* given by Foucault include, the college – in its nineteenth-century form – military barracks, psychiatric clinics, cemeteries, gardens, museums, libraries and boats (cf. Michel Foucault, 'Des espaces autres', in *Dits et écrits IV*, Paris: Edition Gallimard, 1994, p. 752).
6 For example, the recent case of pollution of the French coast by the oil tanker, *Erika*, shows up the difficulty in establishing responsibility for such catastrophes within a multinational corporational context.
7 Cf. 'Matières' and 'Images calculées', in *Les Immatériaux*, Paris: Editions du Centre Georges Pompidou, 1985.
8 See Paul Virilio's interesting analysis on 'the transfer of war from the actual to the virtual', in Virilio, *La machine de la vision*, Paris: Editions Galilée, 1988, p. 141.
9 Jean-François Lyotard, *Discours, Figure*, Paris: Editions Klincksieck, 1971, p. 180.
10 Cf. 'Référence inversée', in *Les Immatériaux*. Paris: Editions du Centre Georges Pompidou, 1985.

11 Jean Baudrillard, *Simulations*, trans. P. Foss, P. Patton and P. Beitchman, New York: Semiotext(e), 1983, p. 4.
12 Baudrillard, *Simulations*, pp. 10–11.
13 For Paul Virilio the contemporary world runs the risk of a terrifying implosion of space and time, and furthermore, of a general de-realisation, if not a universal dissolution.
14 Here we are following the distinction made by linguist Emile Benveniste between the Latin and Greek terms for 'the city'. In the Latin model, the primary term designates the inhabitant himself – *civis* – while in the Greek model the primary term designates an abstract entity or Idea – *polis*. This is the reason for us to introduce two distinct terms: 'media-*city*' and 'media-*polis*'.
15 Here we introduce the notion of 'anabole', which comes from the Greek δναβολη 'ascent, rise', as opposed to the notion of 'symbol', which comes from συμβολη, 'bringing together'. If we notice that the animal world is dominated by reality and by indexical signs, that the languages use rather iconic signs and that the culture is constructed as a symbolic world which becomes increasingly autonomous, then we should also acknowledge that the *anabole* is already operating within an existing tendency to abstract and double the real.
16 See note 14.
17 Here we are proposing a second notion, related to the notion of the symbol. In contrast to the *anabole* which indicates a sign dominated by its signifier, we might introduce the notion of the *catabole* for signs that have a quasi-invisible signifier. The word is derived from the Greek καταβολη, 'putting below'.

Index